THE VICEREGENCY OF

Antonio María Bucareli

IN NEW SPAIN, 1771–1779

THE TEXAS PAN-AMERICAN SERIES

THE TEXAS PAN-AMERICAN SERIES is published with the assistance of a revolving publication fund established by the Pan-American Sulphur Company and other friends of Latin America in Texas. Publication of this book was also assisted by a grant from the Rockefeller Foundation through the Latin American translation program of the Association of American University Presses.

Antonio María Bucareli.

THE VICEREGENCY OF
Antonio María Bucareli
IN NEW SPAIN, 1771–1779

BY BERNARD E. BOBB

UNIVERSITY OF TEXAS PRESS · AUSTIN

TO MARNA

PREFACE

IT IS SOMEWHAT SURPRISING that so few studies have been published of individual viceroys who served the Spanish Crown in the New World, for the viceroy was, generally, a powerful figure whose competence, methods, attitudes, and character were of vital importance to millions of people, as well as to the status and progress of the Spanish empire. This investigation of Bucareli, who governed a key area in a significant time, has seemed to me, therefore, to be a worthwhile undertaking. It has come to include both a study of the man and of the system of viceregal administration as it had developed by the latter part of the eighteenth century.

The work has been in process for more than a dozen years, and the course of its evolution has been marked by the assistance of many persons. Dr. John W. Caughey first pointed out the possibilities of the subject and provided guidance and encouragement, especially during the sometimes discouraging early stages of the study. The American Philosophical Society provided financial assistance, making possible visits to Spain and Mexico for study in the appropriate archives. The staffs of the Archivo General de Indias in Seville and the Archivo General de la Nación in Mexico City were most helpful and cooperative. Finally, my colleagues in the Department of History at Washington State University and the administration of the University have not only encouraged my efforts, but have contributed materially to the completion of the study by making available the necessary time for research. To all these persons I wish here once more to express my gratitude.

B. E. B.

Pullman, Washington

CONTENTS

ILLUSTRATIONS

MAPS

ABBREVIATIONS USED IN NOTES

Good

AGI   Archivo General de Indias, Seville, Spain

AGN   Archivo General de la Nación, Mexico City, Mexico

CVB   Correspondencia de los virreyes, Bucareli

IG   Indiferente General

Leg.   Legajo (a fascicle of documents)

Mex.   Audiencia de México (AGI section)

RC   Reales Cédulas (AGN section)

THE VICEREGENCY OF
Antonio María Bucareli
IN NEW SPAIN, 1771–1779

The Man and the Setting

A SPANISH VESSEL nine days out of Havana put in at the harbor of Veracruz on August 23, 1771. Aboard was a distinguished passenger, the recent Governor and Captain General of Cuba Antonio María Bucareli y Ursúa, come to assume his duties as viceroy of New Spain.[1] The next seven and a half years were destined to comprise for him a notable climax to a long career in the service of the Spanish Crown. These same years have also been described as providing for Mexico "a palpable example of what this soil can be when a virtuous and able man undertakes with decision the difficult task of developing its elements of richness."[2]

The New Spain which Bucareli came to govern represented the most challenging assignment he had yet been given. The most treasured of the Spanish American viceroyalties, it was a magnificent administrative complexity of kingdoms, provinces, colonies, presidencies, judicial divisions, and local governments. Its people constituted a cultural and social entity whose composition was even more complex and diverse than its political organization, and whose membership extended all the way from the savage Apache to the cultured gentleman of the Enlightenment. Within its vastness were included the arid, dangerous provinces of the north, the mysterious regions of the south, the mining camps of the silver belt, and the insalubrious gulf coast. Spectacularly situated in the ancient Valley of Anáhuac was its

[1] Bucareli to Alejandro O'Reilly, September 7, 1771, AGI, Mex., Legajo 1242.
[2] Manuel Rivera Cambas, *Los gobernantes de México*, Vol. I, p. 422.

capital, Mexico City, the metropolis of the New World. In common with all complex societies, that of the viceroyalty was productive of a series of seeming paradoxes, such as the contemporaneous existence of theaters and Indian wars, charity and inhumanity, starvation and conspicuous consumption, libraries and illiteracy, collectivized villages and latifundia, pagan superstition and Christian devotion. Historically, it was the seed of the Mexican nation.

As of 1771 New Spain theoretically extended from Guatemala to Louisiana and Oregon. In actuality Spanish control was delineated by a northern boundary running roughly from the northernmost California settlement eastward approximately through present-day southern Arizona, northern New Mexico, and central Texas. Adjacent governmental units were Louisiana, administered from the captaincy-general of Cuba, and the captaincy-general of Guatemala, which included the present Mexican state of Chiapas.

Prior to the establishment of the intendancy system in 1786, the viceroyalty was divided into major governmental units under varying names. These were: (1) the kingdom of Mexico, or New Spain, the most important area; (2) the Nuevo Reino de León, with approximately the same boundaries as Nuevo León has today; (3) the kingdom of Nueva Galicia, which lay to the north and west of Mexico; (4) the colony of Nuevo Santander, today Tamaulipas and part of southern Texas; (5) the province of Texas, or Nuevas Filipinas; (6) the province of Coahuila; (7) the province of Nueva Vizcaya; (8) the province of New Mexico; (9) the province of Sonora and Sinaloa; (10) the province of California. Subordinate administrative units included *alcaldías mayores, alcaldías menores, cabildos,* and *ayuntamientos.*[3]

---

[3] More detailed accounts of the governmental system may be found in a number of sources, of which a few are suggested here. Clarence H. Haring, *The Spanish Empire in America*, especially Chaps. IV, VII, VIII, and IX. Herbert Ingram Priestley, *José de Gálvez, Visitor General of New Spain, 1765–1771*, Chap. II. This work is cited hereafter as *José de Gálvez*. Wistano Luis Orozco, *Legislación y jurisprudencia sobre terrenos baldíos*, Vol. I, pp. 155–166. This work is cited hereafter as *Legislación y jurisprudencia*. Anonymous, "División política de Nueva España hasta la promulgación de la Real Ordenanza de Intendentes," *Boletín del Archivo General de la Nación*, Vol. III, No. 3 (Mayo–Junio, 1931), pp. 328–334.

The population, estimated at nearly 5,000,000 persons,[4] was divided into closely-defined castes based on color and place of birth. At the top were the peninsular-born Spaniards, called *gachupines,* followed by the American-born whites, or *criollos,* and the *mestizos* of Indian-white mixture. Below them were the various lower castes, such as mulattoes, *sambos* (Indian and Negro), Negroes, and a great diversity of combinations.[5] The Indians were considered a race apart, living in a condition of perpetual wardship.[6]

These distinctions of birth were fundamental determinants of the individual's entire existence, not only with respect to social position but also as regulators of his economic and political situation. To the *gachupines* went the vast majority of high offices, both governmental and ecclesiastical, as well as economic advantage. Almost exclusively, they were the viceroys, governors, judges, archbishops, bishops, chief merchants, and grantees of large estates. Always a small numerical minority, they jealously protected their alleged superiority and practiced a rigid snobbishness with respect to all the rest of the inhabitants of the colony, including their own children. These were the Creoles, condemned as congenitally inferior because of the deteriorative effect of the locale of their conception and birth. Restricted thus to the lesser positions within the government and the church, they came to harbor a bitter resentment for the system which artificially and unreasonably placed them in the category of second-class human beings. Even those Creoles who had inherited the land and who lived in relative luxury on their estates were frustrated by this social inequity. The creation of

[4] An incomplete census of 1794 cites the population as 5,200,000. Priestley, *José de Gálvez,* p. 353.

[5] For an amusing and informative work on the social structure of New Spain, see Gregorio Torres Quintero, *México hacia el fin del virreinato español,* cited hereafter as *México hacia el fin.*

[6] There is a fairly extensive literature on the society of New Spain. A few representative works are: Haring, *The Spanish Empire in America,* Chap. XI; Torres Quintero, *México hacia el fin;* Luis González Obregón, *México en 1768;* Manuel Romero de Terreros y Vinent, *Bocetos de la vida social en la Nueva España.* This work is cited hereafter as *Bocetos.* Hubert Howe Bancroft, *History of Mexico,* Vol. III, Chap. XXXIV. This work is cited hereafter as *History.* Lesley Byrd Simpson, *Many Mexicos,* Chaps. XII, XVI, XVIII; Henry Bamford Parkes, *A History of Mexico,* pp. 116–123.

the colonial militia in the latter part of the eighteenth century afforded them a new opportunity to achieve status, though with dire results for the nation that was to succeed the colony.

The lower classes were condemned to an existence which afforded little in the way of promise or hope. The unfortunate *mestizo,* rejected alike by his Indian and white progenitors, was a species of lost soul who sought in vain his rightful place in society. His day of dominance was destined to arrive, but that was many decades after the time of Bucareli. The other mixtures of the various races were subjected to even further discriminations and prohibitions, such as those against owning or learning to use firearms, appearing on the streets after dark, and being admitted to the craft guilds.

The Indian, who constituted a majority of the population, lived several kinds of existence, depending principally upon the degree of his connection with, and dominance by, the white element. In the settled countryside he lived as a virtual serf on the great haciendas; in the cities he tended to be sunk in brutish misery, relying on alcohol for relief. In some outlying areas he continued to live much as his forebears had lived, maintaining his communal system and a culture which had existed for centuries, relatively untouched by things European. In other distant parts of the viceroyalty, such as the deserts of the north, the Indian also maintained his old way of life, except that it was complicated by the necessity of fighting off the persistent advance of the white man's soldiers and missionaries. Despite laws which made of him a minor in a perpetual state of tutelage, and a vast body of legislation designed to protect him from exploitation, the Indian subsisted generally at a very low level of living.

Two incidents serve to illustrate at least a few of the problems Indians faced. One is revealed in an undated letter of the 1770's in which Governor of Texas Barón Juan María de Ripperdá complained to Bucareli that white settlers in his province were seizing Indian children and selling them as slaves. The other revelation derives from a letter to Bucareli from Julián de Arriaga, the secretary of state, in which Arriaga advised the Viceroy that Charles III was disturbed over reports that Indians on haciendas were being driven to work in the fields by making them run alongside horses and whipping them. Bucareli was ordered to advise all *alcaldes mayores,* or local administrative officials, that this must stop. Indians were to be allowed to go to work at their own pace, to be worked only from sunrise to sunset, and to be permitted to rest for two hours at midday. Otherwise, Arriaga concluded, "they are being treated as slaves, and the laws strictly prohibit this." [7]

The heart of the viceroyalty, the source of authority, the symbol of European dominance, was Mexico City. Descriptions of the metropolis in the latter half of the eighteenth century vary considerably, probably because the observers chose different parts of it to describe, and also because its appearance was much improved by a major rehabilitation instituted by the second Viceroy Juan Vicente de Güemes Revillagigedo in the 1790's, thus making descriptions vary according to the time they were recorded. Baron Alexander von Humboldt, writing just after the turn of the century, paints the most attractive picture, one which is occasionally almost breath-taking in the beauty he manages to suggest with his words. Parts of it are worth reproducing: [8]

As the first conquistadores portrayed the old Tenochtitlán, adorned with a multitude of temples which stood out in the form of minarets or Turkish towers, surrounded with waters and causeways, built on islands covered with verdure, and receiving in her streets each hour thousands of boats which gave life to the lake, it must have resembled some cities of Holland, of China, or of the inundated Delta of Lower Egypt. The capital, as the Spaniards have rebuilt it, presents an aspect perhaps less agreeable, but much more respectable and majestic.

Mexico must be counted, without any doubt, among the most beautiful cities the Europeans have built in both hemispheres. With the exception of Petersburg, Berlin, Philadelphia, and some parts of Westminster, there scarcely exists a city of extent which can be compared with the capital of New Spain, for the uniform level of the ground it occupies, for the regularity and wideness of the streets, and for the grandeur of the public plazas. The architecture, in general, is of a style sufficiently pure, and there are also buildings of the most beautiful nature.

[7] Riperdá to Bucareli, AGN, Historia, Vol. 84, No. 9. Arriaga to Bucareli, March 23, 1773, AGI, Mex., Leg. 1509.

[8] Quoted in Artemio Valle-Arizpe, *La muy noble y leal ciudad de México, según relatos de antaño y hogaño,* pp. 286–294.

By a union of unusual circumstances I have seen consecutively and in a short space of time, Lima, Mexico, Philadelphia, Washington, Paris, Rome, Naples, and the major cities of Germany. Comparing the impressions which follow one another rapidly in our senses, an opinion which perhaps I have adopted too lightly may be corrected. In the midst of the various comparisons whose results can be less favorable to the Mexican capital, I must confess that this city has left in me a certain idea of grandeur, which I attribute principally to the character of the grandness which the location and nature of her surroundings give her.

Certainly there is no richer and more varied spectacle than that which the valley presents when, on a beautiful summer morning, the sky clear and with that turquoise blue of the dry and rarefied air of the high mountains, one looks out from any one of the towers of the Cathedral of Mexico or from the top of Chapultepec hill. All the surrounding sides of this hill are covered with the thickest vegetation. Old trunks of ahuehuetes more than fifteen or sixteen meters in circumference raise their leafless tops above those of the schimes, which in their shape or outline resemble the weeping willows of the Orient. From the center of this lonely spot, that is, from the point of the porphyritic rock of Chapultepec, the view covers an extensive plain and very well cultivated fields which run from the foot of the colossal mountains, covered with perpetual snow. The city is presented to the spectator bathed by the waters of Lake Texcoco, which, surrounded with villages and small places, reminds one of the most beautiful lakes of the Swiss mountains.

From all sides great streets of elms and white oaks lead to the capital; two aqueducts built on elevated arches cross the plain, which presents a spectacle as agreeable as it is beautifying. To the north is seen the magnificent convent of Nuestra Señora de Guadalupe, built on the slope of the mountains of Tepeyac, among some ravines, for whose protection were planted some date palms and yuccas. To the south, all the land between San Angel, Tacubaya, and San Agustín de las Cuevas looks like an immense garden of orange trees, peach trees, apple trees, cherry trees and other fruit trees of Europe. This beautiful cultivation forms a contrast with the wild aspect of the bare mountains which enclose the valley and among which are distinguished the famous volcanoes of Puebla— Popocatepetl and Ixtacihuatl. The first forms an enormous cone, whose crater, always burning and emitting smoke and ashes, breaks forth from the eternal snows.

Mexico City is also notable for its good urban cleanliness. Most of the streets have very wide sidewalks; they are clean and very well lighted with reflectors of flat wicks in the shape of scrolls.

Another European who was apparently enchanted by what he saw in Mexico City was Juan Manuel de San Vicente, a member of the suite of Viceroy Carlos Francisco de Croix, Marqués de Croix. Although his observations were made prior to the rehabilitation effected by Revillagigedo, he nevertheless found the city a thing of beauty in the late 1760's. He was particularly impressed with the streets, which he described as wide enough for coaches to go three abreast and still leave room for the foot traffic. Further, they were "all paved and cleaned by the supply of crystalline currents which bathe them . . ." Both public buildings and private houses he pictured as sumptuous, the homes having "crystal panes in the windows, flat roofs, ducts to the street with lead pipes for the overflow, beautifully painted on the interior and exterior, with a well inside most, many fountains, some gardens, and all with the most necessary comforts for their habitation. . . ." [9] One gets the feeling, however, that San Vicente chose to see only the finer sections of the city, and that perhaps he viewed even these through glasses which were rose-tinted.

This suspicion is borne out, or perhaps engendered by, the observations of Francisco Sedaño, a book merchant and lifelong resident of the capital, whose comments are based on a much longer and closer acquaintance with the scene. His portrayal of the heart of the city, that is, the viceroy's palace and the *plaza mayor,* is in total contrast to what Humboldt and San Vicente had to say. Revillagigedo apparently swept the royal palace clean of all nonofficial activities, but prior to his time it was a number of things in addition to being the seat of government. It housed many of the shopkeepers from the plaza which fronted it, and also provided rooms in which their extra goods were stored. A wine shop, a bakery, a billiard parlor, a public card-playing establishment, a bowling area, and a saloon, wherein "pulque was sold publicly and brandy secretly," were included within its walls. Garbage and rubbish were everywhere. The upper corridors were invaded by what Sedaño calls "people of the night," who fouled the area and

[9] *Ibid.,* pp. 238–240.

"with carbon . . . wrote nicknames and painted lewd things." Some zealous captains of the guard "walked the rounds checking the corners" in an attempt to prevent such activities. Sedaño concluded by commenting,[10]

The idle men and women, who spent the night in fandangos and diversions, went to finish the night at the saloon of the palace, to eat, drink, and get drunk. The disorders which were seen there by day and night are not easy to describe; I saw many when I entered the guard as a soldier in the commercial regiment. All was remedied by the incomparable . . . Conde de Revillagigedo, moved by zeal to the honor of God and the welfare of the public.

The *plaza mayor,* as described by Sedaño, was a frightful thing to behold. Much of it was occupied by a market whose shops consisted of shingle sheds or huts owned and rented by the city council. The gallows were a featured attraction of the plaza, as was also the cemetery which adjoined the cathedral along one side. Until the Revillagigedo reform, the plaza was "very ugly and of a very disagreeable appearance. On top of the shingle roofs were pieces of sleeping mats, hats, old shoes, and other rags which were thrown on them. The unevenness of the paving, the mud in time of rain, the gutters which crossed it, the mountains of garbage, excrement of ordinary people and children, rinds and other nuisances, made it difficult to walk." Sedaño offers further detail of a most unedifying nature.[11]

Nor were the streets of the city which San Vicente found so clean and attractive similarly described by Sedaño. He observed that they were "all of them rubbish heaps, even the principal ones; on each corner there was a great mountain of garbage." Although they were cleaned up once a week, "it was not possible to clean a street for more than an hour, because no sooner was a pile of garbage removed than they began to throw more in the same place. At the door of each house a mountain of garbage was inevitable." Apparently some improvement was achieved under the Marqués de Croix, but "soon the filthi-

[10] *Ibid.,* pp. 266–268.   [11] *Ibid.,* pp. 268–271.

ness returned." Under Revillagigedo, however, "the city came to have such a different look, it appeared to be another."[12]

Despite the depressing nature of Sedaño's description of this one section of the capital, it is evident that Mexico City was not entirely and perpetually in such a condition. Contemporary accounts also reveal that life in the metropolis during Bucareli's time need not be dull and uninteresting, either for those inhabitants who had sufficient wealth to pay for entertainment or for the poorer classes who must find diversion and excitement in what went on around them. For the upper element of capital society there were the theater, balls, the daily promenades along the Paseo de Bucareli and through the Alameda, and their own social functions, which apparently were numerous. The lower classes enjoyed the bullfights, fiestas, religious festivals, and other spectacles whose primary function was not entertainment but which provided it nevertheless. Certainly, for example, there was a macabre titillation to be derived from watching the public executions by hanging of criminals caught by the *Acordada*, and the whippings of lesser offenders by the same agency, or from taunting a *mujer emplumada*, a "bad woman," who, for her misdeeds, was stripped of her clothes, covered with honey, daubed with feathers, and then paraded through the streets. The occasional sentences imposed by the Inquisition, although they no longer featured burnings, provided a similar sort of diversion. It is equally certain that the great majority of the people of Mexico City, including the multitude of *léperos*, or beggars, were kept busy in what was for many of them the desperate effort to make both ends meet.[13]

[12] *Ibid.*, pp. 273–274. Evidence of Croix's efforts to clean up the city is to be found in two decrees of November 26, 1769, and February 26, 1771. The first contains detailed instructions on cleaning and paving the streets; the second provides that the streets be swept daily and prohibits dumping dirty water or excrement in them. AGN, Bandos, Vol. 7, p. 48, and Vol. 8, p. 2.

[13] Further information on life in New Spain may be obtained from the works cited in notes 5 and 6. An interesting account, more recently published, is the diary of Felipe de Zúñiga y Ontiveros, covering the years 1775 to 1786. Zúñiga was a successful printer and an astute observer of capital society. Angeles Rubio-Argüellos, "Zúñiga, Impresor del Siglo XVIII en México," *Anales de la Asociación Española para el Progreso de las Ciencias*, Vol. XXII, No. 3 (1957), pp. 507–561.

Labor in New Spain was very tightly organized and minutely regulated. Every artisan was a member of two recognized groups—his *cofradía,* which was a lay brotherhood with a religious orientation, and his guild. There were *cofradías* not only for such crafts as weavers and masons, but also for the liberal professions and government workers. The guilds were governed by ordinances which were usually promulgated by the *cabildo* and confirmed by the viceroy. These ordinances set forth in precise detail the manner in which the guild member must practice his craft, even to the extent, for example, of prescribing for tanners that from May 1 to September 1 all hides being processed in a lime pit must be covered with four fingers of water, with a fine of four gold pesos for any tanner who failed to conform with the rule. The quality of the product was similarly regulated, as is demonstrated by the weavers' regulation specifying the number of threads that must be used in the weft of cloth woven for the habits of the various religious orders, including further differentiations for each order and the several parts of each habit. The guild system of New Spain was essentially medieval in character and clearly must have acted as a powerful deterrent to competition and free trade. Most of the guilds had been organized in the sixteenth and seventeenth centuries, with only a few remaining to be established in the first half of the eighteenth century.[14]

Out of this economic pattern and out of the economic activities of the people of the viceroyalty it was the major function of the viceroy to extract an annual profit for the Crown. During Bucareli's era, efficient and productive management of the royal revenues was especially important, for although the international situation did not erupt during his term, an eruption was clearly imminent; and once-great Spain, by now revitalized and resurgent, had real need for an effective marshaling of all her resources. After devoting three-quarters of a century to a program of recovery from the decadence brought on by Habsburg ineptitude, the Spanish Crown now felt itself to be once more ready to assume the status of a first-rate power. Long preparation,

[14] Francisco del Barrio Lorenzot, *Ordenanzas de gremios de la Nueva España,* pp. I–VI, 289–298.

patience, and severe disappointment had gone into achieving this hopeful position.

The revitalization of Spain and her empire had its beginnings in 1700 with the ascension to the throne of Philip V, the first Bourbon ruler of the nation. Although the French-trained Philip was something of a failure in the field of international relations, he did initiate a program of governmental and economic reorganization for both the mother country and the colonies which put his nation on the long, slow road to recovery. His successor, Ferdinand VI, by wisely withholding his convalescent country from participation in the European wars of his period, allowed Spain to enjoy fourteen years of much-needed peace, during which the improvements introduced by Philip V took firm root.

Consequently, when Charles III, the greatest of the Spanish Bourbons, assumed the crown in 1759, he found himself ruler of a nation and an empire ready for further progress and eminence, provided the program for achieving such ends was instituted and administered by wise, capable persons. Charles himself assuredly met these criteria, and he did well in his search for aides who possessed the requisite qualifications. His success is attested to by the progress Spain made during his reign. After careful study by a special committee, the customary restrictive commercial policy was considerably liberalized, with a consequent increase in general prosperity. Administratively, he made many changes in both the higher and lower levels of the national and colonial governmental machinery. The result was an improvement in the quality of administration and a significant increase in the royal revenues.

In the field of international relations, however, Charles III reverted to the policy of his father, Philip V, engaging in costly wars which only hurt his country. His era was one of particular significance with respect to the imperial ambitions of the various European colonial powers. Especially important for the period here under consideration was the situation which grew out of the Seven Years' War, in which Spain was a participant on the losing side as an ally of France. By the Treaty of Paris in 1763, France lost her entire American empire to

England, with the exception of Louisiana, which Louis XV ceded to Spain. Spain, besides losing Florida to England, was also forced to ransom Havana and Manila, both of which had been captured by England, and was compelled to grant England logging concessions in Honduras. France, in her humiliation, could think only of securing revenge, an attitude which led directly to the vital help that she gave to the rebellious English colonists in America, thereby contributing to a further readjustment of the colonial scene.

The defeat which Spain suffered in 1763 was also a motive for planning retaliation on the common enemy, England; but Charles III was reluctant to commit his country and his empire to war until he could strengthen his defenses and improve the condition of the royal treasury. To this end he initiated a program designed to bolster his armed forces at the same time that he accelerated his policy of administrative and financial reform at home and in the colonies. One aspect of this activity was manifested by the general inspection entrusted to José de Gálvez in the most valuable and also the most endangered area in Charles III's American empire, the Viceroyalty of New Spain.

Beginning in 1765, the visitation lasted until 1771, and although Gálvez was delayed for awhile in his reform program because of his conflict with Viceroy Joaquín de Montserrat, Marqués de Cruillas, once Cruillas had been replaced by the more amenable Marqués de Croix, the changes came rapidly. The revenue system was extensively overhauled, Crown monopolies were strengthened and increased, the Jesuit Order was expelled from the viceroyalty (as it had been from Spain), the California settlements were established, and, generally, a thorough reorganization, or perhaps one should say refurbishing, of the entire system was initiated.

Priestley points out that Gálvez instituted no significant modification in the fundamental aspects of the colonial system, but that he merely initiated "an enforcement of more rigid adherence to the paramount interest of the mother country in the productive wealth of New Spain."[15] With respect to the general results of the visitation, Priestley recognizes two broad consequences. One is based on the "too little, too

[15] Priestley, *José de Gálvez*, p. 388.

late" concept, which suggests that the relatively enlightened reforms
of Charles III served only to emphasize the need for a more thorough
and more genuinely liberal reorganization of the system, especially in
the light of the crescendo of criticism of monarchy and empire which
characterized the final decades of the eighteenth century. The other
indicates that Gálvez' policies had the effect of alienating or irritating
specific segments of the Mexican citizenry, such as the commercial
elements, the mineowners, the clergy, the Creoles, and, with reference
to the expulsion of the Jesuits, the general public. According to
Priestley, the end result of both of these factors was a contribution
to the sentiment for independence.[16]

Other historians emphasize additional considerations in analyzing
the significance of the Gálvez visitation, or, more precisely, the period
of the Bourbon reforms. Parkes, Motten, Hussey, Whitaker, and
Haring, for example, all make reference to the general liberalism of
the eighteenth century and to the principles of the Enlightenment.[17]
Most of them suggest that the Gálvez visitation was part of the broader
process whereby these principles were introduced into New Spain, a
process which in turn contributed to the growing ferment which was
destined to produce rebellion shortly after the turn of the century.

Of primary interest here, however, is the question of what specific
evidences of these phenomena are discernible during the period of the
Bucareli viceregency. Following directly upon the visitation, and running its course almost exactly in the middle of Charles III's reign,
during a time when the Crown was pursuing a series of clearly-defined
and critical objectives, the Bucareli administration might be expected
to manifest many evidences of the new order and its impact on
Mexican society. Oddly enough, however, evidences of this sort are
difficult to find. An explanation of this surprising result may have
considerable significance, and appears to be based on several factors
operative at the time. For one thing, it is suggested that the impact of

[16] *Ibid.*, pp. 232, 389.
[17] Parkes, *A History of Mexico*, pp. 133–143. Clement G. Motten, *Mexican Silver and the Enlightenment, passim.* Roland D. Hussey, "Traces of French Enlightenment in Colonial Hispanic America," in *Latin America and the Enlightenment*, pp. 23–51. Arthur Preston Whitaker, "The Dual Role of Latin America in the Enlightenment," in *ibid.*, pp. 3–21. Haring, *The Spanish Empire in America*, pp. 344–347.

the principles of the Enlightenment on that minority of the Mexican people who were significantly receptive to them was not immediate and explosive in its effect. Instead, a rather lengthy period of digestion and assimilation was necessary. Additionally, the facilities for the dissemination of such principles were scanty; the deterrents to their acceptance, such as the habits of traditional thinking, the presence of a powerful opposition, and the divided nature of colonial society, were effective counteragents; and the process, first, of acceptance, and then of implementation, of these principles required not only example and encouragement from outside sources, but also the propitious moment. Finally, the personality and character of Bucareli himself must be considered.

The hypothesis is here offered that the period of Bucareli's viceregency was a transitional one, during which the seeds of the Enlightenment, of change, even of rebellion, were sown but had not yet begun to sprout. Personally, Bucareli served as a sort of bridge between the old and the new. Fundamentally conservative, he tended to resist change; but he was not blindly stubborn in matters of this sort, and his soldierly habit of obedience further mitigated his conservatism, although the conservative instinct was always present in some degree. He fulfilled a rather special function, serving as the "straw boss" of the crew that was expected to install the new order with a minimum of harmful repercussion. Fortunately for the Crown, his talents were precisely suited to the task. Not a planner or a visualizer in terms of broad points of view, he was, instead, an efficiency expert with a splendid capacity for internal diplomacy. By exercising these talents from his executive position for a period of seven and a half years, he softened the harsh nature of some of Gálvez' measures and, by placating those who were prone to resent certain aspects of the new order, secured a general acceptance of the change without sacrificing many of its essential elements. Evidence that his success was dual is the fact that revenues climbed steadily during his term and that the Crown was exceptionally pleased with his performance, while, at the same time, the inhabitants of the viceroyalty afforded him a degree of respect and affection far beyond that granted a great majority of the other viceroys.

This circumstance may help explain why there is so little evidence of revolutionary ferment or significant social discontent during Bucareli's years as viceroy. It is not claimed that there were no signs of restlessness at all, or that the authorities did not feel it necessary to maintain vigilance against the introduction and diffusion of dangerous or offensive doctrines.

In this connection the thesis of Xavier Tavera Alfaro helps explain both the absence of evidence of revolutionary sentiment—at least in the form of published protest—during the 1760's and 1770's, and the appearance of such literature in the 1780's. He points out that when José Alzate y Ramírez began publishing his *Diario Literario* in 1768, in which he concerned himself with philosophical discussion and scientific inquiry, he quickly brought upon himself the disapproval of Viceroy Croix. Croix, upon the occasion of the expulsion of the Jesuits, had issued a decree asserting that the duty of every good Spanish subject was to obey, not to discuss, an action which indicates that the official attitude was not favorable to discursive journals. Therefore, within a very short time Croix found it necessary to suppress Alzate's publication because its final issue contained "propositions offensive . . . to the law and to the nation." Despite public interest in such publications, similar periodical works of that period met the same fate. However, by 1788, when Alzate brought out his new journal, *Gaceta de la Literatura de México,* the official attitude had become more liberal and, despite the new magazine's tendency toward violent criticism of the traditional order, it was not suppressed. In fact, in 1791 Viceroy Revillagigedo urged official support for such journals.[18]

During Bucareli's viceregency there was observable a strange mixture of suppression and permissiveness with respect to new concepts and philosophies, which perhaps represented the transitional nature of the time, both in Spain and Mexico. On the one hand, for example, the Crown was most vigorous in its proscription of a utopian book called *The Year 2440,*[19] and decreed severe penalties for anyone caught

[18] Xavier Tavera Alfaro, "Periodismo Diechiochosco," *Historia Mexicana,* Vol. II, No. 1 (Julio–Septiembre, 1952), pp. 110–115.

[19] See my note on this subject in *Hispania* (Vol. XLII, No. 4 [December, 1959], p. 573), in which the text of the pertinent Royal *Cédula* is reproduced. Professor Otis Fellows, through Professors Mario Pei and R. G. Mead, Jr., was kind enough to

with copies of certain stamps dealing with "The Universal Judgment." [20] Also, as the following chapter on the church points out, the Inquisition spent a great deal of time checking on the importation and circulation of reading material. On the other hand, as this same chapter also says, it is clear that books forbidden to the common man were widely read by the privileged classes, while in such areas as mining, the Crown specifically encouraged the spirit of scientific inquiry.

That the problem of treasonable or offensive sentiments was not a major one to Bucareli is evidenced by the absence of the subject from both his personal and official correspondence. In view of the time and place, it seems logical to conclude that, although the content of eighteenth-century liberalism was not considered a fit subject for consideration by the masses, or whatever part of them were sufficiently literate, it was nevertheless being read, discussed, and, to a degree, appreciated by the privileged element in society in mother country and colony, and this to the extent that it was accepted and was not, therefore, a subject for especial official action. Certainly New Spain was not, during Bucareli's time, a mass of seething discontent, with an ideological foundation in the revolutionary doctrines of the era. Neither was it, however, a realm of ignorance, isolated from the intellectual currents of the world around it. As Whitaker suggests, all of Spanish America played a dual role with respect to the Enlightenment —passively, as an object lesson or horrible example, and actively, as a participant.[21] And in New Spain, Bucareli, only partially aware of his role in the larger sense, was a skillful agent for introducing the people of Mexico to the new order.

This forty-sixth viceroy of New Spain, whose full name, with all honors and titles, eventually came to read El Bailío Frey Don Antonio María Bucareli y Ursúa, Laso de la Vega, Villacís y Córdoba, Caballero Gran Cruz, y Comendador de la Bobeda de Toro en el Orden de San Juan, Gentil Hombre de la Cámara de Su Majestad, con entrada,

---

inform me that the prohibited book, titled *L'An 2440*, with the subtitle *Reve s'il en fut jamais*, was published by the French writer Louis-Sebastien Mercier in 1770.

[20] Bucareli to Arriaga, August 27, 1772, AGN, CVB, 1771–1772, Vol. 5, No. 41 or 554, pp. 397–398.

[21] Whitaker, *Latin America and the Enlightenment*, pp. 3–4.

y Teniente General de los Reales Ejércitos, was born in Seville on January 24, 1717. His parents were Luis Bucareli, Marqués de Vallehermoso, and Ana Ursúa Laso de la Vega, Condesa de Gerena. His distinguished family secured a dispensation whereby he was made a member of the military order of San Juan de Jerúsalem at the age of five, and at age fifteen he became a cadet in the brigade of Royal Carabineers. His military career, while not spectacular, was certainly notable. He fought with distinction in campaigns in Italy and Portugal, reorganized the entire Spanish Cavalry as inspector general of that arm, and served as inspector of all coastal fortifications of the Kingdom of Granada, achieving finally the rank of lieutenant general. In 1766 he entered the field of colonial administration when he received the appointment as governor and captain general of Cuba. His service in this assignment was so meritorious that he was rewarded with the promotion to the viceregency of New Spain in 1771. Here, after his seven and a half years as viceroy, death ended a notable career of service to three Spanish kings. There is no record or indication of his ever having married.[22]

Bucareli viewed the assignment to New Spain as both a disappointment and a challenge. The job in Cuba had been arduous and frustrating, frustrating principally because of the difficulty of securing adequate funds for carrying on the necessary activities of government. A large part of these funds came, ordinarily, as subsidy from New Spain, but with Gálvez in the midst of his reorganization of the viceroyalty during these same years, there was no surplus left for Cuba. Bucareli's major tasks in Cuba were numerous and difficult, but by 1770 he regarded them as completed, and he was eager to return to Spain. Out of his restlessness he wrote to Alejandro O'Reilly: [23]

[22] No study of Bucareli's career prior to 1771 has been published. Brief sketches of his life may be found in the following sources: Luis J. Bustamante, *Enciclopedia popular cubana,* Vol. I, pp. 279–280; Francisco Calcagno, *Diccionario biográfico cubano,* Vol. I, pp. 130–131; Jacobo de la Pezuela y Lobo, *Diccionario geográfico, estadístico, histórico de la Isla de Cuba,* Vol. I, pp. 190–191; and an unsigned note bearing the comment, *"Se puso todo para la Gaceta del Martes 7 de Septe de 79,"* in AGI, Mex., Leg. 1276.

[23] Bucareli to O'Reilly, May 14, 1770, AGI, Mex., Leg. 1242. Alejandro O'Reilly was one of Bucareli's few close friends. Their personal correspondence has been

In truth, I assure you that never in my life have I been so bored. The debts increase, and the creditors clamor . . . The Viceroy [Croix] does not dare address me on the matter, and is content with informing the Intendant that on this occasion he can send nothing.

And some months later: [24]

The mail arrived from Veracruz . . . The funds which arrived do not cover loans and troop salaries . . . My letters to the Viceroy are pathetic, although I have been careful with the wording so that nothing will offend him . . . I inform the King of everything, . . . and since my health is wasted away . . . I ask the King for the remedy which will stop the damage which the service suffers, permitting me to return to Spain. Five years is as much as a man can serve well in America. . . .

The threat of an outbreak of hostilities with England silenced Bucareli on the subject of his relief for several months, but by May, 1771, he was back to the topic again. In his monthly letter to O'Reilly he complained: [25]

I was counting on the time when, the fears of war having vanished, they would agree that a governor who had served five years in Havana with great fatigue . . . would merit relief, but all is silence. My strength dissipates, and we are in the hot season, which mistreats me so in this climate. I am much saddened not to deliver the command.

In the meantime, O'Reilly had returned to Spain and was working to secure Bucareli's return to the mother country. At one point he was able to assure the Cuban Governor that the job of inspector general of Cavalry was his as soon as it was vacated. However, he also discovered that there was a strong feeling in the court in favor of

---

preserved for the period 1766–1777, and is almost the only source of anything approaching intimate information on Bucareli. O'Reilly commanded the expedition which brought French Louisiana under Spanish control. Bucareli was his immediate superior in this assignment, and when O'Reilly returned to Spain in 1770 to become inspector general of Infantry, he served as a source of information on events at the court and as a promoter of Bucareli's interests there. See Vicente Rodríguez Casado, *Primeros años de dominación española en la Luisiana,* and O'Reilly's letters to Bucareli, AGI, Mex., Leg. 1242.

[24] Bucareli to O'Reilly, August 30, 1770, *ibid.*
[25] Same to same, May 10, 1771, *ibid.*

Bucareli's promotion to New Spain.[26] This sentiment finally prevailed, of course, and in a letter of May 17 O'Reilly informed Bucareli that the decision had been made and that the official notification would leave Spain in the July mail. He also revealed that Gálvez had been requesting relief for some time and had suggested that his brother, Matías de Gálvez, succeed him as visitor-general, but that the Crown had decided to discontinue the visitation and to limit the change to the appointment of a new viceroy.[27]

It is interesting and informative to note the flood of paperwork which began to flow immediately as a consequence of the appointment. On June 9 the Council of the Indies, which was, below the Crown, the supreme agency in Spain for governing the American colonies, issued the requisite order and directed that the following official notices be sent: to the treasury officials, ordering them to pay Bucareli's salary and collect the *media anata;* to Bucareli, allowing him twelve servants and dependents; to Bucareli, ordering him to read and obey all *cédulas* sent to his predecessors; to Bucareli, citing a *cédula* of 1603 which prescribed the single-subject, marginal-brief form for official correspondence; to Bucareli, advising him that if he should receive a royal appointment involving a member of his family, he must not fill it; to the treasury officials, ordering them to pay the salaries of a viceregal guard of twenty-four soldiers and one captain; to Bucareli, allowing his Negro slaves to carry arms while accompanying him, but at no other time; to the *oidores,* or judges, of the *Real Audiencia,* advising them that the Viceroy was not to interfere in cases before their court; to the Archbishop, ordering him to punish any errant cleric pointed out to him by the Viceroy; to the Archbishop, advising him to cooperate with and assist the Viceroy, with copies to the six bishops of New Spain (Puebla, Michoacán, Oaxaca, Yucatán, Guadalajara, and Durango); to the Provincial of the Dominican Order, ordering him to assist Bucareli in those matters pertaining to

[26] O'Reilly to Bucareli, December 26, 1770, and January 24, February 24, March 24, and April 24, 1771, *ibid.*

[27] *Ibid.* Same to same, May 17, 1771, *ibid.* Copies of the official appointment, dated May 23 and bearing the King's rubric, are in AGI, Mex., Leg. 1239 and Leg. 1509.

his position, with copies to the provincials of six other religious groups and the generals of two Orders; and, to the Mexico City *cabildo,* ordering them to cooperate with and assist the Viceroy, with copies to the *cabildos* of nine other cities.[28]

The effect of the news of his appointment was evidenced by an immediate alteration in the tone of Bucareli's correspondence, an alteration indicative of both his character and his attitude. Complaints about his boredom ceased, to be replaced by professions of humility in view of the honor visited upon him and promises to do his utmost in the service of the Crown. He did confide to O'Reilly, however, that he had no wish to be "an eternal viceroy," and that all he desired upon his return to Spain was the Cavalry assignment.[29] It is clear, nevertheless, that whereas the Cuban job had indeed become a chore of which he desired to be relieved, the appointment as viceroy of New Spain meant that he had achieved the top of the colonial administrative ladder, and he recognized it as a challenge as well as a position of great trust, vast responsibility, and vital importance.

Bucareli brought to the viceregency a preparation that was, in many respects, nearly perfect. He was not simply a bureaucrat, but had seen active service of various kinds. Since one of his principal functions was to defend his area, his experience—both as a commander of troops in the field and as inspector of fortifications—stood him in good stead. He had also had some experience with formal diplomacy during the war in Portugal. Additionally, his years as governor of Cuba had acquainted him with the things of the New World, the Caribbean scene, the problems of colonial administration, the relevant legislation, and the intricacies of the system. The only possible deterrent to his achieving notable success as viceroy was his desire to retire to Spain upon the completion of the Cuban assignment; but there is never the slightest indication that this desire either intruded upon, or interfered with, his fulfillment of his viceregal duties. It should be further pointed out that he approached these duties not in a plodding sense, or with the achievement of the essential minima as his goal, but

[28] AGI, Mex., Leg. 1239.
[29] Bucareli to Arriaga, July 11, 1771, AGI, Mex., Leg. 1509. Bucareli to O'Reilly, July 12, 1771, AGI, Mex., Leg. 1242.

rather with a zeal for doing an excellent job. He was, above all, a devoted servant whose devotion superseded all other considerations. That he brought to the office a degree of fundamental conservatism befits the age in which he lived and the nature of his career. That he viewed his job and the world with the eyes of a Spanish aristocrat is only natural, and that he did not bring to New Spain the attitudes of a twentieth-century liberal, as some of his critics apparently expect of him, should not be surprising.

Within a month of the time he received notification of his new assignment Bucareli had cleared the way for his departure from Cuba. Expressing regret at having to leave his "beloved Havaneros," he sailed from the island on August 14 and reached Veracruz on August 23, having stopped briefly at Campeche en route in order to send word ahead to Croix informing him of his expected time of arrival. He decided to remain at Veracruz until September 9 for the dual purpose of allowing Croix time to arrange for turning over the command and to give himself an opportunity to inspect the adjacent coasts, especially the fortress of San Juan de Ulúa. He commented to O'Reilly, with rather uncharacteristic levity, "The Marqués . . . is sorry to be relieved. Mexico must be a rare enchantment, which makes me begin to warn myself so that I will not be surprised when my successor arrives." [30]

Inasmuch as all that stood between Bucareli and his official assumption of command was a matter of ceremony, he began acting as viceroy even before he left Havana and continued this technically illegal policy en route to Mexico City. There is a certain humor in the situation which led him to issue a viceregal order before he actually had the right to do so. It arose from the fact that some of the coastal provinces were suffering from a locust plague, and Bucareli ordered food distributed to the afflicted inhabitants while he was still in Havana. Upon his arrival in Veracruz he discovered that the plague was still present. Characteristically, he reorganized the system of combatting the infestation; instead of merely furnishing food to the needy, he began paying exterminators a bounty for each *arroba* (about twenty-five

[30] Same to same, September 7, 1771, *ibid.*

pounds) of locusts collected, lowering the cost to the royal treasury by 75 per cent. The King then became personally interested in this rather plebeian problem and advised Bucareli to try the proven remedy of putting pigs to pasture in the infested area, cautioning however, that the pigs must be bled every fifteen days lest they suffocate on their own blood. Bucareli dutifully followed the royal suggestion, but reported that it had failed to work because of the mountainous terrain.[31]

While in Veracruz he inspected the fortress of San Juan de Ulúa and consulted with Engineer Agustín Crame on the matter. It was Bucareli's opinion that much work needed to be done on the castle, but that any decision must await his review of past projects and an inspection of the road to Perote and the state of the fortress being built there.[32]

The trip to Mexico City from Veracruz was taken in slow stages. Bucareli left Veracruz on September 9, reached Perote on the fourteenth, was met by Croix in San Cristóbal on the twenty-second, where he received the viceregal baton, and arrived in Mexico City on the twenty-third, where he took the oath of office before the *Real Audiencia.*[33]

If one were to select the single factor which harassed Bucareli more than any other, he could come up with only one choice—money. Insufficient funds had been the cause of many of his difficulties in Cuba, and questions of finance pervaded virtually every aspect of his administration of the viceroyalty, as subsequent chapters will make clear. It was not only with respect to public funds, however, that he was concerned; problems of his personal fortune also caused him a great

[31] Bucareli to Arriaga, October 18, 1771, No. 20, AGI, Mex., Leg. 1509. Arriaga to Bucareli, February 20, 1772, *ibid.* Bucareli to Arriaga, June 25, 1772, No. 444, *ibid.*

[32] Bucareli to Arriaga, September 8, 1771, No. 1, *ibid.* Bucareli's official correspondence was numbered, and his premature assumption of authority led to the existence of two letters bearing this same number, the later one dated October 4, 1771, after he had officially become viceroy. It was most unusual for him to be guilty of a breach of protocol.

[33] A detailed account of his progress from Perote to San Cristóbal is found in AGN, Historia, Vol. 335, No. 3, pp. 2–2v. Official notification of his assumption of office is the subject of Bucareli to Arriaga, October 4, 1771, No. 1, AGI, Mex., Leg. 1269.

deal of difficulty and embarrassment. Although his family was highly placed, it was not wealthy, and he was forced to rely almost entirely on his salary. The problem became pressing the moment he assumed the viceregency.

His annual salary as viceroy was 40,000 pesos, but he was compelled to pay immediately to the royal treasury a tax called the *media anata,* or one-half of one year's pay. He had saved practically nothing while in Cuba, where his salary had been 16,000 pesos, he had been compelled to borrow from his brothers to make the trip to New Spain, and, as a consequence, found himself in debt to the amount of 44,000 pesos without having either established a household befitting his station or paid the expenses of the traditional public entry. In a plea to the King, he made his case very well: [34]

Ever since I received the Cuba appointment I have held as a maxim not to be leagued with lenders, which might force me to be indebted to the inhabitants of the areas I govern. I accomplished this only because I was able to oblige my brothers to be responsible for the payment of whatever was necessary to outfit me, and when I was cleared of debt at the cost of worry and economies little suited to my station and the practice to which I am accustomed, I am again faced with the necessity of a similar new debt, while the salary I count on can scarcely suffice to cover the obligations of each year. I am aware that I must deposit 40,000 pesos for the *residencia* and must count on the cost of the return to Spain.

For relief he requested that he be excused from paying the *media anata* and that he be granted the same annual 20,000-peso *ayuda de costa,* or special allowance, which his predecessor had received.[35]

Although Charles III did not grant Bucareli everything he asked for, he did make sufficient concessions to ameliorate his viceroy's predicament. The *ayuda de costa* was ordered instituted, and Bucareli was permitted to pay the *media anata* in five annual installments rather than having to make the payment all at once. The royal deci-

---

[34] The *residencia* was a mandatory investigation of an official's conduct during his time in office and was held after he had left the position. He was compelled to deposit the equivalent of one year's salary, to be used to meet possible claims made against his administration.

[35] Bucareli to Arriaga, October 3, 1771, No. 5, AGI, Mex., Leg. 1509.

sion not to dispense with the *media anata* was based on the general principle that it would be bad policy to excuse any official from paying this tax. None of the relevant correspondence mentions the problem of the *residencia* payment.[36]

Bucareli was still having personal financial difficulties after a year in office, for he appealed to the Crown once more for assistance. He pointed out that from August 7 to September 23, 1771, he had been between appointments and had therefore received no salary. He requested some kind of allowance for this period.[37] It was the King's decision that he be paid on the scale of the salary allotted to the governor of Cuba, or 16,000 pesos per year.[38] Apparently this still did not relieve Bucareli sufficiently, for in September, 1774, motivated by a new royal dispensation with respect to the *media anata,* he asked that he receive a refund of the 9,440 pesos he had paid up to that time.[39]

His problems were solved, however, in mid-1776, when his salary was raised to 60,000 pesos, with the 20,000-peso *ayuda de costa* to continue in effect.[40] Even so, upon his death in 1779 his total estate amounted to less than 150,000 pesos, with something less than 100,-000 pesos of this amount in cash.[41] With reason, no one has ever cast the slightest doubt on his financial integrity.

It is perhaps not extravagant to assert that, rather than a "term" as viceroy, Bucareli's period in New Spain should be called a "sentence"; and in a sense it was a death sentence, not only because he died in office, but very possibly because he worked himself much harder than he should have. His final service for the Crown was something akin to being in prison. There is no indication that he ever left Mexico City after arriving there, and clearly it was not the place he wanted most

---

[36] Arriaga to Bucareli, January 25 and February 1, 1772, *ibid.*

[37] Bucareli to Arriaga, August 27, 1772, No. 538, *ibid.*

[38] Arriaga to Bucareli, January 23, 1773, *ibid.*

[39] Bucareli to Arriaga, September 26, 1774, in Rómulo Velasco Ceballos, *La administración de D. Fray Antonio María de Bucareli y Ursúa,* Vol. I, pp. 250–251. This work is cited hereafter as *La administración de . . . Bucareli.*

[40] Bucareli to Gálvez, June 26, 1776, AGN, CVB, 1776, Vol. 80, No. 2304, pp. 13v–14.

[41] A copy of Bucareli's will is located in AGI, Mex., Leg. 1276.

to be in. He was held there, so to speak, against his will. Despite his devotion to his king, he nevertheless was genuinely desirous of returning to Spain as soon as he was satisfied that there was no longer a pressing need for his presence in the colonies and as soon as he could convince the Crown of this fact. Before he had completed three years of service as viceroy he wrote concerning his relief to O'Reilly, "It does not suit me that it be delayed, because the viceroyalty is not well served by him who takes over its duties for a long time. The will of the King will always guide my operations, some months will pass, and I will look for reasons which may incline his pity." [42] In September, 1776, upon the completion of his fifth year as viceroy, Bucareli formally requested that he be relieved of the job; but although Charles III acknowledged that his petition was a just one, he expressed it as his royal will that Bucareli continue in New Spain until a proper successor could be found. [43] This decision was, in effect, the final denial of the appeal from the death sentence, for the vital successor was never found.

There can be no doubt that the viceregency was a killing job if the man appointed to it made a sincere effort to fulfill his duties. Fisher aptly describes the complexity of the system, the maddening minutiae with which the viceroy must be concerned, the endless and distracting red tape, the cumbersomeness of administration, and the inferiority and dishonesty of many of the subordinates on whom the viceroy must rely. [44] Bucareli himself verified this description in part when he commented, "Rest in the viceregency is not possible. All the government of the kingdom has to deal with the Secretariat, and, as a consequence, with the Viceroy. I cannot subject my disposition to leaving pending from one day to another what can be disposed of . . . because otherwise confusion would enter." [45] On another occasion he was led to

[42] Bucareli to O'Reilly, June 26, 1774, AGI, Mex., Leg. 1242.
[43] Bucareli to Gálvez, April 26, 1777, No. 2851, AGI, Mex., Leg. 1275. There is another copy in Legajo 1377. The letter of resignation was not located, but the letter here cited contains Bucareli's acknowledgment of the royal refusal of his request and concludes with an expression of his willingness to continue to work zealously in his assignment.
[44] Lillian Estelle Fisher, *The Intendant System in Spanish America,* pp. 2–5.
[45] Bucareli to O'Reilly, February 25, 1773, AGI, Mex., Leg. 1242.

declare, "Here one lives always agitated in these distances, a residence of little pleasure despite all the grandeur of the job I hold, because the responsibilities are insufferable, decisions necessary in many cases, and the confusion of antecedents more than you can imagine." [46] And again, "This is an intolerable fatigue, but there is no remedy . . ." [47]

Some idea of the nature of the Viceroy's daily existence may be gained from a brief description which he had occasion to offer his friend in reply to O'Reilly's complaint about the difficulties of his own position in Madrid: [48]

Mine is no more pleasing, for I spend ten hours a day at my desk, and still cannot complete what I would like, because on Court days they interrupt me at each step with appeals. My greatest relief is the three days a week when Poyanos usually eats at my house and gives me afterwards an hour of conversation until three o'clock, and another of chatting from eight to nine, with the exception of some Sundays when I go to the theater, more to comply with the public expectation than because it entertains me. At ten I am in bed, and the day rules my departure from it after drinking chocolate. I eat alone, which is a martyrdom, and I go to bed unfailingly at ten. And these are those whom the world calls the fortunate ones, which perhaps they were in another time, and which they would be in this time if I were capable of letting the others do that for which I am responsible.

It is clear that Bucareli was lonely, a consequence stemming perhaps in part from the fact that he apparently did not customarily have numerous close friends and in part from his conviction that a governor must not become too intimately involved with those whom he governs. The "Poyanos" to whom he refers was Colonel Ignacio Poyanos, commander of one of the regular Spanish Army units stationed in New Spain and hence a fellow military officer. His death in June, 1775, was a great blow to Bucareli, and there is no indication that anyone replaced him as Bucareli's closest friend and confidante during the remainder of his viceregency.[49]

[46] Same to same, June 26, 1772, *ibid.*

[47] Same to same, August 27, 1772, *ibid.*

[48] Same to same, January 27, 1773, *ibid.*

[49] Same to same, December 27, 1774, and O'Reilly to Bucareli, December 15, 1775, *ibid.*

Despite the loneliness, the sense of imprisonment, and the frustrations of the job, Bucareli was indefatigable in his efforts to serve the Crown well. Additionally, he developed, or perhaps brought with him to New Spain, a philosophical attitude which stood him in good stead. On one occasion he wrote, "When . . . one walks the Royal road, although suddenly the reasonless is vexing, one must give it little care. I am on this matter a bit of a philosopher, in the respect that I am never indisposed by other remonstrances than those I can make to myself." [50] Another time, again in a letter to O'Reilly, he said, "You already know that I have no other party than that which I judge most convenient for the Service, that I take the good where I find it, and that what I believe harmful I am not capable of embracing." [51]

In addition to zeal and a proper philosophy, any man who served as viceroy for nearly eight years must have been in good health. The climate of Havana had given Bucareli frequent cause for complaint on this score, but it is clear that the climate of Mexico City agreed with him—he remarked only days after his arrival there that "it cannot be bettered." [52] That he was aware of the physical hazard of working too hard is evidenced by his statement, "We are not made of bronze, the years pass, and our strength is not the same in all things, whereby it is necessary to take care to conserve it with precautions which we have not used in earlier years." [53] Until his final brief illness, he apparently was ill enough to be absent from work on only one occasion, when a cold and a high fever kept him in bed for two days.[54] No mention of any other illness was found in the record, personal or official.

It is difficult to assess which phases of his rather long viceregency were most trying for him, inasmuch as he was subjected to different kinds of stress at different times. Obviously, the months immediately following his assumption of command were excessively demanding of his time and his energies. Bucareli was a meticulous administrator, and he discovered quickly that the state of administrative affairs in New

[50] Bucareli to O'Reilly, February 25, 1773, *ibid.*
[51] Same to same, November 27, 1772, *ibid.*
[52] Same to same, October 5, 1771, *ibid.*
[53] Same to same, May 29, 1773, *ibid.*
[54] Same to same, December 27, 1771, *ibid.*

Spain did not approach his standards. Furthermore, he was stepping up from the relative simplicity of governing a single island to the complexity of managing the affairs of a vast and diverse viceroyalty. It is no wonder that he moved very slowly at first. Had he not been at least partially prepared for the situation, the results most certainly could have approached the disastrous. Excerpts from an early letter to O'Reilly can perhaps best demonstrate his reaction to these first months as well as the magnitude of the problems he faced: [55]

. . . ask God to grant me strength to disentangle myself from the chaos of difficulties which enclose me in the confused management of these vast provinces, in which, to now, I walk in shadows, because nothing is concluded. My predecessor rushed through much in the last days in order to close out his affairs, and things are not usually perfected when done in haste. Add to this the fact that I find a Secretariat so disarranged that there is no Index of the previous government, and that the Marqués de Croix has left me no summaries of subjects.

That Monte Rey, the Californias, and provinces of Sonora and Sinaloa neither have their subsidies arranged, nor is it easily discovered how they are governed; that in the Province of Nueva Vizcaya, the frontiers of Chihuahua, the war with the Indians continues, and that the troops with which we oppose them are in charge of the nephew of the *Visitador,* who, despite what they say about his having spirit, at his age has not had experience, a matter from which I hope to be relieved of worry because of the *Visitador's* desire that his nephew accompany him to Spain; . . .

That in this state in which the Indian frontiers are, they have set forth a new *reglamento* for presidios, which you will have seen printed, which amounts to that having removed some [presidios], they change the location of many [others] and specify reserves of supplies when the Treasury neither has them nor can the arrears of two years, which are owing, be satisfied.

In similar vein he discussed a variety of other difficult situations, such as the delay in the organization of the militia, the occupation and disposition of property of the expelled Jesuits, and the lack of written summaries of other problems, and concluded:

[55] Same to same, October 27, 1771, *ibid.*

Neither are you nor am I accustomed to leaving so many loose ends, because it is not the way to serve the King well. I am killing myself to achieve it, and it is true that in my daily conversations with the *Visitador* he gives me an account of antecedents, but they will never be sufficient; meanwhile, I document by writing to clarify the facts.

You will say that this letter offers only confused ideas, but I have no others, and I must move with great caution and not without a lack of confidence, to discover what is possible and what convenient. You give me time and God give me health, so that when, without obstacles I may begin to make decisions, all things will be clearly placed.

José de Gálvez had been instructed to remain in New Spain for several months after the departure of Croix in order to wind up the affairs of the visitation—including the writing of a full report—and to instruct Bucareli in the situation of the viceroyalty. The relationship between the two men was very cordial, and Bucareli found that the daily sessions with the *Visitador* helped materially in getting him oriented.[56] Nevertheless, the amount of information which he was expected to absorb greatly disturbed the Viceroy. On the eve of Gálvez' departure for Spain in February, 1772, Bucareli, in transmitting a copy of the *Visitador's* report, made the following comment: [57]

I send Gálvez' report on the things he has done here. The length of the report, the many documents attached, and the nature of its subjects mean that although for four months I have had daily conferences with him, it is not easy to learn it all. To this report is added another infinity of *expedientes* [files of documents on a particular subject] left behind, some with recommendations and some without. I need to examine them to see what is practical to do, because not everything believed possible on paper is possible in execution, especially in so vast an area . . . For these reasons I cannot soon give a solid opinion on the state of the viceroyalty in all parts. It must await investigation, experience, and some handling of affairs.

A part of Bucareli's concern arose from the fact that he regarded his primary task as much greater than merely continuing to administer

[56] Same to same, December 27, 1771, *ibid*.
[57] Bucareli to Arriaga, February 22, 1771, No. 204, AGI, Mex., Legs. 1509, 1370.

New Spain on the basis of a well-established and traditional system. Instead, he viewed the Gálvez visitation as an agency-of-change which had departed the scene with its work only partially done, or, to use his own words, he deplored "the confusion which reigns between a half-new system not established, and the old." [58] It was particularly difficult for a man of Bucareli's fundamental conservatism to move with confidence in an ambient of change, especially when such change was operative by virtue of somewhat uncertain or vague superior directives. His letter of March, 1772, to O'Reilly is indicative of his concern, for in it he said, "I count six months of continuous investigations and I still am not informed about what is convenient, either in the army or the militia, or in the management of the Treasury, so that I walk with much caution in order not to contradict the innovations or to stop supporting them without having knowledge of their utility." [59] Bucareli was accustomed to what he called the "old way," and felt it necessary to move carefully lest he upset, almost by instinct, the new order which Gálvez had merely begun to install.

However, by the end of the first year of his viceregency, although he still complained occasionally to O'Reilly about the complexities and difficulties of his position, it is clear that he was beginning to get the job under control and to move with greater confidence.[60] From that time until his death in April, 1779, he was truly the governor of New Spain. To be sure, there is no intention to assert that once this confidence and control were established, everything went smoothly and crises were not permitted to arise. As subsequent chapters will reveal, there were many critical moments, numerous occasions on which Bucareli was troubled and uncertain about which course to follow. It would be surprising were it otherwise when one considers the time, the place, and the man.

[58] Bucareli to O'Reilly, December 27, 1771, AGI, Mex., Leg. 1242.
[59] Same to same, March 27, 1772, *ibid.*
[60] See, for example, same to same, September 26, 1772, *ibid.*

The Church in New Spain

F EW INSTITUTIONS have been of such continuous significance in Mexican history as the Roman Catholic Church. Understanding its position is essential to understanding one of the fundamental influences on Mexican development from the time of the Conquest until today. Its virtual religious monopoly among the Mexican people and its favored political and economic status during many centuries have been conditioning factors of tremendous importance in terms of the nature of Mexican societal development. As one of the most notable of the several privileged corporations which the Spanish system tended to produce, such as the military and the merchants' guild, the church contributed in creating popular acceptance of the concept that such elite groups are a proper component of civilized society. Also worthy of note is the fact that this church was the central factor in maintaining the religious peace which prevailed during the entire colonial period, a circumstance of great import when one considers the significance of religious unrest in the English colonial empire of the same period.

Aside from the royal government itself, no institution in the Spanish colonies was of greater importance than the church, and between these two entities, State and Church, there was arranged by an early date a mutually profitable *modus vivendi* based upon the *Patronato Real,* or Royal Patronage, whereby Rome recognized the King of Spain as administrative head of the church in the Spanish Indies. Royal rights to dominance over the church in America began with the papal grants of Alexander VI in 1493 and 1501, and of Julius II in 1508. Possessing little machinery for administering the American church, and finding that the Spanish rulers tended to be cooperative in religious matters, the popes readily granted to the Crown the handling of tithes and the nomination of church officials. In 1574 Philip II was able to set forth explicitly the basis for his claims to the patronage, for by that time the exercise of this right by his predecessors had given it a sanction not thereafter disputed.[1] Although lesser frictions between Church and State lasted until the end of Spanish rule in America, steady royal resistance to papal pretensions found the *patronato* firmly established and secure at the close of the colonial period.

The eighteenth century, however, witnessed the introduction of new factors which tended to place a strain on the heretofore generally harmonious union. The Enlightenment, of which the Spanish Bourbons, and especially Charles III and his ministers, were advocates, contained a strong element of anticlericalism. As a consequence, although the customary harmony apparently continued to prevail, numerous evidences of the changing attitude of the Crown were manifested. The expulsion of the Jesuits, the decline of the Inquisition, the liberal reforms in the ecclesiastical organization proposed by Charles III, all suggest the nature of the new point of view. It is not here proposed that there occurred any extensive or fundamental rupture between Spanish Church and State during the eighteenth century. It is suggested, however, that there came to exist a paradoxical situation wherein the traditional partnership, although apparently still in effect, was actually undergoing modification in the direction of greater independence and dominance on the part of the Crown. In many cases lip service and insincere gestures replaced genuine respect. Bucareli's relations with the church serve to demonstrate this.

Since the king could not by himself supervise in detail the exercise of the patronage throughout his empire, he delegated the authority to his major subordinates, who in this office bore the title of vice-patron. The viceroys of the eighteenth century regarded the *patronato* as a

---

[1] Donald E. Smith, *The Viceroy of New Spain,* p. 232.

function of importance in so far as it gave them a measure of prestige among the people they ruled. Actual church administration was handled by church officials, and the viceroys' influence was rather indirect. In a general way they were to see that the king's prerogatives were not infringed upon by excessively zealous ecclesiastics, and to prevent the latter from quarreling among themselves to the harm of both the government's and the people's interests.[2]

Specifically, the bulk of the vice-patron's tangible powers involved his part in nominations for, and appointments to, positions in the church. Candidates for major prebends and cathedral positions were nominated by the governing chapters, or ecclesiastical *cabildos,* of the cathedrals. It was the viceroy's function to see that such prebends did not long remain vacant, to appoint a royal assistant to attend the nominating sessions in the king's name in order to assure regular procedure, and to pass the nominations on to Spain for the monarch's final choice. With respect to the regular Orders, wherein prelates were elected by the governing chapters, the viceroy's obligation extended to seeing that the elections were impartial and properly decorous. An appointed royal assistant usually sufficed for this purpose, but such elections were occasionally so partisan that a greater show of authority was necessary. In minor appointments, such as to curacies, the viceroy was the ultimate authority, choosing one priest from a list of three presented by the prelate concerned; in most cases he selected the name which headed the list.[3]

Less tangible but perhaps more significant was the vice-patron's function as a sort of combined policeman, moderator, and overseer. This he sometimes exercised in conjunction with the prelates, sometimes through them, and occasionally independently of them. Opportunity to exercise his authority arose when disturbances involving ecclesiastical personnel occurred and the responsible prelate either would not or could not correct the situation. In such cases the viceroy conceived interim measures and then submitted a report to the king for final

[2] *Ibid.* Bancroft, *Mexico,* Vol. III, pp. 685–686.

[3] Marqués de Croix, Instrucción de el Virrey Marqués de Croix que deja a su Subscesor Dividida en cinco Puntos, AGN, CVB, 1772, Vol. 24, pp. 407–456. This document is cited hereafter as Instrucción.

decision. A similar responsibility demanded the vice-patron's vigilance in seeing that the *institutos,* or regulations, of cathedrals were observed. Again, his first step was to notify the prelate of the violation before taking further action himself.[4]

When Bucareli succeeded the Marqués de Croix in 1771, Croix, in his Instruction, discussed the ecclesiastical phase of administration in some detail. His first comments are indicative of his general attitude, and later remarks by Bucareli indicate that he apparently shared this point of view. Croix said:[5]

> The viceroy exercises the *Patronato* as vice-patron, and although it is necessary to conserve it, since it is the jewel which the King holds as the most esteemed in the Kingdom, it is well that with the ecclesiastic state one proceed with great circumspection, maintaining good correspondence and harmony with the bishops and prelates of Orders, because the people are by nature inclined to trouble and to augment any discord whatever, light as it may be, and there usually results harm to the public from whatever quarrel there may be among the heads who govern.

Croix may well have had in mind, as he wrote these words, his own experience wherein he and the Archbishop had become engaged in what took on almost the proportions of a feud over the question of the placement of seats at the Fourth Mexican Provincial Council.[6] More broadly, it is evident that the Marqués regarded his official relations with the church as a matter to be governed in significant degree by public opinion. His Instruction contains no reference to the need for proper respect for the hierarchy, no sign of awe or humility before the authority of the prelates or what they represented.

Bucareli indicated the similarity of his point of view when he commented, in a letter to his friend Alejandro O'Reilly in 1772, "The new Archbishop has arrived and taken possession. He appears to be an able and docile man. You already know that dealing with the prelates is one of the delicate points of America; but I hope to conciliate him in the best service of the King, avoiding rivalries."[7]

[4] *Ibid.*   [5] *Ibid.,* pp. 437v–438.
[6] Croix to Bucareli, November 13, 1771, AGN, Historia, Vol. 335, No. 3, pp. 4–5v.
[7] Bucareli to O'Reilly, September 26, 1772, AGI, Mex., Leg. 1242.

Further evidence is supplied by Bucareli's report, again to O'Reilly, on the Fourth Mexican Provincial Council, which ended its sessions early in his viceregency: [8]

Our Mexican Council is about to conclude; I attended it because it appeared necessary, and I am friendly with the prelates, the reciprocal lack of confidence which prevailed having been ended.

The people are content, and I will go immediately [to the closing ceremonies] from the ceremonial of entry, which is tiring and costly, the one for one who has much to do and the other for one who cannot maintain himself unless the King gives the 20,000-peso *ayuda de costa* which his predecessor had.

P.S. The Fourth Mexican Council ended with much peace, and my attendance. On the thirty-first I made the ceremonial entrance, a very serious act, and one which demonstrates vividly the Greatness of the master whom we serve.

It is probable that both Bucareli and Croix were representative of their class and status, and of their period as well, in this less-than-humble attitude which they displayed toward the church and its dignitaries. Croix is famous for his defiance of the Inquisition, for which Simpson labels him "an emancipated son of the Age of Reason." [9] Bucareli gave other indications that he too was concerned largely in only an official capacity about his relations with the religious hierarchy. There is no intention to suggest that either of these viceroys was not a sincere communicant of the faith. Bucareli in particular was deeply concerned with his religious belief. In his will he specified that he was to be buried beneath the floor of the Shrine of the Virgin of Guadalupe near the door through which he had always entered to pray. He also provided that four thousand Masses be said for his soul, at one peso each, and that twelve silver statues be made for the Guadalupe Shrine, also to be paid for from his relatively small estate. [10] However, both Croix and Bucareli apparently distinguished between the church as the agency of faith and the church as a temporal power capable, if not carefully watched, of infringing upon the rights guar-

[8] Same to same, October 27, 1771, *ibid.*

[9] Simpson, *Many Mexicos,* p. 169.

[10] April 8, 1779. AGI, Mex., Leg. 1276.

anteed by the *patronato,* which each of them guarded with zeal. In this sense they may be regarded as precursors of some of the Mexican liberals of the mid-nineteenth century.

One of the first problems of a religious nature which Bucareli faced upon assuming office was a continuance of the controversy which had led to the coolness between Croix and the Archbishop. The Fourth Mexican Provincial Council—the first since 1585—had been convoked in January, 1771, and was still in session when Bucareli became viceroy. Called by the King, it was attended by all the prelates of New Spain to consider some twenty points proposed by Charles III.[11] Croix had attended the opening session, but was chagrined to discover that the location of the viceroy's dais did not comport with his idea of the respect due the King's alter ego. He had previously remonstrated with the Archbishop over this matter on the occasion of his reception as an incoming viceroy and had twice carried his plea to the King without receiving a final decision.[12]

On October 10, 1771, soon after his assumption of command, Bucareli attended the council because, as he said, "it seemed necessary." He approached the cathedral attended by a large entourage of officials and noblemen. The council members, apprised of his coming, emerged from the cathedral in a procession, led by the Archbishop, and met the Viceroy halfway across the *plaza mayor,* or central square. They conducted Bucareli into the cathedral and thence into the chapter room where the sessions were being held. Some alteration had been made in the location of the viceroy's dais, but it still did not comply with the proper ceremonial standards. After Bucareli and the Archbishop had delivered formal speeches in Latin, the prelates escorted the Viceroy

[11] Several *consultas* of the Consejo de Indias in 1769 discuss reform of both the regular and secular clergy as the fundamental purpose of the provincial councils which were ordered in Lima, Bogotá, and Charcas, as well as in Mexico (AGI, IG, Leg. 3026A). On August 21, 1769, the King issued a *Tomo Regio* addressed to all metropolitans, ordering them to assemble the councils to consider twenty points of reform set forth in this *cédula.* Archbishop Francisco Antonio Lorenzana of New Spain, on January 10, 1770, sent out the convocatory order, setting January 13, 1771, as the date of assembly. Jesús García Gutiérrez, *Apuntamientos de historia eclesiástica mejicana,* pp. 61–62. This work is cited hereafter as *Apuntamientos.*

[12] Croix, Instrucción, AGN, CVB, 1772, Vol. 24, pp. 408–408v. Croix to Bucareli, November 13, 1771, AGN, Historia, Vol. 335, No. 3, pp. 4–5v.

outside the cathedral. On October 26, Bucareli again went to the cathedral to participate in the closing ceremonies. Surprisingly, he did not mention the unmeet seating arrangements when he reported on the council to Spain, perhaps because he saw that there was no need, inasmuch as Royal Assistant Joachín de Rivadeneyra had attended all sessions of the council and submitted a detailed account of the entire affair.[13] It is also likely that he let the matter drop in the interest of mending viceregal relations with the hierarchy.

The fact that the resolutions of the council were never approved by the King, the Council of the Indies, or the Pope has occasioned some dispute. Charles III issued a *cédula* in October, 1772, in which he commented on various minor aspects of the council and ruled that thereafter the viceroy's chair must be placed on the same level as that of the archbishop; but he specifically warned against relying on the council's resolutions as authority for any action until they had been approved by the Council of the Indies and by the Pope.[14] Bancroft asserts that approval was never given because Fiscal José Antonio Areche objected to the conduct of Archbishop Lorenzana.[15] García Gutiérrez is not in agreement with this explanation nor with one which suggests that the Council of the Indies withheld its approval because the Mexican Provincial Council had not displayed a sufficient amount of regalism. He offers his belief that the Spanish court was still upset over the Jesuit expulsion, and that Lorenzana, transferred to Toledo shortly after the adjournment of the council and then promoted to a cardinalcy, had neither the time nor the inclination to press for approval until the resolutions had become outmoded.[16] Apparently the matter will remain a mystery.

[13] Bucareli to Arriaga, October 28, 1771, AGN, CVB, 1771–1772, Vol. 5, Libro 8, pp. 49–62. Rivadeneyra's report had apparently been sent to Spain in installments during 1771 as the council progressed. His account for the period after Bucareli's arrival was sent with the above cover-letter, in which Bucareli makes no mention of the problem of the dais.
[14] AGN, RC, 1772, Vol. 101, No. 100, pp. 398, 401. There is also a copy in AGI, IG, Leg. 3026A.
[15] Bancroft, *Mexico,* Vol. III, p. 376.
[16] García Gutiérrez, *Apuntamientos,* pp. 62–63. It should be noted that royal action was evidently taken on some aspects of the resolutions. For example, in AGI, IG,

The basic reason for calling the council had been to seek ways of improving the religious establishment, principally in terms of greater efficiency and stricter observance of regulations. With this in mind, a comprehensive program of *visitas* (inspections) and reforms for the regular Orders had been projected for some time, and in the council the Archbishop spoke about it at length. He urged the prelates of the various Orders to anticipate the recommendations which the inspectors might make and thus please the King.[17] In view of the disturbances which subsequently occurred, it would undoubtedly have been better had all necessary reforms been accomplished in this manner. Some *visitas* were executed, of course, with a minimum of discord. For example, Charles III appointed the Archbishop to supervise the inspection and reform of the Orders of the Agonizantes and San Antonio Abad, each of which had only one house in New Spain.[18] The matter was handled smoothly and to the satisfaction of the King.[19] Other *visitas,* however, gave rise to disputes, threats, resignations, and general upheaval.

Such was the case of the Bethlemites. The story of this attempted inspection and reform is replete with charges, denials, countercharges, and contradictions to the extent that to relate the facts clearly and confidently is almost impossible. In many ways it approximates a farce. To begin with, both the *visitador,* Fray Andrés de la Santísima Trinidad, and his secretary became ill shortly after reaching New Spain, occasioning a delay in launching their project. Next, a member of the Order, Fray Antonio de la Madre de Dios, had apparently denounced the General of the Order in a written representation and had

Leg. 65, there is a *consulta* in which the Council of the Indies expresses its opinion on paragraphs 231–244 of the council's report; and in AGN, Historia, Vol. 96, No. 25, pp. 1–82, there is a Royal *Cédula* (pp. 2–5), dated October 21, 1775, in which twenty-two points drawn up by the council are settled by the King.

[17] Rivadeneyra's report, Bucareli to Arriaga, October 28, 1771, AGN, CVB, 1771–1772, Vol. 5, Libro 8, pp. 50v–51.

[18] Royal *Cédula,* August 20, 1772, AGN, RC, 1772, Vol. 101, No. 54, pp. 97–98. Same date, *ibid.,* No. 55, pp. 99–100. September 23, 1772, *ibid.,* No. 92, p. 386.

[19] Royal *Cédula,* February 14, 1778, AGN, RC, 1778, Vol. 113, No. 71, pp. 99–100. This *cédula* is an acknowledgment and an acceptance of the Archbishop's report, cited as having been dated July 27, 1774.

been living in a Franciscan college since the denunciation for reasons one may deduce. About the time Fray Andrés was getting well enough to begin his job, Fray Antonio reported to Bucareli that the *Visitador* had excused him from giving further evidence in the matter. Fray Antonio claimed that this was because the general and the *Visitador* had an agreement whereby Fray Andrés was to be made vice-general once the *visita* was satisfactorily concluded.

To complicate matters further, the General and his governing chapter were on the verge of leaving New Spain to set up headquarters in Peru, but their departure was delayed pending the completion of the inspection. To add to the confusion, a dissatisfied group of Bethlemites had previously appealed to both Charles III and the Pope, challenging the legality of the governing chapter that had elected the General. A reply to this appeal was momentarily expected.

Bucareli ordered the General's transfer to Peru suspended pending clarification. The General protested the ruling. Two Assistant Generals chose this moment to charge their leader with irregularity in the method he had used in designating which of the brothers should accompany him to Peru. Bucareli upheld his suspension of the voyage, but in reporting the whole story to the King in May, 1772, he stated that in his opinion the *visita* could not proceed successfully so long as the cause of the trouble was to be found at the top of the organization. He suggested the appointment of a new and fearless *visitador* and at the same time solicited royal guidance in the matter.[20]

Apparently the King offered no solution to the problem. The Bethlemite General periodically petitioned Bucareli to lift the suspension of the voyage until, in April, 1773, Fray Andrés reported that his investigations revealed no reason why the General should be further delayed. Fiscal Areche approved the report, and Bucareli removed his prohibition on the Peru trip.[21]

Peace, however, appears not to have appealed to the Bethlemites. As soon as the General began to prepare for his departure, Fray

[20] Bucareli to Charles III, May 25, 1772, AGN, CVB, 1771–1773, Vol. 6, Libro 5, No. 30, pp. 43–45v.
[21] Bucareli to Arriaga, April 27, 1773, AGN, CVB, 1773, Vol. 37, No. 903, pp. 46–47v.

Andrés notified Bucareli that trouble was again brewing because the General, in contravention of Bethlemite custom, intended to defer the election of a vice-general until the new headquarters was set up in Peru, instead of holding the election in New Spain before he left. Bucareli demanded an explanation from the General. The latter protested briefly, but finally assembled his governing chapter and set an early date for the election. Confident that the matter was settled, Bucareli urged the General to maintain peace in his Order and reported the incident to Madrid.[22] The election was held and followed the Bethlemite pattern—a riot threatened. Bucareli found it necessary to dispatch a judge from the *Audiencia* and a body of troops to the scene to achieve a peaceful conclusion.[23]

The General finally made his belated journey to Peru, leaving in New Spain the recently-elected vice-general. It soon became clear, however, that the presence of the General was not an essential ingredient in the recipe for discord. In spite of Bucareli's hope for peace and his efforts toward that end, new quarrels broke out in the Order. This time the cause of disturbance involved the degree of subordination owed the *Visitador* by the Vice-General and his governing chapter. Increasing steadily in fury, the argument reached a point wherein abusive and threatening lampoons were posted on the door of the secretary of the *visita*. The frightened Secretary and Fray Andrés begged Bucareli's protection. In turn, the Vice-General represented to the Viceroy the irregular conduct of Fray Andrés and argued that the trouble was all the *Visitador's* fault. In the interest of peace, however, he offered to resign his position and "retire to the corner of his cell to finish quietly the few days of life left to him." [24]

As a result of the fear engendered by the lampoons, four friars were transferred to other Bethlemite houses. Within a few days, with the Vice-General's permission, one of them returned to the Mexico City house. When the *Visitador,* still afraid, immediately protested this return, Bucareli requested the removal of this friar and asked

[22] Same to same, May 27, 1773, AGN, CVB, 1773, Vol. 38, No. 952, pp. 26–28.
[23] *Ibid.,* marginal note.
[24] Bucareli to Arriaga, October 27, 1773, AGN, CVB, 1773, Vol. 44, No. 1154, pp. 18–19.

that the other three remain where they were. The Vice-General complied, but asserted that the *Visitador's* fears were groundless.

Peace reigned briefly. Fray Andrés soon began insisting, however, that the prevalent disunity could be dispelled only through the resignation of the Vice-General. Fiscal Areche felt that the whole inspection should be suspended and an appeal made to the King for a complete readjustment of the situation. Bucareli and the *Real Acuerdo,* his advisory council of major ministers, felt, however, that one more attempt at pacification should be made, exhorting both the Vice-General and the *Visitador* to mend their ways. As an alternative, they felt that perhaps the King could be induced to turn the inspection over to the Archbishop. In his report Bucareli stated that if the King did not supply a solution, the upheavals would never cease, the petitions would continue to pour in, and the *visita* would never be completed.[25]

It was completed, nevertheless, possibly because the Viceroy's exhortations for peace had some effect. Fray Andrés accomplished his mission, but in making his final report in October, 1773, he bypassed the Viceroy and sent his account directly to the King.[26] Evidently the issue was peacefully settled inasmuch as no further mention of the *visita* appears in the Viceroy's correspondence or in the Royal *Cédulas* for the remaining years of Bucareli's term.

Although there existed some confusion in the conduct of the Carmelite *visita,* which extended from 1773 through 1775, it did not produce upheavals comparable to those of the Bethlemite affair. Initially, a problem was posed when the *visitador,* Fray Julián de Jesús María, and his secretary arrived from Spain and began their inspection in Puebla without first reporting to the Viceroy in Mexico City, in contravention of the royal instructions they carried.[27] This difficulty was straightened out without any untoward incident, but shortly thereafter, the peculiar nature of the King's instructions produced a puzzling situation. As His Majesty had directed, the

[25] *Ibid.,* pp. 19–20v.

[26] Bucareli to Charles III, October 27, 1773, in Velasco Ceballos, *La administración de ... Bucareli,* Vol. II, p. 302.

[27] Royal *Cédula,* October 27, 1773, AGN, RC, 1773, Vol. 103, No. 115, pp. 273–274.

Visitador established himself in the Carmelite house in Mexico City
while his secretary set up headquarters in the Querétaro convent.
Inasmuch as there were sixteen Carmelite establishments throughout
New Spain, the necessity of traveling from one house to another in
order to accomplish the *visita* properly seems obvious. Nevertheless,
when Fray Julián applied to Bucareli for permission to visit the
other houses, the Viceroy, on the Fiscal's advice, replied that the
King's orders allowed no such activity, and that as a result the
Visitador and his secretary must secure the necessary information
by means of reports from the other fourteen convents.[28]

Under this handicap the two Carmelites pursued their investigations and seem to have done a creditable job. They recommended
establishing a maximum for the total number of Carmelite friars
to be allowed in the sixteen houses, basing the figure on the facilities
and income of each convent.[29] A tendency toward disunity among the
friars, based on partiality for the region from which each had come in
Spain or the New World, led the *Visitador* to suggest a plan designed
to eliminate such provincialism. He further suggested the periodical
dispatch of *visitadores* to see that discrimination on a regional basis
did not occur. Finally, he outlined a constructive program for improvement of the educational and teacher-training system which the
Carmelites employed. Both Bucareli and the King approved the report
and the recommendations.[30]

Not only with respect to inspections did Bucareli exercise a re-
straining and decisive power. In a variety of other incidents within the
ecclesiastical establishment he made use of his position as vice-patron
to take corrective measures, sometimes as a sort of mediator, sometimes
in the character of a judge. One such instance he inherited from his
predecessor, the Marqués de Croix. At the request of the Bishop
of Durango, the Marqués had placed under arrest the dean of that
cathedral for certain derelictions. Shortly after Bucareli's arrival in

[28] Bucareli to Arriaga, October 27, 1773, AGN, CVB, 1773, Vol. 44, No. 1155, pp. 21–22.
[29] Same to same, March 27, 1775, AGN, CVB, 1775, Vol. 65, No. 1763, pp. 33v–35.
[30] Royal *Cédula*, July 27, 1778, AGN, RC, 1778, Vol. 114, No. 172, pp. 338–341v.

New Spain, he was ordered to release the Dean from arrest and put him at the disposition of the Fourth Mexican Provincial Council. Since the council had already adjourned when the royal order arrived, Bucareli sought the Archbishop's advice on what to do with the prisoner. They agreed that since the Dean had never been tried for his alleged offense, the most suitable solution was to return him to his old office after a strict warning from the Archbishop, with the expense of his long round-trip and his detention in Mexico City serving as a penalty. The Viceroy also wrote to the Durango ecclesiastical *cabildo* urging it to endeavor to maintain a tranquil atmosphere in its cathedral. To the home government Bucareli suggested that it might have been more salutary to transfer the Dean to Spain, whereby he would lose his benefice and would thus serve as an example to other would-be troublemakers.[31]

Obviously, not all cases were this simple. In November, 1772, the *cabildo* of the Valladolid cathedral was engaged in voting on candidates to be presented to the *Viceroy* by the three-candidate system for the purpose of filling vacant curacies. Two members of the *cabildo*, Canon Juan Antonio de Nagera and Prebendary Nicolás de Villanueva, protested to Bucareli that all was not proper in the *cabildo's* procedure. They brought charges of nepotism against some of the *cabildo's* members, revealing the log-rolling technique whereby this had been accomplished.[32]

As evidence, Nagera and Villanueva described specific instances of misconduct wherein twelve of the twenty-one members of the body, by a prearranged system of nomination and balloting, had forced their will upon the remainder of the members. The protesters cited the cases of two deserving clerics for whose advancement the public clamored, but whose aspirations were doomed because both the cantor and the canon penitenciary were sponsoring their nephews. Asserting that "flesh and blood prevailed," they formally protested such deplorable activities in a nominating session, citing a Royal *Cédula*

[31] Bucareli to Arriaga, December 20, 1771, in Velasco Ceballos, *La administración de . . . Bucareli*, Vol. II, pp. 289–290.

[32] Bucareli to Charles III, January 27, 1773, AGN, CVB, 1771–1773, Vol. 6, Libro 5, No. 74, pp. 95–95v.

which forbade voting for one's relatives. Their protest was ignored. When the two of them withdrew from the *cabildo,* the rest of the members continued with the nominations. As a result, Nagera and Villanueva requested that Bucareli anticipate the report of the royal assistant, whom the Viceroy had appointed to attend the session, and take proper action if he found any irregularities.[33]

Capitular Vicar Pedro Jaurrieta, the cantor of the Valladolid cathedral, had a different version to present. He acknowledged the fact that the nephews of several *cabildo* members had been nominated for vacant curacies, but he protested that such procedure was in no way illegal, inasmuch as the *cédula* cited by Nagera and Villanueva had been directed exclusively at the Mexico City cathedral. In support of this contention the cantor pointed out that the Valladolid ecclesiastical authorities had never received a copy of the *cédula.* Furthermore, he said, in his eighteen years as a church official he had frequently seen cases of churchmen voting for nephews and even for brothers without any objection being raised. He revealed that Nagera, on another matter, had protested a situation which he had previously accepted because on the earlier occasion it had been to his advantage. Finally, Vicar Jaurrieta made clear the reasons for the *cabildo's* selections in the specific cases to which the protesters had objected, and concluded by asking the Viceroy to accept the triads as presented.[34]

Bucareli felt that he needed more information before making a final decision, and to this end he called for the minutes of the *cabildo's* meetings, showing how the members had voted and revealing the reasons why they felt it proper for a member to vote when his own relatives were among the candidates. Also, since the report of the Royal Assistant had been only general in nature, Bucareli wished to confer with him personally. With these needs supplied, the Viceroy, after consultation with the Fiscal and the Archbishop, arrived at the following decisions: that the cases presented by Nagera and Villanueva were not strong enough to warrant changing the triads or questioning the honesty of the *cabildo;* that the *cabildo's* selections should be accepted; that the prearranged system of voting on candidates was in the

[33] *Ibid.,* pp. 96v–99.   [34] *Ibid.,* pp. 99–105.

interest of efficiency, and that the merits of the candidates really had been considered; that the best and most reasonable members of the *cabildo* had agreed with the cantor; and, that if the selections were delayed, many benefices would remain vacant, to the harm of the parishioners. He therefore issued a decree approving the triads and appointing to office the clerics whose names appeared first on the lists. To Nagera and Villanueva he wrote that he found the disturbances they had caused extremely unpleasant, and he admonished that thereafter they strive to achieve a spirit of peace and harmony.[35]

These decisions were typical of Bucareli—to support the higher authorities, to urge harmonious conduct, and above all, to avoid open ruptures which would injure the reputation of Church or State. The Crown, in turn, supported his decisions with blanket approval. To prevent similar disturbances in the future, however, the King issued a *cédula* prohibiting the nomination of subjects for prebends or curacies within four grades of relationship to any member of the nominating board, thus vindicating the dissidents, at least in principle.[36]

There were several other occasions on which Bucareli exercised his authority as vice-patron to mediate or adjudicate disputes among members of the ecclesiastical family. Major instances involved a clash between a group of Franciscan missionaries residing in the Apostolic College of Pachuca and the authorities of the college,[37] and complaints from certain Dominicans concerning the laxity with which their superiors were conducting the finances and missionary efforts of that Order in New Spain.[38] In both instances Bucareli acted to rectify the situation, although, of necessity, he had to submit his decisions to the Crown for ultimate approval.

[35] *Ibid.*, pp. 105–111v.
[36] Royal *Cédula,* April 1, 1774, AGN, RC, 1774, Vol. 104, No. 77, pp. 130–132v.
[37] Bucareli to Charles III, October 27, 1774, AGN, CVB, 1771–1778, Vol. 14, No. 195, pp. 122–127; and Velasco Ceballos, *La administración de . . . Bucareli,* Vol. II, pp. 310–314.
[38] Anonymous Dominican to José de Gálvez, March 25, 1778, AGN, RC, 1778, Vol. 115, No. 103, pp. 148–154. Royal *Cédula,* November 13, 1778, *ibid.,* pp. 146–147v. Gálvez replaced Arriaga as secretary of state early in 1776.

That the Crown was determined to maintain its cognizance of intrachurch conflicts is made evident by a Royal *Cédula* set forth in 1775. The Commissary General of the Franciscan Order, in issuing patents to some of his delegates in the New World, forbade the members of his Order to make any appeal to the Council of the Indies or to the King. Inasmuch as the prohibition obviously interfered with the *Real Patronato,* Charles III instructed his viceroys to collect all copies of the order and to instruct Franciscan prelates that in all cases where the law permitted, members of their Order were to be allowed to appeal to the Crown for protection.[39]

The religious establishment in New Spain was not, of course, a static thing. Ecclesiastical and civil heads regularly worked together to reorganize, expand, and make more efficient the functioning of the church. Charles III gave considerable stimulus to the secularization of curacies in which the missionary element, although no longer needed, was still present. The Marqués de Croix, in his Instruction, reviewed the progress of the secularization program under his government. He pointed out that, although theory demanded that a curacy should have missionary status for only ten years, secularization at the end of such a period was rare, because the Indian neophytes usually were not yet satisfactorily indoctrinated, and also because they did not have sufficient wealth to support a secular cleric, whose mode of life was more expensive than that of a regular. For these reasons, said Croix, he had proceeded cautiously with the secularization program. He had, however, achieved some reorganization through closing down regular houses holding fewer than eight clerics, consolidating these small groups into larger monasteries, and turning over to seculars some of the parishes thus vacated.[40]

With the reasonable assumption that Bucareli, staying in character, also moved with caution, it is apparent that he did effectuate a secularization program of notable extent. In June, 1773, he reported on the number of curacies and *doctrinas* (Indian villages newly consecrated to the faith) which, to that date, had been secularized and

[39] Royal *Cédula,* February 22, 1775, AGN, RC, 1775, Vol. 106, No. 49, pp. 71–72v.

[40] Croix, Instrucción, AGN, CVB, 1772, Vol. 24, pp. 440–440v.

partitioned, the partitioning probably because of population increases within the areas involved. The report reveals eleven curacies secularized—five in the diocese of Mexico, six in the Valladolid bishopric. Of the eleven, one had been under Dominican control and ten under Franciscan. In the same period, in agreement with the Archbishop and the Bishop of Puebla, Bucareli had divided sixteen old curacies, creating sixteen new ones. The dioceses involved were those of Puebla and Mexico City.[41] The entire change, he said, had been achieved with the greatest tranquillity. There is evidence that further secularization took place in the Mexico diocese and also in the Bishopric of Valladolid in Michoacán, with the Dominicans, Franciscans, and Augustinians feeling the effect of the change.[42]

Secularization at all costs was not Bucareli's policy, as his management of the organization of the San Hipólito Order in Oaxaca demonstrates. At one time, this entire Order had been subordinate to the provincial who resided in Mexico City. Because of the difficulties of communication and because of regional sentiment on the part of distant houses, several distinct provinces had been created, among them Mexico, Puebla, and Oaxaca. During Croix's administration it was proposed that the provinces of Puebla and Oaxaca be joined, with a consequent secularization of ten curacies in the Oaxaca province. The proposal remained unsettled until after Bucareli became viceroy.

He investigated the matter with great care, calling for reports from numerous civil as well as ecclesiastical authorities. In the interest of harmony and efficiency he decided in favor of the *status quo* and against secularization. He pointed out that the subordination of the Oaxaca group to Puebla would revive the old animosities prevalent when the Mexico City provincial had been in command, especially since there existed no precedent for Puebla's dominance. He pictured the inevitable struggle that would result over which group of leaders should obtain the prelacies in the new enlarged province. In view of

[41] Bucareli to Arriaga, June 26, 1773, and inclosures, AGN, CVB, 1773, Vol. 39, No. 999, pp. 29v–30, 145–146.

[42] Royal *Cédula*, October 20, 1778, AGN, RC, 1778, Vol. 115, No. 78, pp. 109–109v. Also see AGI, Mex., Legs. 1275 and 1276, which contain several *expedientes* on projected secularizations in 1778.

this decision against uniting the two provinces, the inadvisability of secularization becomes apparent, for to do away with ten of the twelve curacies which the Order had in Oaxaca would have made untenable the maintenance of the two remaining parishes. The inability of the secular clergy to cope with the variety of languages in the area, the scarcity of learned secular clerics in the bishoprics, and the greater expense of secular administration, all militated against the secularization proposal. For these several reasons Bucareli ordered the continued independent existence of the Oaxaca province of San Hipólito Mártir, the continuation of the same prelates then in control, and the retention of the ten curacies involved.[43]

Two other instances of ecclesiastical reorganization under Bucareli fall more appropriately under other headings. With respect to the creation of a new bishopric to be called Nuevo Reino de León, the primary concern seems to have been financial rather than ecclesiastical.[44] Similarly, Bucareli's action in uniting two colleges in order to achieve greater efficiency is basically an educational matter.[45]

Up to this point consideration has been given only to problems encompassed within the ecclesiastical establishment of New Spain. With the exception of the King and the Viceroy, who appear in their roles as patron and vice-patron, the personnel has been exclusively of a religious character. Obviously, the church did not exist in a vacuum, since it was an important part of the life of virtually every Spanish subject. Ironically, those who perhaps hailed its existence with the greatest joy were the criminals, inasmuch as each edifice provided them with a haven of refuge because of the immunity from arrest which they enjoyed there.

When Croix became viceroy, he found that a large number of criminals used these asylums as bases of operation. According to him, "they insolently left them by day and night to commit robberies

[43] Bucareli to Charles III, October 27, 1773, in Velasco Ceballos, *La administración de ... Bucareli,* Vol. II, pp. 304–307.

[44] Same to same, November 26, 1774, AGN, CVB, 1771–1778, Vol. 14, No. 198, pp. 128v–131v.

[45] Same to same, November 25, 1774, AGN, CVB, *ibid.,* pp. 143–147.

and killings, and returned to said refuges, changing from one to another."[46] Aware that a Royal *Cédula* in 1764 had simplified the method of arresting such enemies of society, Croix, after extensive inquiry, found that it had been sent to New Spain and had been published, but that the efforts of the Vicar General had succeeded in its being given an interpretation which made it generally ineffective. Croix ordered the *cédula* republished and dispatched to ecclesiastics and lower courts. The Crown approved his action in 1768, thereby, said Croix, depriving the criminals of their immunity to the end that they might be more easily apprehended.[47]

Evidently he was too optimistic, for in 1772 Charles III asked the Pope for greater restriction of the right of asylum. In his Brief of September 12, 1772, Clement XIV reiterated the types of crimes which did not merit asylum, and, more importantly, directed that the number of churches offering immunity be reduced to one or two in each town, depending on the size of the settlement.[48] The King issued a Royal *Cédula* in November wherein he specified how the Brief was to be enforced. He indicated his preference that parish churches managed by secular clergy be selected rather than those under control of regulars, unless the regulars were subject to secular jurisdiction because of their position as parochial personnel.[49]

In compliance Bucareli instructed the Archbishop and the bishops of New Spain to be prompt in designating which churches were to offer immunity, to post edicts imparting this information on the doors of all churches, to send copies of the edicts to the respective *ayuntamientos* (town councils) and judges, and then to report to him. Of interest administratively is the fact that Bucareli also sent notices to the Dean of the *Audiencia* of Guadalajara and to the governors of Yucatán and Nueva Vizcaya, although these officials held title as vice-patron independently of the viceroy. In the interest of consistency

[46] Croix, Instrucción, AGN, CVB, 1772, Vol. 24, p. 410v.

[47] *Ibid.,* pp. 410v–411.

[48] AGN, Bandos, 1771–1774, Vol. 8, No. 55, pp. 167–176. Also, AGN, RC, 1773, Vol. 103, No. 118, pp. 279–289.

[49] AGN, Bandos, 1771–1774, Vol. 8, No. 55, p. 166v. Also, Royal *Cédula*, November 2, 1773, AGN, RC, 1773, Vol. 103, No. 118, pp. 278–278v.

Bucareli told them to report to him what measures they might take in effecting the asylum program. He also ordered the *cédula* and Brief reprinted and a copy sent to all justices in order that each might be aware of his powers under it.[50]

Reports began to reach the Viceroy early in 1774. The Bishop of Guadalajara requested permission to designate places of asylum in two ecclesiastical provinces whose vice-patronage actually belonged to Bucareli, in addition to those within his own diocese. Receiving this permission, he reported that he had marked as refuges the head church in each curacy. Similar reports came from the Governor of Yucatán, who included Campeche province within his jurisdiction, the Archbishop, the Bishops of Oaxaca, Puebla, Michoacán, and Durango. In most cases the prelates had designated as asylums, in addition to each parish church, the cathedral in the major city or cities of the province. Bucareli approved their selections, and the edicts were published. By the end of 1774 the new immunity provisions were in effect except in Durango, where the size of the diocese precluded such quick action, and among several missions in Tampico from which the Archbishop had not at that date received a reply to his instructions.[51] Considering the time and the place, the matter had been rather expeditiously managed.

Another aspect of the ecclesiastical establishment with which wrongdoers were concerned, but toward which they certainly manifested no such kindly feeling as they did toward the asylum provision, was the Inquisition. It is clear, however, that by the time of Bucareli the Holy Office, once so terrifying a force, had declined in power and importance. The advent of Rationalism, both in Spain and in her American empire, had helped to reduce the Tribunal to a relatively low state. It remained a very busy agency, but much of its business was of an almost piddling nature. Its activities are interesting, of course, and, additionally, serve to provide a certain insight into some aspects of the way of life of colonial society.

For one thing, the Holy Office had jurisdiction over a wide variety

[50] Bucareli to Charles III, December 27, 1774, AGN, CVB, 1771–1778, Vol. 14, No. 207, pp. 147–148v.
[51] *Ibid.*, pp. 148v–157.

of offenses, not all of them clearly religious or moral. Indexes to the 169 volumes of documents of the Tribunal covering the Bucareli period reveal this diversity. Persons were accused of and tried for: heresy, sorcery, casting spells, bigamy, polygamy, writing or possessing anti-*gachupín* poems, sacrilege, drunkenness, indiscreet remarks, rebaptism, sodomy, bestiality, suspicious declarations and acts, malpractice in confession, soliciting, pornography, insulting the pope, denying being a Catholic, invoking demons, making Protestant notes in a book, anti-Catholic utterances, misusing images, engaging in improper songs and dances, curing by superstitious devices, adultery, reading or possessing prohibited books, libel, perjury, illegal confession, painting demons on one's legs, irreverence, calumny, making a pact with the Devil, impersonating a priest, possessing stamps which insulted the King, and other offenses.[52]

One receives the impression that being denounced to the Inquisition was a fairly strong possibility for the common man or woman of New Spain, although it should be pointed out that a great many self-denunciations fill the records, especially for offenses of a religious nature. Penalties were frequently light, such as a required performance of penitence, fines, or brief imprisonment. Such was not always the case, however. For example, a Negro, found guilty of killing his sweetheart with a bludgeon, was imprisoned for five years and then brought before the house in which he had committed the crime, where his right hand was cut off.[53]

The large number of bigamy and polygamy cases is revelatory. It is possible that many of them arose from the attitude toward marriage held by various of the Indian cultures, wherein a mutual decision by husband and wife to dissolve the union was sufficient to satisfy their particular society, but not the Holy Office. However, the extensive uses of aliases in these cases, and the designation of the offenders as "*mestizo*," "*coyote*," and so on, indicate that such an explanation is only a partial one.

Also impressive is the frequency of the charge of soliciting made against priests. The offenders seem to have been found fairly im-

[52] AGN, Indice del Ramo de Inquisición, Vols. 11, 12.
[53] *Ibid.*, Vol. 11.

partially among both the regular and secular members of the clergy. In view of the number of entries in the indexes concerned with proscribed books, it is apparent that the Holy Office devoted a great deal of time to this facet of its functions. Many of these entries, to be sure, do involve prohibitions against specific works. It has been amply demonstrated, however, that the effort of both Church and State to censor the reading material to which Spanish subjects had access was something of a failure.[54] Many persons of high rank or influence were either wholly or partially exempt from such restrictions. For example, shortly after Bucareli arrived in New Spain he received a letter from the Inquisitor General welcoming the Viceroy to his new job and giving him official permission to read any prohibited books he might desire.[55] American and British smugglers stood ready to supply those Spanish subjects who were not thus favored. Further, the addiction of many members of the governing class, both in Spain and in the colonies, to numerous works on the Index Librorum Prohibitorum, made of the prohibition a law which lacked public support for enforcement. The indexes of cases indicate that the Tribunal spent more time in checking the contents of boxes of books arriving at Veracruz and considering licenses for individuals to read certain books than it did in prosecuting persons for violations of the law.

By the late eighteenth century, relations between the Holy Office and the viceroys had become generally peaceful. Croix's armed defiance of the Tribunal seems to have been an exceptional incident rather than a usual occurrence. The allegation is that Croix insulted the Holy Office and was summoned to appear before it forthwith. He brought with him a battery of artillery, which he posted at the ready before the Tribunal building. Inside and before the court, he informed the Inquisitors that they had ten minutes in which to complete their business with him, for at the end of that time the guns would begin to demolish the building. The President Inquisitor quickly assured him that there was no need for further conversation, whereupon Croix strode out and returned to the viceregal palace. This story,

[54] See, among others, Arthur Preston Whitaker (ed.), *Latin America and the Enlightenment*.
[55] AGN, Inquisición, Vol. 1114, p. 2.

with minor variations, appears in nearly every anthology of anecdotes about colonial Mexico.[56]

The Marqués made manifest the relationship of the two agencies when he advised Bucareli that although the viceroy should maintain harmonious relations with the Holy Office, nevertheless, if the Tribunal should attempt to extend its jurisdiction into the royal domain, the viceroy was empowered to bring the dispute to a judgment wherein he himself was the presiding justice.[57]

Bucareli's concern with the Inquisition was minor. The welcoming letter which he received from the Inquisitor General has already been mentioned. He did have one small clash with the Tribunal, but his handling of it is indicative of the relatively low status to which the court had fallen. When the Princess Carlota was born in 1775, royal orders called for a general celebration of the event. Bucareli sent a copy of the order to the Inquisitors, requesting that they hold a special mass, but he inadvertently used the phrase *"ruego y encargo"* (I request and charge), which he customarily used in transmitting orders to subordinates. The Inquisitors were incensed. They cited the Royal *Cédula* of May 15, 1769, which regulated the language to be used in such circumstances, and protested that Bucareli's usage was "opposed to the regalia and the privileges and exemptions of the Holy Office." They returned his letter, suggesting that he destroy it and replace it with a more suitable document. In reply Bucareli simply enclosed two copies of the recently-printed Royal *Cédula* concerning the celebration, with no comment whatever.[58] Presumably, he could have replied in kind, thus starting some sort of feud with the Inquisitors; but such an action would not have been characteristic of his methods. On the other hand, his failure to apologize or to humble himself indicates that the Holy Office was no longer the fearsome agency it once had been.

In Bucareli's official correspondence with the Crown only five Inqui-

---

[56] See, for example, Luis González Obregón, *Epoca Colonial, México Viejo,* pp. 511–514.

[57] Croix, Instrucción, AGN, CVB, 1772, Vol. 24, p. 417v.

[58] Bucareli to the Tribunal of the Holy Office of the Inquisition, August 14, 1775, AGN, Inquisición, Vol. 1162, pp. 197–205.

sition cases make an appearance, none of them of any great significance. The most important two concern convictions for polygamy,
with sentences involving transportation to Spain for review and ultimate imprisonment in Africa.[59] In neither instance was the case itself
cause for comment. Instead, a dispute arose as to which agency—Inquisition or royal treasury—should pay for the transportation.[60] Not
surprisingly, Charles III decided that thereafter the Holy Office should
stand the expense of such journeys.[61] Aside from these minor matters,
or perhaps by virtue of their very singularity in the realm of relations
between Court and Executive, it is apparent that the Inquisition did
not stand forth as an agency of any great concern to the Viceroy.

In view of the fact that the Jesuit Order had been expelled from
New Spain in 1767, one would be justified in assuming that, aside
from the property they left behind, the Jesuits would be of less
official interest to Bucareli than was the Inquisition, but this was not
the case. The 1767 expulsion was temporal in nature; that is, it was
the action of the King of Spain and applied only to Spain and its
empire. Papal action came on July 21, 1773, when Clement XIV
issued a Brief wherein he suppressed the Company of Jesus throughout the whole world. In October Charles III passed this Brief to New
Spain, with orders that it be published and made known to all his
vassals.[62]

In compliance Bucareli disseminated the required information
throughout the viceroyalty. His job, however, did not end there.
When the Jesuits left New Spain in 1767, ten remained in the
College of the Holy Spirit in Puebla, unable to make the voyage because of advanced age or illness. Charles III exhibited a constant
interest in these stragglers, and in the *cédula* which accompanied the

[59] Bucareli to Arriaga, April 26, 1773, AGN, CVB, 1773, Vol. 37, No. 904,
pp. 47v–48. Same to same, December 27, 1774, AGN, CVB, 1774, Vol. 62, No.
1654, pp. 46–46v.
   [60] Same to same, December 27, 1775, AGN, CVB, 1775, Vol. 72, No. 2027,
pp. 46v–48.
   [61] Gálvez to Bucareli, August 12, 1776, AGN, RC, 1776, Vol. 108, No. 77,
pp. 158–159.
   [62] AGN, Bandos, 1771–1774, Vol. 8, No. 38, pp. 91–122. A copy of the Brief is
included.

Brief he gave Bucareli explicit instructions with regard to this group. Obediently, the Viceroy ordered the Administrator of Temporalities to meet with them and read the Brief and *cédula*. The former regulars were then to surrender their distinctive Jesuit garb and don the dress of secular priests. Further, the Administrator was to impress them with the benefits they would enjoy if they would leave New Spain and settle down in the place assigned them in the Papal States. Bucareli also ordered the commissioner of the college to have a doctor examine the former Jesuits and present certified evidence of their state of health, with special alertness for any simulated illnesses. Resulting reports showed that eight of the ten agreed to absolute obedience to the *cédula* and Brief. The other two were adjudged insane and therefore incapable of making a proper response. None of the ten was found physically able to travel.[63]

Despite the fact that Charles III, in his 1767 expulsion order, and Clement XIV, in his Brief of suppression, both forbade the people to make any mention of the expulsion or the suppression, murmurs of dissent continued to be heard. To put a stop to such talk, the College of Cardinals, at the direction of Pius VI, in 1776 issued an order which reiterated the prohibition and the penalties prescribed for transgressors.[64] The King relayed the order to New Spain, where Bucareli issued it in the form of a decree.[65]

Shortly before Bucareli died, the King once more inquired into the status of the former Jesuits remaining in New Spain. The Viceroy's correspondence reveals no acknowledgment of, or answer to, the royal inquiry, and it is probable that the matter was carried over into the following administration. Noteworthy is the fact that the request for the report mentions that only seven of the original ten remained alive at that time.[66]

Whenever the Jesuits are the subject of consideration, it brings to mind the vast wealth the Order is alleged to have amassed. In truth,

[63] Bucareli to the Count of Valdellano, February 24, 1774, AGN, CVB, 1771–1778, Vol. 14, No. 141, pp. 10v–18.
[64] January 23, 1776, AGN, Bandos, 1775–1776, Vol. 9, No. 47, pp. 303v–304.
[65] October 19, 1777, *ibid.*, pp. 304–305.
[66] Antonio de Toranco [?] to Bucareli, October 21, 1778, AGN, RC, 1778, Vol. 115, No. 86, p. 123.

the church generally achieved considerable material prosperity. However, not all ecclesiastical income remained with the church, inasmuch as the government took a significant share of such wealth. The chief means of royal taxation of the church were these: taxing the salaries of ecclesiastics through the collection of the *media anata* and the *mesada;*[67] the sale of bulls of the Santa Cruzada,[68] which used the church as an instrumentality of government revenue, thereby diverting money which probably would have gone into the hands of prelates; and, the collection of tithes—the chief source of church income —which was paid into the royal treasury. The revenue from tithes went largely to maintain the religious establishment, but not entirely. The *noveno,* or one-ninth of tithe collections, was reserved for the temporal needs of the Crown.[69]

By the time of Bucareli, however, the financial relationship between Church and Crown was well established and mutually accepted. Specific instances of investigation and reform were usually initiated in Spain, where the King apparently noted deficiencies general throughout his empire and consequently dispatched corrective orders to all his major subordinates. Such a case was that wherein Charles III suspected local ecclesiastical agencies of laxity and carelessness in the management of revenue, as a consequence of which many curacies continued to receive support from the royal treasury which they could not rightfully claim. He ordered Bucareli, as well as all other viceroys, along with governors and subordinate officials, to investigate

[67] The *mesada,* paid by newly-appointed officials, secular and ecclesiastical, represented one month's income. Every new ecclesiastical officer, from the archbishop down, who received an income of 100 ducats or more, paid a *mesada* figured from the annual average yield of the benefice during the preceding five years. The *media anata*—half the first year's salary and a third of all other emoluments accruing to the position—replaced the *mesada* for secular officials in 1631, and for the higher clergy (those receiving an annual salary of more than 300 pesos) in 1753. Lesser clerics continued to pay only the *mesada.* Haring, *The Spanish Empire in America,* pp. 292–293.

[68] Bulas de la Santa Cruzada were indulgences sold to provide funds for wars against the infidels. The stipulation was that the funds so obtained must be employed in the extension of the faith. The cost of the indulgences varied in time, place, and the capacity of the various individuals to pay. The bulls were published in America every other year. *Ibid.,* p. 286.

[69] Donald E. Smith, *The Viceroy of New Spain,* pp. 235–236.

the matter and institute reformative measures.[70] The evidence of what Bucareli did about it is scanty, and has, perhaps, a dubious relationship. A document issued by him and dated July 5, 1775, some three years after the promulgation of the above order, calls for a census of curacies, designed to reveal the sources of revenue and the annual income and expenses of each church.[71] If this was accomplished and the resulting information properly used, the King's desires were fulfilled.

A similar situation, although more general in nature, involved the observance of a law already in the code which proclaimed as invalid testamentary dispositions made by moribund persons in favor of their confessors, Orders, or convents. To make the prohibition effective, not only was the disposition declared illegal, but the notary public who drew up such a document lost his license. Bucareli performed his duty by publishing the corresponding edict.[72]

The two instances just discussed demonstrate the relationship between Bucareli and the church in financial matters. They are typical in that they reveal the relative unimportance of the issues involved and stress the fact that by the 1770's major policies had been satisfactorily settled and agreed upon.

Less predictable were the results of daily contact between ecclesiastical personnel and government agencies or officials. Croix warned Bucareli of the dangers of a situation of this nature when, in his Instruction, he discussed the viceroy's obligation to protect the Indians. He pointed out the obviousness of the fact that both curates and *alcaldes mayores*—judicial and administrative officials of districts and municipalities—customarily oppressed the natives through their demands for taxes and services. When these two agencies united, he said, the Indian was genuinely in trouble, and when the two agencies disagreed, the result was a multitude of trials, with the priest venting his anger at the *alcalde* by persuading his parish Indians to attend court and support his side of the argument. He noted that in anticipation of such situations, a provision already existed for investigating Indian complaints to ascertain whether they had been instigated by

[70] Royal *Cédula*, January 21, 1772, AGN, RC, 1772, Vol. 100, No. 16, pp. 48–49.
[71] AGN, Bandos, 1775–1776, Vol. 9, No. 11, pp. 48–48v.
[72] *Ibid.,* No. 20, pp. 209–212.

white persons, and if so, by whom. But it was generally accepted, he said, that Indian declarations and testimony did not deserve a high rating of reliability because the natives customarily said what the *alcalde* or the curate wanted them to. In his opinion, these reasons made mandatory a cautious approach to Indian affairs of this nature.[73]

Higher officials than *alcaldes* were not immune from objecting to certain ecclesiastical activities. In 1772 the Governor of Yucatán complained that the Bishop of that diocese had, without either the Governor's consent or the Viceroy's approval, appointed and removed at will the chaplains for the garrison on the Isla del Carmen. The Bishop, in defense, argued that ever since the establishment of the garrison the disputed power had belonged to the prelate, and that custom therefore supported his claim. Bucareli investigated the matter and discovered that from 1716 to 1741 the chaplains had been chosen by civil authorities, from which fact he deduced that "the indolence, carelessness, or lack of intelligence of those who governed said island since 1741 has given a motive for the Governor of the Bishopric of Yucatán to endeavor to take for himself a faculty opposed to the Ordinances of the Army and the Laws of *Real Patronato.*" Bucareli therefore informed the disputants that the right of nominating chaplains belonged to the captain of the presidio concerned, although the nominees must be selected from among persons approved by the ordinary. He concluded, as usual, by enjoining the opponents to maintain a reciprocally harmonious relationship.[74] The King approved Bucareli's solution as a whole, but added some refinements about the technique of nomination.[75] Both parties appear to have accepted the Viceroy's decision without argument.

The locale for discord between spiritual and temporal agencies next shifted to Puebla, a city where conflict seems to have been the rule rather than the exception. In 1774 an old dispute broke out anew between the *ayuntamiento* and the Bishop of Puebla. Trouble had

[73] Croix, Instrucción, AGN, CVB, 1772, Vol. 24, pp. 412–412v.

[74] Bucareli to Arriaga, March 27, 1773, AGN, CVB, 1773, Vol. 36, No. 869, pp. 86v–91.

[75] Royal *Cédula,* November 21, 1775, AGN, RC, 1775, Vol. 106, No. 167, pp. 307–308v.

originally flared in 1770, and the ephemeral character of Croix's mediation of that year became apparent when Bucareli received complaints from both sides on the same matter. The issue was typical, involving as it did questions of precedence, prestige, and seating arrangements at joint *ayuntamiento*-ecclesiastical *cabildo* meetings. Over these minor points a great deal of excitement was manifested. Bucareli handled the situation with commendable tact and firmness. His solution was simple—he requested a detailed report from the parallel authorities in Mexico City and relayed the information to Puebla. He informed the disputants that this was the proper procedure, that they would henceforth employ it, and that thereafter they would endeavor to get along peacefully.[76] No protests followed.

Aside from the *Vida Común* controversy, discussed in the following chapter, the existence and activities of the church in New Spain during Bucareli's command followed a generally peaceful and well-recognized path. The excitement of the Jesuit expulsion gradually dissipated, the increased independence and dominance of the Crown were more clearly evidenced, and the religious establishment continued much as it had before—monopolistic, entrenched, wealthy, secure. Although a lessening in the degree of devotion to the church as a temporal agency may have been discernible within the upper element of colonial society, reflecting a similar shift in the mother country, there was no noticeable accompanying rumble of discontent with the singularity or the position of the church, either from this same upper class or from the vast majority of the common people, who remained its faithful communicants. The conflicts which occurred were contained largely within the organization itself and were more in the nature of minor squabbles than struggles of serious import.

With respect to Bucareli himself, perhaps the most easily recognized, and perhaps therefore the dominant trait of his conduct as vice-patron, was his desire for a harmonious and peaceful functioning of the ecclesiastical establishment. In almost every instance considered—the Bethlemite affair, the Dean of Durango case, the Valladolid trouble, the secularization problem, the Yucatán argument—he looked beyond

[76] Bucareli to Charles III, September 26, 1774, AGN, CVB, 1771–1778, Vol. 14, No. 186, pp. 83v–92v.

62 *Viceregency of Bucareli*

an immediate solution and invariably endeavored to impress the parties involved with the necessity of avoiding discord in the future.

This does not mean, of course, that he lacked firmness in dealing with the existing controversies. He recognized them as controversies and solved them in accordance with the dictates of his code, of which the major premises are not difficult to identify. In most cases Bucareli tended to support the men in authority, probably because he recognized the desirability of a government's presenting at least an outward appearance of unity. In his decisions as a vice-patron, this attitude is especially apparent, and the reason for it is obvious—the mutual bulwarks of Church and State should not exhibit any cleavage. And to avoid occasion for such cleavage, Bucareli was usually careful either to leave the management of a problem to the official concerned, or to consult with the proper prelate before rendering a decision involving any of that prelate's subordinates.

In general, Bucareli appears to have been a good vice-patron, although the lack of opportunity to compare him with other viceroys in this respect makes such judgment tentative. He gave evidence of knowing what his duty was, he executed faithfully the orders of the patron, and, at the same time that he maintained friendly relations with the ecclesiastical authorities, he also retained their respect.

The Vida Común *Controversy*

L ATE IN FEBRUARY, 1778, after more than six years as viceroy, Bucareli wrote to José de Gálvez, "In these matters, one always moves in darkness. Nothing has agitated my spirit so much in this command."[1] With these somber phrases he was assessing a situation which, when reviewed today, is almost comic opera in nature, even to the extent of having a stereotyped plot wherein sorely-beset males are frustrated and driven almost frantic by the unpredictable and seemingly groundless machinations of a group of women.

The Viceroy was referring to the *Vida Común* controversy, in the course of which he struggled in vain to restore peace among the nuns of New Spain. Early in the campaign he said, with prescience, "The ire of women is more fearful than that of men, because once they make it known, they have little place for reflection and are less concerned over consequences than that their caprice be fulfilled."[2] There can be no doubt but that he would have taken issue with Croix's statement that ". . . nuns give no trouble, because of the docility with which they are governed by their prelates."[3] The entire dispute, which greeted Bucareli when he took command and which was still unsettled

[1] Bucareli to Gálvez, February 24, 1778, AGN, CVB, 1773–1779, Vol. 7, Libro 15, No. 239 or 3568, p. 15v.
[2] Bucareli to the Bishop of Puebla, February 19, 1772, AGN, CVB, 1771–1772, Vol. 5, Libro 8, No. 21 or 233, p. 235.
[3] Croix, Instrucción, AGN, CVB, 1772, Vol. 24, p. 441v.

when he died, centered around the efforts of the Crown and prelates to reform the nuns' mode of life by establishing in the nunneries the *Vida Común*, or Common Life.

In the latter half of the eighteenth century the life of a nun was not so austere as might generally and logically be presumed. Young ladies of good family entered convents, bringing with them a sizable and required dowry.[4] Each nun had a cell, apparently comfortably furnished. In most cases she also had several servants to see to her well-being, and the physical work necessary for maintaining the convent was also done by servants. Furthermore, the nunneries customarily adopted female children, and under the doting care of the nuns these girls were educated and cared for. There were also a number of secular women in the convents, neither nuns nor servants, whose function apparently was to serve as companions to the nuns and to help care for the children. In general, the life of a nun offered both peace of mind and physical comfort.

The small cloud on the horizon made its appearance during Croix's administration when some shod nuns in several of the convents in Puebla became concerned about the laxity of their rules and appealed to their bishop to institute a reform. The bishop investigated and found that the rules and constitutions of each of the convents prescribed the *Vida Común,* and that this mode of life had been observed in these convents until about a century before, when relaxation set in.[5] As a result, the Archbishop of Mexico and the Bishop of Puebla undertook to supplant this easy mode of existence in the convents under their control with one more in keeping with the purposes of a religious life and the vows which the nuns took in their professions. The *Vida Común* which these prelates proposed to establish contemplated the replacement of individual cells with common dormitories, the expulsion of children and secular women from the convents, and a drastic reduction in the number of servants.

---

[4] For an interesting account of the luxuriousness of the ceremony of profession, see Romero de Terreros, *Bocetos,* pp. 203–204.

[5] Royal *Cédula,* August 17, 1780, AGN, RC, 1780, Vol. 119, No. 138, pp. 285–285v. This is a most useful document, for in it Charles III reviews the entire course of the controversy from its origins to the date of issue.

The reaction of the nuns foreshadowed future events. From Puebla the inmates of La Concepción Convent protested to the King, who ordered that the problem be turned over to the Fourth Mexican Provincial Council and that no change from the old life be instituted until that body reached a decision. Three other Puebla convents appealed to Croix, protesting the divergence of the proposed new life from the one they had professed. The Marqués passed their appeal to Charles III, advising the nuns meanwhile to obey their prelate and to have hope that all would be composed.[6]

This was the situation when Bucareli assumed command. His first Instructions on the matter from the home government were dated October 23, 1771, and included one of the petitions sent to Spain by Croix. The King ordered Bucareli to turn the document over to the religious council if it was still in session; if that body had adjourned, he was to send it to the Bishop of Puebla for his action.[7] A similar directive was sent two months later, with the remainder of the petitions enclosed and with the same instructions as to their disposition.[8]

During January, 1772, pressure built up and an explosion was in the making. The situation compared with, or perhaps even exceeded, the Bethlemite dispute when one considers the degree of confusion which grew out of the charges and countercharges. The Bishop of Puebla, Francisco Fabián y Fuero, acknowledged the receipt of the petitions returned from Spain, and promised to take corrective action.[9] He must have moved aggressively, for the early products of his measures were two new petitions from Santa Inés Convent, both

[6] Croix, Instrucción, AGN, CVB, 1772, Vol. 24, pp. 441v–442v. There were also similar appeals from several of the Mexico City convents, the details of which are contained in a *consulta* of the Consejo de Indias of June 30, 1773, with an account of the specific action taken in their case. It turned out to be inconclusive. AGI, IG, Leg. 3043.

[7] Arriaga to Bucareli, October 23, 1771, AGN, RC, 1771, Vol. 99, No. 129, pp. 304–304v.

[8] Same to same, December 20, 1771, *ibid.,* No. 134, pp. 330–331.

[9] Fabián to Bucareli, January 18, 1772, AGN, CVB, 1771–1772, Vol. 5, Libro 8, No. 21 or 233, pp. 201–202 (inclosure No. 5). Bucareli acknowledged the receipt of the petitions and the pertinent Instructions in two letters to Arriaga dated January 27 and March 21, 1772, numbered 179 and 250, respectively, AGI, IG, Leg. 3042.

dated January 22, one to Bucareli [10] and the other to the *Audiencia*.[11] The latter appeal was much longer and in greater detail. The nuns complained that the Bishop had done the following things: ordered all the cells torn out, although their construction had been costly; used threats to make them accept the *Vida Común;* removed twenty-two nuns to a separate part of the convent, where he was starting a new Order without royal license; accused the remaining nuns of not obeying the constitution of the convent; forced them to accept eight special confessors who gave counsel consonant with the Bishop's policy; enticed nuns to the new Order by illegal promises; and, allowed four unqualified women to become nuns, using the community wealth for their dowries. They asked that their case be heard in court and that a lawyer in Mexico City be appointed to act in their behalf. Finally, they requested that the prelate be suspended until the case was settled.

On the twenty-fifth, the Bishop reported to Bucareli that two more nuns had joined the group that actually was practicing the *Vida Común*. He claimed that those who still refused to participate had been influenced by the principal confessor, who, when asked by the nuns what they should do about the matter, had "imprudently" answered, "Commend yourselves to God, and do what may appear." The Bishop, finding legal precedent in a Bull of 1748, therefore assigned "eight learned confessors of virtue, prudence, and the greatest experience and maturity" to counsel the nuns.[12] The licenses of other clerics to confess were revoked.[13]

In reply to Fabián's report, Bucareli told of receiving the petition from Santa Inés Convent, but commented that he had not replied to it, inasmuch as the Bishop was the one in charge of the matter. He warned that two centuries of abuse in the observance of religious vows called for caution and tact in applying a remedy.[14]

[10] Fabián to Bucareli, January 18, 1772, AGN, CVB, 1771–1772, Vol. 5, Libro 8, No. 21 or 233, pp. 199–201 (inclosure No. 4).

[11] *Ibid.*, pp. 209–221 (inclosure No. 8).

[12] *Ibid.*, pp. 202–204 (inclosure No. 6).

[13] Order of the Bishop of Puebla, January 22, 1772, *ibid.*, pp. 204–205 (inclosure No. 6). This is the order appointing the eight new confessors.

[14] January 26, 1772, *ibid.*, p. 208 (inclosure No. 7).

The explosion came on February 11. On that day, two more Santa Inés nuns agreed to active practice of the *Vida Común* and hence moved over to the corresponding part of the convent. Upon hearing the news, two demented nuns ran to the convent gate, crying aloud that they wanted to get out. A number of other clamorous nuns joined them there, while, at the same time, several servants mounted to the tower and began ringing the bells. The vicar general, apprised of the reason for the turmoil, sent word to the Governor of Puebla, who hurried to the convent and managed to achieve a temporary tranquillity. The Bishop transmitted the story to Bucareli via special courier on the morning of February 15.[15] A later communique, released at 6:00 P.M., revealed that quiet still reigned and that the number of nuns who continued unrepentant for their part in the upset had been reduced to five.[16]

In his reply of February 19, Bucareli said that the upheaval had disturbed him greatly. He noted sorrowfully that the whole affair had become public knowledge and that the people, as usual, were enlarging on the story. (It was in this letter that he made the comment about the ire of women being more fearful than that of men.) Nevertheless, he declined to make a decision or order any change, and continued to leave the matter to the discretion of the Bishop.[17]

On the twenty-fourth, Bucareli reported the entire course of events to Spain, and in so doing revealed his motivations and his methods. He regarded the problem as a grave one, and tended to put his faith in the Bishop, whose judgment he trusted. He felt further that, inasmuch as a majority of the nuns at Santa Inés had accepted the *Vida Común,* those nuns who still resisted should not be encouraged in their obstinacy. Therefore, fearing that either the *Audiencia* or the Fiscal would react favorably to the nuns' petition and thus recommend stopping the Bishop in his course, Bucareli called a meeting of the *Real Acuerdo* and made clear his ideas on the subject. He pointed out that the Santa Inés situation was being watched by other convents that desired to evade the *Vida Común* system, and that for the bishop

[15] February 15, 1772, *ibid.,* pp. 193–196 (inclosure No. 1).

[16] *Ibid.,* pp. 196–197 (inclosure No. 2).

[17] *Ibid.,* pp. 233–235 (inclosure No. 9).

to fail in this case would do greater harm than was superficially apparent. The *Real Acuerdo* saw his point, for the resulting opinion of the Fiscal on the nuns' petition supported the Bishop, as did the *Audiencia's* recommendations.[18]

Within less than two weeks the Viceroy's wishes were fulfilled. Bishop Fabián reported complete calm at Santa Inés, with all those who agitated on the eleventh having repented. In his report the Bishop answered one by one the charges made against him by the nuns in their petition to the *Audiencia,* and his defense seemed valid.[19] He also enclosed a letter to Bucareli from the nun who was the principal author of the petition and who had been the ringleader in the resistance. She renounced completely the claims she had made, blaming her rebellious actions on her own ignorance.[20] One month later, March 26, 1772, Bucareli relayed to Spain the Bishop's reports that quiet still prevailed and that the future promised continued peace.[21]

The Puebla nuns did remain quiet long enough for another group of convents to take the center of the stage. Sometime late in 1770, the nuns of the royal Jesús Mariá Convent in Mexico City had complained to the Crown about being forced to accept the *Vida Común.* Charles III, in reply, ordered a return to the old mode of life for these nuns until the Mexican Provincial Council could decide their case. When the council decided in favor of the *Vida Común,* the Jesús María nuns, joined now by those of six other convents, immediately protested the council's decision, claiming that the Archbishop, by illegal methods, had persuaded the councilors to rule against them, and that as a result they were suffering new oppressions. Again Charles III ruled in favor of the nuns, ordering once more a restoration of the old manner of life, this time until he himself had reached a final decision.[22]

[18] Bucareli to Arriaga, February 24, 1772, *ibid.,* pp. 187–192. This is the cover-letter for the inclosures cited in notes 9–17 of this chapter.

[19] Fabián to Bucareli, February 22, 1772, *ibid.,* pp. 244–251.

[20] María Ana de San Joaquín to Bucareli, *ibid.,* pp. 253–254 (inclosure No. 4).

[21] Bucareli to Arriaga, March 26, 1772, *ibid.,* pp. 381–383. Fabián to Bucareli, February 29 and March 21, 1772, *ibid.,* pp. 383–385 and 385–386 (inclosures Nos. 1 and 2).

[22] Royal *Cédula,* August 6, 1772, AGN, RC, 1772, Vol. 101, No. 33, pp. 42–45v.

The Puebla group, meanwhile, tired of standing in the wings, decided once more to occupy the limelight. A change of personnel had altered the situation by this time—March, 1773—for Bishop Fabián had been transferred to Spain, and his place had been taken by Bishop-elect Victoriano López Gonzalo. In this fresh disturbance the nuns of Santísima Trinidad Convent joined those of Santa Inés in accusing the new diocesan of excesses in his efforts to impose upon them a greater austerity. He had, they claimed, expelled all the children from the convents within a period of twenty-four hours, further reduced the number of servants, weighed the nuns down with innumerable menial duties, and threatened with severe punishment anyone who complained about the new life. The King commissioned the Archbishop to investigate the matter, with the instruction that if he found that the Bishop-elect had forced the nuns to accept the *Vida Común* against their will, he was to order the customary restoration of the old mode of life until the King could settle the matter himself.[23]

When Bishop-elect López heard of the Archbishop's commission, he urged Bucareli to persuade the prelate not to institute any changes because, according to López, it would cause great trouble. The Viceroy spoke soothingly to López and enjoined him to cooperate with the Archbishop.[24] Instead of complying, however, López tried to block the Archbishop's investigation to the extent that the latter protested to Bucareli. The Viceroy carried the matter to the *Audiencia* and the Fiscal, and upon their advice once more urged López to cooperate. This he did in the extreme, offering to resign. The Archbishop accepted his offer and transferred him to a position in Mexico City.[25] On the basis of what occurred later, it is apparent that the Archbishop then ordered a restoration of the method of life observed in the Puebla convents prior to the introduction of the *Vida Común.*

By this time, then—the end of 1773—the Puebla and Mexico City convents were once more under the old system, and from lack of evi-

---

[23] Royal *Cédula,* June 26, 1773, AGN, RC, 1773, Vol. 102, No. 183, pp. 326–333.

[24] Bucareli to Charles III, September 26, 1773, in Velasco Ceballos, *La administración de . . . Bucareli,* Vol. II, pp. 294–296.

[25] Same to same, December 27, 1773, *ibid.,* pp. 296–298.

dence to the contrary it would appear that elsewhere throughout the viceroyalty the prelates made no attempt to embark on a *Vida Común* program. Any further action on the matter depended entirely on Charles III, and his decision was not long in coming. On May 22, 1774, he issued a Royal *Cédula* which ordered the establishment of the *Vida Común* in all the nunneries of New Spain not practicing it at that time. He allowed each nun a choice between the common life and the old manner of life, but new entrants must henceforth promise to observe the *Vida Común* if they should reach the stage of professing. The *cédula* granted the nuns fifteen days to decide on their choice, during which period they could seek counsel from their superiors and their confessors or other learned persons. At the end of this period, the immediate prelate was to go to each convent to take the nuns' statements. Prelates were ordered to give equal treatment to all, regardless of which choice they might make. The King pointed out that the common life was the perfect life, and that therefore it was only proper that the officials of each convent, such as the abbess or prioress, should be nuns who had chosen it. He added, however, that if, unfortunately, there were fewer than three *Vida Común* nuns in a convent, others could hold office, but only until new entrants should change the situation. With respect to children and secular women, the *cédula* forbade their presence in convents unless the convent rule provided for the education of the children. Private-life nuns were allowed not more than one servant apiece, and the servants necessary for convent maintenance were permitted for each *Vida Común* group.[26]

In the cover-letter accompanying the *cédula* the King, with vast optimism, ordered an end to the trouble over the *Vida Común*. He specified that all officials involved were to gather all pertinent documents on the matter, place them in a sealed bundle, and close the file. To paraphrase Roeder only slightly, it may be said, with respect to Charles III, that kings "are accustomed by their activities to a con-

[26] Royal *Cédula*, May 22, 1774, AGN, Historia, Monjas, Vol. 134, No. 3, pp. 6–11. This is the original of the *cédula*. There are numerous copies, e.g., AGN, RC, 1774, Vol. 104, No. 119, pp. 214–219.

formity of opinion which affects their judgment."[27] It was obviously his belief that for him to order a thing done was to have it done. He committed the basic error of underestimating the foe, docile and defenseless as the nuns may have seemed.

The *cédula* reached New Spain in August, and on the ninth of that month Bucareli ordered three hundred copies printed and distributed to prelates, courts, ecclesiastical *cabildos,* and *ayuntamientos* of cities in which there were nunneries.[28] It was done, and the trouble started. Victoriano López, who had resigned his position as Bishop of Puebla during the earlier disturbances, once more filled that post. On August 16 he notified the nuns in his five convents of the common-life *cédula,*[29] and within three days news filtered back to him that a rumor, starting in Santísima Trinidad Convent, had spread that the *cédula* did not legally apply to the Puebla houses. The idea, López said, allegedly had its origin in the Governor's office.[30] Meanwhile, he began immediately a program for the gradual departure of children and secular women from the convents, making arrangements to care for those who had no other means of support.[31]

In the first week of September the Bishop of Puebla began his visits to the convents to receive the nuns' statements on acceptance of the *Vida Común.* At the first two he noticed signs of tension, but no

[27] Ralph Roeder, *Juárez and his Mexico,* Vol. I, p. 38.

[28] AGN, RC, 1774, Vol. 104, No. 119, pp. 224v–225, indorsement. This indorsement is on a second copy in *ibid.,* pp. 220–224v.

[29] In a letter to Bucareli, dated August 13, 1774, López discusses in detail his plans for executing the provisions of the *cédula.* AGN, Historia, Monjas, Vol. 134, No. 3, pp. 183–184v. The precise date on which he announced its measures to his convents is computed from a letter of September 1, in which he mentions that date as the conclusion of the fifteen-day waiting period.

[30] López to Bucareli, August 20, 1774, *ibid.,* pp. 185–185v.

[31] María Magdalena de Jesús, subprioress of Santa Catalina Convent, to López (August 25, 1774, *ibid.,* No. 25, pp. 205–206) is a report on the progress of removing the children from this convent. López to Bucareli, August 27, 1774, *ibid.,* No. 9, pp. 189–189v. Same to same, same date, *ibid.,* No. 10, pp. 190–191v. Bucareli to López (August 30, 1774, *ibid.,* No. 13, p. 134) acknowledges receipt of the preceding three letters and approves the system. López to Bucareli (September 1, 1774, *ibid.,* No. 14, pp. 194–196) is the letter in which López indicates the conclusion of the fifteen-day waiting period.

trouble occurred. Of the seventy-four nuns in San Gerónimo Convent, thirty-eight had accepted the common life, among them all the officers of the house. Of those in Santísima Trinidad the count was thirty-two out of forty-seven.[32] In his visits to the other three convents the Bishop encountered some outright opposition; furthermore, their acceptances of the *Vida Común* did not reach such a high percentage— twenty-four of seventy-seven, seventeen of forty-eight, and twelve of fifty-eight.[33] López ascribed the difficulties to lack of screening with respect to the pre-entry backgrounds of these nuns, and he also stated that he was on the trail of an outsider who was deliberately trying to cause trouble.[34]

It was not long after the announcement of the *Vida Común cédula* that petitions against its provisions began to appear. The nuns of Santa Catalina in Puebla were first, choosing the expulsion of children from the convents as their reason for complaint. They argued that the *cédula* forbade only the entry of children in the future, and did not apply to those already living in the convents. They contended further that the law allowed those nuns who so chose to continue the old mode of life, and that inasmuch as the care of children had been part of that life, it would be unjust to the nuns to expel them. They offered several other arguments, based largely on a wishful interpretation of the *cédula* in question.[35] Others lent their voices to this protest against expelling the children, notably, the secular women of La Concepción Convent of Mexico City,[36] and, oddly, the *ayuntamiento* of the same place.[37]

On the Fiscal's advice, Bucareli uniformly rejected all appeals on the subject. With respect to that of the Santa Catalina nuns, he ruled that

[32] López to Bucareli, September 10, 1774, *ibid.,* No. 18, pp. 198–198v.
[33] Santa Catalina, Santa Inés, and Purísima Concepción, respectively, *ibid.,* No. 21, p. 202v.
[34] López to Bucareli, September 17, 1774, *ibid.,* pp. 201–203v.
[35] Thirty-nine nuns of Santa Catalina Convent to Bucareli, August 30, 1774, *ibid.,* pp. 210–213v.
[36] Bucareli to Arriaga, October 27, 1774, in Velasco Ceballos, *La administración de . . . Bucareli,* Vol. II, pp. 323–324.
[37] Same to same, September 26, 1774, AGN, CVB, 1773–1775, Vol. 11, Libro 9, No. 76 or 1529, pp. 104–106v.

their interpretation of the *cédula* was incorrect, that the signers represented only a minority of the nuns and a minority of the governing chapter, and that the petition should not have come to him in the first place, but should have gone to the Bishop of Puebla.[38] In his report to Spain he said, "Since all these matters are delicate because of the weakness of the sex, I felt it well to leave to the judgment of the Bishop of Puebla the rest of the measures he may see as opportune . . . and to console them with sweet and benign persuasions." [39]

The matter of support from the *ayuntamiento,* however, involved neither delicacy nor weakness, and in this more familiar situation Bucareli was much more blunt. He informed them that the *cédula* was to be enforced, that an end must be made of the matter, and that all documents dealing with the subject must be collected and permanently filed. The *ayuntamiento* was immediately called into session, from which there was sent to Bucareli a most humble letter of withdrawal from the matter and a copy of the petition which they had intended to send to the Viceroy and the King. Bucareli summarized the incident when he said, "In this state, and satisfied that by such smooth and moderate means an end has been achieved to the pretensions of the city, I have ordered canceled, filed, and closed, as the May 22 Royal *Cédula* orders, all papers passed to me." [40] The sequence is indicative of the relative position of local government in New Spain, even so notable an agency as the *cabildo* of Mexico City.

The surrender of the *ayuntamiento,* however, was not typical of the reactions of others affected by the new order. It may be said that, in general, the struggle was joined, and that for the next several years both sides won victories and suffered defeats. The clashes were not spectacular, nor did they occur uniformly throughout the viceroyalty. The convents of Puebla stand out as the leaders of the resist-

[38] Fiscal's opinion and Bucareli's decision on petition from Santa Catalina nuns, dated August 30, 1774, AGN, Historia, Monjas, Vol. 134, No. 16, pp. 212v–217. Bucareli to López, September 21, 1774, *ibid.,* No. 29, pp. 209–210v. Bucareli to Arriaga, September 26, 1774, AGN, CVB, 1773–1775, Vol. 11, Libro 9, No. 78 or 1531, pp. 107v–109.

[39] *Ibid.,* p. 109.

[40] Bucareli to Arriaga, September 26 and September 28, 1774, *ibid.,* No. 76 or 1529, pp. 106–106v, and No. 81 or 1563, pp. 112–113.

ance. In other sections there was almost no objection to the *cédula*.[41] The Archbishop of Mexico turned in a generally acceptable count of the number of children, secular women, and servants expelled from his convents.[42] Because of a petition from the nuns of Santa Clara de Jesús Convent in Querétaro against the *Vida Común,* an investigation was instituted, with the result that the responsible Franciscan provincial was adjudged to be too indulgent in the matter of leaving servants in the convents, and instead of relief the nuns got fewer servants.[43] There was some tendency, perhaps because of steady pressure from their prelates, for nuns who had at first rejected the *Vida Común* to change their minds and enter the new life.[44]

Those who did choose to continue to resist, however, resorted to a variety of devices to secure their ends. Some professed a desire to accept the *Vida Común,* but argued that they were in such a small minority in their convent that they did not care to oppose the general opinion.[45] Four nuns in two convents in Mexico City promised to enter upon the *Vida Común,* but when the time came for the ceremony they asserted that they had lost the patents given to them and were no longer interested in the change. It became apparent that the abbesses

[41] The Bishop of Guadalajara reported complete acceptance of the *Vida Común* in the six convents under his control. Bucareli to Arriaga, September 26, 1774, *ibid.,* No. 73 or 1526, pp. 100–100v. From Michoacán the Bishop reported full acceptance in Valladolid and only a few refusals in Pátzcuaro. Bishop of Michoacán to Bucareli, September 11, 1775, AGN, Historia, Vol. 136, No. 1, pp. 2–3. Fray Pedro Rivas, the Dominican provincial of Oaxaca, also reported that only a few nuns in his convents remained under the old rule. Rivas to Bucareli, October 4, 1774, November 8, 1774, and April 16, 1776, *ibid.,* No. 2, pp. 33–33v, 4–4v, and 42.

[42] Bucareli to Arriaga, October 27, 1774, in Velasco Ceballos, *La administración de . . . Bucareli,* Vol. II, pp. 324–325.

[43] Arriaga to Bucareli, August 18, 1775, AGN, RC, 1775, Vol. 106, No. 194, pp. 359–359v. Another copy is in AGN, Historia, Monjas, Vol. 134, No. 2, p. 15.

[44] Same to same, November 22, 1775, *ibid.,* pp. 18–18v. Bucareli to Arriaga, April 26, 1776, AGN, CVB, 1776, Vol. 12, Libro 13, No. 154 or 2213, pp. 14–14v. Bucareli to Gálvez, July 27, 1776, *ibid.,* No. 160 or 2397, p. 29. Same to same, August 27, 1776, *ibid.,* No. 164 or 2473, pp. 35–35v. Same to same, December 27, 1776, *ibid.,* No. 183 or 2680, pp. 56–56v. Gálvez to Bucareli, October 22, 1776, AGN, RC, Vol. 109, No. 48, p. 128.

[45] Bucareli to Arriaga, September 26, 1774, AGN, CVB, Vol. 11, Libro 9, No. 77 or 1530, pp. 106v–107v.

of the two convents were involved in the conspiracy.[46] Petitions seeking exemptions from various provisions of the *cédula* descended on Bucareli, but he was enabled to ignore them or pass them along to the prelate concerned by virtue of a royal order which forbade the admission of any appeal.[47] Convent elections provided a source of resistance in a variety of ways. For example, the private-life nuns of two Puebla convents planned to meet in advance of the date set for the elections and choose a prioress from their own number, after which they would obey her and publicize their action by ringing the convents' bells. The plot was discovered and only barely forestalled.[48] An interesting by-product of this incident was the flushing of a local citizen, one Rafael Manzanares, who had been encouraging the nuns to resist the *Vida Común* program.[49] It is possible that he was the disturbing influence mentioned by López the preceding September.

As the skirmishing continued through 1775 and 1776, it became clear that, although the nuns were winning an occasional victory in Mexico City and elsewhere, the Crown was generally having its way— except in Puebla. Whether because of greater unity, a firmer determination, better leadership, or sheer stubbornness, the Puebla nuns emerged as the most successful opponents of the *Vida Común,* and, ergo, the Bishop of Puebla as one of the most beset men in New Spain. Ignoring the royal prohibitions against petitions and appeals, the nuns continued to pour forth their resentment.

[46] Same to same, August 27, September 26, and November 26, 1774, *ibid.,* Nos. 71 or 1487, 74 or 1527, and 96 or 1637, pp. 96–98v, 101v–103, and 126v–127.

[47] Same to same, April 26, 1775, *ibid.,* No. 110 or 1816, pp. 190–190v. The royal order was dated January 19, 1775.

[48] Same to same, May 27 and June 26, 1775, Nos. 1830 and 1852, AGI, Mex., Leg. 1374.

[49] Manzanares had previously been apprehended for stirring up trouble and had been warned to desist, but had ignored the warning. This time, Bucareli ordered the Governor of Puebla to give Manzanares twenty-four hours to leave the city and eight days in which to report to the *alcalde mayor* in Valladolid. He was also to be forbidden to communicate with the Puebla nuns by any means. Unfortunately, Manzanares could not be located in Puebla to be told of his new status. He was last seen, according to Bucareli, in the vicinity of the village of Tepeaca. Bucareli to Arriaga, May 27 and June 26, 1775, Nos. 1830 and 1852, *ibid.* The King approved this method and urged its use on other troublemakers. Arriaga to Bucareli, August 23, 1775, AGN, Historia, Monjas, Vol. 134, No. 3, pp. 16–16v.

In August, 1777, Bucareli received notices from Spain that the Puebla nuns had again complained of the oppressions inflicted on them by Bishop López in his efforts to get them to accept the *Vida Común.* The King ordered the Viceroy to take whatever corrective action he deemed best.[50] In informing López of the King's command, Bucareli could be no more specific than the royal order had been— he simply repeated the generality that the nuns complained of oppression and cautioned the prelate against undue molestation of his charges.[51]

Either the Bishop of Puebla was a dishonest man with a glib tongue, or the dissident nuns in his convents untruthfully impugned his character. His reply to Bucareli's letter was a masterpiece of injured innocence and self-defense. He protested the absence of specific charges, asking that the nuns explain "which are the molestations and oppressions which have been done to them, in what manner, and by what persons," in order that he might make clear the falseness of the claims. He pointed out that, far from urging nuns to accept the *Vida Común,* he and his vicar general did not admit those who applied for it until they had proved their worthiness. The Bishop then remarked the increasing tendency of the dissidents to neglect their normal religious duties, such as attending confession and communion, and asked how he could be accused of urging such persons to accept the common life, which demanded greater religious devotion and a finer spirit than they were wont to express. He made the final point that these nuns who broke their own vows in such notorious fashion had to be corrected, and that although such correction had no connection with accepting the new life, the nuns created the connection artificially and dishonestly because they knew of the intercession they might thus obtain from the King.[52]

Although López' defense appears to have fallen on deaf ears, those same ears were able to hear the continued complaints of his rebellious nuns. Their persistent clamors reached even as far as Rome, with the result that the papal nuncio in Spain delivered a note to

[50] Gálvez to Bucareli, May 10, 1777, *ibid.,* pp. 20–20v.

[51] Bucareli to López, August 13, 1777, *ibid.,* pp. 21–21v.

[52] López to Bucareli, August 23, 1777, *ibid.,* pp. 22–27.

Charles III on behalf of the sisters. Once more, and this time more sternly, the Puebla ordinary was ordered to desist from his oppressions and pay heed to that part of the *Vida Común cédula* which enjoined him to treat with equal gentleness all elements of his convents.[53] Let the badgered Bishop speak for himself this time. Beginning with a reference to his previous letter of defense, he said:

> I have nothing to add, except that the dissidents . . . continue in the same indolence, refusing almost all Acts of Community. . . . I also continue inactive . . . because an experience so extended and distressing has persuaded me that the ills of these tempted ones, who, by the grace of God are few, however much in their petitions they may multiply the signatures, one feigning those of many, are not subject to any human remedy, and much less to that of oppression and molestation, which I have never considered. . . . It is so clear and notorious to everyone, that to . . . substantiate it with documents would, it seems to me, give body to the shade and obscure the very light. From all this, Your Excellency will recognize the artifice and caprice with which the dissidents, badly advised and believing thus to achieve their intent, have directed their appeals, and that with respect to the cited royal order, I have nothing to do but offer to God the inexplicable bitterness which [I feel] on seeing my conduct accused as disobedient to the King's wishes . . . and which [I feel] on considering that I must account to God for the direction of souls who . . . have the daring temerity to carry even to the throne such enormous impostures. . . .[54]

Bucareli faced a puzzling situation. With growing forcefulness Charles III had several times ordered him to see that the oppression of the Puebla nuns was stopped. The Viceroy had relayed these injunctions to Bishop López, adding his own cautioning statements. The prelate had replied, convincingly, that no oppression existed. And yet the dissident inmates of the Puebla houses continued to cry out against the alleged persecutions to which they were being subjected. Even while López was preparing his second reply, Bucareli received a

---

[53] Gálvez to Bucareli, September 6, 1778, *ibid.,* p. 28. This is the cover-letter for Gálvez to the Bishop of Puebla, *ibid.,* pp. 29–29v. The letter concerning the papal interest is Gálvez to Bucareli, *ibid.,* pp. 31–31v.

[54] López to Bucareli, January 13, 1778, *ibid.,* pp. 34–35.

petition from one of his nuns begging relief from his harsh rule.[55] Who was right?

In an effort to find out, Bucareli adopted the suggestion of Fiscal Guevara that he appoint three agents to make secret inquiries in Puebla and report their findings to the Viceroy. As agents he chose Felipe Venancio Malo, archdean of the Puebla cathedral; Francisco Xavier Sánchez Pareja, prebend of the cathedral; and Colonel Gaspar de Portolá, governor of Puebla.[56] Classified as "Very Confidential," the Instructions ordered the agents to ascertain the following: the way in which the Bishop and his subordinates had treated and were treating the nuns; the method used to put in effect the 1774 *cédula* on the *Vida Común;* whether or not the nuns received a choice in the matter; whether those who did not accept the *Vida Común* were getting equal treatment with those who had; whether the non-*Vida Común* group continued the same mode of life they followed at the time they professed; whether peace and paternal charity for all was being evidenced in the convents; whether each nun not observing the *Vida Común* was allowed one servant; what molestations were being inflicted on the nuns, or whether they were in any way being oppressed.[57]

The agents discovered that getting at the truth was difficult, if not impossible. In the introduction to his report Sánchez Pareja averred that when he approached individuals in search of information, he found them either indifferent, partisan, or fearful of being considered partisan, and that therefore they gave ambiguous answers or did not reply truthfully.[58] Portolá reported that his chief informant had exacted a promise that he would not reveal the informant's identity.[59] Charles III later said of the reporters that "they differed among themselves and were so inconclusive" that no clear decision could be

[55] Phelipa Francesca de San José (a nun in Santa Catalina Convent in Puebla) to Bucareli, October 31, 1777, *ibid.,* pp. 32–32v.

[56] Fiscal Guevara to Bucareli, January 26, 1778. Bucareli's indorsement and approval dated February 3, 1778, *ibid.,* pp. 36–37.

[57] February 3, 1778, *ibid.,* pp. 38–38v.

[58] Sánchez Pareja to Bucareli, February 28, 1778, *ibid.,* pp. 47–47v.

[59] Portolá to Bucareli, February 21, 1778, *ibid.,* pp. 41–45v.

reached.[60] Thus was marked up another failure in the effort to settle the *Vida Común* controversy.

At this point, with the reports of his agents before him, Bucareli recapitulated the entire course of events and offered his suggestions. By way of introduction, he defined the nuns as persons "who for so many years have made trouble for this government through the difficulty it has always had in ascertaining the reality of the measures proposed and the measures followed by such learned prelates as he who occupied and today occupies that bishopric, and the constant, inflamed appeals of nuns in order that the Rule they professed shall not be altered." He spoke briefly of events prior to the issuance of the 1774 Royal *Cédula* on the *Vida Común,* and then credited this measure with ushering in an era of tranquillity. He averred that, in general, the prelates of New Spain had executed the King's wishes with creditable tact and energy. The Bishop of Puebla, he said, had succeeded in establishing the *Vida Común* in his convents among the more stable elements of their inmates,

but at the same time, he is the prelate on whom the most war has been made by those who seemed resolved to abandon the whole thing before being convinced. . . . I feel that the expositions and complaints of those who held to the private life are enlarged, and that they are mixed with antecedents which have no connection with events since 1774, whereby the remedy was given for each one to follow the party her spirit told her to. . . . The measures of the Puebla Bishop, zealous, impartial, desirous that the King be obeyed, and that all nuns, common life or private life, observe what is set forth, seem to me to be credible. . . . And since . . . they still complain, the whole thing needs a remedy difficult to administer. . . . In these matters, one always moves in darkness. Nothing has agitated my spirit so much in this command.[61]

[60] Royal *Cédula,* August 17, 1780, AGN, RC, 1780, Vol. 119, No. 138, p. 292A. The reports are located with Bucareli's cover-letter of March 28, 1778, in AGN, CVB, 1773–1779, Vol. 7, Libro 15, No. 244 or 3628, pp. 20v–21, 155–172. The designation of dates on this volume is incorrect, inasmuch as it contains documents beginning in 1778 and has none earlier than that date.
[61] Bucareli to Gálvez, February 24, 1778, *ibid.,* No. 239 or 3568, pp. 10–16v.

From the foregoing it is obvious that Bucareli believed Bishop López' version of the Puebla situation and did not credit the claims of the nuns. The nuns, however, either did not care what the Viceroy thought, or, more probably, were unaware of his sentiments, for they continued to complain and to turn out petitions to headquarters higher than Bucareli's.

The situation did not improve significantly during the summer of 1778, and, as a result, in August Charles III decided to institute another investigation, this one to be open and official, with the authority and prestige of the throne behind it. The Instructions did not reach New Spain until November, 1778, and the report of the investigation was not completed until after Bucareli's death in April, 1779. As a result, the Viceroy was unable to participate in what was, for the era at least, the last scene in this prolonged drama.

Appointed as investigators were Inquisitor President of the Holy Office Manuel Ruiz de Vallejo, and Vicente Ruperto de Luyando, an *oidor* of the *Audiencia* of Mexico. Their general instructions were to "go together to Puebla to re-establish peace . . . in the convents of shod nuns." In modern terms the specific points of inquiry which the inspectors were to follow, and which numbered twenty-three, appear to be generally slanted in favor of the nuns and against the Bishop. Many of them seem to consist merely of the charges made against López, preceded by the word "If." For instance, "If the present bishop, vicars, and subordinates have prevented the publication of secrets of the convents so that the oppression the nuns are subject to will not be discovered," and "If they have deprived the private-life nuns of the cells which their fathers bought them, giving them a door on the street, like the habitations of seculars," are fairly typical examples of the shade of the wording. The inspectors were instructed not to make a mystery of the investigation or its objectives, and to question not only the Bishop and his subordinates, but to allow every nun to speak freely. *Vida Común* nuns were to be asked under oath if they wished to continue with the new life, and private-life nuns were to be promised help in transferring to other convents if they so desired.[62]

[62] The original Instructions are in AGN, Historia, Vol. 1337, Gálvez to Luyando, pp. 1–4, and Gálvez to Vallejo, pp. 5–7v. There is a copy in AGI, IG, Leg. 3043.

When Bucareli delivered the Instructions to the inspectors, Inquisitor Vallejo admitted that the job posed a problem for him. He said that he had been a friend of Bishop López for many years, that he had stayed with him in Puebla for eight days in the year just past, and that, on his request, the Bishop had given one of his relatives a position. Bucareli was well acquainted with the Inquisitor, however, and felt that these facts would not influence his judgment. He told him, therefore, to proceed to Puebla and begin with his work.[63]

The inspectors reached Puebla on December 19, and three days later began their interviews with the top echelon of the city's ecclesiastical society, or, to use their words, "the subjects of the first rank of the Orders who, because of their independence, status, graduation, learning, and virtue (of which we also inform ourselves), we believe will be able to clarify in large part the points included in the royal order."[64] They did not restrict themselves, however, only to the illustrious, but also interrogated some lesser folk. Altogether, they interviewed forty-nine persons in addition to every nun in the six convents. They finished their work in Puebla early in February, and on the thirteenth of that month returned to Mexico City, where they began to write their report.[65]

Sifting such a large volume of material, reducing it to proper terms, and reaching the definite answers which the King had requested was a lengthy undertaking. The final report totaled 1,062 pages, and was turned over to the Viceroy late in March, 1779.[66] Whether Bucareli read it is not surely known, but he died on April 9, and the report is not mentioned in any of his final papers. At his death the reins of government were taken over by the *Audiencia,* which forwarded the report to Spain on April 26.

Undoubtedly, the person who awaited most anxiously the outcome

[63] Bucareli to Gálvez, February 24, 1778, *ibid.,* No. 239 or 3568, pp. 10–16v.
[64] Luyando and Vallejo to Bucareli, December 27, 1778, *ibid.,* pp. 264–264v. This is an inclosure in Bucareli to Gálvez, December 29, 1778, *ibid.,* No. 281 or 4202, pp. 100v–101.
[65] Bucareli to Gálvez, February 24, 1779, *ibid.,* No. 288 or 4324, pp. 111–111v.
[66] AGN, Historia (Vol. 137) contains more than 750 pages of documents on the inspection, including the interviews held in Puebla. It does not contain, however, a copy of the final report.

82 *Viceregency of Bucareli*

of the investigation was Bishop López; but outrageous fortune had not yet exhausted her supply of slings and arrows in so far as he was concerned. A series of rather unlikely mishaps combined to delay a decision in the matter. The original of the report was thrown into the sea to avoid its being captured by the English, and, inexplicably, the duplicate which customarily would have been sent in the next mail was not dispatched.[67] Not until late September did the new viceroy, Martín de Mayorga, become aware of the omission and remedy it by sending the duplicate,[68] and not until August, 1780, did the King make known his decision.

The patience of the long-suffering Bishop was at last adequately rewarded, for Charles III exonerated him completely. Mayorga was instructed to inform López of the following royal decision:

His Majesty has resolved that in his royal name Your Excellency manifest to the Reverend Bishop of Puebla, don Victoriano López Gonzalo, that it has been his royal pleasure to have seen his conduct in that clamorous affair fully justified, and the prompt fulfillment which the same prelate has given to the cited Royal *Cédula* of 1774 and to the orders which have been set forth as a consequence.

Finally, His Majesty wishes that Your Excellency assure said Reverend Bishop of how satisfied is his royal spirit with the suave and prudent means with which he has cooperated in order that the efficacious and pious desires with which His Majesty has procured and procures the spiritual well-being of those nuns may be fulfilled, and that he hopes that he will continue with the same fervor contributing to the execution of the Royal *Cédula* which with this same date he has deigned to set forth, confirming that of May 22, 1774.[69]

The new Royal *Cédula* referred to was, first of all, a confirmation of the 1774 *cédula,* as the King pointed out. Additionally, it granted to each Puebla nun eight days from the time of announcement to decide

---

[67] Gálvez to Mayorga, September 16, 1779, AGN, RC, 1779, Vol. 117, No. 143, pp. 259–259v.
[68] Mayorga to Gálvez, September 26, 1779, AGN, CV, 1779, Vol. 123, No. 122, pp. 57v–58.
[69] Gálvez to Mayorga, August 17, 1780, AGN, RC, 1780, Vol. 119, No. 136, pp. 57v–58.

once more on which way of life she would choose, and allowed any nun to change from one to the other during this period, except those nuns who had professed since the 1774 *cédula* had been installed and who must remain in the *Vida Común*. No appeals were to be permitted, and any petition received by higher authorities was to be returned to the proper prelate for action against the petitioners as disturbers of the peace.[70] According to his Instructions, Mayorga notified Luyando and Vallejo of the new *cédula* and advised them that they had been appointed to proceed to Puebla to put the regulation into effect.[71] This phase of the struggle, at least, had come to an end.

There is more to be derived from a study of the *Vida Común* controversy than the lesson that one should never underestimate the power of a woman. The conflict also represents one of the hazards of attempting a program of reform, much as the reform may be needed, justified as it may be in terms of its objectives. By extension, if such a minor change involving so few persons could cause so much excitement and occupy the time of so many officials and clerks, the dangers of a major-reform effort may be more clearly understood.

Bucareli's handling of the situation is revelatory in several respects. His confident use of his position to cow the *Audiencia* and the *Real Acuerdo* on one occasion and the *ayuntamiento* of Mexico City on another is demonstrative of the power and prestige of the executive in the Spanish system. In some respects, Bucareli occupied the unenviable position of the man in the middle during much of the campaign, serving as a sort of semiresponsible relay between the King and the Bishop. There was little of an effective nature that he could do, and yet his monarch apparently expected him to do something.

Finally, the controversy demonstrates clearly the extent to which the *patronato real* had been expanded by the latter part of the eighteenth century. Dictation by the Crown of the mode of life of an entire segment of ecclesiastical personnel was never challenged by any religious authority—not even by Rome itself. Instead, the Pope merely

[70] *Ibid.,* No. 138, pp. 285–299. This document also contains a complete review of the subject, as well as the praise and exoneration of Bishop López already cited.
[71] Mayorga to Gálvez, March 7, 1781, AGN, CV, 1781, Vol. 128, No. 957, pp. 116–116v.

inquired of the Crown about the conduct of one of his own bishops, while the prelates concerned hastened to do the bidding of the temporal patron. The *Vida Común* controversy helps to reveal that the Church was indeed the lesser partner in the Spanish combination of Church and State.

The Captain General and Defense

HISTORIANS ARE more deeply concerned with significance than
with any other facet of their craft, and to them significance
means, most importantly, an understanding of, and an explanation for, what follows as the result of an event or situation. In
this sense, one of the most meaningful aspects of the Bucareli viceregency was one part of the policy which was followed with respect to
defense. In view of the problems of the era, this should not be surprising; and in view of the Viceroy's powers and functions, his actions in
this field must be noted and weighed.

Parallel with the viceroy's position as civil head of the government
was his status as military head or captain general of the viceroyalty.
As bearer of this title he was the supreme commander of all military
personnel. He had control of coastal defenses, conquests, new discoveries, and new settlements. He was in full charge of military justice and sat as a court of appeal in civil or criminal cases concerning
persons who enjoyed the military *fuero,* or privilege. It was an important power.[1]

It was also an important responsibility, especially in the decades
which followed the Seven Years' War, for during these years a new
and grand defensive design was initiated by the Crown for the entire
empire. The results of the Seven Years' War were, of course, fundamental determinants of subsequent Spanish policy in almost all areas

---

[1] Croix, Instrucción, AGN, CVB, 1772, Vol. 24, pp. 443–444v; Haring, *The
Spanish Empire in America,* p. 124. For a good general discussion of the viceroy as
captain general, see Donald E. Smith, *The Viceroy in New Spain,* Chap. 4.

of action. Spain's defeat by England was nearly disastrous, and the certainty that England would not remain content with the *status quo* for long constituted a powerful motivation for the Spanish Crown to improve its situation before it was too late. The primary need, obviously, was greater strength, a basic component of which was defensive strength, not only with respect to the peninsula itself, but also with respect to the entire empire. Therefore, at the same time that a general program of inspection, introspection, and reform was begun by Charles III for Spain itself, the specific decision was made that overseas military establishments must also be strengthened. By his decision as to how this should be achieved, this Spanish Bourbon unwittingly contributed to the making of the petard by which his grandson was destined to be hoist.

Prior to the Seven Years' War, the defenses of New Spain could be described as scanty, especially in so far as troops were concerned. The only permanent military units in the viceroyalty were the viceroy's guard of halberdiers, a few infantry companies called *compañías de palacio,* and a variety of other small units stationed in the ports and on the northern frontiers.[2] In addition, merchants and several of the craft guilds in the principal cities maintained small private armed forces, a sort of urban militia. The organization of professional units in New Spain was begun in 1762, partly with regiments from the mother country. At about the same time, efforts were initiated to create a regular colonial militia, distributed by battalions throughout the provinces.[3]

This militia was a key element in the Crown's new defensive plan. Inasmuch as the great majority of its membership would serve without pay except for the one month a year during which they would engage in an assembly and maneuvers, it was the answer to the prohibitive cost of maintaining an adequate military force composed of regular troops. Such a description is an oversimplification of the official plan, to be sure, but it is not far removed from the general, and unwarranted,

[2] Lyle N. McAlister, *The "Fuero Militar" in New Spain, 1764–1800,* pp. 1–2 and Table 1, Appendix I, p. 93. This work is cited hereafter as *"Fuero Militar."* See also Haring, *The Spanish Empire in America,* p. 124.

[3] Haring, *ibid.,* pp. 124–125.

optimism with which the program was ordered into effect, an optimism which was, typically, more prevalent among officials in Spain than among those closer to the situation in the colonies.[4]

That the formation of the militia was not going to be an easy task should have been apparent from the experience of Viceroy Marqués de Cruillas when he tried to organize the defenses of New Spain during the crisis of the Seven Years' War. He found that Mexican males seemed to have an almost congenital aversion for military service, the people generally resisted the program, all kinds of necessary matériel were very difficult to acquire, and all accomplishments turned out to be ephemeral. His efforts after the war to maintain a necessary part of what he thought he had achieved during the war, and the subsequent work of Lieutenant General Juan de Villalba y Angulo, proved to be, if not fruitless, certainly not so productive of solid gains as had been hoped for.[5]

Bucareli's predecessor, the Marqués de Croix, was the next to try his hand at this unrewarding task. In his Instruction he apprised Bucareli that, although it was conjectural whether such troops would serve any useful purpose, the King had ordered an increased number of militia units. He indicated that upon his arrival in 1766 he had found the militia on little more than a paper basis, but that through a series of

[4] Orozco y Berra offers the interesting suggestion that, although defense was the long-range objective of the militia program, a more immediate goal was the creation of loyal groups with which to handle the Jesuit expulsion. He says, further, that the expulsion so weakened the traditional bond between Church and State that the Crown, seeking to restore this lost support, turned to the militia for such replacement. Finally, he suggests that the public disturbances growing out of the expulsion alerted the Spaniards to the fact that the colonials had no real love for Spanish domination and were merely awaiting the opportune moment to rebel. The new military program was designed to provide adequate preparation should that moment arrive. Manuel Orozco y Berra, *Historia de la dominación española en México*, Vol. IV, pp. 138–143. This work is cited hereafter as *Historia de la dominación española*.

[5] For a detailed consideration of this phase of the Cruillas administration, see María del Carmen Velázquez, *El estado de guerra en Nueva España, 1760–1808*, pp. 31–61. This work is cited hereafter as *El estado de guerra*. For Villalba's work, see Lyle N. McAlister, "The Reorganization of the Army of New Spain, 1763–1767," *Hispanic American Historical Review*, Vol. XXXIII (February, 1953), pp. 1–32.

inspections its status had been improved. Croix explained that there existed a general fund derived from a tax on cacao imports in Veracruz, plus special funds in various major cities, to support the organization. Ultimately, he said, the militia would cost the treasury nothing, and in case of war it provided a ready defensive force, while in peacetime it served to preserve law and order. In addition, the Marqués commented favorably on certain units, including a squadron of lancers in Veracruz and, in Mexico City, the *Comercio* infantry regiment, the silversmith company, also infantry, and two cavalry companies composed of bakers and pork butchers. These units guarded the government buildings when the regular troops were called outside the city.[6]

Two factors affecting the militia program were operative when Bucareli assumed the viceregency: first, Spain was at peace, and war did not appear imminent; second, Bucareli's primary task was to strengthen the financial status of New Spain, an objective which had precedence even over considerations of defense. Consequently, within ten days of his arrival he ignored Croix's advisement that the King desired a larger militia by discharging from active service as of September 30, 1771, three militia battalions serving in the capital, offering as his official reason the opinion that ". . . in time of peace . . . this expense ought to be avoided and the royal treasury freed of it." Writing to his friend Alejandro O'Reilly, Bucareli could speak a bit more frankly. He told him that not only had he dismissed the militia companies, but that, acting on a royal order to Croix, he had ordered the Battalion of Flanders returned to Spain and could do the same with the Battalion of Savoy in view of the prevailing peace. He then commented, "For war, those who come from Spain as reinforcements are better, without the vices of diminution which here appear inevitable."[7]

Shortly after taking this action, Bucareli volunteered his opinion on the potentialities of New Spain's militia. On his journey from Veracruz to the capital he had inspected a number of militia units. A few he rated equal to similar outfits in Havana, which he regarded highly.

[6] Croix, Instrucción, AGN, CVB, 1772, Vol. 24, pp. 443v–445.

[7] Bucareli to Arriaga, October 5, 1771, in Velasco Ceballos, *La administración de . . . Bucareli,* Vol. II, p. 125. Bucareli to O'Reilly, October 5, 1771, AGI, Mex., Leg. 1242.

Most of them, however, he found poorly armed, badly mounted, and inadequately instructed. They would inspire, he said, as little confidence in the man who had to command them in case of war, as respect in those who might face them as enemies. Reports from other towns indicated that most units were incomplete, the method of levying personnel was frequently unjust, and bribery was not uncommon for avoiding service. It was necessary, he asserted, to undertake a complete reestablishment of the backward system, seeking at the same time to achieve this goal with less burden on the heavily-indebted treasury.[8]

The King's hearty approval of Bucareli's dismissal of the three Mexico City battalions[9] led the Viceroy to suggest a similar fate for three units on active service in Veracruz—two infantry companies and a lancer squadron. Charles III told him to use his own judgment. Bucareli therefore informed the Governor of the port city that inasmuch as the regular infantry regiment and the two dragoon companies stationed in Veracruz were a sufficient garrison force, the militia units would be dismissed as of July 1, 1772, and the men set free to pursue their civilian occupations full time. A nucleus of officers and noncommissioned officers would remain on active duty, however, and would periodically give military instruction to the personnel on inactive status. In reporting his decision to Spain, Bucareli attached detailed statements which revealed that the dismissal would result in an annual saving of 27,456 pesos to the Crown.[10] Governor Juan Fernando Palacios carried out the Viceroy's order on schedule, and three more militia units stopped drawing the King's pay.[11]

The Viceroy was not yet finished with his retrenchment program. In

[8] Bucareli to Arriaga, October 21, 1771, in Velasco Ceballos, *La administración de . . . Bucareli,* Vol. II, pp. 125–127. Carmen Velázquez points out that practically every military authority who arrived in New Spain in the eighteenth century speaks of working on the armed-forces problem as though he were the first to encounter it and must therefore start from the very beginning. *El estado de guerra,* p. 112.

[9] Arriaga to Bucareli, January 23, 1772, AGN, RC, 1772, Vol. 100, No. 20, p. 53.

[10] Bucareli to Arriaga, May 24, 1772, and inclosure, AGN, CVB, 1772, Vol. 24, No. 378, pp. 22–24.

[11] Same to same, June 24, 1772, AGN, CVB, 1772, Vol. 25, No. 436, pp. 15–15v. Crown approval was expressed in Arriaga to Bucareli, August 20, 1772, AGN, RC, 1772, Vol. 101, No. 51, p. 92.

Guadalajara a militia company of *pardos,* a colored caste, was employed in guard duty and, in addition, provided a detachment of one officer and sixteen men to the port of San Blas every six months. As with the Mexico City and Veracruz units, Bucareli felt that it worked a hardship on civilians to be thus separated from their families and to lose touch with their civilian occupations. Furthermore, there were two incomplete regular Army units in New Spain, the Companies of Volunteers of Cataluña, which were not usefully employed. Bucareli suggested filling the ranks of these units, with Catalans if possible, and assigning one company to take over the job of the militia company in Guadalajara. Every one or two years the two Catalan companies could trade assignments. Again Bucareli had a statement ready to show that the maneuver would save money. The plan was carried out in 1773.[12]

Dismissal and consolidation were not the whole of Bucareli's military personnel policy, although the lack of certain documents makes necessary an element of conjecture with respect to his actions during the first three years of his viceregency. As mentioned already, Croix had informed Bucareli of the King's desire that the militia be expanded; and yet, from his arrival in September, 1771, until January, 1775, no action was taken to form new units. Scattered and scanty sources seem to indicate that a halt to the expansion program was ordered by the Crown as of the time Bucareli assumed command, with the decision on whether to resume the program or not resting with Bucareli. This decision was to be based on a thorough survey of the situation, conducted, apparently, by him and by whatever methods he felt desirable.

The evidence that such was the policy is as follows. In a letter to O'Reilly, dated October 27, 1771, Bucareli said, "The delay in the establishment of the militia you will have known about via the last reports from the Marqués de Croix and by what I say in my letter to the Bailío [Arriaga]."[13] (These "last reports" are among the missing

---

[12] Bucareli to Arriaga, May 26, 1772, AGN, CVB, 1772, Vol. 24, No. 395, pp. 41–42v. Same to same, March 23, 1773, AGN, CVB, 1773, Vol. 36, No. 839, pp. 34–37v.
[13] AGI, Mex., Leg. 1242.

documents mentioned above.) O'Reilly provided the next relevant comments when he wrote, on December 25, 1771, "The Conde de Croix has sent me many papers on the militia, but until you can inform yourself and reveal what you understand, all will remain suspended." [14] Then, on January 25, 1772, O'Reilly wrote, "No job will be provided in that militia until you, with full knowledge of its state, report what it seems to be to you and request what suits you." [15]

Bucareli apparently was depending in part on the assistance of an inspector to aid him in reaching a decision.[16] Although Field Marshal Pascual de Cisneros was appointed Inspector of Troops for New Spain late in 1771, he did not arrive until September, 1772, thus delaying the decision.[17] Cisneros then embarked on a lengthy inspection tour of the viceroyalty, a tour interrupted for several months by illness.[18] It seems reasonable to assume, therefore, that the militia program was suspended pending Bucareli's investigation and decision, that Bucareli chose to await the results of an inspection by an aide, and that the delay in Cisneros' arrival and his tour all combined to produce a rather lengthy hiatus in the expansion program.

The suspension was not concluded by Cisneros' submitting to Bucareli an ambitious plan for an expanded militia program in October, 1773, nor even by his delivering the documents relating to his inspection of all militia units,[19] with the recommendation that immediate action be taken on the above plan. The Viceroy directed Cisneros to convene a junta of high military officers to draw up a provisional set of ordinances for the proposed new units. Meanwhile, Bucareli requested of the Fiscal a report on possible sources of funds to support the project, while he himself turned to an investigation of the

[14] *Ibid.*   [15] *Ibid.*

[16] Bucareli to O'Reilly, October 27, 1771, *ibid.*

[17] O'Reilly to Bucareli, December 25, 1771. Bucareli to O'Reilly, September 26 and October 27, 1772, *ibid.*

[18] Bucareli to O'Reilly, November 27, 1772; April 27, June 26, and July 28, 1773, *ibid.*

[19] Cisneros, Statement of Provincial and Urban Units formed . . . , note 2, AGN, CVB, 1776, Vol. 80, of No. 2342, p. 416v. Cisneros here refers to the fact that he submitted his plan on October 3, 1773.

history of the matter and reflection on its ramifications for New Spain.[20]

Not until December did he transmit to Spain the results of his cogitation on Cisneros' plan and the potentialities of his viceroyalty with respect to it. The inspector called for an initial establishment of ten battalions of infantry and two regiments of cavalry and dragoons. If these proved successful, four more infantry battalions would be formed. He acknowledged the backwardness of the militia units then in existence and previously established, but he felt that he saw the reasons for such failure and believed he had the cure for it. Bucareli agreed that the idea was good, and he revealed that the treasury would by now be able to stand the added expense. He was still hesitant about endorsing the plan, however.[21]

It must be pointed out that Bucareli's feelings about the entire project were strong, and were based on a combination of rather astute observations and personal bias. His dubiety about the program sprang fundamentally from his attitude toward the men who must compose the units. In contrast to his high regard for Cubans, Bucareli quickly acquired a low opinion of the people of New Spain. With special reference to the inhabitants of Mexico City and Puebla his tone was almost bitter. One-third of the capital militia, he said, spent their time in jail, not only for desertion and other common offenses, but also because they sold their uniforms and arms as quickly as they were issued. It was impossible to train them, for they could not be instructed while they were naked, and yet to issue them clothing and equipment was to ensure that it would be pawned at the first opportunity. Punishment did not frighten them, nor did they have any sense of honor. Europe had nothing like them, nor did Cuba. Furthermore, such persons did not learn by example, for when they were scattered among regular troops from Europe, they only filled the jails and hospitals and ruined the regular discipline. He described the *bajo pueblo* generally as homeless, shameless, perpetually drunk, given to gambling, and totally without ambition. Of O'Reilly he besought, "Tell me, what militia can these be?" And then, with resignation, "Fine people and a fine system for one who did well in Havana." He was saddened, he said, by "the large amounts of funds which the King has spent without utility and the many good officers who have been wasted. The certain fact is that after seven years there is no militia, and they have cost the King much." [22]

Was there no other segment of the population he could turn to? All hard labor, he said, was done by the Indians. The rigors of war demanded such robust men as these, but government policy forbade instructing Indians in the use of firearms. The other castes did not produce individuals of this type, while Spaniards were customarily available in sufficient numbers only to fill executive positions and to handle the viceroyalty's trade. Bucareli concluded by saying, "All that reason dictates, based on experience, has shown that a useful, regulated militia is not possible in this kingdom." [23]

In addition to his low opinion of the people, Bucareli's attitude toward Cisneros did not augur well for the militia program. The Viceroy had hoped that one of two old friends, Poyanos or Pimiento, would receive the appointment as inspector.[24] Cisneros was, therefore, a disappointment, and since he had had to come only from Cuba, his delay in reaching New Spain did not improve the Viceroy's attitude.[25] Bucareli's comment to O'Reilly shortly after Cisneros reached Veracruz is indicative: "Cisneros arrived; all that he has seen seems good to him, and he intends to establish a useful militia. If it were you who gave me this opinion, I would be calmed, but I am still not so in the matter." [26] Some months later, in a sharply caustic manner that was not typical of him, Bucareli virtually skewered the inspector when he wrote to O'Reilly:

[22] Bucareli to O'Reilly, November 26 and December 27, 1771, and July 27, 1772, AGI, Mex., Leg. 1242. Bucareli to Arriaga, December 27, 1774, AGN, CVB, 1774, Vol. 62, No. 1645, pp. 11–21v.

[23] *Ibid.*, pp. 21v–23.

[24] Bucareli to O'Reilly, October 27, 1771, AGI, Mex., Leg. 1242. His reference to them in this letter uses only last names.

[25] Same to same, September 26, 1772, *ibid.*

[26] Same to same, November 27, 1772, *ibid.*

Cisneros goes effectively, making his lightning departures, to examine those that are called militia units. He has sent me nothing on the matter, but in our conversations I observe that he finds everything done, that he is not approaching wisdom, nor does he foresee the consequences of giving a bad opinion. You know that no one exceeds the limit prescribed by his talents, and you know that what fell to this individual is not of great extent. Otherwise he is a good man, although with the misfortune of always disgusting those who must obey him and serving little those who command him. Nevertheless, I will observe his results with care.[27]

The last sentence is a more valid reflection of the character of Bucareli than those which precede it. Indeed, one of his earlier comments on the militia problem reflects to an impressive degree his general objectivity and fair-mindedness. Appealing to O'Reilly for help, he said, "Give me your frank opinion, for I am not so partial to my own that I stop yielding to reason, and I only seek the advantages of the Service." [28] Nowhere does he offer better proof of his sincerity in making this statement than in the matter of the militia program. Despite his feeling that the character of the Mexican people made a useful militia an impossibility, and despite his initial low opinion of Cisneros, nevertheless, in view of the importance of the matter, and Cisneros' certainty that his plan was feasible, Bucareli agreed to allow the inspector to offer proof of his belief.

With an eye to the fact that Veracruz was the most logical point of possible attack, the Viceroy agreed that Cisneros should proceed with the formation of two battalions in Córdova and Orizaba, since they were nearest the seaport and their inhabitants probably more accustomed to the climate. On the success or failure of these demonstration battalions would rest the fate of the inspector's plan. Although Bucareli proposed to give them a fair trial, his letters to Arriaga and O'Reilly indicated clearly that he held little hope for a profitable result. With O'Reilly he was somewhat more frank:

I believe that the *expediente* on the militia will go in this mail, and my decision to make the final proof by means of the two battalions of Córdova and Jalapa. . . . I have said to you before, my principal doubt

[27] Same to same, April 27, 1773, *ibid.*
[28] Same to same, May 27, 1772, *ibid.*

is not that they can be formed, but . . . whether one can count on their
strength; this appears incredible, but such is the population of the country. . . . We shall see what this proof of militia produces. It is time to
look for the disillusionment. . . . The matter is of the first importance,
but my mode of thinking does not permit making known to the King as
advantageous to his service what I do not see as certain to be.[29]

Before Cisneros left Mexico City, he delivered to Bucareli the
provisional set of ordinances his junta had drawn up for the proposed
unit.[30] An interesting and informative document, it set forth the following organizational plan. The first battalion, with headquarters in
Córdova, and including Orizaba, San Andrés Chalchicomula, and
Tehuacán de las Granadas in its area, was to be composed of eight
infantry companies and one company of grenadiers. The total strength
of the latter unit was to be sixty-six men and officers, while each
infantry company was to have ninety members. Each company was to
enlist ten supernumeraries, and it was considered desirable that all the
men in the unit come from the same pueblo if possible.

A certain number of regular Army personnel known as the "veteran
base" were scattered through each unit to serve as instructors to the
militiamen. For example, in an infantry company there would be, in
order of descending rank: one militia captain, one regular lieutenant;
one militia sublieutenant; one regular first sergeant; two militia second
sergeants, two drummers, and two first corporals, all regulars; two first
corporals, four second corporals, and seventy-four soldiers, all militiamen. The second battalion, with headquarters in Jalapa and including
Perote, San Juan de los Llanos, and other small settlements in its area,
was to be of the same structure as the first, with minor variations in
the battalion staff. The regiment, therefore, was to total more than
eighteen hundred men. All members were to enjoy military privilege.

In the absence of facilities for a proper draft, the authorities were to
enlist only men of established residence who were least involved in
agriculture. Exemptions from service were many, including: lawyers,

[29] Bucareli to Arriaga, December 27, 1774, AGN, CVB, 1774, Vol. 62, No. 1645,
pp. 23–26. Bucareli to O'Reilly, December 27, 1774, AGI, Mex., Leg. 1242.
[30] It is one of the inclosures in Bucareli to Arriaga, January 27, 1775, AGN, CVB,
1775, Vol. 63, No. 1696, pp. 27v–29v, 85–107.

cabildo scribes; major domos of cities, *villas,* and ecclesiastical communities; officials and subordinates of the Cruzada and the Inquisition; only sons of widows or sexagenarian fathers; doctors; druggists; surgeons; bloodletters in villages where there were no surgeons; veterinarians; administrators and employees of royal *rentas;* syndics of San Francisco; sacristans and the necessary servants of churches; schoolteachers; and certain other classes specifically exempted by royal declaration.

The rest of the ordinances dealt in detail with such varied matters as rules of conduct, policing, discipline, nominations for and assignment to positions, licenses to marry, leave, change of residence, and special privileges. Added as appendexes were five tables on organization and pay.[31]

Cisneros left Mexico City for Córdova on January 19, 1775, and during February and March he labored to organize these two important battalions. Early in April he reported the job done. Attached to his report were the names of the men he proposed as militia officers, from which list Bucareli was to make temporary appointments, the final decision resting with the Crown. Bucareli had no trouble selecting the colonel of the regiment—one Josef Manuel de Zevallos "spontaneously" offered to contribute 6,000 pesos to help pay for uniforms, and this generosity, plus the man's standing and record, assured him of the position. Choosing the lieutenant colonel, who was to command the second battalion with headquarters in Jalapa, presented difficulties. The most eligible person was Juan de Segura, but when Cisneros approached him on the matter, Don Juan proclaimed himself aggrieved at not being offered the colonelcy. After a cooling-off period, the inspector made several efforts to see Segura again, but this man who would not accept second place refused to grant Cisneros an audience. When the Viceroy heard of this, he instructed Cisneros that in the future he was never again to look to Segura *"for any matter of service."* He also ordered the new units equipped with armament from the royal warehouse in Puebla.[32]

[31] *Ibid.*
[32] Bucareli to Arriaga, April 26, 1775, AGN, CVB, 1775, Vol. 66, No. 1798, pp. 20–22.

Almost unbelievably, Bucareli was enthusiastic about the new units. There is no clear way to account for this apparent about-face. In his official correspondence he made no reference to his changed opinion nor to any variation in the situation which might explain his new orientation. Instead, he spoke most highly of Cisneros' zealous efforts and ventured his opinion that the formation of these battalions offered "not vague hopes" for achieving what to then had been difficult, and, finally, that with this example the task might be easier in other locations.[33] His personal letters to O'Reilly are only slightly more helpful, although they do indicate, somewhat indecisively, a gradual modification of his ideas. Whereas in December, 1774, he had expressed firm doubt of the feasibility of the whole project, in January, 1775, he stated that the results of the Córdova experiment ought to be "very interesting"; in February he felt that "it ought to be of service to us in the government"; and by April he had come to the conclusion that the new units would be "most useful." [34] This is one of the very few times in his viceregency that Bucareli's conduct was enigmatic.

The remainder of 1775 proved to be a quiet period in so far as the militia program was concerned, but 1776 was different. In February the new Córdova-Jalapa regiment held its first general assembly and maneuvers. Cisneros attended the exercises and reported favorably on what he saw.[35]

At the same time that this was going on in Mexico, Gálvez in Spain was writing a dispatch to Bucareli in which he predicted, perhaps unwittingly, the end of the peace which Spain had enjoyed since the end of the Seven Years' War. He stated that in spite of the cordiality then existing between Madrid and London, the conflict going on between England and her North American colonies threatened the neutrality of even those nations that had no desire for war. He therefore advised the Viceroy that the King desired immediately a complete statement of the defensive status of New Spain, including a listing of

[33] *Ibid.*, pp. 20–23v, 159.
[34] Bucareli to O'Reilly, December 27, 1774; January 28, February 24, and April 26, 1775, AGI, Mex., Leg. 1242.
[35] Bucareli to Arriaga, February 25, 1776, AGN, CVB, 1776, Vol. 76, No. 2169, pp. 39v–40.

all that was lacking for a thorough defense and that must be sent from the peninsula. He concluded with the warning that Bucareli was to incur no extraordinary expenses nor exhibit publicly any signs of undue concern over the defensive situation, but that he must anticipate the needs of his command in that respect.[36]

Bucareli received the letter in May and immediately wrote a lengthy reply. Although it dealt in large measure with the need for armaments and with problems relative to various coastal forts, the parts devoted to the militia are significant. The Viceroy noted that since the experiment with the Córdova-Jalapa regiment had turned out so well, he was awaiting only the King's order to proceed with the rest of Cisneros' plan, and for this purpose he urged that thirty regular Army officers be sent to serve as instructors. If the threat of war increased, he said, he would personally take over the formation of the militia units, substitute a militia company for the fusileer unit in Guadalajara, and place on active service one of the Veracruz militia battalions.[37]

Two months later, July, 1776, Gálvez informed Bucareli that the threat had indeed increased—that it was now twofold. The Portuguese had precipitated war by conducting raids along the borders of the Buenos Aires viceroyalty. Charles III was suspicious of England, despite repeated reassurances from that country that she would remain neutral so long as the war was confined to South America. Bucareli was therefore again warned to be alert for any surprise move on the part of England. The Viceroy replied that he was directing his efforts to improving New Spain's defenses, citing briefly the steps he planned to take.[38]

[36] Gálvez to Bucareli, February 28, 1776, AGN, RC, 1776, Vol. 107, No. 50, pp. 87–88v.

[37] Bucareli to Gálvez, May 27, 1776, AGN, CVB, 1776, Vol. 12, Libro 13, No. 155 or 2238, pp. 16–20. The request for the specific number of thirty officers was based on Cisneros' estimate of the number needed in response to Bucareli's query on the matter. Same to same, same date, AGN, CVB, 1776, Vol. 79, No. 2255, pp. 18v–19. Gálvez immediately requested Inspector General Count O'Reilly to choose the thirty officers. Gálvez to Bucareli, August 26, 1776, AGN, RC, 1776, Vol. 108, No. 103, pp. 216–216v.

[38] Gálvez to Bucareli, July 27, 1776, AGN, RC, 1776, Vol. 108, No. 56, pp. 121–121v. This letter merely ordered Bucareli to seek additional revenue from

It is apparent that this dangerous international situation led Charles III to approve the whole of Cisneros' plan for an expanded militia. On July 9 Gálvez informed Bucareli of the royal decision. When the Viceroy passed this information to the inspector, Cisneros signified that his choice for the location of the next new militia regiment was the Tlaxcala-Puebla area.[39] Late in November Cisneros went to Tlaxcala to begin the job.[40] Inasmuch as the promised regular Army officers from Spain had not as yet arrived, the requisite numbers for the new unit were secured from the regiments of Granada and La Corona stationed in New Spain. When the thirty officers did come from the peninsula, they were to be assigned to the next new militia regiment to be formed.[41]

Cisneros had learned a great deal in the course of organizing the Córdova-Jalapa regiment, and much of the preliminary work had been done by the time he reached the new area. In the single month of December, therefore, he was able to complete his task and report to the Viceroy not only the establishment of the new regiment, but also of an additional battalion of *pardos* in Puebla. It developed, however, that there were not enough of this colored caste in the immediate Puebla area to make a full battalion; consequently, the unit was redesignated as the eighth company in the *pardo* battalion previously formed in Córdova. When Cisneros reported these various units as organized, he did not mean, of course, that they were as yet in any sense a fighting force. This initial establishment consisted only of enlisting the men, assigning them to units, and nominating officers. Training was done on

---

tobacco and pulque in order to help pay for the anticipated expenses of the war contemplated with Portugal. Another dispatch of the same date, not available in the original but quoted in its entirety by Bucareli in his reply cited in the text, reveals Charles III's plan to send an expedition of nine thousand men to Buenos Aires, and it is following this statement that his distrust of England is expressed. Bucareli to Gálvez, October 27, 1776, AGN, CVB, 1776, Vol. 21, Libro 13, No. 170 or 2535, pp. 42v–43v.

[39] Bucareli to Gálvez, October 27, 1776, AGN, CVB, 1776, Vol. 84, No. 2567, pp. 49–49v.

[40] Same to same, November 26, 1776, AGN, CVB, 1776, Vol. 85, No. 2600, p. 23v.

[41] Same to same, November 26, 1776, *ibid.*, No. 2601, pp. 26–26v.

Sundays and holidays, with a full month of each year devoted to general assemblies and maneuvers.[42]

During the last two years of Bucareli's viceregency—from January, 1777, to April, 1779—the European situation deteriorated rapidly, and Spain, by virtue of her alliance with France, was dragged into war against England. As a consequence, among other military preparations in New Spain, the militia program was accelerated. In May, 1777, Cisneros reported the formation of a battalion of *pardos* in Mexico City. As was his custom upon receiving such news, Bucareli immediately ordered the requisite equipment and armament supplied to the new unit. In reporting this fact to the Crown, the Viceroy indicated that the establishment of a new regiment of *blancos*, or whites, was presently underway in the capital.[43] In October the two Veracruz companies of *pardos* and *morenos*—another of the colored castes—were called to active service to help the seaport's regular garrison forces, which had been hard hit by a fever epidemic. February, 1778, produced the inspector's report on the formation of a dragoon regiment in Puebla.[44] In April Cisneros re-formed, revitalized, and expanded the eighteen companies of the Toluca infantry regiment,[45] and in October he practiced the same revision with the infantry regiment of Mexico City.[46] At this point, Cisneros' original plan had reached completion.

As already mentioned, somewhere along the line during this stepped-up program Bucareli lost his conviction that the formation of efficient militia units in New Spain was an impossibility. Apparently he was converted through hearsay evidence alone, for there is no indication that he participated personally in the program or inspected any of the

---

[42] Same to same, January 27, 1777, AGN, CVB, 1777, Vol. 87, No. 2718, pp. 26–29.

[43] Same to same, June 26, 1777, AGN, CVB, 1777, Vol. 92, No. 3044, pp. 16v–18.

[44] Same to same, March 27, 1778, AGN, CVB, 1778, Vol. 101, No. 2668, pp. 41v–44.

[45] Same to same, April 26, 1778, AGN, CVB, 1778, Vol. 104, No. 3717, pp. 27–28v.

[46] Same to same, October 27, 1778, AGN, CVB, 1778, Vol. 111, No. 4044, pp. 1–4.

units. Nevertheless, he relayed, with obvious acceptance, the enthusiastic report of Cisneros on the annual maneuvers of the Tlaxcala-Puebla regiment in November, 1777, and the statement of Gaspar de Portolá, governor of Puebla, that this unit and the battalion of *pardos* could "in no way . . . be distinguished from any veteran unit of the army."[47] In March, 1778, Bucareli passed along similar views on the Córdova-Jalapa regiment, and in February, 1779, he repeated his praise of the Tlaxcala-Puebla unit.[48]

The story of the militia under Bucareli leads to certain conclusions, although some of them must be conjectural, at least in part. Clearly, the militia forces were significantly expanded. The earliest available statement on militia strength during Bucareli's term is dated January 24, 1772.[49] It shows a total effective strength of 6,837 men, including the units from Mexico City that Bucareli had already retired, and the Veracruz battalions soon to be dismissed. It is a safe assumption, therefore, that the militia strength on paper reflected little actuality. In addition, in view of Bucareli's attitude, his determination to save money, and the state of peace which prevailed during his early years as viceroy, it is probable that this disparity between statement and fact became even greater. With the rise of a war threat, the rescue of the treasury from heavy debt, and the emerging confidence of Bucareli in Cisneros, the picture changed, as has been shown.

In existence on paper at the time of Bucareli's death were the following militia units: white infantry—the regiments of Querétaro and

---

[47] Same to same, November 26, 1777, AGN, CVB, 1777, Vol. 97, No. 3348, pp. 13v–14.

[48] Same to same, March 27, 1778, and February 24, 1779, AGN, CVB, 1778, Vol. 101, No. 3667, pp. 41–41v, and *ibid.*, 1779, Vol. 116, No. 4281, pp. 19–19v. An inclosure in the latter communication is a diary kept by Cisneros for the thirty days of the Tlaxcala-Puebla regiment's 1779 annual assembly. *Ibid.*, pp. 221–227. The commander of this regiment obviously took the whole thing very seriously, inasmuch as he wrote to Gálvez suggesting that militia officers wear their uniforms at all times. Gálvez solicited Bucareli's opinion, and in reply the Viceroy said that although he commended the man's zeal, the idea was not practical. Bucareli to Gálvez, September 26, 1778, AGN, CVB, 1773[8]–1779, Vol. 7, Libro 15, No. 273 or 4006, pp. 93–94.

[49] Bucareli to Arriaga, January 24, 1772, AGN, CVB, 1772, Vol. 20, No. 165, pp. 185–186.

Puebla, the lancer squadron of Veracruz, and the Legions of El Principe and San Carlos (mixed infantry and cavalry); colored infantry—the *pardo* battalions of Mexico and Puebla, the *pardo* company of Veracruz, and the *moreno* company of Veracruz. The total effective strength of these units would be approximately 14,000 men.[50] It is doubtful that Bucareli, had he called on them for active service, would have secured an effective force in such numbers. It is equally probable, however, that the militia in 1779 was greatly improved over the militia of 1771, as international and financial conditions warranted, or even demanded, and that Bucareli, as captain general, must be given his share of credit after he changed his mind about the potentiality of militia in New Spain. However, since war did not come to New Spain during this period, and since these troops therefore never underwent trial by combat, the efficacy of the entire program, in this respect, is left in doubt. Conceivably, the whole effort may be judged as having been in vain.[51]

On the other hand, there were destined to be several long-range and deeply significant consequences of this military venture. As Orozco y Berra points out, the burst of activity produced by the events of 1762– 1763 interrupted two centuries of colonial peace, during which the Mexican people had been generally unaware of, and uninterested in, matters of war. He suggests that the militia program had the effect of accustoming Mexicans to the noise of arms and causing them to lose their fear of such things through the simple factor of familiarity.[52] Although the revolutionary role of the Creole militia was destined to be less central in New Spain than it was elsewhere in the Spanish empire because of the unique beginnings of the independence movement in that sector, it ultimately made its influence felt on the side of separa-

---

[50] Citing the documents concerning militia strength would involve the identification of nearly 50 volumes in the 108 volumes of Bucareli's correspondence in the AGN. Usually, the dispatch consists of a cover-letter in the first part of a volume and the inclosure or strength report in the second part.

[51] McAlister points out that when war with England made it necessary to call out some of the provincial militia regiments in 1781–1782, Viceroy Mayorga found them to be in deplorable shape, and the urban units were not much better. *"Fuero Militar,"* p. 55.

[52] *Historia de la dominación española,* Vol. IV, p. 135.

tion. There is a splendid irony in the Crown's insistence on the militia
program despite the multiple discouragements and unexpected high
cost which attended its achievement. That the militia, created to defend
the empire, should become a weapon for dissolution of the empire,
was a shocking denouement, if such it really was.

The irony is compounded, moreover, and especially is this true with
respect to Mexico, when one considers an even more significant consequence of the program. As McAlister demonstrates with great effectiveness, the virtual forcing of the military profession on the people
of New Spain by the mother country provided a beginning for the
growth of the praetorian tradition, destined to be the curse of Mexican
national existence for generations.[53] To be sure, the seed fell on soil
fertile in more ways than one. José-María Luis Mora's astute analysis
of the Spanish tendency to create privileged corporations within, but
independent of, the body politic helps explain the facility with which
the military element exploited its position once it became aware of the
advantages so readily available.[54] And the obvious unpreparedness of
the Mexican people for self-government at the time the nation was
born virtually guaranteed success for an element thus favored. According to McAlister, the key factor in, first, luring the colonial
militiaman into an appreciation of his position and, then, holding the
Mexican soldier to this attitude, was the military *fuero,* or privilege,
whereby very fruitful benefits were his merely by his wearing of the
uniform.[55] As one views the role of the Mexican Army in Mexican
history, he may well conclude that Spain has had her revenge on her
rebellious child, deeply and at great length.

What of Bucareli in all this? What part did he play in getting the
process underway? And did he foresee any of the harmful results
which grew out of his actions? Probably not. Don Antonio appears to
have possessed a rather fundamental optimism and naïveté. Thoughts
of rebellion and resistance to authority seemed seldom to cross his
mind or find expression in either his personal or official writings. As
Mendizábal and Carmen Velázquez find him "more generous" in his

---

[53] *"Fuero Militar."*
[54] José-Mariá Luis Mora, *Méjico y sus revoluciones.*
[55] *"Fuero Militar."*

attitudes toward society than many of his official colleagues, so does he seem to have been. On some occasions he had a surprising tendency to see the little man's—perhaps society's—point of view. One gets the feeling that to him, with his basic and unruffled loyalty to the Crown and to Spain, the idea that any significant number of Spaniards, peninsular or American, could feel otherwise was unthinkable. Only non-Spanish subjects could be anti-Spanish. Individuals or classes could be misguided, victims of bad habits or bad social attitudes, but never disloyal.

The story of the regular Army in New Spain during Bucareli's viceregency is neither so complex nor so significant as is that of the militia. Aside from questions of military justice and unit location, the Viceroy was involved only casually or not at all in such matters as organization, training, and effectiveness. When Bucareli became viceroy, the regular Army force was relatively small, composed of the following units with effective strength as shown: [56]

Unit	Men	Horses
Second Infantry Battalion of Savoy .	549	
Infantry Regiment of Granada . .	1,140	
Infantry Regiment of La Corona . .	1,090	
Regiment of Dragoons of Spain . .	492	480
Regiment of Dragoons of Mexico .	483	492
	3,754	972

In the course of Bucareli's viceregency there was no extensive change either in units or in number. He started out as he had with the militia. In September, 1772, Charles III ordered that if the Viceroy did not feel that the Savoy battalion was needed in New Spain, it would be well to return it to the peninsula.[57] Bucareli replied that in view of the general peace then prevailing, he saw no reason for keeping the battalion in New Spain, and that, as soon as its members who were natives of the viceroyalty and who desired to stay there could be

[56] Bucareli to Arriaga, June 26, 1772, and inclosure, AGN, CVB, 1772, Vol. 25, No. 438, p. 16, and *ibid.*, Vol. 26, of No. 438, p. 218.

[57] Arriaga to Bucareli, September 17, 1772, AGN, RC, 1772, Vol. 101, No. 78, pp. 366–366v.

transferred to the fixed La Corona regiment, the unit would be prepared for embarkation. He also commented to O'Reilly that, besides the other disadvantages of leaving regular Spanish troops in New Spain, such as the deterioration in discipline and morale, it cost the royal treasury four times as much to keep a battalion in the colony as in Spain.[58] Late in February, 1773, he disposed that the battalion leave Mexico City on March 3 in order to sail from Veracruz on April 10.[59]

That same year, Bucareli put wheels in motion to replace in part the soldiers who had left for Spain. During the preceding viceregency, Croix had begun the formation of two companies called the Volunteers of Cataluña. As of mid-1772 these units, although far below strength, were doing garrison duty in Real del Monte and Guadalajara. For humanitarian reasons, and to save money, as related in the section on the militia, Bucareli suggested the completion of the organization of these units and the dismissal of the *pardo* company in Guadalajara, which was acting as a police force and was furnishing a detachment for service in San Blas. Charles III approved of the idea and decided on a strength of three officers and seventy-nine men for each company.[60] The plan was carried out, and the two companies were entered on the roster as part of the regular Army force in New Spain.[61]

In recruiting men for these units an effort was made to secure Catalans, but when not enough men from Catalonia were available, other Spaniards had to be included. No such restrictive policy was feasible as a general rule, however, and especially was this true with respect to any unit that garrisoned Veracruz. The climate of this seaport held such terrors for most of the people who dwelt inland that recruiting for service there obtained a minimum response. The difficulty was increased by the fact that the climate was genuinely bad, the

[58] Bucareli to Arriaga, January 27, 1773, AGN, CVB, 1773, Vol. 34, No. 759, pp. 64v–65. Bucareli to O'Reilly, January 27, 1773, AGI, Mex., Leg. 1242.

[59] Bucareli to Arriaga, February 24, 1773, AGN, CVB, 1773, Vol. 35, No. 813, pp. 45v–46.

[60] Arriaga to Bucareli, February 19, 1773, AGN, RC, 1773, Vol. 101, No. 141, pp. 478–479.

[61] Bucareli to Arriaga, March 27, 1773, AGN, CVB, 1773, Vol. 36, No. 839, pp. 34–37v. The King approved the method the Viceroy employed to do the job. Arriaga to Bucareli, September 11, 1773, AGN, RC, 1773, Vol. 103, No. 78, p. 213.

casualties among units stationed in Veracruz were high, and there existed a real need for replacements. At one time Bucareli went so far as to provide that criminals guilty of offenses not involving moral turpitude be used to fill out the ranks of such depleted units. Cisneros had inspired the idea, and the matter was submitted for comment to the Colonel of the Corona regiment garrisoning Veracruz—who expressed disapproval—to the Auditor of War—who approved—and to the Governor of Veracruz—who was opposed—before Bucareli ordered that it be executed. The Viceroy also suggested to the authorities of the *Acordada* that they keep this need in mind when sentencing criminals in the future.[62] On occasion Bucareli was extremely realistic.

Whether to move different units in and out of Veracruz frequently, or to leave one unit there to suffer and perhaps achieve a measure of acclimatization, was a question which plagued Bucareli constantly. To add to the unit-location problem was the King's disagreement with his viceroy over how many troops were needed to garrison Mexico City, a station which inevitably deteriorated the character and morale of the resident troops.[63] It was in 1776 that the vacancies in the Crown regiment in Veracruz became so numerous that Bucareli fell back on the use of criminals, apparently thus operating on the principle of leaving the same unit there for an extended period.[64] His decision had only begun to take effect, however, when orders came from Spain specifying that the Veracruz garrison was to be changed every six months, that is, all the other units in New Spain were to alternate with the Crown regiment. Bucareli immediately ordered the Granada regiment to Veracruz and transferred the first battalion of the Crown regiment to Mexico City and the second battalion to Perote.[65]

In the same mail with the above royal order came notification that the Asturias regiment of two battalions was leaving the peninsula for

[62] Bucareli to Gálvez, October 27 and November 26, 1776, AGN, CVB, 1776, Vol. 84, No. 2562, pp. 41–46v, and *ibid.*, Vol. 85, No. 2612, pp. 36–37v.

[63] Arriaga to Bucareli, February 21, 1772, AGN, RC, 1772, Vol. 100, No. 61, p. 110. Bucareli to Arriaga, May 24, 1772, AGN, CVB, 1772, Vol. 24, No. 379, pp. 25–27.

[64] See note 62, above.

[65] Bucareli to Gálvez, January 27, 1777, AGN, CVB, 1777, Vol. 87, No. 2717, pp. 24–25.

New Spain. Bucareli designated Córdova and Orizaba as temporary locations for the new outfit, sending an official there to arrange for quarters and the hospital facilities he knew would be needed.[66] The bulk of the Asturias regiment reached Veracruz in late June, 1777. The figures on the status of the troops are appalling. As of June 20, 976 fit men disembarked; 53 had died en route; 36 were in the hospital; and 148 were sick and convalescent. As of July 15, a hospital count showed 382 entrants, 12 deaths, 123 releases, and 242 still hospitalized.[67] One ship carrying two companies was separated from the convoy and did not arrive until later. A final summary revises the figures thus: 104 died en route; 56 died in Veracruz; an unspecified number caught [*sic*] scurvy and died later.[68]

The entire regiment, or what remained, settled down in Córdova and Orizaba to recuperate. Meanwhile, the old trouble was back to harass Bucareli. For reasons which are not stated he had left the Granada regiment in Veracruz for nearly a year without relief, and fever had hit the unit hard. As a result of representations from the Governor of Veracruz, Bucareli permitted the sick to leave the area for a more healthful climate. He also approved the activation of the two *moreno* and *pardo* companies in Veracruz to help with the garrison duties. Fearing that to leave the Granada unit in the seaport would ruin the regiment permanently, Bucareli saw as his only recourse to return the Crown regiment once more to the station it had occupied for so long. The Granada regiment was ordered to Córdova and Orizaba, ousting the Asturias regiment, which was divided between Perote and Mexico City.[69]

The Asturias regiment, because of its disastrous journey from Spain, and the Granada and Crown regiments, because of their association with Veracruz, were all seriously under strength. A royal order of

[66] *Ibid.,* pp. 25–26.
[67] Same to same, July 27, 1777, AGN, CVB, 1777, Vol. 93, No. 3100, pp. 4v–5v. The inclosures to No. 3099, of which a copy is not available, include, by ships, a list of the sick and dead, statements of vacancies at the time of disembarkation, and daily hospital reports for the period June 30–July 15. *Ibid.,* pp. 65–68.
[68] Bucareli to Gálvez, January 27, 1778, AGN, CVB, 1778, Vol. 99, No. 3484, pp. 7v–8v.
[69] *Ibid.,* pp. 8v–10.

August, 1776, had opened these units to *mestizos* and *castizos limpios* (different mixtures of white and Indian blood), but it had little effect on recruiting. Bucareli urged the unit commanders to seek recruits more aggressively, but he also informed Gálvez that the best solution was to send replacements from Spain.[70] Charles III agreed with his viceroy, and in September, 1778, Bucareli received word that 500 men, composed of 300 conscripts and captured deserters and 200 veterans, would soon leave the peninsula.[71] Early in December, 300 of these replacements reached Veracruz, and Bucareli divided them equally among the three under-strength regiments.[72]

This was the last major change in troop strength during his term. When he died in April, 1779, the following regular Army units were under his command: infantry—the regiments of Granada, Asturias, and the Crown, and the First Free Company of Volunteers of Cataluña; dragoons—the regiments of Spain and Mexico; artillery—the First and Second Fixed Artillery Companies. The Second Cataluña Volunteers was in the interior provinces, a separate command along the northern frontier, under Teodoro de Croix. These units, excluding the last-named, had a total effective strength of 4,527 men as of March 27, 1779. Their vacancies numbered 716.[73]

Although it is clear that Bucareli did not concern himself greatly with the internal affairs of these regular units, he did carry through one measure of genuine merit which has undoubtedly contributed to his reputation for benevolence. Retired soldiers apparently were of little interest to the government they had served, for it was not until 1761 that the Spanish Crown organized formally a *Cuerpo de Inválidos,* or a system for taking care of old veterans. The system was in effect in Spain only, however, and did not apply to the empire. Buca-

---

[70] *Ibid.,* pp. 10–11. Same to same, April 26, 1778, AGN, CVB, 1778, Vol. 104, No. 3728, pp. 34–34v.

[71] Same to same, September 26, 1778, AGN, CVB, 1778, Vol. 110, No. 3994, pp. 1–1v.

[72] Same to same, December 27, 1778, AGN, CVB, 1778, Vol. 114, No. 4172, pp. 1–1v.

[73] Inclosure in same to same, March 27, 1779, AGN, CVB, 1779, Vol. 116, of No. 4381, p. 251.

reli, motivated perhaps by his long career as a military man, began to investigate the matter soon after he became viceroy. He sought a method whereby veterans worthy of help could be supported without overburdening the treasury. His first move was to solicit reports from leaders in the two big military centers, Mexico City and Veracruz, concerning the number of *inválidos* extant. For the rest of the vice-royalty he dispatched circular letters to the officials of the royal sub-treasuries.

He found that such an organization already existed, but that it was poorly managed and inadequate. The monthly allowance was given directly to the veterans, who immediately spent it on liquor. An initial clothing allotment had been made in 1768, but none since then. Consequently, the old soldiers were customarily seen on the streets, half-naked, begging for food, the object of public scorn. Bucareli's proposed remedy contemplated a maximum body of 200 veterans, a method of selecting them, a system of supply and maintenance, assignment to such jobs as they could do, and a plan for internal management. He estimated that in view of the small number of regular Army units normally stationed in New Spain, the number of eligible veterans probably would not reach the maximum figure. At the time of his report—July, 1772—there were 155 men eligible for the unit.[74]

Because of the various questions and answers which had to be passed back and forth between Madrid and Mexico City, it was not until July, 1774, that final approval was given to Bucareli's plan. He moved immediately to its execution. The 200 veterans were to be divided into three companies, two composed of men physically capable of light duties, one in Veracruz and one in Mexico City, and one composed of completely disabled men, to be located in Mexico City also. Only enlisted men were eligible. The monthly allowance was 10 pesos for sergeants, 8 pesos for corporals and privates. From this amount, deductions were to be made in advance for food and clothing. The veteran's maintenance was thus assured, for he was not given the chance to

[74] Bucareli to Arriaga, July 26, 1772, and inclosure, AGN, CVB, 1772, Vol. 28, No. 465, pp. 24–28v.

spend his entire allotment on riotous living.[75] As nearly as can be ascertained, the program went into effect late in 1774 or early in 1775.[76] There can be no doubt that the measure was needed, and credit must be given to Bucareli for his part in its execution.

Not all of his problems with respect to the defense establishment and its ramifications were so easily or so successfully handled as the *Cuerpo de Inválidos*. One of the most harmful aspects of the restrictive colonial system was the prohibition on manufacturing, which made especially troublesome the problem of an adequate supply of artillery. Most of the artillery in New Spain came from the mother country, although some was shipped from the Manila foundry. Inasmuch as Spanish foundries and mines were inadequate even for Spain's needs, the shortage was keenly felt.

Bucareli's correspondence with the home government offers frequent examples of the difficulties occasioned by this situation. Early in 1772, in compliance with a royal order, he disposed that all unserviceable cannon be collected at Veracruz for shipment to Spain to be recast.[77] On two occasions in 1773 tests were ordered made on new, possibly defective, cannon in Veracruz. Fortunately, they proved to be all right, but had they been defective, there would have been no alternative but to return them to Spain for recasting, while the viceroyalty would have remained less well defended.[78] In 1777 most of the cannon in Acapulco were sent to the new Manila foundry for reworking.[79]

Characteristically, Charles III decided to remedy this old situation. On April 1, 1776, he ordered Bucareli to initiate action to establish a foundry for bronze artillery somewhere near Veracruz, so located that its output could be transported by water to wherever it might be

[75] Same to same, July 27, 1774, and inclosure, AGN, CVB, 1774, Vol. 56, No. 1448, pp. 6v–9, 56–57.

[76] Arriaga to Bucareli, January 19, 1775, AGN, RC, 1775, Vol. 106, No. 12, p. 15.

[77] Bucareli to Arriaga, March 22 and April 25, 1772, and inclosures, AGN, CVB, 1772, Vol. 22, No. 255, pp. 21–23, and *ibid.*, Vol. 23, No. 347, pp. 36–37, 177–178.

[78] Same to same, March 27, June 26 and inclosures; and August 27, 1773, AGN, CVB, 1773, Vol. 36, No. 845, pp. 43v–45; *ibid.*, Vol. 39, No. 996, pp. 28–28v, 115–117v; and *ibid.*, Vol. 41, No. 1066, pp. 27–28.

[79] Bucareli to Gálvez, June 26, 1777, AGN, CVB, 1777, Vol. 92, No. 3059, pp. 39–40v.

needed.[80] The urgent need for the foundry was emphasized several months later when Gálvez, in reply to a request from Bucareli for military supplies, explained, somewhat apologetically, that the bronze artillery ordered was not available in Spain, and that it behooved the Viceroy to hurry the establishment of the foundry.[81]

Bucareli undoubtedly intended to see the foundry quickly located and organized, but he regarded the matter as one of extreme importance, and this, in combination with the usual slow pace of colonial administration, served to delay the project. His first move was to send *Fundidor Real* (Royal Smelter) Francisco Ortúzar and Engineer Captain Pedro Ponze to examine prospective sites near Perote, after which they were to go to Veracruz to report their findings to Brigadier Engineer-Director Manuel de Santisteban and Artillery Captain Diego Panes. Having completed their reconnaissance, Ortúzar and Ponze proceeded to Veracruz and recommended a site one league from Perote. Santisteban endorsed their choice, but Ponze held out for further exploration, arguing that the foundry was to supply not only the fort at Perote, but a much wider area. Bucareli agreed, putting further reconnaissance in Santisteban's charge. The latter asked for funds to finance further investigations, which, surprisingly, Bucareli granted without his usual warning about economy.[82]

Panes and Ponze were chosen for the job, and during April and May, 1777, they examined the territory from Orizaba to the Alvarado River, finally recommending a site near Orizaba on the estate of the Marqués de Sierra Nevada. Before a decision could be made, however, repairs would have to be made on the Orizaba-Veracruz road, and it would be necessary to build a bridge over a certain arroyo.[83] Rains delayed the two examiners from surveying the road for a time, but they finally gave the site their unqualified approval.[84] Bucareli, regarding

---

[80] Same to same, July 27, 1776, AGN, CVB, 1776, Vol. 81, No. 2404, pp. 57v–59.

[81] Gálvez to Bucareli, October 6, 1776, AGN, RC, 1776, Vol. 109, No. 21, pp. 36–37.

[82] Bucareli to Gálvez, March 27, 1777, AGN, CVB, 1777, Vol. 89, No. 2818, pp. 22v–29.

[83] Same to same, May 27, 1777, AGN, CVB, 1777, Vol. 91, No. 2993, pp. 42v–45.

[84] Same to same, June 26, 1777, AGN, CVB, 1777, Vol. 92, No. 3058, pp. 38–39.

the job as finished, ordered the two officers to return to Veracruz, thus ending the special daily allowance the treasury was paying them.[85]

The Viceroy passed their report to his fiscal and thence to Santisteban for his opinion. The latter agreed that the Orizaba site seemed to be a good choice, but pointed out that there remained still another district to be reconnoitered. Once more, therefore, Bucareli ordered Ponze to take up his travels. Meanwhile, Royal Smelter Ortúzar had looked over the Orizaba site and had declared it excellent in every respect.[86] This was in November, 1777, but not until February, 1778, did Ponze report that he had found nothing as good as the Orizaba location. Santisteban agreed with his findings and this time had no suggestions to offer about areas still unexamined.[87]

In the meantime, plans had been drawn up based on the Orizaba site. The entire file was sent to Spain. And there the matter ended.[88] Inasmuch as no reason for dropping the project is found in Bucareli's correspondence, the only recourse is to hazard a guess. In the light of developments during the last years of Bucareli's viceregency—the growing war threat, the Buenos Aires expedition, and reiterated requests from Spain for more and more money to support an active policy—it is possible that the artillery project was shelved as too expensive at that precise time. The urgent need for funds is doubly demonstrated by the history of the attempt to build a shipyard near Veracruz during this same period.

In the first third of the eighteenth century a shipyard had existed on the Coatzacoalcos River on the coast south of Veracruz. The construction of vessels had proved too costly both in money and lives, however, and around 1734 the Crown had ordered the yard abandoned. In the mid-1770's, as a consequence of the danger of Spain's being drawn into a war with England, and of the conflict with Portugal along the Brazilian border, Charles III decided to expand his Navy, and to

---

[85] Same to same, July 27, 1777, AGN, CVB, 1777, Vol. 93, No. 3104, pp. 12–12v.

[86] Same to same, November 26, 1777, AGN, CVB, 1777, Vol. 97, No. 3344, pp. 5v–8.

[87] Same to same, February 24, 1778, and inclosures, AGN, CVB, 1778, Vol. 100, No. 3754, pp. 4v–6v, 43–54, 90–99.

[88] Velasco Ceballos, *La administración de . . . Bucareli*, Vol. II, p. 169.

this end directed Bucareli to investigate the possibility of rebuilding this old shipyard or of constructing a new one in the same vicinity. Furthermore, it was the King's desire that the Viceroy, without publicity, seek to raise money in New Spain from ecclesiastical *cabildos,* the Mexico City *consulado,* the *Cuerpo de Minería,* and similar bodies to pay for several fifty- to sixty-cannon ships and several thirty- to forty-cannon frigates.[89]

Bucareli received this order in July, 1776. He replied that he intended to send Colonel Engineer-in-Chief Miguel del Corral and a Navy officer from San Blas to inspect the old Coatzacoalcos site and also to look over the nearby Alvarado River, but that their reconnaissance would be delayed until October inasmuch as the rains had been unusually heavy that year. With respect to the matter of financing the project by means of donations rather than with royal funds, he made a number of revealing comments. He said that he must await an opportune moment for making the requests of the various organizations, because they did not have "those great funds which they had at other times." The *cabildos* of Durango, Oaxaca, and Mérida he dismissed as poor. Mexico City, Valladolid, Guadalajara, and Puebla could give something, he thought, but all together they could not equal the product of one honest and efficient administration of the royal revenues. At that time, he said, the *Real Hacienda* was out of debt and its income was increasing; nevertheless, its income would not suffice to pay for a war, and for that reason he intended to build "good faith" in order that, when the time came, he could confidently ask for donations, a method he had not as yet been forced to use. He proposed, therefore, to wait until after the arrival of the fleet and the conclusion of the subsequent Fair, at which time chances of success would be at their maximum.[90]

The story of the quest for the shipyard location is similar to that of the artillery foundry. This search was more elaborate, more expensive,

[89] Gálvez to Bucareli, April 23, 1776, AGN, Marina, Astilleros, Vol. 39, 1776–1777, No. 11 [?], pp. 1–2 (arbitrary pagination).

[90] Bucareli to Gálvez, July 27, 1776, AGN, CVB, 1776, Vol. 12, Libro 13, No. 159 or 2353, pp. 25v–29. This letter repeats the April 23 letter from Gálvez cited in note 89, above.

and more confusing, but the pattern was the same. Beginning with the letter of July, 1776, just cited, Bucareli wrote at least one report on the subject every month until September, 1778.[91] Topics discussed included the depths of passages over bars at river mouths, the availability of various types of wood for shipbuilding, adequacy of nearby labor and food supply, the climate, and methods for defending the yard. A considerable area was examined, numerous juntas were held, and experts were interrogated. The project came to an end in August, 1778, when Bucareli sent to Spain a copy of the entire file on the matter, with maps, drawings, and estimates of cost.[92] As with the artillery foundry, it was completely developed on paper, but it advanced no further.[93]

Ironically, the fund-gathering campaign was a great success, and in few other situations during his viceregency did Bucareli demonstrate more spectacularly his deftness in handling people of his own class and the acuity of his analysis of their motivations. He started with sources whose generosity he was certain of, in order to be able to use them as examples for later possible donors. The *Consulado* of Mexico City delivered nobly, offering 300,000 pesos, although only the two top men in the organization knew precisely the purpose of the gift. Bucareli turned next to Pedro Romero de Terreros, the Count of Regla, on whom he counted "with no less certainty than on the *Consulado.*" The Count offered to pay for two ships, a donation which Bucareli regarded as being worth from 300,000 to 450,000 pesos.[94] At this opportune moment there arrived notice of the royal decision allowing the formal

---

[91] All but one of these are found in three of the "Very Confidential" volumes at the beginning of the Bucareli correspondence series in the AGN. These are: AGN, CVB, 1776, Vol. 12, Libro 13; *ibid.*, 1777, Vol. 13, Libro 14; and *ibid.*, 1773[8]–1779, Vol. 7, Libro 15. The single nonconformist is in *ibid.*, 1778, Vol. 104, No. 3743, pp. 51–51v. Most of these letters are also scattered through Legs. 1376–1381, AGI, Mex.

[92] Bucareli to Gálvez, August 27, 1778, AGN, CVB, 1773[8]–1779, Vol. 7, Libro 15, No. 269 or 3927, pp. 88–90v.

[93] Velasco Ceballos, *La administración de . . . Bucareli,* Vol. II, p. 169.

[94] Bucareli to Gálvez, August 27, 1776, AGN, CVB, 1776, Vol. 12, Libro 13, No. 162 or 2423, pp. 32v–33. In return for this generosity, upon Bucareli's recommendation, the King granted the titles of Marqués de San Francisco and Marqués de San Cristóbal to Regla's sons. Velasco Ceballos, *La administración de . . . Bucareli,* Vol. II, p. 169. Regla to Gálvez, April 19, 1777, AGN, CVB, 1777, Vol. 13, Libro 14, of No. 219 or 3220, pp. 77–79.

creation of the *Cuerpo de Minería.* Bucareli's account of his tactics in this circumstance is a masterpiece of frankness. "I thought this an appropriate time to point out to the Deputies . . . that at present the Royal Treasury has unusual expenses. This insinuation, made in general terms, produced the effect it was intended to, for immediately the Deputies offered me 300,000 pesos." As a reward, Bucareli suggested that Joaquín Velázquez de León, general director of *Cuerpo de Minería,* be given a position on the *Audiencia* of Mexico, and that Lucas de Lassaga, its administrator general, would be satisfied if his brother, Diego, was made a lieutenant colonel in the Fixed Regiment of the Crown.[95]

Using these splendid donations as a lever, Bucareli began to widen his field of activities. The Archbishop visited the Viceroy in his offices, and Bucareli found the occasion appropriate to point out to the prelate how urgent were the defensive needs of the viceroyalty. Within forty-eight hours an 80,000-peso gift was forthcoming.[96] The way was now prepared for an appeal to all the bishoprics, using as spurs to their generosity the needs of Spain, the certain gratitude of the King, and the zeal expected of every Spanish subject. The precincts began reporting in almost immediately, with Puebla first in line with an offer of 50,000 pesos.[97] From this point on, the contributions poured in from a variety of sources, such as: the *ayuntamiento* of Veracruz, 50,000 pesos; the bishop and *cabildo* of Valladolid, 80,000 pesos; the *Consulado* of Cádiz, 120,000 pesos; the City of Mexico, 80,000 pesos. There were numerous lesser contributions of several thousand pesos each, including one from Josef de Prado y Ulloa of Oaxaca, who tendered his gift immediately upon being informed that he had just become an *alcalde mayor.*[98] By the end of August, 1777, the Viceroy

[95] Bucareli to Gálvez, November 26, 1776, AGN, CVB, 1776, Vol. 12, Libro 13, No. 181 or 2607, pp. 52v–53. The rewards were quickly paid, with Velázquez de León receiving an appointment as *Alcalde del Crimen* of the *Audiencia.* Same to same, May 27, 1777, No. 2996, AGI, Mex., Leg. 1377.
[96] Same to same, April 26, 1777, No. 2854, AGI, Mex., Leg. 1377.
[97] Same to same, same date, No. 2855, *ibid.*
[98] Same to same, June 26, 1777, No. 3029, AGI, Mex., Leg. 1382. Legajos 1377 and 1380–1382 contain numerous reports of contributions, as does also AGN, CVB, 1777, Vol. 13, Libro 14.

had raised 1,285,000 pesos, and other donations were received after that date.[99] The final total exceeded 1,300,000 pesos, to which Bucareli planned to add enough of the Crown's money to reach 2,000,000 pesos. "It is apparent," he said, "that none of the shipyards which the King possesses has been able to begin with such a solid foundation."[100] Don Antonio had certainly done his share.

In the eyes of military experts, of equal or perhaps greater importance than armed forces, ships, or artillery were the fortresses which guarded New Spain's seacoast and the principal route from Veracruz to Mexico City. Foremost among these was the castle of San Juan de Ulúa. Running parallel with the beach about one-half mile north of Veracruz was Gallega Shoal, which, at high tide, was covered with three feet of water. Placed on this shoal to protect the anchorage was the Castle. The fort, quadrilateral and irregular in shape, was built after the sacking of Veracruz by pirates in 1683. Additions were made in 1742 and 1762 in order to withstand possible attacks by enemies better prepared and more determined than pirates. Another survey had been made in 1766, and a new construction program was begun which was still in progress when Bucareli became viceroy.[101]

As he approached Veracruz on his voyage from Havana in 1771, Bucareli expressed surprise at "the smallness of the fortress which defends its port, and the only safeguard of the kingdom." His apprehension made him waste no time in proceeding to its inspection, and he found the fort inadequate in many respects. In search of a

[99] Bucareli to Gálvez, August 27, 1777, No. 3158, AGI, Mex., Leg. 1381. This letter cites the figure quoted, while Leg. 1380 contains a number of letters reporting subsequent donations.

[100] Velasco Ceballos, *La administración de . . . Bucareli*, Vol. II, p. 169. Although the Coatzacoalcos shipyard was not built with this money, some of it, at least, went into ship construction. In 1779, after Bucareli's death, 50,000 pesos was sent to Havana to pay for starts on two vessels in that shipyard. *Audiencia* to Gálvez, April 26, 1779, AGN, CV, Vol. 118, No. 27, pp. 23v–24.

[101] Relation of the . . . state of the fortifications of the Castle of San Juan de Ulúa . . . , May, 1772, AGN, CVB, 1772, Vol. 24, of No. 367, pp. 90–100. Detailed relations of fortifications existing in . . . the Castle of San Juan de Ulúa . . . , June 30, 1774. Signed by Segismundo Fons (engineer in charge of construction) and four others, AGN, CVB, 1774, Vol. 57, No. 1497 and inclosures, pp. 7v–8, 47–52v. Croix, *Instrucción*, AGN, CVB, 1772, Vol. 24, pp. 445–445v.

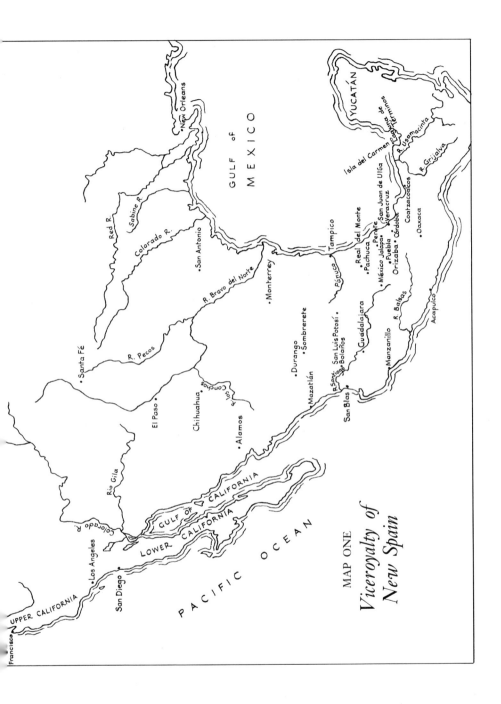

MAP ONE

Viceroyalty of New Spain

King Charles III of Spain.

Reproduced from Manuel Rivera Cambas, Los gobernantes de México, Vol. I, p. 466.

remedy, he requested separate proposals from Engineer and King's Lieutenant Agustín Crame and Engineer-Director Manuel de Santisteban. Crame presented an elaborate and costly plan involving, besides additions to the Castle itself, extensive construction of battery sites and outposts. Santisteban's first proposal was too simple to satisfy the Viceroy, and his second plan, although more elaborate, was still less complex than Crame's. Bucareli sent both projects to Spain, with a letter stating his opinion of them and of the defensive situation of his command.[102]

His ideas with respect to New Spain's defense, offered within the first eight months of his stay there, are of extreme interest. After his inspection of the Castle, he took the road for Mexico City, passing through Jalapa and coming out on the plains of Perote, where he inspected the fort being built there and examined maps of the surrounding area. Basing his opinions on these few personal observations and on the projects of Crame and Santisteban, he presented a general commentary on the points he regarded as significant with respect to defense.

He focused his attention on Veracruz, which, he said, was the only dangerous port in the kingdom from the standpoint of enemy attack. Its only defense was San Juan de Ulúa, and he felt that in its present state it could be captured, "wherewith the enemies of the Crown would have a second Gibraltar in these dominions," resulting in ruin for New Spain. He regarded as extremely unlikely an attack at any other coastal point, and he was confident that so long as the Veracruz fortress held out, the interior was secure. He saw no need to build up the fortifications of Veracruz itself, to strengthen the artillery batteries on its flanks, or to adopt Crame's suggestion for fortifying the nearby height. The Castle was the key. While it held out, the commander of the land forces in the interior could be gathering his units and choosing his own time of attack. Bucareli concluded, therefore, that the major task was to decide on the desirable expansion of this fortress and proceed to its execution as vigorously as possible.[103]

[102] Bucareli to Arriaga, May 24, 1772, and inclosures, AGN, CVB, 1772, Vol. 24, No. 367, pp. 9–13, 90–100.
[103] *Ibid.*

Crame's and Santisteban's reports and Bucareli's commentary were sent to Spain in May, 1772. Moving with what would appear to be dangerous lethargy in a matter of such importance, the Crown handed down no decision until April, 1774, and even this did not call for action, but disposed only further discussion. Arriaga apparently did not feel qualified to pass judgment on the issues raised and therefore turned the file over to three prominent military figures in Spain— Captain General Pedro Abarco de Bolea, Conde de Aranda, Lieutenant General Antonio Ricardos, and Field Marshal Antonio Cermeño —with a request for their opinions. They obliged, at length and in detail.

Aranda and Cermeño were in agreement that Santisteban's plan was preferable, not because of its intrinsic superiority, but because Crame's project, although excellent in theory, called for a prohibitive amount of money. Ricardos, however, dissented. Submitting a minority report, he challenged the two basic principles of everybody else's argument. First, he disagreed that the Castle of San Juan de Ulúa was the key to the defense of New Spain, and second, he averred that the addition of more fortifications to the Castle would serve only to weaken rather than strengthen it. He pointed out that the enemy was not obliged to attack the fort. Attackers could anchor and disembark at Punto de Antón Lizardo—a short distance from Veracruz—take the seaport, blockade the Castle, and proceed with their invasion. Furthermore, the fortress garrison in no way constituted a threat to the enemy's forces. Finally, he said, if the proposed additions were made, it would mean that the current which kept the anchorage free of sand would be blocked off, while these same additions would put a part of the Castle within easier striking distance of enemy foot-forces and artillery. Ricardos admitted, however, that since it was probable that the Castle would be maintained, it must be improved as much as possible. To this end, he selected what he considered the best parts from both Crame's and Santisteban's reports, weaving them into a workable project.[104]

[104] Arriaga to Bucareli, April 23, 1774, and inclosures, AGN, RC, 1774, Vol. 104, No. 95, pp. 165–166 (cover-letter), 167–174 (Ricardos' opinion), 175–178 (joint opinion of Aranda and Cermeño).

Even with all this expert opinion available, Charles III still could not come to a final decision. He ordered Bucareli to convene a junta in Veracruz, consisting of Governor of Veracruz Lieutenant General Juan Fernando Palacios, Santisteban, Crame, Artillery Colonel Nicolás Devis from Havana, and one more engineer of Bucareli's choosing. After examining the complete file, including now the opinions of the Spanish experts, this junta was to decide on what was the best solution to the problem. Ricardos' ideas had had some effect, as evidenced by the King's warning that the junta should keep in mind a possible enemy landing at Lizardo, followed by a blockade of San Juan de Ulúa and an invasion of the interior. Charles III therefore advised leaving the Castle garrison small, in order not to draw strength away from the land forces. He also suggested that, once a decision was reached, the work should be started at once, keeping the Castle always in the best possible defensive state in case of surprise attack.[105]

In July, 1774, Bucareli reported that he had sent out the necessary orders for convening the junta, selecting Second Engineer Segismundo Fons as the fifth member.[106] The body completed its recommendations in December. It had ignored Ricardos' intelligent observations with respect to the Castle's not being the key to New Spain. Instead, the report called for additions to the fort which would cost more than even Crame's elaborate project. Bucareli figured the ultimate cost at more than 2,000,000 pesos and the time necessary to do the job at not less than ten years. Inasmuch as the treasury was already paying heavily for the fortifications at Cuba, Puerto Rico, the Island of Tris, and Perote, while San Blas and California were becoming increasingly expensive, he felt that 200,000 pesos annually was the maximum that could be allowed for San Juan de Ulúa. He anticipated that after 1777, when Perote would be finished, the annual subsidy of 144,000 pesos for that project could be added to the Castle fund. Since the season of storms was soon due in Veracruz and the beginning of the work would have to wait for this to pass, Bucareli was able to send the junta's recommendation to Spain for the King's approval before em-

[105] *Ibid.*, pp. 165–166.
[106] Bucareli to Arriaga, July 27, 1774, AGN, CVB, 1774, Vol. 56, No. 1469, pp. 28–29.

120   *Viceregency of Bucareli*

barking on such an expensive program. Despite the cost, he supported the junta's report as the solution to New Spain's defense problem.[107]

Charles III followed suit. He approved the plan, ordering Bucareli to start work immediately and to dispose the payment of the 200,000-peso annual subsidy. He also inquired about the defensive plan for the entire viceroyalty which he had apparently instructed the Veracruz junta to produce.[108]

This body had proceeded to a consideration of such a plan as soon as it completed its sessions on the Castle. The narrowness of its point of view with respect to what constituted the danger zone of the viceroyalty is manifested by the title of the report—"A Plan of Defense for the Kingdom of New Spain on the Coasts Collateral to Veracruz Comprehended between Alvarado and Zempoala." The plan was based on the stubborn insistence that the English (the enemy is openly named) must attack the Castle of San Juan de Ulúa. Therefore, having already recommended measures to make this fortress invincible, the junta regarded as remaining to be arranged only the proper defenses for the adjacent coasts and the roads to Mexico City.[109]

Since the fifty-eight-page length of the document precludes a detailed discussion of its contents here, certain general observations must suffice. Two major sections are devoted to a careful description of the coast on either side of, and the country behind, Veracruz. It discusses roads, rivers, bridges, terrain, vegetation, water supply, and numerous other pertinent points. A third section treats of the defensive force necessary to repel an enemy expedition of from sixteen thousand to eighteen thousand men, attacking, of course, San Juan de Ulúa. Faint hope is shown for much help from the militia, although the necessity of using it is recognized. Other sections are devoted to troop training, strategic quartering, transportation, livestock, supply of food and

[107] Same to same, December 27, 1774, and inclosures, AGN, CVB, 1774, Vol. 62, No. 1644, pp. 7v–11, 121–130.
[108] Arriaga to Bucareli, June 19, 1775, AGN, RC, 1775, Vol. 106, No. 132, pp. 225–226.
[109] A Plan of Defense for the Kingdom of New Spain . . . , January 17, 1775, AGN, CVB, 1773–1775, Vol. 11, Libro 9, of No. 120 or 1912 (inclosure No. 1), pp. 251–252v.

equipment, outposts, and plans of operations in various circumstances. Throughout the document there runs a sense of inferiority in the face of the threat of English arms. The attitude is almost wholly defensive, and success seems to be reduced to dependence on two interrelated factors—a tenacious resistance on the part of the Castle garrison, and the effect of the climate on the physical and spiritual condition of the enemy troops.[110] One must almost conclude that the only really effective defense for the Mexican viceroyalty would have been for Spain to remain at peace with England.

Bucareli took steps to get the construction work on San Juan de Ulúa underway as soon as he received royal approval of the junta's plan. Throughout the remainder of his viceregency he gave frequent proof of his conviction that this job was an important one. To assure a good beginning, he took his best engineer, Santisteban, off the Perote project and sent him to Veracruz to establish procedure and to draw up a list of tools and equipment which had to come from Spain. Bucareli also offered complete administrative cooperation in matters of supply, labor, and funds.[111]

The work apparently proceeded satisfactorily for about eighteen months. Then, in March, 1777, Bucareli reported having received an anonymous letter from Veracruz which suggested that progress on the fort was not as it should be. He moved carefully. From March through August he conducted a remote-control inquiry into the manner in which Engineer Colonel Segismundo Fons was handling the job. Bucareli was finally convinced that the work was being done too slowly. Reports indicated that Fons was behind schedule, that inadequate stockpiles of materials often slowed down the entire project, and that the excuses given for these conditions were weak. Fons was removed from his position, apparently not in disgrace, and sent to Spain to begin another job. Second Engineer Miguel del Corral, lately returned from the useless shipyard-site reconnaissance, took over Fons's duties as head of construction.[112]

[110] *Ibid.*, pp. 253–279v.
[111] Bucareli to Gálvez, September 26, 1775, and October 27, 1776, AGN, CVB, 1775, Vol. 71, No. 1969, pp. 1–2, and *ibid.*, Vol. 84, No. 2560, pp. 38v–40v.
[112] Same to same, September 26 and October 26, 1777, AGN, CVB, 1777, Vol. 95, No. 3237, pp. 12–16v, and *ibid.*, Vol. 96, No. 3305, pp. 24v–25v.

From the time of this change until Bucareli's death no other unusual developments occurred. In his last letter on the subject, however, Bucareli was forced to admit that his estimates on the ultimate cost of the additions and the time necessary to complete them had both been too optimistic. From November 6, 1775, when actual construction began, until December 31, 1778, the Crown had spent 447,016 pesos, 4 tomines, 6 grains on the project. Computations based on this figure made clear that 2,000,000 pesos would not suffice to complete the job. The original estimate had been figured on a basis of 5 pesos per cubic *vara* of masonry, whereas the actual cost thus far had been 16 pesos, 4 tomines. Consequently, the final cost would be more than 4,000,000 pesos, and completion would be delayed twenty-four years unless the work was speeded up. Bucareli speculated that if materials could be adequately supplied, and if the work could go on without interruption, the job could be finished in from eight to ten years.[113] There can be no doubt that having to write this report was a bitter experience for Bucareli, who had so frequently expressed his belief in the importance of the work and the necessity for its prompt completion.

No such lamentable developments accompanied the construction of the new fortress near the pueblo of Perote. This village was situated in the hills above Veracruz, out of the hot climate and a short distance past Jalapa on the main road from the seaport to Mexico City. Ever since the shocking capture of Havana by the English in 1762, the Spanish Crown had worried about the possibility of a similar fate for the Mexican capital. Deciding that the Veracruz defenses were inadequate insurance, in 1770 Charles III ordered a fortress built in the above location. It was to serve as a fort and as a convenient and healthful place to quarter troops and store supplies for use along the tropical coast when occasion arose.[114] Construction proceeded regularly, with

[113] Same to same, March 27, 1779, and inclosure, AGN, CVB, 1779, Vol. 116, No. 4330, pp. 13–14, 58–58v. Bucareli's arithmetic does not make sense on the basis of these figures. However, he may be including some factors apparent or known to those close to the matter and not clear to us.

[114] Velasco Ceballos, *La administración de . . . Bucareli,* Vol. II, p. LV. See also note 115, below.

only a few minor alterations in the original plan. The work was completed on December 31, 1776, and to Bucareli fell the honor of selecting the names for the fortress and its four main bastions.[115] Another fortress problem which Bucareli inherited from his predecessors and whose ultimate solution remains something of a mystery was that of the Presidio del Carmen on the Island of Tris. This island is a long, narrow piece of land which almost completely seals the entrance to the Laguna de Términos, just north of Campeche. A garrison had been maintained on the island since 1716, quartered in wooden barracks. In 1758 Viceroy Agustín de Ahumada, Marqués de [las] Amarillas, submitted a plan to the Crown for a new stone fort, the Presidio del Carmen, which was approved in a royal order of May 12, 1759. Apparently no action followed, because the order was repeated to the Marqués de Cruillas on May 13, 1764. In the next two and a half years 20,000 pesos was allotted to the project, procedural instructions were issued, and a considerable amount of construction material was sent to the island. Bucareli initiated an investigation of the status of the project in 1772 and discovered that the materials had been ruined by the climate, that 19,000 of the 20,000 pesos had been expended, and that no construction had been begun.[116]

He reported the facts to Spain and was ordered to carry the investigation further.[117] He consulted his engineer-director, Santisteban, who recommended a new reconnaissance of the proposed fortress site with the object of making a plan for proceeding with construction. The

[115] Bucareli to Gálvez, January 27, 1777, AGN, CVB, 1777, Vol. 87, No. 2711, pp. 18–18v. Documents concerning Perote are found throughout Bucareli's correspondence in the AGN between the years 1771–1777. Apparently no fortress was ever really finished. AGN, Historia, Vol. 327, is devoted entirely to Perote, and indicates that discussion on additions was begun in 1780, with documents on the subject running until 1789.

Orozco y Berra criticized the location of the fortress, pointing out that it was built on a site so far from the *Camino Real* that it could serve no useful purpose in defending the interior from invasion. *Historia de la dominación española,* Vol. IV, pp. 143–144.

[116] Bucareli to Arriaga, November 26, 1772, and inclosures, AGN, CVB, 1772, Vol. 32, No. 663, pp. 30–30v, 131–143.

[117] Arriaga to Bucareli, March 20, 1773, AGN, RC, 1773, Vol. 102, No. 77, p. 145.

124   *Viceregency of Bucareli*

Viceroy therefore ordered Antonio Oliver, the governor of Yucatán, to appoint an engineer to make such a survey.[118] In May, 1774, Bucareli forwarded to Spain a plan drawn up by Second Engineer Juan de Dios Gonzáles, whom Oliver had selected to carry out the Viceroy's instructions. Bucareli was shocked at the cost of Gonzáles' project—583,411 pesos—but since Santisteban averred that the plan was acceptable in every way, the Viceroy sent it to Spain and awaited the King's reaction.[119]

Meanwhile, by royal order a military commission had been created in New Spain to draw up a special *reglamento* for the troops stationed at that time in the old presidio and those who would subsequently garrison the projected fortress. After a trip to the Island of Tris to look over the scene at first hand, this three-man board submitted its completed regulation in July, 1774. Bucareli approved the ordinances, adding a section providing for the retirement of veterans, and ordered them printed and made effective as of January 1, 1775.[120] Charles III approved the *reglamento* and the bonus which Bucareli had paid to the three commissioners for their good work and for the hardships they had endured as the result of a shipwreck on their return journey.[121]

Here the matter appears to end. No evidence has been found that the Crown ever rendered a decision on the plan submitted by Gonzáles. Furthermore, although Bucareli, in December, 1774, spoke of the expenses of the construction on the Island of Tris while citing various treasury expenditures to demonstrate that the maximum annual allotment for San Juan de Ulúa could be only 200,000 pesos, the Presidio del Carmen does not again appear in his correspondence. Also, it was

[118] Bucareli to Arriaga, April 26, 1773, AGN, CVB, 1773, Vol. 37, No. 899, pp. 41–43.
[119] Same to same, May 27, 1774, AGN, CVB, 1774, Vol. 54, No. 1405, pp. 27–30v.
[120] Same to same, October 27, 1774, and inclosures, AGN, CVB, 1774, Vol. 60, No. 1565, pp. 17–21v, 185–221, 223–225, and map on unnumbered page. Besides the *reglamento,* the commissioners also submitted a report on the history, geography, and economy of the island, which is cited as the second inclosure, pp. 223–225.
[121] Arriaga to Bucareli, April 12, 1775, AGN, RC, 1775, Vol. 106, No. 80, pp. 126–126v.

customary to submit semiannual reports of expenditures and progress on both Perote and San Juan de Ulúa, but no such statements for Carmen are found. Velasco Ceballos expresses his belief that the project was dropped.[122] There is good reason to support the possibility. The plan came up for approval at about the time Spain's relations with Portugal and England began to get tense. It was also during these years that the Crown began to ask for increased funds for war purposes and the shipyard idea also disappeared into limbo. The best assumption seems to be that there simply was not enough money to allow for the completion of the Island of Tris project. Again, Bucareli had wasted his time by royal order.

One further defense site demanded his attention. On April 21, 1776, Acapulco suffered a severe earthquake which did extensive damage to the Castle of San Diego in that seaport. Bucareli sent Engineer-Captain Miguel Constanzó to survey the damage and submit his recommendations on the matter. Constanzó reported that the old fortress was both obsolete and beyond repair, whereupon he submitted plans for a complete new structure, to be built on the same site as the old one. Bucareli passed the documents to Santisteban for his opinion, and when the latter signified his approval, the Viceroy forwarded the file to Spain, urging prompt action.[123]

In Spain, Gálvez in turn submitted the plans to an expert, Commandant General of Engineers Silvestre Abarca, who approved them. Charles III therefore ordered Bucareli to allot funds for the project and to proceed to its execution.[124] The Viceroy sent the order to Santisteban, directing that he draw up a list of equipment and labor needed and also appoint an engineer to handle the job. Bucareli assigned a monthly subsidy of 6,000 to 8,000 pesos for the project, with the provision that this figure would be increased or decreased in accordance with the availability of materials in the Acapulco area.[125]

<hr>

[122] Velasco Ceballos, *La administración de . . . Bucareli,* Vol. II, pp. LIV–LV.
[123] Bucareli to Gálvez, October 27, 1776, AGN, CVB, 1776, Vol. 84, No. 2558, pp. 35–37.
[124] Gálvez to Bucareli, March 12, 1777, AGN, RC, 1777, Vol. 110, No. 185, pp. 286–286v.
[125] Bucareli's endorsement on *ibid.,* June 18, 1777, p. 287. The information in

Santisteban selected Engineer-Captain Ramón Panón to direct the work, and Panón proceeded immediately to Acapulco with the necessary equipment and laborers. Working with interim Governor Domingo Elizondo, he drew up a plan of procedure, arranged contracts for the acquisition of materials, and reported that the first stone of the new fortress was laid on March 16, 1778.[126]

As with the Presidio del Carmen, the Castle of San Diego now disappears from the Viceroy's correspondence. However, in view of the fact that the work was actually begun and the allotment made, and that the project was a minor one, it seems probable that the job was completed, although not during Bucareli's viceregency.[127]

How successful was Bucareli as captain general? Not surprisingly, his record is a variable one, with success noted in this instance, failure in that one, and something in between in still another. Certain aspects of this phase of his job must have had a welcome familiarity to Lieutenant General Bucareli. Although the militia program constituted a relatively new concept in New Spain, it was not thus to him, for he had come directly from a similar program in Cuba, and his military career assuredly had made him familiar with activities of this kind. It is problematical whether his change of attitude toward the militia was genuine. His early disrespect for the organization was based on his observations of the units on his way to the capital and on his opinion of the common people he encountered in Mexico City. His later enthusiasm was, basically, merely an extension of what Cisneros and other subordinates relayed to him. Inasmuch as the period of his viceregency saw a complete change in the world situation, it is possible that the increasing threat of war, the new solvency of the treasury, and his growing trust in Cisneros led him to manifest an appearance of ac-

---

this endorsement was reported to Spain in Bucareli to Gálvez, June 26, 1777, AGN, CVB, 1777, Vol. 92, No. 3070, pp. 53–54v.

[126] Bucareli to Gálvez, April 26, 1778, and inclosure, AGN, CVB, 1778, Vol. 104, No. 3716, pp. 22–27, 625–629. The inclosure includes a drawing of the proposed new fortress.

[127] *Ibid.*, p. 26v. In this letter Bucareli revealed that he had been called upon once again to exercise his talent for name selection. A letter from Bucareli's successor, Mayorga, to Gálvez, February 24, 1781, indicates that construction was still going on on the fortress. AGN, CV, Vol. 128, No. 904, pp. 63–64.

cepting the militia since it was the only force available in strength. Without the ultimate proof of combat, one can only guess that he did a creditable job in his administration of the militia program. The significant consequences of the program were, of course, beyond both his time and his vision.

His management of other aspects of the job receives a variable rating, as has been suggested. His apparent uncertain handling of the problems attendant upon garrisoning Veracruz merits criticism, whereas his work in establishing the retirement program for old soldiers deserves high praise. His customary caution was amply demonstrated in the relatively unproductive projects involving the shipyard and the artillery foundry, from which perhaps the only solace that can be derived is the knowledge gained about several areas previously almost unexplored.

Finally, the time wasted on, the slow progress in the construction of, and the miscalculations made with respect to, the Castle of San Juan de Ulúa lead to certain reflections. In a way, the entire episode was typical of the time and place. The measure of failure that is ascribed to Bucareli must be tempered with the thought that the incident serves to demonstrate once more that the viceroy's job was much too big for one man, and that the system of colonial administration called for a detrimental devotion to detail on the part of the chief executive, this despite the number of subordinates he commanded.

The Interior Provinces

CARCELY HAD the echoes of conflict died away in Tenochtitlán before hopeful Spanish *conquistadores*, driven by a lust for gold, were pushing their way outward from the Aztec capital like spokes from the hub of a wheel. So strong was this drive, so eager were they to believe and prove the tales about such wondrous places as the Seven Cities of Cíbola, that disillusionment was slow in coming. Even after the dream of quick and easy wealth was dissipated, however, the urge of empire and the magnetism of a multitude of human souls to be saved continued to draw the vassals of the Spanish Crown ever farther into the reaches of the Mexican viceroyalty. And as the vast spaces of North America began to be filled in by other white nations, there was added the motive of defense against possible encroachment.

Such were the forces which, combined, explain the existence of a thin line of Spanish settlement far to the north and northwest of the viceregal capital in the middle of the eighteenth century. Although some of the country was productive of agricultural and mineral wealth, much of it was of little value, and the reason for holding it is not clear unless one adverts to the motives listed above. An additional unattractive feature of the entire area was the stubborn and warlike character of the Indian inhabitants, who steadfastly opposed each forward step of the Spaniard and ceaselessly tried to make him retreat. Thus is explained the line of presidios and missions along the frontier, for in this area the sword was allied with the cross long beyond the usual period of time.[1] Warfare along this frontier was constant. When Bucareli became viceroy, he inherited from the Marqués de Croix much the same set of problems originating in the hostility of the Indians that the Marqués had inherited from his predecessor, and so on. During Croix's vice-regency, however, certain steps had been taken with respect to the Interior Provinces which were to affect significantly Bucareli's relationship to the area.

The most important of these was an inspection of the entire line of presidios by the Marqués de Rubí from 1766 to 1768.[2] That there were unsatisfactory features in the existing arrangement had been apparent for some time. Royal *Cédulas* in September, 1759, and January, 1764, ordered an investigation, but the consequent efforts of Viceroy Marqués de Cruillas did not satisfy Charles III.[3] Rubí was therefore commissioned in 1765 to do the job thoroughly. After more than two years in the field, he submitted his recommendations to a council of war in Mexico City early in 1769. They dealt principally with the problem of presidio location. Rubí listed those forts which he regarded as improperly situated and proposed that they be relocated to the end that a more efficient defensive barrier against the Indians might be established.[4]

During these same years, 1767–1769, *Visitador* José de Gálvez and Colonel Domingo Elizondo were co-leaders of a military expedition into Sonora and Sinaloa (a single province) designed to quell a prolonged and destructive uprising of the Seris, Pimas, and Sibubapas. Although much energy and several hundred thousand pesos were

[1] For the annals of the frontier provinces see Hubert Howe Bancroft, *History of the North Mexican States and Texas,* Vol. I, and, by the same author, *History of Arizona and New Mexico.*

[2] For the Rubí inspection see Herbert E. Bolton, *Texas in the Middle Eighteenth Century,* pp. 378–383; Alfred B. Thomas, *Forgotten Frontiers: A Study of the Spanish Indian Policy of Don Juan Bautista de Anza, Governor of New Mexico, 1777–1787,* pp. 3–5. This work is cited hereafter as *Forgotten Frontiers;* and Lawrence Kinnaird, *The Frontiers of New Spain: Nicolás Lafora's Description, 1766–1768.*

[3] Priestley, *José de Gálvez,* p. 288.

[4] Croix, Instrucción, AGN, CVB, 1772, Vol. 24, p. 453.

expended, favorable results were few. Indeed, as though disdainful of the Spaniards' clumsy maneuverings in force, additional groups of Indians arose. In New Vizcaya the Apaches terrorized the province with such boldness that Gálvez urged the governors of Coahuila and New Mexico to aid the stricken province by attacking these Indians along their respective borders.[5] But Governor Jacobo de Ugarte y Loyola in Coahuila and Governor Fermín de Mendinueta in New Mexico were too busy with their own Indian problems to spare any of their precious troops for such a purpose, while in Texas, Governor Barón de Ripperdá was similarly occupied. There was no improvement, but rather a further deterioration of the situation between 1769 and 1771.[6] Bucareli therefore was faced with a threatened disaster the moment he became viceroy.

In his Instrucción, Croix's summary of conditions in the Interior Provinces was not completely dismal, but news of a more depressing nature soon began to reach Bucareli. Letters from Governor José Fayní of New Vizcaya,[7] Bernardo de Gálvez, who was in charge of all frontier defenses,[8] and Ugarte in Coahuila,[9] depicted continuous uprisings, mostly by the Apaches, against which the Spanish defensive forces were totally inadequate.

Bucareli's approach to the problem is doubly revealing. First, Ugarte had asked for reinforcements, and in commenting on this request, the Viceroy said, "I know well that the maxim of presidio captains is to

[5] Priestley, *José de Gálvez,* pp. 267–278.

[6] Croix, Instrucción, AGN, CVB, 1772, Vol. 24, pp. 446–449v, 452–453. These pages comprise Croix's summary of the situation in the Interior Provinces, including his commentary on the Rubí inspection.

[7] Bucareli to Arriaga, January 22, 1772, AGN, CVB, 1771–1772, Vol. 5, Libro 8, No. 11 or 141, pp. 91–94. Fayní's letter, dated June 11, 1771, had been sent directly to Spain. Arriaga sent it to Bucareli for his information and action with a letter of October 26, 1771. Therefore, although it was the earliest of the three letters cited, Bucareli received it last. In his covering letter Arriaga relayed the King's Instructions that Bucareli ascertain the true situation in New Vizcaya, inasmuch as José de Gálvez, on almost the same day as Fayní, had reported the Indians under control and a state of peace extant. In his reply Bucareli stated that Fayní was apparently correct in his statements.

[8] Bucareli to Arriaga, November 26, 1771, in Velasco Ceballos, *La administración de . . . Bucareli,* Vol. I, pp. 14–15. Ugarte's letter is dated November 4.

[9] Same to same, November 26, 1771, *ibid.,* pp. 15–16.

augment the number of their garrison, and their allotted force always seems small to them." Second, in the early months of his viceregency Bucareli exhibited an exceptionally strong tendency to move with even more hesitancy than his customary caution bade him to proceed with during the rest of his term. Probably this slowness stemmed from his uncertainty, which in turn was based on his self-stated lack of knowledge concerning his new command. Consequently, he took no immediate steps to relieve the beleaguered provinces. Instead, he forwarded Bernardo de Gálvez' letter to Lieutenant Colonel Hugo O'Conor, who had replaced Gálvez as commandant, for O'Conor to use in recommending what he might regard as necessary for adequate frontier security. It is well to recall that Bucareli was somewhat dubious about Bernardo de Gálvez' ability to handle the job, as is revealed by a comment, previously quoted, in a letter to O'Reilly, in which he said, "the troops with which we oppose them are in charge of the nephew of the *Visitador,* who, despite what they say about his having spirit, at his age has not had experience, a matter from which I hope to be relieved of worry because of the *Visitador's* desire that his nephew accompany him to Spain. I have arranged that Don Hugo O'Conor relieve him." The relief did not come soon enough, however, for two months later Bucareli reported, again to O'Reilly, that O'Conor was delayed in assuming his command because "the *Visitador's* nephew had gone out with many hopes of quieting the Indians, and returned with a wound." [10] In addition to the report which he requested from O'Conor, Bucareli also solicited Fayní's estimate of the situation, and if the information thus gathered indicated the necessity for heavy financial expenditures, he proposed to consider the matter in a junta of War and Finance. [11]

Fayní reported first. He pictured New Vizcaya as a province which had been steadily approaching ruin for several years. He had, he said, appealed repeatedly to both Arriaga and the Marqués de Croix for additional troops with which to increase the existing garrisons and to man new presidios. Deploring the Spanish tendency toward fruitless

[10] Bucareli to O'Reilly, October 27 and December 27, 1771, AGI, Mex., Leg. 1242.
[11] Bucareli to Arriaga, November 26, 1771, in Velasco Ceballos, *La administración de . . . Bucareli,* Vol. I, pp. 15–16. See also note 7, above.

pursuits of the Indians into their own territory, he advocated first a strengthening and solidifying of the line of presidios, after which punitive expeditions might be undertaken. He stated that his province, harassed for so long, could not support financially the necessary augmentation of defenses, and he acknowledged the probability that the cost would be heavy. But he pointed out that in view of the small likelihood that the Apaches would voluntarily make peace, force was necessary. In conclusion, Fayní noted that any elaborate plan, however good, would take time, and that the urgency of the situation demanded some sort of immediate, stop-gap action.[12]

O'Conor's report was in greater detail and even more depressing than Fayní's. Characterizing the state of the provinces as "fatal," he reported that in less than two months the Apaches had killed 45 persons, wounded 21, captured an unknown number, burned houses, destroyed furnishings, and stolen a large number of mules and horses. He acknowledged that the savages were experts in warfare, but he cursed them for their "cowardice and baseness of spirit" which drove them to attack and then flee into the rough mountains rather than face Spanish troops. The soldiers he found almost incapable of effective action because of their small numbers, their lack of equipment, and their poor mounts. The Chihuahua garrison, numbering 108 officers and men, was, he said, nearly naked, without arms or horses, unpaid, of inferior quality and "known pusillanimity." O'Conor revealed that Bernardo de Gálvez had formed the unit from the beginning, inasmuch as the former company under Captain Lope de Cuellar had simply dissolved, leaving Gálvez with no heritage when he assumed command. It was his opinion that only through the creation of new presidios along the Río de los Conchos and Agua Nueva and an increased number of troops could the situation be remedied.[13]

---

[12] Fayní to Bucareli, February 1, 1772, inclosure No. 1 in Bucareli to Arriaga, April 24, 1772, in Velasco Ceballos, *La administración de . . . Bucareli,* Vol. I, pp. 35–38.

[13] O'Conor to Bucareli, February 18, 1772, inclosures Nos. 2 and 3 in Bucareli to Arriaga, April 24, 1772, in Velasco Ceballos, *La administración de . . . Bucareli,* Vol. I, pp. 38–41.

As a consequence of these reports, Bucareli called a junta of War and Finance for mid-March, 1772. Although his Instruction to this council acknowledged the urgent need for succoring New Vizcaya, his main concern was how best to accomplish this end with the least possible expense. He requested that the council consider plans for effecting the transfer of presidios as recommended by Rubí and formalized in a *reglamento* by the Marqués de Croix. He also stated his opinion that by raising from 70 to 100 the number of troops in the Chihuahua garrison, and by sending in 300 more men, the Indians could be halted and New Vizcaya made secure.[14]

The junta rejected for the time being O'Conor's proposal of two new presidios. Instead, it decided that the transfer of the five presidios listed by Rubí for removal should be begun at once. The first one, Julimes, was to be moved to the junction of the Conchos and Río Grande, where it had previously been. The other four, Cerro Gordo, San Sabá, Santa Rosa, and Monclova, were to be relocated on the banks of the Río Grande, separated by approximately equal distances along a line 140 leagues long which extended from the above junction to the Río San Juan Bautista. It was hoped that in this manner the frontiers of New Vizcaya and Coahuila would be protected. The junta allotted 3,000 pesos to each presidio captain to pay for the expense of the transference and new construction. The council also approved the 30-man increase for the Chihuahua garrison and ordered the creation of three more companies of equal size, i.e., 100 men, in New Vizcaya. These new units were not only to assist with the regular defensive duties, but were also to serve as a special patrol in the area left uncovered in the course of the transfer of the presidios until the move was accomplished. In view of O'Conor's report on the lack of equipment among the soldiers and the need to arm the new units, the junta ordered sent from the capital 550 carbines, an equal number of muskets, and a one-year supply of flints and balls. However, each soldier had to pay for his weapons by deductions from his already

[14] Bucareli's endorsement following Fayní's and O'Conor's letters, March 15, 1772, inclosure No. 4 in Bucareli to Arriaga, April 24, 1772, in *La administración de . . . Bucareli,* Vol. I, pp. 41–43.

meager salary. Powder was furnished by the Crown. Surplus pieces were to be sold to local inhabitants if they wished to buy them.[15]

The frontier Indians were not concerned, of course, with all the reporting, conferring, and planning taking place. In June, 1772, Bucareli declared himself sorely troubled over the continued Apache and Comanche ravages in New Vizcaya, Coahuila, and New Mexico, and the impotence of the King's forces to punish the culprits. When a group of Apaches conducted a raid near Chihuahua, capturing 400 horses and killing 5 guards, they escaped unscathed because the garrison had no mounts with which to pursue them. In one day in Coahuila, Lipan Apache groups, in scattered attacks, killed 23 whites, captured 22, and took 954 head of livestock. Reporting this disaster, Governor Ugarte protested the presidio-transfer plan, arguing that the removal of San Sabá, Santa Rosa, and Monclova could only make the province more vulnerable. From New Mexico the Governor reported similar troubles with the Comanches, expressing his fear that when the winter snows were gone from the mountains the attacks would increase. As a solution he proposed mandatory consolidation of the widely-scattered settlers into fortified pueblos, from which they could respond in force to any Indian threat.[16] Bucareli regarded the proposal as too defensive, however, and in its place recommended the construction of a presidio near Taos, from which an offensive could be mounted. Significantly, he confined himself to this recommendation and took no step to put the proposal into practice.

His active measures since the conclusion of the junta had been restricted largely to effectuating the plans of that body. He had ordered O'Conor to take preliminary steps for the transfer of the five presidios, to increase to 100 men the Chihuahua garrison, and to recruit the 300 men for the three flying companies. Sonora Intendant Pedro Corbalán was instructed to send to Chihuahua the 100,000 pesos held

[15] Bucareli's summary of the recommendations of the junta, April 2, 1772, inclosure No. 5 in Bucareli to Arriaga, April 24, 1772, in Velasco Ceballos, *La administración de . . . Bucareli*, Vol. I, pp. 43–52.

[16] Extract of reports from the Interior Provinces, inclosure in Bucareli to Arriaga, June 26, 1772, AGN, CVB, 1772, Vol. 25, No. 451, pp. 35–40.

in Pitic for buying the gold from Cieneguilla, which had not been produced as expected.[17]

O'Conor began to carry out his orders. On May 23 he reported from Chihuahua that local industry had completed enough lances, shields, and cartridge cases for the expanded forces. Horses had been secured at the cost of great effort, inasmuch as Apache raids and an extended drought had cut seriously into the supply of this essential element. Preliminary steps for the presidio transfers were nearly finished, and, although Ugarte opposed the project, O'Conor felt that the Governor's reasoning was weak and that Rubí's plan would prove to be efficacious.[18]

During the summer of 1772 little news of a startling nature came out of the Interior Provinces, although O'Conor did manage a few small successful attacks on the Apaches. Bucareli confined himself to advising the presidio captains to use suavity and prudence in their dealings with the Indians,[19] and to warning O'Conor not to trust the Apaches, even when they appeared to be defeated,[20] which was probably the most unnecessary thing Bucareli ever did. In keeping with the system, it was not until September that the Crown got around to approving the recommendations made by the junta the preceding April. The King ordered Bucareli to give freely of money and supplies to achieve peace in the interior area, and Arriaga promised the Viceroy an early decision on a new *reglamento* for the presidios of the Interior Provinces, based on Rubí's report.[21]

In this same September events in Texas, heretofore much quieter than its sister provinces farther west, compelled Bucareli to give closer consideration to its problems. Texas faced a greater diversity of Indian

---

[17] Bucareli to Arriaga, June 26, 1772, AGN, CVB, 1772, Vol. 25, No. 451, pp. 53, 58.

[18] *Ibid.*, pp. 53–54.

[19] Same to same, July 26, 1772, in Velasco Ceballos, *La administración de . . . Bucareli,* Vol. I, p. 65.

[20] Same to same, August 27, 1772, AGN, CVB, 1772, Vol. 29, No. 525, pp. 16–17.

[21] Arriaga to Bucareli, September 18, 1772, AGN, RC, 1772, Vol. 101, No. 81, pp. 369–370.

enemies than the other provinces, for, in addition to the Eastern Apaches, numerous tribes, called the Indians of the North, inhabited Texas. Among others, these included the Bidais, Taovayas, Tuacanos, Tayshas (Texas), and Comanche groups. Texas' salvation thus far had derived from the numerous animosities which these tribes maintained among themselves. The Apaches, however, were the common foe of all the others. Although the Indians of the North were generally regarded as being more tractable than the ever-hostile Apaches, they had occasionally been guilty of destructive attacks against the Spaniards. Governor Barón de Riperdá had recently consummated peace treaties with several of these northern tribes, but it was rumored that the Bidais and Texas groups were contemplating an alliance with the Apaches, and there had occurred an increased number of raids which each group blamed on another. Furthermore, all these Indians were demonstrating a disturbing dexterity with the growing number of firearms which were being supplied to them by English traders and Spanish subjects from Natchitoches. If Ripperdá took the Northern Indians to task for the recent series of hostilities, attacks might develop into open war, in which case there was no doubt that the Apache alliance would be effected and with disastrous results. Bucareli counseled Riperdá to observe scrupulously the treaties he had made, endeavoring, at the same time, however, to catch in the act the groups of Indians who were making the raids in order that their punishment could not be challenged by their fellow tribesmen. Also, he was to make every effort to attract the Indians to settle down in controlled reductions, thereby diminishing their opportunity for making sudden attacks on remote settlements.[22]

Meanwhile, in Spain the King's experts had been studying for nearly a year the recommendations made by Rubí and adopted in a directive which Croix produced just before he left New Spain. In September, 1772, Charles III approved his councilors' proposals based on these

[22] Bucareli to Arriaga, September 26, 1772, AGN, CVB, 1772, Vol. 30, No. 569, pp. 15–18. Bucareli repeated these same observations one month later, adding a few bitter comments on the Louisiana Spaniards who were supplying arms to the Indians. Same to same, October 27, 1772, AGN, CVB, 1772, Vol. 31, No. 611, pp. 30v–33.

documents, but the approval did not come in time for copies to be sent to Bucareli in that month's mail. Nevertheless, Arriaga informed the Viceroy of the royal decision and told him that O'Conor had been promoted to colonel and was to be the first commandant inspector of the *Provincias Internas.*[23]

Appropriately, Bucareli chose almost this precise moment to put in writing his reflections on the whole problem of the interior area— its defects, its difficulties, and possible solutions.[24] He began with a summary of the reasons why no immediate improvement in the general situation could be expected. He stated that, until the five presidios were transferred to the Río Grande, until O'Conor could start a general campaign, until presidio garrisons could begin to fight outside their walls, and until the several governors could agree to correlate their strategy and convince their people of the advantage of being united to oppose the Indian wherever he might strike—until all this had come about, destruction by the savages would continue and Spanish victories would be infrequent.

One of the great defects which Bucareli noted was the location of the presidios. Not only were they too far apart, but they did not cover the routes ordinarily used by the Indians to enter the area of Spanish settlement. There resulted, therefore, the anomaly of admitting peacefully to some presidios the same Indians who had just come from assaulting another fortress. Presidio captains acknowledged the truth of this statement, but they argued that their forces were so small that they did not dare start hostilities every time the superior Indian groups appeared, especially since help from other presidios was so far away. Bucareli predicted that if he called together a junta of these captains they would conclude that the only remedy was more troops, an expense which the treasury could not and need not stand.

Another thing which complicated the general problem for the Viceroy was the diversity of opinions he received whenever he sought information. He said that he could solicit advice on a single question

[23] Arriaga to Bucareli, September 29 (?), 1772, AGN, RC, 1772, Vol. 101, No. 97, pp. 392–392v.
[24] Bucareli to Arriaga, October 27, 1772, AGN, CVB, 1772, Vol. 31, No. 609, pp. 23–29.

from governors, missionaries, presidio captains, *ayuntamientos,* and private citizens, but that their replies would all differ as to ideas, fact, methods, and proposals. He then asked how an executive, many leagues away from the area concerned, could determine the truth of the matter, and how could he risk lives, money, and territory by making a decision based on such a baffling variety of statements.

The Viceroy next observed that the presidios had always been disorderly places in need of corrective measures. When Brigadier Pedro de Rivera had made his general inspection in 1724, he found a lack of subordination and discipline among the soldiers and ignorance of their jobs and their arms. He effected some reforms in presidio arrangement and troop supply, but overall, conditions stayed bad. Repeated royal orders from 1753 to 1767 failed to produce any improvement until finally Rubí was ordered to conduct his inspection.

Bucareli had nothing but praise for Rubí and his work. He lauded his methods, the detail and subject matter of his reports, his observations on the land and the Indians, and his recommendation for relocation of certain presidios to form a defensive line stretching all along the northern frontier.[25] It is well that such was the Viceroy's attitude, for as he was giving it expression, the new regulation governing the interior presidios mentioned by Arriaga a month earlier was on its way to New Spain, and its provisions coincided in large part with what Rubí had proposed.

The plan was properly ambitious, contemplating as its end point the complete subjugation of the Indians and the attainment of peace throughout the *Provincias Internas.* In a letter which accompanied the regulation Arriaga relayed to Bucareli the major preliminary steps which would have to be taken. First, there had to be a review of all presidial troops and a weeding out of all personnel not fit, physically or spiritually, for the demands of the coming campaign. These men were to be replaced with sturdier individuals. Second, all efforts were to be made to complete as quickly as possible the transfer of the five presidios as proposed by Rubí. Cognizant of the need for good arms and equipment, the regulation prescribed what each soldier was to carry. To supply the necessary weapons, the Barcelona armory was

25 *Ibid.*

devoted to manufacturing them, and their shipment to New Spain was to be promptly accomplished. Finally, Bucareli was accorded the faculty of instituting any changes in the regulation which he saw as more feasible in the light of current conditions.[26]

The new regulation provided Bucareli with a guide to follow in his management of the problems of the Interior Provinces, and, as a consequence, 1773 saw the beginning of an active and theoretically coordinated plan to alleviate the conditions which had for so long been a source of worry and wasted effort. In keeping with this more aggressive attitude, Bucareli reported in January that, in accordance with the royal order of the preceding September, 100 veteran troops from the two regular dragoon regiments in New Spain were ready to leave for Durango, the capital of New Vizcaya, where they were to be placed under O'Conor as replacements for his flying companies. This same dispatch also revealed that Bucareli had simplified the financial procedure in order that O'Conor would not be delayed in his activities through any temporary lack of funds. Furthermore, the governors of New Vizcaya, Sonora, and Coahuila were ordered to furnish the Commandant Inspector with whatever he might ask, although Bucareli did put his brand on these instructions—the warning not to spend money needlessly.[27]

Meanwhile, the Viceroy was drawing up a set of Instructions to guide O'Conor in the effectuation of the new regulation. The frontier commander's first job was to dislodge by offensive action a group of Mescalero Apaches who were raiding out of the Bolsón de Mapimí. Next, he was to select the new sites for the presidios of Julimes, San Sabá, Cerro Gordo, and Monclova, review and revitalize these garrisons, and then move on to follow the same procedure with the garrisons of Janos, San Buenaventura, Paso del Río del Norte, and

[26] Arriaga to Bucareli, October 12, 1772, AGN, RC, 1772, Vol. 101, No. 104, pp. 407–409. The full title of the new regulation is "Reglamento e instrucción para los presidios que se han de formar en la línea de frontera de la Nueva España resuelto por el Rey N.S. en cédula de 10 de septiembre de 1772." O'Reilly claimed the credit for getting this discretionary authority included in the plan. O'Reilly to Bucareli, August 26, 1772, AGI, Mex., Leg. 1242.

[27] Bucareli to Arriaga, January 27, 1773, AGN, CVB, 1773, Vol. 34, No. 741, pp. 44v–47.

Huejoquilla. Next in line for this treatment were the Sonora strong-holds of Santa Gertrudis del Altar, Túbac, Terrenate, and Fronteras. In view of the magnitude of this part of the job, the establishment of the new order in Texas and New Mexico was to be in the hands of their respective governors. Ripperdá had a large program to carry out. He had to see to the abandonment of Los Adáes and Orcoquizac presidios, the extinction of Los Adáes, Nacogdoches, and Ais missions, the re-formation and enlargement of the San Antonio and Bahía de Espíritu Santo garrisons, and settle a detachment in Arroyo de Cíbola. Mendinueta's task was simpler—he had merely to re-form the Santa Fé garrison and establish a 30-man detachment at Robledo.[28]

Bucareli's reports to Spain were based on dispatches from O'Conor and the several governors of the Interior Provinces. From the Viceroy's letters it would appear that conditions began to improve immediately, although Indian eruptions of course did not cease. O'Conor's campaign in the Bolsón de Mapimí, classified as "remarkable" by Thomas, suc-ceeded in dislodging the Apaches and driving them north.[29] In January, 1773, Bucareli reported that Governor Matéo Sastre of Sonora had convinced the Tiburón Island natives that they should make peace and move into reductions.[30] In March he indicated his certainty that the Seri tribe was about to follow suit, although he was still working on the problem in September.[31] By October he was able to write in a mildly boastful tone of the new peace which had come to the frontier, especially in New Vizcaya. As evidence, he cited a letter from the curate, *alcalde,* and inhabitants of San Bartolomé, who averred that the extraordinary absence of hostile Indians had allowed a harvest without equal in twenty years. Furthermore, in this province a force of

[28] Same to same, February 24, 1773, AGN, CVB, 1773, Vol. 35, No. 799, pp. 19–23. Two other letters from Bucareli to Arriaga on this same date reported: tranquillity in New Vizcaya due to the new vigilance engendered by O'Conor; and the departure of the two regular dragoon detachments for Durango on February 12 and 15. *Ibid.,* Nos. 793 and 798, pp. 9v–10, 16v–19.

[29] Thomas, *Forgotten Frontiers,* p. 6. Bucareli to Arriaga, April 26, 1773, AGN, CVB, 1773, Vol. 37, No. 888, p. 31v.

[30] Arriaga to Bucareli, May 12, 1773, AGN, RC, 1773, Vol. 102, No. 128, p. 232.

[31] Same to same, June 18, 1773, AGN, RC, 1773, Vol. 102, No. 167, pp. 294–294v. Bucareli to Arriaga, September 26, 1773, AGN, CVB, 1773, Vol. 42, No. 1099, pp. 15v–18v.

friendly Tarahumaras was on its way to attack an Apache encampment, while several presidio captains were leading forces on a small-scale offensive campaign.[32] At year's end he revealed that a unit of Lipan Apache warriors had taken the field for Spain in Coahuila, and that New Vizcaya had gone for four months without the loss of one human life or a single head of livestock. A less cheerful note was sounded in New Mexico, where the Comanches were making successful sorties, but Bucareli was optimistic about future improvement there. Also, O'Conor, in his eagerness to pursue the enemy, had not been sufficiently attentive to the presidio-transfer program, which the Viceroy told him to accelerate.[33]

The year 1774 was one of mixed victory and defeat. As usual, a period of peace in one area was apt to mean increased eruptions in another. O'Conor and his assistants traveled widely throughout New Vizcaya, Coahuila, and Sonora, concerned mainly with finishing the presidio program, but also occasionally taking to the field against marauding savages. Presidio captains embarked more frequently on offensive expeditions in these three provinces. In Texas, Ripperdá managed to maintain the uneasy peace that he himself had created, although Bucareli repeatedly expressed concern over the Governor's rather casual treatment of some of the tribes. New Mexico continued to be the scene of perhaps more violence than was the case elsewhere. Although the Comanches were the principal offenders, Gila Apaches and Navajos also contributed occasionally to Governor Mendinueta's problems. The settlers, aided by an appreciable number of Indian allies, fought back with creditable zeal, winning one especially overwhelming victory in September under the leadership of an old Indian fighter, Carlos Fernández.[34] Despite such victories, Bucareli regarded

[32] Bucareli to Arriaga, October 27, 1773, AGN, CVB, 1773, Vol. 44, No. 1144, pp. 12v–14v.
[33] Same to same, December 27, 1773, AGN, CVB, 1773, Vol. 46, No. 1221, pp. 8–10v.
[34] For a succinct but detailed account of the fighting in New Vizcaya, Coahuila, and Sonora in 1774, see Thomas, *Forgotten Frontiers,* pp. 7–9. The New Mexico story is told with translations of documents by the same author in *The Plains Indians and New Mexico, 1751–1778,* pp. 169–177. This work is cited hereafter as *Plains Indians.*

New Mexico's condition as dangerous. Nevertheless, the Viceroy felt that the forces available to O'Conor should finish their job in the New Vizcaya-Coahuila-Sonora sector before any extensive help could be sent to Mendinueta. He therefore offered the Governor only encouraging words rather than material assistance.[35]

By the spring of 1775 O'Conor had progressed sufficiently with the rebuilding of the frontier defenses to be ready to take concerted action against the Apaches. His plan originally contemplated using more than 2,200 men, but Mendinueta of New Mexico, lacking horses, was unable to contribute the 600 requested of him. Nevertheless, it was still one of the largest bodies ever gathered to fight the Apaches in this area. The general strategic plan called for Ugarte and the captains of the Río Grande presidios to drive the Apaches westward before them. Since the Indians' escape route to the north was to be blocked by the New Mexico detachment, they would be forced to take refuge in the mountains west of the Río Grande—the Mogollons, Mimbres, and Gilas. Meanwhile, it was contemplated that another New Mexico detachment and the Sonora contingent would be moving in from the west, while O'Conor was moving northward from Carrizal, following the Sangre de Cristo, thus enclosing the Apaches in a trap. Despite the inability of the New Mexico forces to participate, the eastern commanders did their part, O'Conor and Crespo from Sonora[36] met as planned, and together they administered a series of fifteen defeats to the enemy. In all, the Spaniards killed 138 warriors, captured 104 Indians of various types, and recovered 1,966 animals. The campaign occurred during the months of September, October, and November, 1775.[37]

The battle went still worse for the Apaches in 1776. First Lieutenant Diego de Borica in New Mexico conducted a successful campaign through the Sierras of Magdalena and Ladrones, and O'Conor

[35] Bucareli to Arriaga, September 26, 1774, AGN, CVB, 1774, Vol. 58, No. 1524, pp. 12–15.

[36] Bucareli reported in April, 1773, that Governor Matéo Sastre of Sonora had died, and that he had been replaced temporarily by Lieutenant Colonel Francisco Crespo. Bucareli to O'Reilly, April 27, 1773, AGI, Mex., Leg. 1242.

[37] Thomas, *Forgotten Frontiers,* pp. 9–11.

hit the savages five more blows in lesser actions. From Father Francisco Garcés in Zuñi came a report that the Apaches in that area indicated that all of their western tribesmen were returning with their families and horses, fleeing from the Spanish offensive and seeking peace. Confirmation of this report came from the troop commanders of Sonora and New Vizcaya, who were continuing their attacks on the enemy. Finally, one more hard blow was administered to the Apaches, this time by the Comanches. Running before the Spaniards, the groups of Apaches congregated in the Sierras of Guadalupe and Sierra Blanca, and here a large Comanche force fell on them, killing several hundred.[38]

By 1776, then, the line of presidios recommended by Rubí had been established and the Indians had been forced to retreat. O'Conor, broken in health, requested a transfer to a less arduous position and was rewarded with the governorship of Guatemala. Thus was marked the end of an era and the beginning of a new concept with respect to the Interior Provinces. Additionally, a consideration of the history of the area from 1776 to 1779 has special significance for the student of Bucareli and his viceregency.[39]

The importance of the year 1776 to the Interior Provinces derives specifically from a set of Instructions issued by Charles III on August 22 to Teodoro de Croix.[40] These Instructions appointed him governor

[38] *Ibid.,* pp. 12–15.

[39] The colonization of California and the administration of the Interior Provinces are the only two phases of Bucareli's viceregency which have received any significant amount of published study. The administration of the Interior Provinces has been the special concern of Alfred B. Thomas, who, in some of his writings, has been highly critical of Bucareli, an attitude with which I am not in total agreement.

Two of Thomas' works have already been cited. Others are: "Governor Mendinueta's Proposals for the Defense of New Mexico, 1772–1778," *New Mexico Historical Review,* Vol. VI, No. 1, January, 1931; *Teodoro de Croix and the Northern Frontier of New Spain, 1776–1783,* cited hereafter as *Teodoro de Croix;* and "Antonio de Bonilla and Spanish Plans for the Defense of New Mexico, 1772–1778," in *New Spain and the Anglo-American West* (Vol. I). For excellent treatment with emphasis on the eastern sector, see Herbert E. Bolton, *Texas in the Middle Eighteenth Century,* and *Athanase de Mézières and the Louisiana-Texas Frontier, 1768–1770* (Vols. I, II).

[40] He was the nephew of the Marqués de Croix and had held several offices in

and commandant general of the Interior Provinces of New Spain, which meant Texas, Coahuila, New Vizcaya, Sonora and Sinaloa, New Mexico, and the Californias. This tremendous area thus became a separate governmental unit independent of the Viceroyalty of New Spain, with certain minor exceptions which will be noted later.

Why the King chose this precise time to create the interior command is perhaps open to speculation. In the Instructions the Spanish monarch noted that New Spain encompassed a vast area and that its viceroy had a multitude of duties, obligations, and responsibilities. For these reasons, in 1752 the Crown had begun to consider a proposal to erect a separate command of the interior because of the obvious difficulty of governing the territory efficiently and with the requisite promptness from Mexico City. The Marqués de Croix and José de Gálvez had urged its creation in 1768, and in 1769, said Charles III, he had decided the question positively.[41]

Thomas ascribes a different motive to the decision of the King and to the Council of the Indies, a motive which reflects on Bucareli's competence. He says, "By 1776, the threatened collapse of the entire northern frontier of Mexico, sapped by maladministration, increasing Indian attack, and the recent acquisitions [Louisiana and the Californias] demanded attention." And again, "The year 1776 brought a crisis on the northwestern frontier. The continued decline of the provinces there was apparent to the Council of the Indies, if not to Bucareli." [42] Thomas cites Velasco Ceballos in support of his assertion that Bucareli frequently misrepresented frontier conditions in his reports to Spain.[43] This is possible, but one wonders from what other

---

New Spain during his uncle's viceregency. He accompanied the Marqués back to Spain in 1771. A Caballero of the Teutonic Order, he used this title in his signature. His rank in the Army was that of brigadier.

    [41] Royal *Cédula*, August 22, 1776, in Velasco Ceballos, *La administración de . . . Bucareli*, Vol. I, p. 332.

    [42] *Teodoro de Croix*, p. 17. For a somewhat more detailed discussion of Bucareli's competence in this matter than I give here, see Bernard E. Bobb, "Bucareli and the Interior Provinces," *Hispanic American Historical Review*, Vol. XXXIV (February, 1954), pp. 20–36.

    [43] Thomas, *Plains Indians*, pp. 48–49.

source than the Viceroy the Council of the Indies secured the information regarding the "threatened collapse" and the decline that was "apparent," which led to the creation of the commandancy-general. There may have been anonymous letters to the council, or direct reports from the provincial governors, such as the one by Fayní in 1772; but the procedure in this case and in all similar cases, of which there were many in other phases of administration, was to send the documents in question to the viceroy with an order for explanation. No evidence has been found that there were such reports on the Interior Provinces, and there is no reason to believe that the Spanish authorities changed methods in this one instance. It is logical to believe that the reasons for the creation of the new command were those given by Charles III in the Instruction.

Croix's function in his new post was outlined in detail by the King's Instruction. Charles III delineated the new commandancy-general as the provinces of Sonora, Sinaloa, the Californias, New Vizcaya, and the subordinate governments of Coahuila, Texas, and New Mexico, with the line of presidios running from the Gulf of California to the Bay of Espíritu Santo. Croix was to abide by the *reglamento* of September 10, 1772, which O'Conor had struggled to put into effect. The second point in the Instruction was important and was destined to be the source of much trouble. It ordered that Croix, although he was directly subordinate to the King, was to keep the Viceroy informed of the situation in the Interior Provinces for the latter's information, and also in order that the Viceroy might give the Commandant General such supplies and help as he needed and requested. Croix had the faculties of the superintendent general of royal *hacienda* and royal patronage. He was ordered to establish his capital at Arizpe, in Sonora, and to erect a mint there to remedy the chronic shortage of specie in the interior. His principal job was not clearly defined, that is, it was variously indicated in separate paragraphs. One stated it as "the defense and extension of the great territories included in your command." Another defined it as "the conversion of the numerous nations of heathen Indians who live in the north of western America." Much of the Instruction was devoted to the Californias, their importance, and the special care to be taken with respect to their develop-ment.[44] Croix thus became the virtually independent chief of a vast area, but in possession of a cushion on which to rely if necessary—help from the Viceroy of New Spain.

Bucareli first saw the Instruction on December 22, when Croix, just arrived in Mexico City, displayed the original, which he was carrying with him. The Viceroy ordered that the secretariat immediately gather together all documents relating to the Interior Provinces and begin making copies for delivery to Croix.[45] He also notified the provincial governors of the change, with instructions to direct subse-quent reports to the new chief; ordered the Tribunal of Accounts to prepare a financial statement on the Interior Provinces; and directed Miguel Constanzó to draw a map of the new commandancy-general.[46]

The date on which trouble between Croix and Bucareli began cannot be specifically stated. Thomas states that Bucareli's animus against Croix originated in the King's decision to create the com-mandancy-general, that the Viceroy regarded this as a reflection on his administration, since his optimistic picture of conditions in that area had not deceived the King or his council. Also, Velasco Ceballos notes that Bucareli submitted his resignation on September 26, 1776—one month and four days after the date on the Instruction and Royal *Cédula* naming Croix to his new command, that is, August 22—and concludes that the resignation was an expression of Bucareli's resentment. Thomas concurs with this conclusion.[47] It is doubtful, however, that, even with uncustomary expedition, the document could have reached Bucareli on or before September 26; in fact, Bucareli re-ported that he received his own copy of the *cédula* and Instruction on December 24, two days after Croix had presented him with the

[44] Instruction of Charles III to Teodoro de Croix, August 22, 1776, in Velasco Ceballos, *La administración de . . . Bucareli,* Vol. I, pp. 332–342.

[45] Bucareli's endorsement on the Instruction, December 22, 1776, *ibid.,* p. 342.

[46] Bucareli to Gálvez, December 27, 1776, AGN, CVB, 1776, Vol. 86, No. 2638, pp. 15–17. Charles III expressed himself as being "very satisfied with the prompt-ness and exactitude" of Bucareli. Gálvez to Bucareli, March 19, 1777, in Velasco Ceballos, *La administración de . . . Bucareli,* Vol. I, p. 348.

[47] Velasco Ceballos, *La administración de . . . Bucareli,* Vol. II, p. XXVI, and Vol. I, p. 409, note 1; Thomas, *Teodoro de Croix,* p. 28.

original.[48] There is every indication that Bucareli's resignation had no connection with Croix's appointment or the creation of the new command. Indeed, the only surprising aspect of Bucareli's resignation is the fact that he had not submitted it earlier. It was his desire to return to Spain upon completion of his Cuba assignment. Writing of this desire in August, 1770, he said, "Five years is as much as a man can serve well in America."[49] After more than three years as viceroy, Bucareli wrote appreciatively to O'Reilly of the latter's efforts to arrange for Bucareli's appointment as inspector general of Cavalry in Spain, saying, "You already know that for a long time I have desired my return [to Spain] . . ." And, a few months later, "I cannot continue much longer as viceroy, nor is any appointment in America attractive to me."[50]

During his first few months in Mexico City, Croix spent his time acquainting himself with the problems of his new command and organizing his staff. Thomas notes that not until March 31 did Bucareli turn over to Croix some 156 pertinent documents, with a lengthy explanatory index written by the Viceroy. Thomas also points out that Bucareli's index was restricted largely to the work of O'Conor, which does not seem strange, and comments that the Viceroy felt that the provinces were in a promising condition, in spite of reports from the frontier telling of Indian unrest, raids, and uprisings.[51]

In April, with these documents and the governors' reports before him, Croix wrote to Gálvez:[52]

Thus . . . I look upon a dismal stage. Although some [Bucareli] try to persuade me that the provinces under my command have taken on a better aspect than that which they had in 1771 . . . I cannot reconcile these

[48] Bucareli to Gálvez, December 27, 1776, AGN, CVB, 1776, Vol. 86, No. 2638, P. 15.
[49] Bucareli to O'Reilly, August 30, 1770, AGI, Mex., Leg. 1242.
[50] Same to same, November 26 and December 27, 1773, and February 26, 1774, *ibid.*
[51] Thomas, *Teodoro de Croix,* pp. 20–21. Bucareli's index to the documents which he delivered to Croix is a diffuse document detailing the history of his and O'Conor's handling of the Interior Provinces, including comment on California. AGN, CVB, 1777, Vol. 89, of No. 2819, pp. 166–203v.
[52] Thomas, *Teodoro de Croix,* p. 22.

favorable reports with the adverse ones that are frequently proffered in this capital and with those sent from the Interior Provinces. . . . It would please me greatly if the first ones were true, but on the other hand the second ones frighten me . . . for I see the greater disasters they foreshadow.

In May, June, and July of 1777, accounts of Indian depredations on the frontier continued to reach Croix in Mexico City. Although he regarded the picture as a black one and despaired of bringing immediate relief to the provinces, he ordered certain steps taken for troop redistribution and augmentation with militia. He then left Mexico City on August 4.[53] Thomas condemns Bucareli for his tardy delivery of the pertinent documents to Croix, but makes no comment on the fact that Croix had been appointed on August 22, 1776, had been in Mexico City since December 22, and had complained repeatedly that his new command was in terrible shape, but had remained in the capital for four months after receiving his archival material instead of getting out to the frontier to see the situation at first hand and take some action.

In Querétaro, Croix received a packet of twenty-four letters from Governor Felipe Neve, Fray Junípero Serra, and Captain Fernando de Rivera y Moncada in California. Because he felt inadequately informed about California, Croix forwarded the letters to Bucareli with the request that the Viceroy take the necessary executive steps in the matter. Both Velasco Ceballos and Thomas are critical of Bucareli for his response to this request. The Viceroy returned the packet to Croix with a letter of explanation, from which the two critics select one sentence, the same one, on which to comment. Thomas says:[54]

Bucareli . . . in rather lordly fashion informed Croix that "Neither was your lordship nor am I authorized to separate from our commands any part of the provinces which the king placed under our care." Croix's inter-

[53] *Ibid.*, pp. 26–27.
[54] *Teodoro de Croix*, pp. 18–19. Croix's letter to Bucareli, dated August 15, 1777, is inclosure No. 1, pp. 290–291, in Bucareli to Gálvez, August 27, 1777, AGN, CVB, 1777, Vol. 94, No. 3218, pp. 62v–63. Bucareli's reply to Croix, dated August 27, 1777, is inclosure No. 2, pp. 292–295.

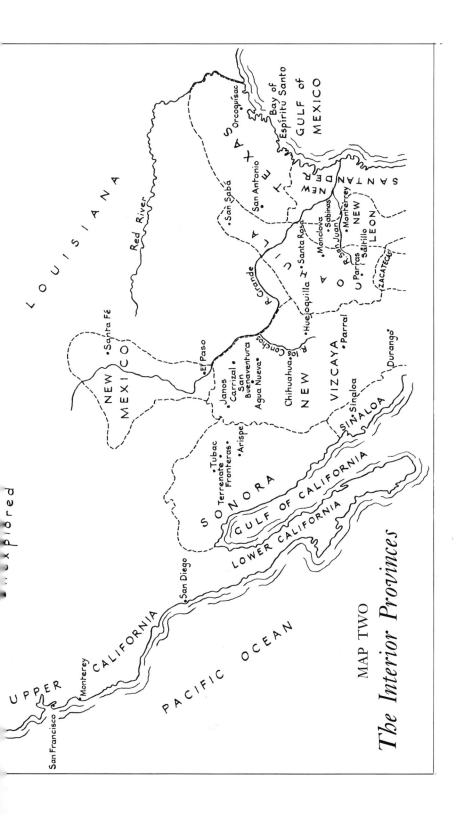

MAP TWO

The Interior Provinces

José de Gálvez.

Reproduced from Herbert I. Priestly, *José de Gálvez,* as
taken from Lucas Alamán, *Disertaciones* . . . , Vol. III,
p. 296.

est in the efficient administration of the provinces rather than in his prerogatives stands in sharp contrast to Bucareli's refusal to succor California and seek a definition of powers later.

Velasco Ceballos labels the Viceroy's reply "unjust, hard, and short." He does concede, however, that technically Bucareli was correct.[55] There was much more to Bucareli's letter than these two writers indicate. The Viceroy pointed out to Croix, not harshly or impolitely, that California had passed from his control by royal order, that the officials of the province had been informed of the change, and that they had been submitting their reports to their new commander for some time. Then—and this seems a complete refutation of the accusation that Bucareli let California down—the Viceroy told Croix what he, Bucareli, would do about every one of the points raised in the California letters if he were still in command of the area. Bucareli sent Gálvez a copy of both Croix's letter of appeal and his own reply, with an explanatory covering letter. It is hard to understand how anyone could find fault with the Viceroy's action in the matter; apparently Charles III saw no reason for censure, since he approved Bucareli's answer to Croix.[56]

In the meantime, Croix had a second request of the Viceroy, one which was to be repeated many times and for the refusal of which Bucareli is again criticized. On August 22, three weeks after he had left Mexico City and while he was still in Querétaro, Croix wrote a long, despairing letter to Bucareli about the plight of himself and his command. He said that even before he reached Veracruz he had begun to hear "dismal reports of the deplorable, ruinous state" of the Interior Provinces. Since his arrival in New Spain the reports had been worse and worse. Many times, he said, he had contemplated expressing his concern to the Viceroy, but had deferred doing so until he personally saw the area. In Querétaro, however, he had received a depressing report from José Rubio, bad news from Sonora's Military Commander Juan Bautista de Anza, and desperate notices from the several provincial governors. Sonora was threatened with inundation

[55] Velasco Ceballos, *La administración de . . . Bucareli,* Vol. II, p. XXI.
[56] See note 46. The King's approval is repeated in Bucareli to Gálvez, April 27, 1778, AGN, CVB, 1778, Vol. 104, No. 3740, pp. 49–50.

by the Seris, Pimas, Papagoes, Tiburones, and Gila Apaches. New Vizcaya was practically under siege. Coahuila was defenseless before the attacks of the Lipan Apaches. Texas, while not in a state of open warfare, faced trouble it could not handle. New Mexico was on the verge of ruin. The troops were nearly naked, unarmed, undisciplined, without horses, unpaid, and, as a result, almost useless. All this information came from current reports from the frontier officials. Croix made the tactful deduction, therefore, that O'Conor had been "mistaken" in the notices he had sent to Bucareli concerning the conditions of his command.

Consequently, the Commandant General was obliged to ask for help. With only 2,000 men scattered along a frontier more than 700 leagues long, an adequate defense was impossible. He needed, he said, an equal number of reinforcements, and even this was a minimum requirement. In the meantime, he had disposed that each Sonora presidio receive an increase of 20 militiamen, and he asked that Bucareli immediately order the company of fusiliers in Guadalajara to march to Sonora.[57]

In reply to this appeal Bucareli began by commenting on the discordance between the state in which O'Conor ostensibly left the Interior Provinces and their condition as indicated by Rubio and the other officials currently stationed there. He indicated that in the face of this disparity he would reserve his opinion until he should hear what Croix had to report after making a personal inspection of the area. With respect to the increase of 2,000 troops, Bucareli pointed out that the forces at his command did not suffice for the needs of the viceroyalty proper. Furthermore, the annual salaries of this number of new troops would amount to more than 600,000 pesos, in addition to the tremendous cost of outfitting them. Not only was the treasury in no condition to bear such a burden, but Charles III had specifically ordered that the Viceroy not enter into any extraordinary expenses in view of the imminent European war. Consequently, with regret,

---

[57] Croix to Bucareli, August 22, 1777, inclosure No. 1 in Bucareli to Gálvez, August 27, 1777, in Velasco Ceballos, *La administración de . . . Bucareli*, Vol. I, pp. 355–368, 353–355. Croix's long letter is filled with details of explanation, argument, and persuasion.

Bucareli refused Croix's request.[58] Thomas labeled this a "sharp refusal," which it was not.[59]

The Viceroy sent both Croix's letter and his reply to it to Gálvez. In the covering letter he expressed his surprise at the reports on the new command, pointing out that he had received no information on the area for several months. He revealed that there were at that time 1,997 troops on the frontier, that this was a greater number than had been there in 1771, and that their cost, plus that of Croix's staff, amounted to more than 800,000 pesos annually. Greater expenditures were impossible, in his opinion.[60]

Thomas states that Bucareli's hostile attitude toward Croix derived from his parsimony and his contempt for the Mexican population. Bucareli was parsimonious, it is true, but one must consider also the heavy demands that Charles III was making at this time for every extra peso that could be raised. It is also true that Bucareli had a low opinion of the lower castes, but Thomas goes so far as to say that "alleviation of human suffering at no time entered his calculations." He also asserts that Croix's plea for 2,000 men was "quite beyond the vision of this viceroy." On the contrary, Bucareli looked the problem squarely in the eye and recognized the 600,000-peso expenditure there.[61]

In the face of Bucareli's refusal to provide additional troops, Croix's next move was, according to Thomas, "devastating." [62] He repeated his appeal for help but cut his request to 1,000 men, pending the King's decision on the matter. Croix also said that he did not need all veterans, that if Bucareli would give him the fusilier company in Guadalajara plus a few regular officers and noncommissioned officers, he would recruit the remainder in his territory. The devastating part of his action consisted in enclosing a résumé of Indian depredations drawn up by New Vizcaya's Governor Felipe Barri for the period 1771–1776. The totals showed 1,674 persons killed, 154 cap-

---

[58] Bucareli to Croix, August 27, 1777, inclosure No. 2 in Bucareli to Gálvez, same date, see note 57, above.

[59] *Teodoro de Croix,* p. 28.

[60] Bucareli to Gálvez, August 27, 1777, see note 56.

[61] *Ibid.,* pp. 28–29.   [62] *Ibid.,* p. 30.

tured, 116 haciendas abandoned, and 68,256 head of livestock stolen. They did not include military losses and certain other ravages.[63]

Bucareli may well have been staggered, as Thomas says. He expressed his unawareness of these depredations and passed the report to O'Conor for explanation. The rest of his brief reply to Croix was blunt: "As to the increase of strength upon which you insist, I can say nothing more than I told you in my letter of August 27 . . . because the present circumstances of public affairs, of the command, and the affairs of these provinces prevent me from separating any part of the veteran troops." [64] Again Bucareli sent a copy of everything to Gálvez, and again the King approved his viceroy's action.[65]

One month later Croix once more appealed for reinforcements of 1,000 or 2,000 troops. Without these, he said, he could take no positive action, and the provinces would be lost. Bucareli finally conceded in part and ordered the Guadalajara fusilier company to proceed to the frontier. He also promised to help Croix raise two flying companies. In transmitting this information to Gálvez, the Viceroy expressed his concern over thus diminishing the small forces at his command, inasmuch as at this time the few units he had were being hard hit by the fever at Veracruz.[66]

During the last months of 1777 and the first of 1778, Croix finally stopped writing letters and started taking some action. He inspected the presidios of Texas, Coahuila, and New Vizcaya, and on February 8, 1778, reported his conclusions to Bucareli. Although the tone of his letter was less dramatic than his previous ones and showed a greater degree of tolerance, perhaps because he had finally seen for himself the difficulties under which frontier officials had to work, nevertheless he remained convinced that the condition of the frontier was danger-

[63] Croix to Bucareli, September 27, 1777, inclosure No. 1 in Bucareli to Gálvez, October 27, 1777, AGN, CVB, 1777, Vol. 96, No. 3338, pp. 445–447.

[64] Bucareli to Croix, October 15, 1777, inclosure No. 2 in Bucareli to Gálvez, October 27, 1777, *ibid.*, p. 449.

[65] Bucareli to Gálvez, October 27, 1777, *ibid.*, pp. 55–56. Charles III's approval is noted in same to same, July 27, 1778, AGN, CVB, 1778, Vol. 108, No. 3858, p. 9.

[66] Bucareli to Gálvez and inclosures, November 26, 1777, AGN, CVB, 1777, Vol. 97, No. 3354, pp. 20–21, 154–159.

ous. He blamed O'Conor indirectly for this situation, but conceded that the former commandant inspector had faced a huge task and had not received sufficient support from his subordinates. He felt that the new presidio arrangement had produced no benefits and many disadvantages. He repeated his arguments in favor of the 2,000-troop increase, but in the meantime he had drawn up a plan for redistributing his presidial forces and for spreading among them 377 reinforcements.[67]

Bucareli approved both his plan and the added expense it entailed. He notified Croix that he would see to it that the subtreasuries in the Interior Provinces always had ample funds on hand, but urged him to be economical.[68]

In the course of his inspection tour, which he continued through June and July, 1778, Croix held three councils of war in which a general policy was set forth and a coordinated program drawn up. Alliance, war, and peace with various Indian groups were all to be part of the Spanish method, both as coexisting and sequential policies. In July, Croix began putting these plans into practice. By March, 1779, progress had been made. In Texas the Indians of the North made peace with the Spaniards and dissolved an alliance they had made with the Comanches. In Coahuila the Lipan Apaches had been wooed away from the Mescaleros. Attacks were continuing in New Vizcaya, but the Chafalotes, Natagées, and Mescaleros had sued for peace. Spanish forces in Sonora had achieved temporary control over the Seris, although the Gila Apaches still menaced. Contributory to these achievements had been Croix's success in raising more than 500 additional troops from within his own command.[69]

In recounting the above occurrences, Thomas makes no comment on facts which, in the light of his attitude toward Bucareli, would seem in all fairness to call for some interpretation. For example, in his reports Croix continued to ask for additional troops. Since Bucareli

---

[67] Croix to Bucareli, February 8, 1778, inclosure in Bucareli to Gálvez, March 28, 1778, AGN, CVB, 1778, Vol. 101, No. 3640, pp. 16–17, 502–513.

[68] Bucareli to Gálvez, May 27, 1778, and inclosures, AGN, CVB, 1778, Vol. 106, No. 3773, pp. 26–27, 197–200.

[69] Thomas, *Teodoro de Croix*, pp. 35–40. These and subsequent pages contain a detailed account of Croix's plan, the Indian situation, and Spanish progress against the hostiles.

always included copies of Croix's stirring letters in his accounts to Gálvez, it must be deduced, therefore, that Charles III and Gálvez were equally as parsimonious, heartless, unjust, and visionless as the Viceroy, because they took no steps to provide the frontier commander with the men he requested. Gálvez was especially culpable, for he himself had participated in a campaign against these same Indians and therefore cannot be excused because of ignorance. Furthermore, in March, 1779, Croix was still complaining about mismanagement in the presidios, corruption among paymasters, disregard for regulations, and lack of discipline and training.[70] This was two and a half years after he had been appointed commandant general, two years after he had arrived in New Spain, and eighteen months after he had left Mexico City to take an active part in administering his command. Regardless of what the conditions were upon his arrival, in this space of time it does not seem unfair to assert that he should have straightened out some of these things.

However, this is probably too severe a judgment. It is more likely that the territory was too big, communication methods were too slow, Indian resistance was too stubborn, and incentive for the few troops to fight in an exemplary manner was too low, for one man to achieve unqualified success as commander-in-chief.

With certain extensions this idea may be offered in explanation of the seemingly unreasonable amount of trouble which the Spaniards had along the northern frontier. The two factors which seem most responsible for Spanish failures are the Indians, who failed to appreciate the benefits of European religion and vassalage to Charles III; and the position of Spain in international relations, which led her to attempt more than her strength warranted.

The temptation to impose current standards on past performers in the historical scene is, of course, constant, but unfair. Judged by the standards of his time, Bucareli was not so heartless as Thomas makes him out to be. His assistant, O'Conor, probably did the best he could with inadequate tools in an area too vast for efficient control. The Viceroy, titular head of a much more extensive territory, was com-

[70] *Ibid.,* p. 41.

pelled to rely on the reports of his subordinates for his knowledge of conditions. When Croix began to submit reports contrary to those turned in by O'Conor, it is probable that the Viceroy's surprise was genuine. Genuine also was his explanation of why he could not grant Croix the help he asked for—requests from Spain for more money were urgent, the fear of England was well-founded, certain costly and necessary fortifications at Veracruz were unfinished, and the troops on which the Viceroy could rely in case of attack were indeed few in number. Also worthy of note is the fact that the numerous viceregal predecessors of Bucareli had failed to solve the problem of the northern frontier, and when, in the nineteenth century, some of this territory was transferred to the United States, the American Army found these same Indian tribes a stubborn and worthy foe.

On the whole, Bucareli's policies and actions were justified. Croix proved this in part when, in the four years following Bucareli's death, he went ahead and achieved a general frontier peace without the 2,000 men he had so often claimed were indispensable. Only cautious criticisms are called for with respect to Bucareli's handling of the problem of the northern frontier. His was a tremendous job, and the Interior Provinces were not its focus.

The California Colonization

THE SINGLE PHASE of Bucareli's viceregal activities which has received thorough and competent attention from scholars is his management of the problems emanating from the new settlements in California.[1] Charles E. Chapman, in particular, wrote a number of works based on documentary sources which treat extensively of Bucareli's relationship with the young colony.[2] Other aspects of the early colonial years have been investigated by a number of writers, editors, and translators.[3] Most of the significant facts concerning the occupation, therefore, may be regarded as having been adequately pre-

[1] The term "California" is here used to identify the area which Spain labeled "Alta California," that is, the territory extending roughly from San Diego to San Francisco. Lower (Baja) California will be referred to as Lower California.

[2] Charles E. Chapman, *The Founding of Spanish California*, hereafter cited as *Spanish California; A History of California, the Spanish Period*, hereafter cited as *History;* "The Alta California Supply Ships, 1773–1776," *Southwestern Historical Quarterly*, Vol. XIX, No. 2 (October, 1915), pp. 184–194; and "Difficulties of Maintaining the Department of San Blas, 1776–1777," *Southwestern Historical Quarterly*, Vol. XIX, No. 3 (January, 1916), pp. 261–270, cited hereafter as "Difficulties of San Blas."

[3] The immediate background for the occupation is delineated in Priestley, *José de Gálvez*. Many original narratives have been reproduced both in Spanish and English. Francisco Palou's *Notícias de la Nueva California* appears in four volumes in translation by Herbert E. Bolton as *Historical Memoirs of New California*. Palou's *Junípero Serra* has been translated by C. S. Williams. Bolton's *Anza's California Expeditions* presents in five volumes the record of the opening of the land route from Sonora. For an extensive critical bibliography, see John Walton Caughey, *California*, pp. 618–621.

sented. The interpretations placed upon these facts, however, will bear some consideration, especially with respect to the historical observation point from which a particular author views the scene, as well as the basis he may have for reaching his conclusions. Also, there still exist several factual points worthy of presentation.

The occupation of California was not a new idea to the Spanish Crown in the second half of the eighteenth century. Colonization of this area had been contemplated ever since the sixteenth century, but Spanish preoccupation with other affairs, the lack of capital, the distance from an established base, the rigors of the sea approach, and the difficulties involved in crossing the land frontier combined to delay consummation of the project.[4] As usual, events in Europe foreshadowed and predisposed events in America. Thus, in the 1760's, Russian advances from northeastern Asia and English interest in the North Pacific aroused Spanish concern over the California region to a higher pitch than ever before.

Chapman advances the fear of foreign aggression as one of the immediate motives for the occupation, and proceeds to the interesting conclusion that the nature of the resultant colonization was fortunate for the United States, inasmuch as it held the area in a relatively dormant state until the workings of Manifest Destiny brought it into the Union. He places the movement of the late 1760's, however, within the larger framework of the certain, although occasionally sporadic, northwestward advance of the Spaniards from Mexico City. Within this pattern he then concentrates on individuals and, consequently, devotes a great deal of attention and praise to *Visitador* José de Gálvez, who actually engineered the whole thing.[5]

Caughey, on the other hand, minimizes to some extent the degree of agitation caused in Spain and Mexico by current reports of Russian and English ambitions. He says that Charles III ordered Viceroy Marqués de Croix to investigate the Russian threat, but that the order did not call for colonization. Croix passed the royal Instruction to Gálvez,

---

[4] Bucareli's predecessor, the Marqués de Croix, cites a directive of Philip III, based on Vizcaíno's discoveries, which ordered the occupation and settlement of California. Croix, Instrucción, AGN, CVB, 1772, Vol. 24, p. 451.

[5] Chapman, *Spanish California,* pp. viii–x, 68, 91.

who was at that time making a tour of the western provinces. The *Visitador* made the decision that California should be settled. Caughey, therefore, states that the Russian threat was an excuse, and that the real immediate cause for the occupation of California in 1769 was Gálvez.[6]

Viceroy Marqués de Croix substantiates this conclusion, although he naturally gives himself a more significant role. In his Instruction he began the section on the two Californias by going back to 1767. He said that the diversity in the reports he was receiving from Lower California led him to seek better information. As a consequence, when the Jesuit expulsion was pending, he selected Gaspar de Portolá to go to the peninsula as governor to take over from the Jesuits, keep the peace, and report on the character and customs of the natives, the products of the area, and the nature of the coast and seaports to the end that Croix might make wise decisions with respect to that province. It is surprising that the Viceroy of New Spain in 1767 should have to be seeking such information. When Gálvez was organizing his expedition to Sonora, said Croix, he agreed with the *Visitador* that his route should take him to Lower California. Then, while Gálvez was in San Blas, continued Croix,[7]

I received an order from the court revealing to me His Majesty's fears that a foreign nation intended to reconnoiter the coasts of . . . the Californias and make a landing there. I was ordered to take efficacious measures for its security. . . . I passed a copy of the order to the *Visitador* in order that he, having arrived in said province, might take the corresponding measures for its security, in accordance with what the court had ordered, and arrange for an expedition by sea to said port. (Croix had mentioned Monterey as the most likely place for foreign entry.)

Exactly what the Marqués meant when he originally spoke of "the corresponding measures for its security" is not here important, but what Gálvez made of the phrase is important. In light of the usual pace and procedure of Spanish colonial officialdom, the aggressiveness this man displayed during his visitation is surprising, and there is no better example of his methods than the California occupation. When

[6] Caughey, *California,* pp. 118–119.
[7] Croix, Instrucción, AGN, CVB, 1772, Vol. 24, pp. 450–451.

he received the order which Croix relayed to him, he passed from San Blas to Lower California, where he devoted himself to organizing the colonizing expedition. He commandeered two ships, the *San Carlos* and the *San Antonio,* which had been built for use in the campaign against the Indians in Sonora. He also secured additional troops from the mainland and drew on the small supply of materials available on the peninsula. In the first three months of 1769, as a result of the *Visitador's* action, two sea parties and two land parties set out from Lower California for San Diego.[8]

In spite of the severe hardships and fatalities which apparently are the concomitant of pioneering ventures, these original parties accomplished their immediate purpose. In July, 1769, the presidio and mission of San Diego were founded. Early in 1770 they were almost abandoned for lack of food, but the last-minute arrival of a supply ship saved them. In June parallel establishments were made at Monterey, and two more missions—San Antonio de Padua and San Gabriel Arcangel—were founded in 1771.[9] Thus, when Bucareli became viceroy in September of 1771, the settlements in the most distant of his provinces numbered four. Perhaps he was pleased with the thought of the prestige which might be his as a result of his governing a viceroyalty of even greater extent than that of his predecessor; but the difficulties he encountered in administering this new colony make such a nebulous reward as prestige seem poor compensation.

The miraculous relief of San Diego in 1770 was of only temporary duration. Existence in California was precarious for several years thereafter. The Spaniards were few and the Indians were hostile. Since local agricultural production was inadequate, nearly all food had to be brought from Mexico, and the sea route was long and dangerous. The military and the religious did not get along harmoniously. The soldiers caused trouble by their relations with Indian women. Converts to Christianity were few. Supply crises were recurrent. Also, California was an expensive colony, offering no return in goods or produce for the money reluctantly spent by the Crown.[10] These problems were Bucareli's.

[8] Caughey, *California,* pp. 124–126.   [9] *Ibid.,* pp. 127–128, 132, 163.
[10] *Ibid.,* pp. 133–135.

As stated above, Bucareli's executive acts with respect to California constitute the only phase of his administration which has been fully studied and written about by competent historians. I feel, therefore, a certain trepidation in disagreeing in diverse ways and to some extent with such reputable scholars. This negative attitude, however, is directed primarily at the interpretation of facts; with the presentation of the facts there is in general no argument.

The question of the degree of importance which California assumed in Bucareli's eyes is worthy of attention. In various places Chapman avers that ". . . nothing interested him more than the precariously held province in the far northwest," and ". . . nothing in the affairs of the viceroyalty interested him so much or got so large a share of his attention as the problems of the Californias and the route thereto from Sonora." Chapman then quotes the Viceroy as saying on this subject, "It seems as if this has been my only attention in this command."[11]

In another place, in support of his portrayal of Bucareli's character, Chapman says, "My opinion is based upon a reading of several hundreds of his official letters, besides some private correspondence with General O'Reilly."[12] There is no way of ascertaining how many pieces of correspondence Bucareli wrote during his term. It is certain, however, that he sent nearly forty-five hundred official letters to the Minister of the Indies alone. Neither by simple arithmetical count nor by a perusal of the contents of these letters does it appear that California was either his main interest or his principal concern. Financial affairs certainly held the top position. Defensive matters other than those concerning California also commanded much of his interest. In the lengthy Instruction which he gave to the Caballero de Croix when the Interior Provinces passed to the command of the latter, Bucareli allotted to both Californias less consideration than he did to several other topics.[13]

It must be pointed out that Chapman focuses this period of Bucareli's

---

[11] Chapman, *History*, pp. 271, 275.
[12] Chapman, *Spanish California*, p. 96 n.
[13] Inclosure in Bucareli to Gálvez, March 27, 1777, AGN, CVB, 1777, Vol. 89, No. 2819, pp. 166–203v.

special interest in California in the years from 1773 to 1776. From 1771 to 1773, he says, Bucareli "got acquainted with conditions in California, made timely remissions of supplies and decided upon the main lines of his policy." [14] With respect to this early policy, Caughey says, "For two years he was largely occupied with the central and routine tasks of that office. . . . Thus far his attitude was that Alta California was a very incidental part of New Spain." [15] It is my opinion that Caughey assesses the actual situation more precisely than does Chapman, and the only modification of Caughey's statement that might be suggested here is that the Viceroy's failure to take positive steps involving the new settlements derived not only from his attitude toward them but also from his characteristic caution.

Bucareli was always reluctant to move until he felt fully informed about the matter concerned. One month after he became viceroy he wrote to Arriaga of the confusion he faced in his new job. As for California, he complained that nothing was in order with respect to organization, the division of missions between Franciscans and Dominicans, the amount of money to be allotted, or which branches of the treasury the money was to come from.[16] The reader will recall that Bucareli wrote to O'Reilly on the same day, ". . . ask God to grant me strength to disentangle myself from the chaos of difficulties which enclose me in the confused management of these vast provinces, in which, to now, I walk in shadows, because nothing is concluded. . . . Monte Rey, the Californias, and provinces of Sonora and Sinaloa neither have their subsidies arranged, nor is it easily discovered how they are governed." [17]

He was not passive about the problem, of course. In February, 1772, he reported to Spanish Minister of State, Marqués de Grimaldi that he was working on methods for protecting the Chihuahua frontier and on a *reglamento* for the missions of California, "both matters of first importance on which opinions are not in agreement." [18] In April he

[14] Chapman, *Spanish California*, p. 96.

[15] Caughey, *California*, p. 137.

[16] Bucareli to Arriaga, October 27, 1771. Microfilm of typed copy in Bancroft Library indicated as being from AGI, IG, 146–4–2.

[17] Bucareli to O'Reilly, October 27, 1771, AGI, Mex., Leg. 1242.

[18] Bucareli to Grimaldi, February 25, 1772, AGI, IG, 146–4–2. See note 16, above.

wrote to Arriaga that two supply ships should have left San Blas for California on the sixth of that month, but that this fact did not warrant any relaxation on his part because much remained to be done on the matter.[19] He ordered the Commissary of San Blas to see that these shipments were promptly made in the face of the urgent need of supplies in California.[20]

The dearth of what he regarded as trustworthy information continued to bother him. In July, 1772, he complained that the discord between secular and religious authorities in the new settlements gave cause for conflicting reports which, when considered singly, seemed straightforward and well-founded. In an effort to sift out the truth, he sought information from other sources, such as the Guardian of the College of San Fernando, from whence came the Franciscan missionaries to California. The major reason for his hesitancy, however, appeared to be his uncertainty regarding the source of money for the colony's support. Before taking any decisive action, he felt that he must have full information on the outright subsidy to be granted, what could be counted on from the Pious Fund, and how much he must expect to spend on the supply port, San Blas.[21] As always, the keynote of Bucareli's caution was, "How much will it cost?"

One other measure of the Viceroy's in the year 1772 had to do with the supply problem. His October report to Arriaga revealed that he had taken steps to remedy the chronic food scarcity in California. He had ordered Governor Felipe Barri to submit to both himself and to the Commissary of San Blas an estimate of the amount and types of foods he felt would be necessary for a one-year supply. With this as a guide, the Viceroy proposed to see to it that the new settlements would never lack for adequate foodstuffs thereafter.[22]

The year 1773 is singled out by both Chapman and Caughey as the time of awakening for Bucareli with respect to California. Chapman

[19] Bucareli to Arriaga, April 26, 1772, *ibid.*
[20] Same to same, same date, No. 354, *ibid.,* 104-3-3.
[21] Same to same, July 26, 1772, AGN, CVB, 1772, Vol. 28, No. 462, pp. 8-9v.
[22] Same to same, October 27, 1772, AGN, CVB, 1772, Vol. 31, No. 612, pp. 33v-35.

does not make clear why this is so, beyond stating that by this time Bucareli had become sufficiently oriented in his new job to act more specifically than heretofore. Caughey, on the other hand, cites Serra's trip to Mexico City and his apparently effective talks with the Viceroy at this time as one reason, Anza's proposal for an expedition to open a land route as a second reason, and Bucareli's "increasing realization of the strategic value of a Spanish outpost in California" as a third cause.[23] A fourth motivation, and a strong one, was contained in a communication from Spain which Bucareli received on January 17, 1773. It was the new *reglamento* for the relocation and government of the interior presidios. In this Instruction Charles III specified that both the Californias merited "special attention" because upon their possession depended a necessary extension of his dominions, the security of New Spain, and, "above all," the propagation of the faith. Bucareli, therefore, was given a "special charge to sustain and supply said establishments in order that they will not decay and may be extended pending the voluntary reduction of the Indians."[24]

With the Viceroy's attention thus increasingly focused on California, it is natural to ask what he did for the area to merit Chapman's conclusion that Bucareli is "the greatest hero who has ever appeared in the field of California history."[25] This is a strong statement to make about a man who never was nearer to the new settlements than the vicinity of Mexico City.

In considering the "outstanding events" which led to the achievement of Bucareli's policies, Chapman cites first the *reglamento* of July, 1773, for the Californias and San Blas and the Instruction to Fernando de Rivera y Moncada which followed it.[26] It is difficult to understand why Bucareli merits any special praise for these documents. Indeed, Chapman himself provides a significant qualification of such praise when he reveals that the *reglamento* had three sources: a series of recommendations by Juan José Echeveste, one-time purchasing agent for the Cali-

[23] Caughey, *California*, pp. 137–138.
[24] Arriaga to Bucareli, October 12, 1772, AGN, RC, 1772, Vol. 101, No. 104, pp. 407–409.
[25] Chapman, *History*, p. 242.   [26] *Ibid.*, p. 273.

fornias; the supplementary opinion of a junta on these recommendations; and Bucareli's decree adopting Echeveste's ideas, with the changes
proposed by the junta.[27]

Other evidences which Chapman offers in support of Bucareli as a
great hero are the Viceroy's authorization of Anza's expeditions which
opened the overland route to California, and the exploratory voyages
made along the west coast by Juan Pérez, Bruno de Heceta, Juan
Francisco de Bodega y Cuadra, and Juan Manuel de Ayala in the years
1773–1775.[28] It is not clear why Bucareli should merit more credit for
these activities than that, for example, Diego de Velázquez should be
credited with the conquest of Mexico. The projects did not originate
with Bucareli. In fact, during his entire viceregency Don Antonio was
the source of very few original concepts. Why he is to be the recipient
of accolades because California was settled, in part, while he was
viceroy is difficult to comprehend.

This observation gives rise to an interesting speculation concerning
the writing of history in general and of California history in particular.
It is a common and human tendency of the historian to want success
for the topic he is presenting. The biographer offers the most easily
recognized example of the tendency because the temptation is strong
for him to identify himself with his character, a sort of ego projection.

With respect to California, why should Bucareli be held a hero because his administrative ability contributed to making its establishments
less precarious? The criterion arbitrarily selected, the objective sought
after by the historian in this case, is to get the area settled. That is, the
historian avers that there is intrinsic value in having inhabitants of
another civilization occupy the province, although such a premise is
not openly stated. Probably it is not even consciously felt by the
scholar. Whether or not the proposition has merit depends in part on
the historical viewpoint of the writer. What may appear to be advantageous to the observer in California, who is guided by the criterion
stated above, may be harmful and unwise to one in Mexico City or
Madrid, whose lodestone is the well-being of New Spain or the
Spanish empire.

[27] *Ibid.*, p. 289.   [28] *Ibid.*, pp. 273–274.

Few were the benefits which either Spain or New Spain derived from the settlement of California, although politically it may have had a certain value as a factor in the international rivalry with England and Russia. Financially, it was a drain on an already heavily-burdened treasury. Administratively, it was one more problem for a harassed executive. Commercially, it produced nothing of notable value. Its defensive worth was dubious. It did not become a land of opportunity for great numbers of the lower classes. Only to the church was it fruitful through its containment of a considerable number of unsaved souls.

If, therefore, Bucareli is to be credited with the responsibility for making firm the Spanish occupation of California, it would appear that he deserves more condemnation than praise, except for the fact that he did succeed in doing what he set out to do. However, it is here argued that the responsibility was not his. The physical project was initiated by Gálvez on the basis of uncertain orders from Spain. Bucareli therefore found the settlements in existence when he became viceroy. Thereafter he followed orders from Spain and accepted or adapted ideas given to him by Echeveste, Serra, Anza, and various juntas.

The position expressed here is not intended to deprive Bucareli of credit which is properly his. He merits recognition for two things: administrative talent, and the ability to follow orders as a good subordinate should. Somehow he found the money with which to support the enterprise, he chose capable leaders for his sea and land expeditions (but not especially so in California itself), he administered a program which kept the settlements supplied, and he carried out orders. But to give him hero status or to attribute to him nobility of character because of these accomplishments seems to me unwarranted. On the other hand, if he does not deserve credit for the achievement of objectives whose merits are assumed but not stated, neither is he to be blamed for possibly harmful results which may stem from the entire policy.

In 1776 California passed beyond Bucareli's executive control by virtue of the creation of the commandancy-general of the *Provincias Internas*. Although Bucareli continued to administer the dispatch of supply ships from San Blas, the Caballero de Croix assumed responsibility for all other aspects of California's development. If such development is regarded as desirable, Croix's administration was unfortunate for California. Because of his concentration on the Indian problem in the older provinces, he neglected the Anza route, as a result of which the Yuma Indians rebelled and the overland passage was closed.[29] Thereafter, California was forced to look inward for further progress, and such supplies as it received from Mexico had to come by sea.

The maintenance of the southern terminal of this sea route, San Blas, caused Bucareli a great deal of trouble. In common with the California settlements which it supplied, San Blas was a new entity. Furthermore, it was also a creation of the energetic Gálvez. According to Viceroy Croix, the *Visitador* first conceived the idea for a port on the Gulf of California in his conversations with Viceroy Marqués de Cruillas about the transportation of troops and goods to Sonora for use against the rebellious Indians there. It was decided that the ships to be used for this purpose should be built in New Spain, and San Blas was chosen as the site for a shipyard.[30] The selection was not a wise one—the port was poor, the climate was unhealthful, and neither livestock nor agriculture flourished in the vicinity.

Late in 1767 Gálvez sent an agent, Manuel Rivero Cordero, to found the port, and in May, 1768, Gálvez went there himself to see to the administrative establishment called the Department of San Blas. The organization came to have three divisions: the department, the arsenal and shipyard, and the fleet. According to the *reglamento* of 1773, with three vessels in operation the annual running cost was to exceed 55,000 pesos. As the activities of the port expanded, so did the problems and the expense.[31]

Bucareli's first difficulty with the department was administrative. In October, 1772, he reported that as a result of dissension between Commissary Francisco Trillo Bermúdez (the chief administrator) and his subordinates, San Blas was in a "deplorable state." Trillo had placed the *contador,* or official auditor, and two other officials under

[29] Chapman (*History,* pp. 330–342) blames Croix for the Yuma massacre. Thomas (*Teodoro de Croix,* p. 59) seeks to exonerate the Caballero.
[30] Croix, Instrucción, AGN, CVB, 1772, Vol. 24, pp. 449–449v.
[31] Chapman, "Difficulties of San Blas," pp. 261–263.

technical arrest, exiling them to Guadalajara. The exiles and other inhabitants protested Trillo's activities to Bucareli, and the Commissary attempted, of course, to defend himself. In addition, the Tribunal of Accounts informed the Viceroy that Trillo's financial reports were confusing and suspect. As a result of all this Bucareli could not get a clear picture of the role the department was to play in the California financing program.

Information secured directly from the parties concerned did not satisfy the Viceroy. Consequently, he decided to send a secret agent to San Blas to take the Commissary and his subordinates by surprise, assume control of the administrative machinery, and make a thorough investigation. For this purpose he chose Domingo del Barco, a royal official of the Guadalajara *caja,* or financial office. His instructions directed Del Barco to effect an immediate seizure of all papers in Trillo's office, in the royal warehouse, and in the treasury offices. He was to audit the accounts quickly and choose a reliable man to help him put things in order. If he found that the three officials exiled to Guadalajara were unjustly accused, Del Barco was empowered to authorize their immediate release and return to duty.[32]

Del Barco was unable to accept the commission. Of the three officials assigned to the Guadalajara *caja,* one was ill and another was convalescing. It was near the end of the year, when all the accounts were due for audit, and Del Barco had to handle the whole thing by himself. Bucareli turned next to Felipe Clere, a royal official in the *caja* of San Luis Potosí.[33] Available documents do not reveal why Clere could not accept the job, but four months later, in March, 1773, Bucareli submitted a report on the man who finally started the investigation, José del Campo Viergol, the *contador* of the *caja* of Pachuca. According to the Viceroy, Viergol was doing excellent work, expecially with respect to the problem which had been worrying Bucareli the most—the prompt dispatch of food ships for California.[34]

[32] Bucareli to Arriaga, October 27, 1772, and inclosure, AGN, CVB, 1772, Vol. 31, No. 643, pp. 76–77v, 295–296.
[33] Same to same, November 26, 1772, AGN, CVB, 1772, Vol. 32, No. 666, pp. 33–34.
[34] Same to same, March 27, 1773, AGN, CVB, 1773, Vol. 36, No. 842, pp. 39v–41.

Trillo was ousted and Viergol became commissary in his place. Viergol soon fell ill, however, and Bucareli had to seek a fourth man for the job. This time his choice fell on Francisco Hijosa, who retained the position until 1778, when José Faustino Ruiz became commissary.[35]

Adequate, skilled personnel to keep the various activities of San Blas going were a constant source of worry to Bucareli. In 1773, to handle the ships on the proposed exploratory voyages along the California coast, he asked that naval officers be sent from Spain. The King promised to send six officers, but they did not reach New Spain until after Juan Pérez had departed on his first voyage.[36]

In 1776 the master shipbuilder, Pedro de Izaguirre, fell seriously ill. He moved to Compostela, where he recovered partially, but he requested, nevertheless, that he be retired. Such was the lack of artisans of his type that Bucareli had to deny the old man's request until a successor could be found. The Viceroy turned to the chief naval officer in Havana for help, with the expressed view that if one could not be found there, he would have to appeal to the King to send one from Spain.[37] Havana, however, had no shipbuilder it could spare. Meanwhile, Izaguirre had returned to the job in San Blas and, in spite of his illness, was supervising the laying of a new keel, with the hope that when that vessel was finished he would be relieved. In Spain the first man whom Charles III selected managed somehow to evade the summons. Finally, late in 1777, one Francisco Segurola left for New Spain to fill the job, but only under protest.[38]

As activities in San Blas expanded, the need for skilled personnel grew more acute. Late in 1776 Bucareli directed that there be held in the port settlement a junta composed of Navy officers, the commissary,

[35] Same to same, December 27, 1774, AGN, CVB, 1774, Vol. 62, No. 1642, pp. 1–4v. Bucareli to Gálvez, August 27, 1778, AGN, CVB, 1778, Vol. 109, No. 3933, pp. 7–7v.
[36] Bucareli to Arriaga, November 27, 1773, AGN, CVB, 1773–1775, Vol. 11, Libro 9, No. 59 or 1182, pp. 56–58v. This letter cites Bucareli's original request for the officers and indicates that it was written in July, 1773.
[37] Bucareli to Gálvez, November 26, 1776, AGN, CVB, 1776, Vol. 85, No. 2594, pp. 20–22.
[38] Same to same, May 27, 1777, AGN, CVB, 1777, Vol. 91, No. 2981, pp. 29–31v. Chapman, "Difficulties of San Blas," p. 269.

and the pilots, to make recommendations on manpower needs. The council submitted a consolidated request for eighty seamen, two first boatswains, four bloodletters, two master lampmakers, two armorers, and twelve master carpenters. The Viceroy acknowledged that these men were needed, but he cut the number of seamen to fifty and ordered the Minister of *Hacienda* in Veracruz to look for them, enjoining Fleet General Antonio de Ulloa to assist him. It was Bucareli's idea to use these men as instructors in a school for seamen which he intended to found in San Blas. When the Veracruz minister reported difficulty in finding the fifty recruits, Bucareli suggested seeking deserters from merchant ships. Before this idea was put into effect, however, the Veracruz recruiter completed his quota and so notified the Viceroy.[39] The other artisans requested by the San Blas junta were apparently picked up from various parts of New Spain and sent to the port.[40]

Another source of worry concerning the California supply port had its origin in the heavy storms which pounded San Blas in November, 1773, depositing a great amount of sand in the anchorage. A solution was hindered because of the Spanish system, Iberian pride, and Bucareli's character. After the Viceroy had received several complaints about the matter, he sought an opinion from Commissary Hijosa. This minister recommended that the port and shipyard be moved either to Chacala or Matanchel, both nearby. Bucareli then requested an opinion of the senior naval officer in San Blas, Lieutenant Ignacio de Arteaga. Arteaga agreed that a change was necessary, but he suggested that Bucareli should first consult certain other naval officers. Since all but one of these were at sea at the time, the project was delayed. Finally, the *expediente* resumed its travels, growing fatter as it passed through the hands of several Navy officers, Hijosa and Arteaga for the second time, Engineer Miguel Constanzó, and the fiscal. The fiscal wrote a summary of all the preceding opinions, which revealed that Matanchel had a good port but offered only a poor site for a town, while Chacala had these virtues in reverse. He therefore recom-

[39] Bucareli to Gálvez, December 26, 1776, AGN, CVB, 1776, Vol. 86, No. 2648, pp. 40v–44.
[40] *Ibid.* Same to same, February 24, 1777, AGN, CVB, 1777, Vol. 88, No. 2754, pp. 13–14.

mended the Spanish colonial vice—further investigation—throwing in Acapulco as a third possible site.[41]

Inasmuch as Bucareli seldom opposed his fiscal, he turned the matter over to Arteaga again. He then called a junta of *Hacienda,* which suggested only that the Viceroy appoint an engineer to inspect the three ports, excluding Acapulco, and then consult with Arteaga and the other Navy officers as to whether or not San Blas could be rehabilitated and, if not, which of the other two should be chosen. Bucareli sent Engineer Miguel del Corral to San Blas, but Corral was unable to submit a recommendation because the disagreement among the naval officers there with respect to what should be done had reached such a bitter stage that consultation was impossible. Corral went ahead with his investigations anyway, and finally reported that San Blas was not as yet completely unserviceable. The file went once more to the fiscal, who sagely observed that because of the discord, no decision had been reached and no progress made. Bucareli then convened another junta of *Hacienda,* which fell back on the old device which suited such circumstances—it recommended that the whole thing be turned over to the King for decision.

In his report on the matter Bucareli concluded by saying that this was what he had wanted to do all along. If San Blas should become useless, he intended to move the base to Acapulco temporarily. It was much closer to Mexico City anyway, he pointed out.[42] In reply Charles III agreed with his viceroy, adding that ultimately a new and better port could be located on the coast of California.[43] None of these plans for a change of site came to fruition.

In justice to Bucareli, however, he must be given credit for his handling of San Blas as the single port and, indeed, the only base from which the new California settlements could be supplied until Anza opened the land route. The problems were many and serious, inasmuch as California was completely dependent on these supplies from Mexico.

[41] Same to same, July 27, 1776, AGN, CVB, 1776, Vol. 81, No. 2394, pp. 42–44.
[42] *Ibid.,* pp. 44v–48.
[43] Same to same, April 26, 1777, AGN, CVB, 1777, Vol. 90, No. 2896, pp. 44v–45v. In this letter Bucareli repeats the King's comment on the matter.

Bucareli demonstrated commendable administrative ability in solving them.

In the first place, the climate of San Blas was such that it was not feasible to store perishable food there for any length of time. Additionally, only certain months were favorable in so far as the sea voyage to California was concerned. The Viceroy therefore coordinated the arrival of food at the port with the time for ship departures, with the result that supplies reached California safely and in good condition. In a like manner he dealt successfully with the shortage of shipping space and the lack of trained personnel. As Chapman points out, Bucareli's merit in this respect was apparently recognized when, in 1776, although California became a part of the new independent commandancy-general of the Interior Provinces, Bucareli was left in charge of the supply system via San Blas.[44]

It is perhaps just to conclude this chapter on a note of praise for Bucareli in view of the iconoclastic character of my earlier discussion which tends to deprive him of what may be conceived of as the excessive glory attributed to him by Chapman. Bucareli does deserve credit for his handling of California's problems. Only the degree of credit he merits is here questioned. Further considerations of a related but more general nature will be made in the concluding analysis of Bucareli's contributions and comparative standing as a viceroy.

---

[44] Chapman, "The Alta California Supply Ships, 1773–1776," pp. 184–194. This article is a detailed account of Bucareli's solutions of the problems arising from the California supply situation.

The Mexican Mining Industry

THE PERIOD of Bucareli's administration is highly significant for the mining industry of New Spain in several respects. For one, the 1770's mark the beginning of an era of exceptional prosperity for Mexican mining, a prosperity dependent, in part, upon a reorganization initiated under Bucareli and involving characteristics almost unique in colonial Mexico.[1] Additionally, and in part complementarily, this decade witnessed the utilization of the mining industry as an avenue for introducing the ideas of the Enlightenment into New Spain, ideas which were destined to have far-reaching effects, not only on the viceroyalty but also on the nation which succeeded it.[2]

The influence of José de Gálvez, initially as *visitador* general and later as Minister of the Indies, was a primary factor in both administrative reorganization and the transfer of new knowledge.[3] Bucareli's role with respect to both of these processes was typical of his general conduct as viceroy and therefore serves a useful purpose as evidence of his capacities. Suggested policies which represented fundamental change tended to arouse his resistance, whereas those which represented mere modification in detail or the achievement of greater efficiency received his support. It may be said that his general administrative technique

[1] Walter Howe, *The Mining Guild of New Spain and its Tribunal General, 1770–1821*, Preface, cited hereafter as *Mining Guild*.

[2] Clement G. Motten, *Mexican Silver and the Enlightenment*, cited hereafter as *Mexican Silver*.

[3] Both Howe and Motten make this clear. For an excellent account of the Gálvez visitation, see Priestley, *José de Gálvez*.

was not that of an originator, but that, instead, he functioned usually as a sort of combination "straw boss" and efficiency expert. Such an evaluation is borne out by his management of the problems of the Mexican mining industry.

New Spain's mineral wealth was of paramount importance to the economic prosperity of the viceroyalty and, indeed, of the entire Spanish empire. Such names as Zacatecas, Guanajuato, Valenciana, and numerous others recall to mind the flood of silver and gold which the great viceroyalty poured into the royal coffers. Shipments of precious metals to the mother country began to assume important proportions after about 1536, when German experts brought in the knowledge and apparatus necessary for smelting silver ore. Tradition has it that in 1557 Bartolomé de Medina introduced the patio amalgamation process using mercury, whereby a greater percentage of mineral could be extracted from the ore, as a result of which production jumped upward.[4]

Although mineral production in New Spain showed a steady, if somewhat slow, increase over the colonial centuries,[5] it is here suggested that the exploitation of the mines was not so effective as it could have been. Government interest in, and control of, mining was so strong as to act as a deterrent to exploitation by individuals, especially in an industry where risk was great and yield uncertain.[6] Technical backwardness boosted the odds in favor of failure. Digging was experimental, European advances in metallurgy were generally unknown, hoisting apparatus were inefficient and neglected, pits and galleries were unwisely and uneconomically constructed, drainage methods were obsolete, ventilation was inadequate, and proper financial backing was lacking.[7]

Despite the fact that the Crown and its agents evinced a constant interest in the revenue to be derived from mining, the government took little significant action to improve the industry until the great reform-

[4] Motten suggests that this traditional account is not precisely correct in all details. *Mexican Silver,* p. 22. See also Haring, *The Spanish Empire in America,* p. 262.

[5] Howe, *Mining Guild,* Appendix A, pp. 453–459, and Motten, *Mexican Silver,* pp. 12, 68, note 2.

[6] Haring, *The Spanish Empire in America,* pp. 276–277.

[7] Bancroft, *Mexico,* Vol. III, p. 597.

ing monarch, Charles III, turned his attention to it. New Spain found the royal interest personalized in *Visitador* General José de Gálvez. The King instructed Gálvez to take special care in ascertaining the status of the mineral industry, the faithfulness with which royal taxes were being collected, and the method of handling mercury distribution.[8]

In compliance with his instructions Gálvez undertook a thorough investigation of the mining industry. He personally inspected many mines throughout the viceroyalty, conferred with their owners, and held consultations with the leading mining experts. On the basis of his observations, he left with Bucareli a list of deficiencies and proposed remedies which, judging from subsequent developments, constituted in broad outline the new viceroy's program for dealing with the problems of the industry. Briefly, Gálvez recommended the following measures:

1. Effective in March, 1768, the price of mercury had been lowered by one-fourth, resulting in a substantial increase in Crown revenues from silver and from increased sales of mercury. The *Visitador* therefore urged a further cut of one-fourth in the price of quicksilver.

2. Inasmuch as many miners still used the smelting process to extract silver, Gálvez suggested a comparable decrease in taxes collected on smelted silver.

3. Although the Crown had assumed the right of coinage in 1733, it still collected a tax for the now nonexistent privilege. Gálvez felt that this tax, called "duplicate seigniorage," should be done away with.

---

[8] José de Gálvez, *Informe instructivo del Visitador Gener.l de Nueva España al Exmo. S.or Virrey de ella don Antonio Bucareli y Ursúa, en cumplimiento de Real Orden de 24 de Mayo de 1771*, Vol. I, p. 158. MS, Huntington Library, San Marino, California. This document is cited hereafter as Informe instructivo. The King was guided in these Instructions by the recommendations of a special commercial council, which he had convened for the purpose of inquiring into the causes of the decline in American trade and revenues, and possible remedies for such decadence. The council proposed a lowering of the import duties on American gold and silver, and a reduction in the price of mercury. Priestley, *José de Gálvez*, pp. 29, 34.

Mercury became a Crown monopoly in the sixteenth century, shortly after the discovery of the amalgamation process. Arthur Preston Whitaker, *The Huancavelica Mercury Mine*, pp. 9–10.

4. The mining industry was suffering a general decline and was held in bad repute. The solution, according to Gálvez, was a new set of ordinances and the establishment of a mining body patterned after the *Consulado de Comercio,* or merchants' guild.

5. The rich Real del Monte mines had been closed for several years because their owner, the Count of Regla, had ceased operations in the face of repeated uprisings among the workers. Bucareli was advised to establish peace in the area and convince the Count that he should resume production.

6. Gálvez recommended that certain offices, at that time leased, be returned to royal control.

7. Finally, he urged Bucareli to devise some method for halting the extensive contraband exportation of gold.[9]

It is apparent from these recommendations that the mining industry of New Spain was not enjoying a maximum prosperity. Indeed, Gálvez spoke of the backwardness of the industry, and, with reference to the mines, of the "total abandonment or appreciable decadence in which various of them are found."[10] One local official claimed that production had fallen off one-third in recent years.[11] One of the best descriptions of the status of mining in the early 1770's comes from the operators themselves. In a lengthy printed pamphlet delivered to Bucareli in 1774, two mining experts, Juan Lucas de Lassaga and Joaquín Velázquez de León, outlined the condition of the industry, the reasons for its decadence, and the remedies which they judged would be most efficacious in its revival.[12] A summary of their diagnosis is appropriate here, though the pamphlet will be discussed at some length later in this chapter.

After a brief reference to mining as practiced by the Indians, the two experts pointed out the haphazard and negligent manner in which the Spaniards had exploited the mineral wealth of New Spain. Care-

---

[9] Gálvez, Informe instructivo, Vol. I, pp. 160–184.

[10] *Ibid.,* pp. 157, 159.

[11] Priestley, *José de Gálvez,* p. 181.

[12] Juan Lucas de Lassaga and Joaquín Velázquez de León, *Representación que a nombre de la Minería de esta Nueva España, hacen al Rey, Nuestro Señor los apoderados de ella . . . ,* AGN, CVB, 1774, Vol. 59, Libro 2, of No. 1534, pp. 322–377v. This work is cited hereafter as *Representación.*

lessness had frequently been responsible for the piercing of extensive subterranean water deposits, which flooded the mines. Because of ignorance and lack of sufficient capital for costly drainage operations, the owners abandoned many of the mines, leaving in them riches greater than those already extracted. As a consequence, the writers claimed, the oldest and principal mines were being only scantily worked because they were flooded and were mere "useless deposits of great riches and sad monuments of former opulence," not producing a tenth of what they could with even minimum rehabilitation. The experts admitted that there were certain mines which were not in such a bad state, but overall, they said, production was only about a third of what it should be. They averred that making capital available for loans was the principal remedy needed.[13]

A second major factor in mining decadence was the lack of organization within the industry. They pictured the Guild of Miners as headless, disunified, confused, and generally useless, in no way comparable to the *Consulado de Comercio,* the model they aspired to emulate. Closely related to this deficiency was the obsolete set of ordinances by which the industry was regulated. As a remedy they recommended a complete new code of laws. The two reviewers then discussed certain lesser but nevertheless important causes for the substandard status of mining. These included: unscientific exploitation of mineral wealth and a scarcity of expert knowledge or source of instruction; the collection of duplicate seigniorage; the poor transportation system; and the periodic scarcity of mercury.[14]

Despite his early statement that the mining industry was, on the whole, "in a flourishing state,"[15] Bucareli's actions indicate that he recognized the need for improving its condition, although, to be sure, his course was not going to be a precipitate one. Probably on the basis of one of Gálvez' recommendations, Bucareli first turned his attention to the problem of the Vizcaína vein in El Monte mining district near Pachuca.

[13] *Ibid.,* pp. 322, 334v.
[14] *Ibid.,* pp. 339–341, 347–353, 372–376.
[15] Bucareli to Charles III, December 24, 1771, AGN, CVB, 1771–1772, Vol. 6, Libro 5, No. 12, p. 10.

This vein had produced well until early in the eighteenth century, when water invaded the shafts. In 1762 Pedro Romero de Terreros, later the Count of Regla, began draining the mines and, at great cost, succeeded in getting production under way once more. Then, in 1766, the workers rebelled against some attempted changes in the system of payment, killing an *alcalde mayor* and nearly killing Romero de Terreros. The motivation for the rebellion stemmed from an effort to alter the traditional method of payment whereby the workers received a daily wage plus one-half of the ore they carried out above a set amount. This was called the *partido* system. The overseers suspected fraudulent practices with respect to the *partido,* as a result of which it was abolished and various other systems were tried as substitutes. The workers resisted these variations and eventually resorted to violence. Romero de Terreros, already one of the wealthiest men in New Spain, consequently withdrew from working the mines except for leaving some Indians and Negro slaves in three of the nine shafts in order to keep valid his claims under the law.[16] Troops suppressed the revolt, including some later brief spasms of violence, and remained stationed nearby to maintain an uneasy peace.

During the remainder of his viceregency the Marqués de Croix made several attempts to rectify the situation, but when Bucareli assumed office little progress had been made. After a close examination of the antecedents, the new Viceroy expressed his opinion on various aspects of the case, and in so doing affords us insight into several facets of his character and his framework of thought. With respect to the rebellion he said:[17]

Once the restraint of obedience is broken, the common people are be-latedly and poorly reduced to their old subjection, and much less so the mining people, vicious because of their breeding and customs, proud and insolent because they consider themselves necessary and because they are united in order to sustain themselves in whatever dispute.

With reference to the question of abolition or retention of the *partido* system, he stated:[18]

---

[16] *Ibid.,* pp. 10–12.   [17] *Ibid.,* pp. 12–13.   [18] *Ibid.,* pp. 15v–16v.

I hold as one of the principal maxims of good government to make no change in old customs when they are not harmful, or when it is intended to establish them as a result of common recognition and considerable utility. I understand that the practice of *partidos* which the mineworkers have is about as old as the mines, and so universal in the kingdom that there is scarcely a mine where it is not in use.

He then pointed out that if, in an isolated case, an attempt to suppress the *partido* had resulted in such upheaval, a general application of the abolition would drive the workers to desperation and would lead to the abandonment of many mines. He concluded, therefore, that the custom should be retained.[19] On the other hand, the Count of Regla, having prudently retired from the mining scene, was convinced that the *partido* system lay at the root of the trouble, and insisted that it be abolished before he would resume operations. Meanwhile, noted Bucareli, the inhabitants of Vizcaína were unemployed, banditry was on the increase, commerce in the nearby towns was at a standstill, and the royal treasury was not receiving its customary income. "All these considerations have filled me with bitterness," he lamented.[20]

Nevertheless, he had a solution to offer, although he defined it as a "radical remedy." He proposed a new general ordinance for all mines, insisting that, in spite of the fact that from the rest of the mining districts other than El Monte there had been no complaint about the *partido,* uniformity must prevail in order that the workers would not all flock to the preferred workings and leave the less desirable areas depopulated. For guidance in creating the new law Bucareli suggested the formation of mining juntas in all mining districts, to be composed of representatives of both owners and workers. The juntas were to meet in their own areas, thus avoiding the expense of a trip to the capital for a general meeting, and also allowing the poorer members to attend as well as the wealthy. He had not gone ahead with the project, he said, until he could secure royal approval.[21]

In the meantime, Bucareli had endeavored to convince the Count of Regla that he should begin rehabilitating his mines once more, with a

[19] *Ibid.,* pp. 19–24.   [21] *Ibid.,* pp. 25v–27.
[20] *Ibid.,* pp. 24–25v.

view to an early renewal of production. In the correspondence which ensued between the two, Bucareli gradually won over the nobleman, but only by acceding to certain demands for safety precautions which Regla set forth.²² The Viceroy proceeded with the execution of these measures. First, he requested from the royal officials of Pachuca secret reports on the individuals living in Real del Monte who, having been involved in the 1766 tumult, had served their sentences or had received pardons. These luckless persons Bucareli planned to exile from the area in order to ease the mind of Regla and to serve as a warning to other would-be rebels. Next, he ordered that the detachment of cavalry stationed in Pachuca be changed to infantry and be transferred to Real del Monte proper, where it could respond to call more quickly. Finally, the Viceroy promised the Count help in securing additional laborers.²³

Bucareli reported these facts to Charles III in December, 1771. By March, 1772, he had enforced a decree ridding Real del Monte of its known turbulent characters, the troops had been rearranged as planned, and all was ready for Regla to resume operations.²⁴ By October, 1774, major preparations were completed and general drainage was begun.²⁵ Apparently the mines resumed production early in 1775, for in December, 1774, Bucareli appointed a special judge to serve in El Monte district, to be paid by Regla and to assist the Count in securing an adequate flow of labor for the mines.²⁶

²² The gist of this correspondence, seven letters in all, is contained in *ibid.,* pp. 27–27v, but the copies of the letters do not appear in their customary location in the volumes of Bucareli's correspondence, nor did a search in other likely places bring them to light.

²³ *Ibid.,* pp. 27–28v.

²⁴ Bucareli to Arriaga, March 25, 1772, AGN, CVB, 1772, Vol. 22, No. 299, pp. 29–30v. Charles III approved Bucareli's measures and his agreements with Regla. Arriaga to Bucareli, July 20, 1772, AGN, RC, 1772, Vol. 101, No. 21, p. 27.

²⁵ Bucareli to Arriaga, October 26, 1774, AGN, CVB, 1773–1775, Vol. 11, Libro 9, No. 82 or 1595, p. 114.

²⁶ Same to same, December 27, 1774, AGN, CVB, 1774, Vol. 62, No. 1665, pp. 68v–76v. Charles III approved Bucareli's action by a Royal *Cédula* dated April 30, 1777, AGN, RC, 1777, Vol. 101, No. 286, pp. 450–455v.

Although Miguel O. de Mendizábal offers no precise time for the resumption of production, he does say, ". . . the exploitation of the mines of Real del Monte re-

Within the year Bucareli had an opportunity to demonstrate further his willingness to protect Regla from any possible recurrence of rebellion. In November, 1775, eighteen of twenty released prisoners coming to New Spain from Havana aroused the curiosity of Squadron Commander Juan Bautista Bonet. He inquired into their pasts, discovered that they had been deeply involved in the 1766 riots, and notified Bucareli. The Viceroy feared that if they returned to a mining district they would again cause trouble. He therefore ordered the *alcaldes mayores* of six major mining areas to watch for these men, and if they found any of them in their territories, to force the former prisoners to move elsewhere, under threat of further punishment.[27]

In this manner, then, did Bucareli succeed in his first attempt to improve mining production through the rehabilitation of one of New Spain's major abandoned veins. In another similar case, however, the initiation was not the Viceroy's, but came rather from one of the most famous men in New Spain's mining history. José de la Borda had made and lost several fortunes through direct participation in the search for, and the production of, precious metals. When Gálvez wrote about him in 1771 he commented that the old prospector was nearly blind and had retired to Tasco.[28] Nevertheless, in 1768 the Crown had granted him several special concessions with respect to the price of mercury and freedom from taxes, in return for which De la Borda proposed to rehabilitate the once-opulent Quebradilla mine in the Zacatecas district.[29] Apparently he did not immediately take advantage of these concessions, for early in 1777 Bucareli reported that De la Borda had approached him at some unspecified date since 1773, presenting his plan to work the mine. The Viceroy encouraged him, but noted in a letter to Madrid that the obstacles to be overcome were such as to discourage any man other than De la Borda. By March,

---

turned to its old activity and production was maintained in a prosperous state." "Los Minerales de Pachuca y Real del Monte en la época colonial," *El Trimestre Económico*, Vol. VIII (1941), p. 304.

[27] Bucareli to Arriaga, November 26, 1775, in Velasco Ceballos, *La administración de ... Bucareli*, Vol. II, pp. 377–388.

[28] Gálvez, Informe instructivo, Vol. I, pp. 159–160.

[29] Bucareli to Gálvez, October 27, 1777, AGN, CVB, 1777, Vol. 96, No. 3303, p. 19.

1777, he had drained the mine sufficiently to produce ore samples which promised profitable operation.[30]

It would appear that these promises were fulfilled, because within a few months the royal officials of Zacatecas, bearing large rolls of red tape, entered upon the scene. In the ensuing flurry of representations, *expedientes,* indorsements, and opinions, Bucareli demonstrated a commendable capacity for common sense and fair dealing. The royal officials raised doubts concerning De la Borda's position under the royal grant of 1768, but in almost every case Bucareli settled in favor of the old miner.[31] Perhaps he was partly motivated by the genuine admiration for De la Borda which appears in his correspondence about him. As a result, De la Borda was treated generously, inasmuch as Charles III approved wholeheartedly Bucareli's decisions.[32]

Two completed rehabilitations of major abandoned mines in a term of more than seven years is not an outstanding record.[33] It is probable, however, that Bucareli was not to blame. As will be shown below, it was more the system which retarded activity of this type rather than the character of the Viceroy. Nevertheless, it bears repeating that in the two instances related, Bucareli undertook the Regla problem on the recommendation of Gálvez, and with respect to De la Borda's work, the miner himself was the initiator. In the matter of mine rehabilitation, Bucareli demonstrated little initiative. Whether viceregal aggressiveness could have produced a more fruitful result is a matter of conjecture.

[30] Same to same, March 27, 1777, AGN, CVB, 1777, Vol. 89, No. 2848, pp. 73–75. Gálvez acknowledged the report and expressed the King's pleasure in a letter to Bucareli dated July 14, 1777, AGN, RC, 1777, Vol. 11, No. 156, p. 253.
[31] Bucareli to Gálvez, October 27, 1777, in Velasco Ceballos, *La administración de . . . Bucareli,* Vol. II, pp. 384–387.
[32] Gálvez to Bucareli, February 24, 1778, AGN, RC, 1778, Vol. 113, No. 110, pp. 156–156v.
[33] Bucareli took part in the early stages of one more attempt to revive an abandoned deposit. In 1779 two miners formed a stock company to finance the rehabilitation of a series of mines in a hill called La Compaña in the Tasco district. They petitioned the Viceroy for permission to proceed, and Bucareli's report to the Crown was generally favorable. Bucareli to Gálvez, January 27, 1779, AGN, CVB, 1779, Vol. 115, No. 4222, pp. 7v–9v. Before a reply could come from Spain, however, Bucareli died, and the matter was left to his successor.

Perhaps the same thing may be said with respect to the discovery of new mines. It is true that royal revenue from mining increased during Bucareli's term, and in view of the facts on rehabilitation in the same period it seems probable that mines of this type contributed only slightly to the increase. With respect to income from silver, the increase was consistent and occasionally notable, but the increase from gold must be regarded as remarkable. In the six years from 1765 through 1770 the annual revenue from gold, in thousands of pesos, was 76, 69, 73, 92, 83, and 68; in the six years from 1771 through 1776, the figures are 102, 115, 96, 97, 100, and 92. In 1777 the figure dropped to 64, in 1778 to 19, and thereafter through 1789 averaged about 14.[34] The principal source of this increase was the placer mines called La Cieneguilla in Sonora.

Discovered late in the term of the Marqués de Croix, these mines reached boom proportions under Bucareli and were destined to cause him a great amount of trouble. Early in 1772 he received an inquiry from Arriaga, quoting a report from Croix on the Cieneguilla placers and asking for information on their development. Bucareli directed his secretary to gather the required information from the letters of Intendant Pedro de Corbalán, of Sonora, and prepare the report requested.[35] Apparently the report thus prepared was too vague, judging from the rebuke administered by Arriaga when he wrote, ". . . the King orders me to tell Your Excellency that the true measure of such discoveries is for Your Excellency to confirm them through the product of *diezmos* in the *cajas marcas* of the district. Without this test and other reports from experienced miners and their backers, which Your Excellency has in that capital, Your Excellency will have difficulty in verifying the reports which, because of interest or bias, are regularly enlarged."[36]

At this point the Viceroy's correspondence is difficult to understand.

[34] Fabián de Fonseca and Carlos de Urrutía, *Historia general de real hacienda*, Vol. I, pp. 40–43.

[35] Arriaga to Bucareli, November 23, 1771, and attached, undated note bearing Bucareli's rubric, AGN, RC, 1771, Vol. 99, No. 92, pp. 143–144.

[36] Same to same, March 18, 1772, AGN, RC, 1772, Vol. 100, No. 97, pp. 170–170v. The *diezmo* was the tax of 10 per cent on all mined silver and gold. A *caja marca* was a subtreasury office located in a frontier area.

In one letter to Arriaga, dated July 26, 1772, he acknowledged the truth of the King's statement, but plead in extenuation that what news there was from Sonora was contradictory and confusing. He had requested detailed reports of Governor Matéo Sastre, Corbalán, and Colonel Domingo Elizondo, but the first two had not yet given any answer and Elizondo had not finished his report.[37] In another letter of the same date, also to Arriaga, he mentioned the "confused and discordant" reports of Corbalán and Lieutenant Pedro de Tueros, Corbalán's assistant, on the status of the Cieneguilla placers.[38] With or without the reports, however, he was unable to give the King the information the latter desired. Again in October, 1772, in answer to another royal request for details on Sonora mining, Bucareli had to admit that although he had received letters from Corbalán and Tueros, they were still confusing and did not provide the information he had repeatedly asked for. He promised that as soon as he obtained such details he would relay them immediately to the King.[39]

Not until January, 1773, did two of the long-awaited reports reach the capital. They answered most of Bucareli's and the King's questions. They accounted for the expenditure of 180,000 pesos allotted by the Crown for the purchase of gold. Tueros told of the government established, the standard of living of the inhabitants, the condition of the placers, and the possible bonanza they offered, although he suggested that a greater effort would be necessary if they were to prove a bonanza. Corbalán repeated much that Tueros reported, but he also enclosed a number of significant documents of a financial nature. One revealed that as of November 17, 1772, the royal *caja* at Los Alamos had already collected in *diezmos* and seigniorage on gold alone more than 72,000 pesos. Since the total royal revenue for all of New Spain from gold in 1772 was 115,000 pesos, the importance of the Cieneguilla placers is obvious. Other statements revealed the quantity of gold thus far shipped to Mexico, the cost of handling, and the details of the

[37] Bucareli to Arriaga, July 26, 1772, AGN, CVB, 1772, Vol. 28, No. 458, pp. 4–5.
[38] Same to same, July 26, 1772, *ibid.,* No. 459, pp. 5–5v.
[39] Same to same, October 27, 1772, AGN, CVB, 1772, Vol. 31, No. 614, pp. 40–41.

Crown's gold purchases. Bucareli concluded his extract to Arriaga by commenting that he had ordered the Sonora officials to watch carefully for fraudulent extractions of gold, to facilitate the influx of more workers, to maintain good relations with merchants and inhabitants, and to check closely and report in detail on the amounts of gold registered at the Alamos *caja* and the royal revenues derived therefrom.[40]

In February, 1773, the Viceroy received from Tueros a pessimistic report. Written the preceding December, the letter noted that gold production had fallen off but that would-be miners, three-fourths of them Indians, were still pouring in, and that unless some new placers were found they would become discouraged and leave. Furthermore, food was becoming scarce. Tueros expressed hope, however, for an unexploited area which showed promise. In his reply Bucareli could only encourage the Lieutenant in his ideas about this new possibility.[41] Tueros' next letter, written about one month later, indicated that the hoped-for strike had not as yet materialized.[42]

Production stayed steadily at the same level throughout the next two and a half years, in spite of Tueros' gloomy prediction. Then, early in the fall of 1775, new discoveries were made. Tueros now found cause for worry in possible attacks by hostile Indians, asking special troop protection for the mining area. Bucareli complied by issuing appropriate orders to Commandant Inspector Hugo O'Conor, who was then commanding the troops of the interior areas.[43] That Tueros continued his appeals for troop support is evidenced by Bucareli's reference to ". . . the clamors which that officer repeats from time to time,"[44] and

[40] Same to same, January 27, 1772, AGN, CVB, 1772, Vol. 34, No. 740, pp. 40–44. Charles III approved Bucareli's handling of the matter in Arriaga to Bucareli, May 12, 1773, AGN, RC, 1773, Vol. 102, No. 132, pp. 236–236v.

[41] Bucareli to Arriaga, February 24, 1772; Tueros to Bucareli, December 1, 1772; Bucareli to Tueros, February 24, 1773, AGN, CVB, 1773, Vol. 35, No. 797 and inclosures, pp. 15v–16v, 58–59v, 60.

[42] Bucareli to Arriaga, March 27, 1773, AGN, CVB, 1773, Vol. 36, No. 837, pp. 30–31.

[43] Same to same, November 26, 1775, AGN, CVB, 1775, Vol. 73, No. 2037, pp. 7–8.

[44] Bucareli to Gálvez, September 26, 1776, AGN, CVB, 1776, Vol. 83, No. 2497, p. 33v.

by the fact that Charles III at a later date ordered the Viceroy to accede to the Lieutenant's requests.[45] Commandant O'Conor and Governor Sastre did not agree with Tueros. O'Conor expressed his willingness to aid Tueros whenever it might be necessary, but he found the Lieutenant's fears "unbelievable," and characterized the officer as "flighty." Sastre corroborated O'Conor's statements, pointing out the untrustworthy nature of Tueros' past predictions on the same subject. Bucareli was inclined to hold the same opinion.[46]

The disagreement was apparently without much significance, however. In 1776 the royal revenue from gold totaled 92,000 pesos. In 1777 it fell to 64,000 pesos, the lowest since before the initial Cieneguilla discovery, and in 1778 it dropped to 19,000 pesos. The Cieneguilla boom was through.[47]

Silver, not gold, was the cornerstone of New Spain's wealth, and during Bucareli's viceregency royal income from this source climbed. For the seven years preceding his term the annual revenue, in thousands of pesos, averaged 1,380. During the seven full years of his command the average was 1,725. In 1776 it exceeded 2,000, while in 1777 it reached 1,965.[48] The sources of this increase were several. Some undoubtedly came from the rehabilitated mines of Regla and De la Borda. Recognition must also be given to the greater production from established mines brought about by the lowered price of mercury. Finally, a few new major silver deposits were discovered during Bucareli's viceregency, although the big strikes came near the end of his term.

In May, 1772, the governor of Coahuila, Jacobo de Ugarte y Loyola, reported the discovery of two new mines in his jurisdiction and sent some promising ore samples to Mexico City. Bucareli immediately ordered that extra mercury be sent from the nearest royal stores at San Luis Potosí and instructed Ugarte to proceed with the usual

[45] Gálvez to Bucareli, October 18, 1776, AGN, RC, 1776, Vol. 109, No. 37, p. 106.

[46] Bucareli to Gálvez, September 26, 1776, AGN, CVB, 1776, Vol. 83, No. 2497, pp. 34–35.

[47] Priestley, *José de Gálvez*, p. 317.

[48] *Ibid.*

governmental organization for the workers arriving at the mines.[49] The next month Ugarte reported on the progress in the mines, the control he was exercising over labor distribution and wages, and the *partido* percentage being used. In return the Viceroy inquired whether proper care was being taken to protect the royal interests, suggesting the dispatch of a special official to supervise the collection of *diezmos* and seigniorage.[50] Unfortunately, further documentation is lacking on these discoveries, and since the available sources make no mention of the name given the two mines or of the district of their location, it is difficult to trace their later development.

In the last year of Bucareli's viceregency two promising discoveries were made. The first occurred near Hostotipoquillo in Guadalajara province. The regent of the Guadalajara *Audiencia* interviewed the discoverer, who reported that the seam was exceptionally wide, the ore of good weight, and that there were already thirty other excavations under way near his original diggings. Since the area was well populated, development proceeded quickly and smoothly, with less of a boom aspect apparent.[51] The main mine, called Santa María de la Yesca, held up well, and numerous other profitable strikes were made nearby. The royal officials of Bolaños, the location of the nearest *caja,* reported highly satisfactory activity in the taxation process.[52] The greatest profit from these mines, however, came after Bucareli's death.

News of the second major discovery reached the Viceroy less than a month before he died. A militiaman from San Luis Potosí, while searching for a lost horse, came upon a seam of silver of extreme richness. There ensued an immediate rush to the area, with more than two hundred mines registered in less than a month. Accompanying the report of discovery which Bucareli received was a petition from the Commandant of the San Luis Potosí militia. Apparently the soldier-

[49] Bucareli to Arriaga, May 24, 1772, AGN, CVB, 1772, Vol. 24, No. 369, pp. 15–16.

[50] Same to same, June 26, 1772, AGN, CVB, 1772, Vol. 25, No. 452, pp. 40–41.

[51] Bucareli to Gálvez, July 27, 1778, and inclosure, Eusebio Sánchez Pareja to Bucareli, June 26, 1778, AGN, CVB, 1778, Vol. 108, No. 3882, pp. 30–31, 134–135.

[52] Gálvez to Bucareli, April 23, 1779, AGN, RC, 1779, Vol. 115, No. 171, p. 311.

discoverer, who remains nameless in the Viceroy's correspondence, was not to be allowed to enjoy his sudden wealth indefinitely, for his solicitous commanding officer asked to be named as his guardian. The soldier was, he said, "abusing his own good luck, . . . possessed of the sins of drunkenness and gambling, in which he was iniquitously investing the profits of his fortune." In order to gain some measure of control over the riotous conditions in the boom area, the Viceroy transferred certain officials from San Luis Potosí to nearby Los Alamos. Their tasks were to inspect the mines, regulate the flow of silver through the proper channels for taxation, clean up the black market in mercury, investigate the wishes of the soldier-discoverer with respect to a guardian, and effect a general return to law and order.[53] Bucareli, of course, did not live to see his orders carried out.

The foregoing, then, were the major discoveries of new gold and silver deposits during Bucareli's time, or at least those important enough to command space in his voluminous correspondence with Spain. There were other strikes of a lesser nature, and there were profitable new developments in established mining areas, such as in the Valenciana mine in Guanajuato, the veins in the Catorce district in San Luis Potosí, the Veta Negra in Zacatecas.[54] All of these contributed to the increased royal revenue which Bucareli was pleased to report. But the production of precious metals in New Spain at no time approached the potential of the area. Early in his viceregency Bucareli proposed to find out why.

On July 1, 1772, he dispatched to the ministers of all the *cajas* in the viceroyalty a request for detailed reports on the status of mining in each district, to include a listing of mines working at full production, those at only half production, and those abandoned. The reports trickled in— some never came. Finally, in May, 1774, the secretariat drew up an extract of the information received. It indicated a general lack of vigor in the mining industry and offered an infinite number of causes for the decadence; but certain alleged causes were common to nearly all

[53] Bucareli to Gálvez, March 27, 1779, AGN, CVB, 1779, Vol. 117, No. 4378, pp. 38–42v.
[54] Bancroft, *Mexico,* Vol. III, pp. 588–589.

the reports from all the mining districts, and one of these was the need for a new system of mercury pricing, allotment, and distribution.[55]

Mercury had occupied a vital position in the Spanish system since early in the colonial period. Its function as a producer of revenue was twofold. First, as a government monopoly its sale to miners at a controlled price was a profitable business. Second, because the amount of silver a miner produced could be calculated on the basis of the amount of mercury he used, the Crown could keep a close check on production, thereby forestalling fraudulent extraction and sale of bullion without taxation. Francisco de Toledo, a viceroy of Peru, gave impetus to government control when he expropriated the Huancavelica Mercury mine in 1570. Thereafter, quicksilver could not be mined with anything approaching the individual freedom that applied to other metals. A discoverer enjoyed the fruits of his single strike, but all other parts of the same deposit belonged to the Crown. Furthermore, the discoverer's share reverted to the Crown when he died.[56]

The mercury used in New Spain came in large part from the great Almadén mines in Spain. Whenever these deposits failed to produce an ample quantity, the deficit was supplied from Austria, at an increased price. Occasionally it came from China, and, rarely, from Peru.[57] There was no middleman involved in the distribution. A miner secured his supply at one of the *cajas reales,* or subtreasuries, scattered throughout New Spain. He was then obliged to make a return to the *caja* of a corresponding amount of silver, called the *correspondido.* Until this was done, no more quicksilver was forthcoming.[58] One important disadvantage of the system was that a miner could not purchase a small amount of mercury—sales were made only in large lots. The small miner was thus compelled either to use the less

[55] Bucareli to Arriaga, May 27, 1774, and inclosure, AGN, CVB, 1774, Vol. 54, No. 1396, pp. 17–18, 85–107.

[56] Whitaker, *The Huancavelica Mercury Mine,* pp. 9–10.

[57] Bancroft, *Mexico,* Vol. III, p. 583. Howe suggests that the use of Peruvian mercury was not unusual in New Spain. *Mining Guild,* p. 11. On the other hand, in a letter of June 26, 1777, to Gálvez, Bucareli observed that when supplies of mercury from Spain were inadequate, the scarcity of Peruvian mercury made it dangerous to rely on that source. AGI, Mex., Leg. 1381.

[58] Bancroft, *Mexico,* Vol. III, p. 583.

profitable smelting process, to buy illegally from a wealthier miner, if possible, or to go out of business.

Late in Croix's viceregency, Gálvez and Croix acceded to a request from some Zacatecas miners that this ruling be relaxed. They ordered the sale of mercury in small amounts and for cash—that is, without the *correspondido*. When Bucareli assumed office, he confirmed the arrangement.[59] At the same time that he took this action he was study-ing the advisability of recommending a possible change in the price of mercury.

From a cost of 187 pesos per quintal (101.43 lb.) in 1590, de-livered in Veracruz, the price had gradually declined to 62 pesos in 1768, immediately prior to which it had been 82 pesos.[60] This latest cut had come as the result of the combined efforts of Gálvez and Croix, who argued that cheaper mercury would, in the long run, bring a greater income through increased sales of quicksilver and a resultant increased production of silver. Their theory was validated as income from *diezmos* jumped, the mint coined more money, and sales of mercury increased. When the King granted the lower price, he indi-cated that if the theory worked, another cut of one-fourth would be allowed. The *Visitador* and the Marqués joined in urging Bucareli to press for such a decrease.[61]

Although Croix had also proposed this second cut to the King, he had not himself complied with a royal request for a special report on the income from silver taxes since the first decrease. Early in 1772, therefore, Bucareli received from Spain a request for this information, to be accompanied by an expression of his opinion on the matter. The Viceroy in turn asked the superintendents of the *Ramo de Azogues* (mercury branch) and the mint for the required data.[62] If Bucareli subsequently submitted the report, mention of it does not appear in his

---

[59] Arriaga to Bucareli, November 12, 1773, AGN, RC, 1773, Vol. 103, No. 127, p. 305.

[60] Priestley, *José de Gálvez*, p. 242 n.

[61] Gálvez, Informe instructivo, Vol. I, pp. 160–166. Croix, Instrucción, AGN, CVB, 1772, Vol. 24, pp. 432v–434.

[62] Arriaga to Bucareli, November 23, 1771, and Bucareli's attached note of instruc-tions, *ca.* March 1, 1772, AGN, RC, 1771, Vol. 99, No. 93, pp. 145–146 and at-tached unnumbered page.

correspondence. It is not clear, therefore, what part his response or lack of response may have played in the next phase of Crown policy with respect to mercury.

In November, 1773, Bucareli received instructions providing for a significant rearrangement of the mercury distribution system. This alteration was part of a general plan for strengthening the mining industry. Without making any immediate changes, the Viceroy was to convene a special junta of major officials connected with mining, the fiscal, and certain leaders in the industry. He himself was to preside. The junta's task was to establish a method whereby, within a year, mercury distribution to individual miners would be handled by local mining deputations or councils rather than by the royal subtreasuries. Furthermore, the junta was to recommend the lowest feasible price for which mercury could be sold. Finally, it was ordered that the junta discuss a revised set of ordinances for the mining industry and re-establishment along the lines of the *Consulado de Comercio*.[63] Bucareli gave the matter priority, ordering the immediate notification of the members of the junta and setting regular meeting times for the body. Although he allowed the members from outlying areas two months to reach Mexico, it was not until May 13 that the junta held its first session.[64] The members who were professional miners came prepared. They presented a lengthy printed pamphlet outlining their plan for the creation of a powerful mining organization, which was their main interest and about which more will be said later.

With respect to the mercury question, they had several serious objections to the King's plan that retail distribution be handled by local mining deputations. It was pointed out that, in many mining districts, there was no individual wealthy enough to finance the necessary wholesale purchase prior to retailing the metal. Furthermore, they said, it would be a full-time job, and the distributor would have to abandon his mines. As an alternative they suggested that in each dis-

[63] Arriaga to Bucareli, November 12, 1773, AGN, RC, 1773, Vol. 103, No. 127, pp. 305–308.

[64] Bucareli's endorsement on *ibid.*, February 16, 1774. Also, Bucareli to Arriaga, February 21, 1774, AGN, CVB, 1774, Vol. 48, No. 1290, pp. 22v–25v. This letter relates in detail the convening procedure. Same to same, May 27, 1774, AGN, CVB, 1774, Vol. 54, No. 1397, pp. 18v–20v.

trict the miners select a trustworthy merchant, to be known as the *Mercader Repartidor de Azogues,* to handle the job, operating under the supervision of the local mining council. Finally, the mining deputies urged the abolition of the *correspondido,* to be replaced by a system of mutual responsibility in each mining district, with all miners jointly guaranteeing the proper return in silver—possibly a suggestion of dubious value among a group as individualistic as were the miners of New Spain.[65] As for the price of mercury, the junta expressed approval of another cut, without specifying the amount.[66]

At this point there occurred what appears to have been a series of misunderstandings between the Viceroy and the Crown, caused by explanatory letters passing one another on the Atlantic. Bucareli opposed another decrease in the mercury price on the grounds that the recent increase in income from precious metal had resulted from causes other than the first cut—principally from the extraction of higher-grade ores. In addition, because he did not approve of the printed plan for the creation of a mining *consulado,* he decided that the whole matter needed further consideration and consultation with Madrid. He therefore suspended the junta meetings indefinitely.[67] Before his letter telling of his action reached Spain, however, Charles III approved the recommendations of the junta on mercury distribution, but asked when he would get a specific recommendation on the minimum price.[68] This was in October, 1774. The stalemate appears to have lasted for more than a year, although the reason for its prolongation is not clear. Not until March, 1776, does the subject reappear in a letter from Gálvez to Bucareli, reminding the Viceroy that the King was awaiting action on the mercury question.[69] In reply, Bucareli reviewed the entire

[65] *Expediente* marked as inclosure to No. 1397 above. Inclusive dates, November 12, 1773–June 10, 1774, AGN, CVB, 1774, Vol. 54, of No. 1397, pp. 108–128.
[66] Bucareli to Arriaga, September 26, 1774, AGN, CVB, 1774, Vol. 58, No. 1534, p. 32v.
[67] *Ibid.,* pp. 30–33.
[68] Arriaga to Bucareli, October 12, 1774, AGN, RC, 1774, Vol. 104, No. 96, pp. 215–215v.
[69] Gálvez to Bucareli, March 27, 1776, AGN, RC, 1776, Vol. 107, No. 117, p. 215.

situation in detail. He defended himself by stating that when he suspended the junta he had written his reasons for doing so, and that since then he had been awaiting the King's decisions on the questions raised. As a result, he said, the entire subject had been held in abeyance.[70]

Although it did not settle the other questions about mining which Bucareli had raised, the King's answer, dated October 4, 1776, did put an end to the question of the proposed lowering of the price of mercury by ordering another decrease of one-fourth. Since he also desired that miners who smelted silver be granted a parallel compensation, he advised the Viceroy to meet again with the junta to decide on the corresponding alteration of the taxes on this product.[71] Bucareli did not make the price cut immediately effective inasmuch as at that time—early in 1777—the amount of mercury on hand was small, and he feared that a buying rush would empty the warehouses. He chose, therefore, to make the cut effective on May 1, before which date he expected a large shipment of the metal.[72] Not until mid-1777, then, did the lower price which both Gálvez and Croix had urged in 1771 become established. Also, it came about in the face of Bucareli's opposition, although he had not expressed himself strongly or repetitiously on the subject. It is somewhat surprising that it took place at all, in view of the fact that by the time the action was taken, Bucareli had proved himself an extremely capable administrator in financial matters. With respect to mining, however, Charles III demonstrated a strong advocacy of change and a tendency to follow the recommendations of the miners. It is also well to recall that Gálvez, one of the King's most influential subordinates, favored the change.

The question of price did not comprise the whole of Bucareli's concern with mercury. The mining of this metal in New Spain had long been prohibited. Periodic scarcities caused by the disruption of shipping

---

[70] Bucareli to Gálvez, June 26, 1776, AGN, CVB, 1776, Vol. 80, No. 2306, pp. 16–19.
[71] Gálvez to Bucareli, October 4, 1776, AGN, RC, 1776, Vol. 109, No. 11, pp. 16–17.
[72] Bucareli to Gálvez, February 24, 1777, and inclosures, AGN, CVB, 1777, Vol. 88, No. 2776, pp. 34–36v, 173–175.

from Spain, however, occasioned sporadic efforts to get permission to work the known deposits. The threat of war in 1777, coupled with a chronic shortage of mercury caused by increased consumption, led Charles III to request a report from the Viceroy on the quality and status of the viceroyalty's quicksilver deposits, with an eye to their development in case of need. The resulting report, written in March, 1777, offered little promise, but Bucareli requested that an expert be sent from Spain to make an investigation.[73] In June the deputies of the mining industry presented a petition urging that immediate steps be taken to institute an expert appraisal of mercury resources and to put any workable mines on a productive basis. Bucareli agreed with their contention that a new supply was needed, but both he and the superintendent of *Azogues* frowned on the miners' request for the right to work the mines without the usual government supervision. The Viceroy took no action, referring the matter to Spain.[74]

In Madrid, Charles III proved his continued interest in the idea by ordering an expert from the Almadén mines to go to New Spain with a crew of assistants to conduct a thorough investigation into the viceroyalty's possibilities as a mercury producer.[75] As preparation for the future, the King also instructed the *Cuerpo de Minería* of New Spain to select four students to send to the new School of Subterranean Geometry and Mineralogy in Almadén.[76]

Judging from the rather costly and extensive preparations which were made, both Madrid and Mexico held high hopes for the success of the Almadén experts. A large amount of equipment reached Veracruz and was carefully stored pending the arrival of the survey

[73] Same to same, March 27, 1777, AGN, CVB, 1777, Vol. 89, No. 2844, pp. 60v–70. In this letter Bucareli reviewed the history of searches for mercury deposits which had been made during the eighteenth century. He found the results generally discouraging.

[74] Same to same, June 26, 1777, and inclosure, AGN, CVB, 1777, Vol. 92, No. 3031, pp. 5–9, 82–90. The inclosure includes the petition and the several endorsements thereon as it passed from office to office. The cover-letter alone is also found in Velasco Ceballos, *La administración de . . . Bucareli,* Vol. II, pp. 393–396.

[75] Gálvez to Bucareli, July 2, 1777, AGN, RC, 1777, Vol. 111, No. 118, p. 196. Bucareli acknowledged this letter in Bucareli to Gálvez, November 26, 1777, AGN, CVB, 1777, Vol. 97, No. 3389, p. 38v.

[76] Gálvez to Bucareli, July 14, 1777, AGN, RC, 1777, Vol. 111, No. 162, p. 260.

party. The qualifications of New Spain's leading miners were reviewed in order to select local assistants for the visitors.[77] The Spanish party reached Veracruz on July 1, 1778, under the leadership of Rafael Helling.[78] In the capital they conferred with Bucareli and his advisers, were assigned assistants, received 3,000 pesos as expense money, discussed and selected the area to be investigated first, and set out for the mines on August 25.[79]

Late in October Bucareli reported that in nearly two months of steady work the inspectors had found no deposit of any value whatsoever. He ordered them to continue their search, however, and added what amounted to his signature—a warning to avoid unnecessary expense.[80] He did not report again until late in February, 1779, when he told essentially the same story—no deposit of value. Meanwhile, the party had returned to the capital, collected more equipment, and moved on to a new area.[81] The King displayed no discouragement over the initial failure and approved Bucareli's action in continuing the quest.[82] Doubtless Bucareli never saw the letter expressing this approval since it is dated in Spain on March 20, 1779. The inspection continued briefly after his death, but found no worthwhile ore. It is estimated that the expedition cost about 160,000 pesos.[83]

Undoubtedly the major development in the mining industry during

[77] Bucareli to Gálvez, February 24, 1778, AGN, CVB, 1778, Vol. 100, No. 3566, pp. 2–2v.

[78] Same to same, July 27, 1778, AGN, CVB, 1778, Vol. 108, No. 3850, pp. 1v–2.

[79] Same to same, August 27, 1778, AGN, CVB, 1778, Vol. 109, No. 3951, pp. 24–26.

[80] Same to same, October 27, 1778, AGN, CVB, 1778, Vol. 111, No. 4094, pp. 49–51.

[81] Same to same, February 24, 1779, AGN, CVB, 1779, Vol. 116, No. 4302, pp. 29–30.

[82] Gálvez to Bucareli, March 20, 1779, AGN, RC, 1779, Vol. 115, No. 143, p. 210.

[83] Bancroft, *Mexico,* Vol. III, p. 584. Priestley, *José de Gálvez,* p. 376. Bucareli's successor, Martín de Mayorga, continued the effort to find new deposits. On November 18, 1779, he issued a decree which liberalized the terms under which mercury mines could be exploited by individuals. Mayorga to Gálvez, November 19, 1779, AGN, CV, Vol. 124, pp. 23v–26. A letter of May 26, 1780, indicates that the search was still going on, but without significant result. Same to same, AGN, CV, Vol. 126, pp. 241v–242.

Bucareli's viceregency was the creation of the *Cuerpo,* or *Consulado de Minería,* and the multiple ramifications of its organization. That there was a need for some such step was apparent. It was an obvious partial and basic answer to the disturbing fact that the mines of New Spain were not producing their potential of precious metals. Gálvez linked the need for a strong mining guild and the need for a new set of mining ordinances as corollary problems. He averred that the industry was discredited, subject to annoyances and extortion at the hands of petty officials, extensive losses through the ignorance and rebellious character of the workers, and, above all, constantly faced with the fatal consequences of having suddenly to abandon its best mines because of lack of ready funds to pay for maintenance or new equipment. He pointed out that if commerce, which profited from mining, had its own courts and privileges, mining had a still greater right to these things.[84]

Bucareli appears to have done nothing about the matter of his own volition. Indeed, he had been in office for more than two years before any action was taken, and then the initiative came from Spain. It found expression in the order of November 12, 1773, which directed the Viceroy to convene the general mining junta to discuss the mercury problem and, incidentally, to make some progress in the writing of a new set of ordinances wherein would be included the regulations for a miners' association. Inasmuch as there were nearly one hundred mining districts, each with a mining deputation or council, the King ordered that the deputies of only the major areas of Guanajuato, Zacatecas, Pachuca, Tasco, and Sultépec, should meet and choose three or four of their number to represent the entire industry. These men were to attend the junta as advisers, with no right to vote. Specifically named as junta members were Bucareli, who was to preside; the judge administrator of *Azogues;* the superintendent of the mint; the fiscal; and the royal officials of the head treasury in the capital. The Viceroy received discretionary authority to name several other members.[85]

[84] Gálvez, Informe instructivo, Vol. I, pp. 175–176. Priestley says that the *Cuerpo de Minería* owed its existence to Gálvez. *José de Gálvez,* p. 74.

[85] Arriaga to Bucareli, November 12, 1773, AGN, RC, 1773, Vol. 103, No. 127, pp. 305–308.

Bucareli designated the two days a week on which the junta would meet, sent notices of the election procedure to the six major mining districts (adding Bolaños at the fiscal's suggestion), explained the reason for the junta's creation, and requested that the members come prepared to discuss the issues.[86]

In the first meeting, held on May 13, 1774, the junta outlined the procedure it would follow in the later sessions. It was agreed that the three major problems to solve were: the minimum price which should be set for mercury; new ordinances for the government of the mining industry; and the formation of a body similar to the *Consulado de Comercio*. The deputies then decided that they would begin with the third point, inasmuch as from it would emanate the decisions on possible changes and needs in the first two. For this purpose, the mining members revealed that they had already prepared a formal printed memorial which they intended to present to the King. Each junta member was given a copy to study in order that he might the more intelligently discuss it in future sessions. Thus ended the initial assembly. In his report to the King Bucareli mentioned that he would take care that the number of members in the junta remained small because, he said, not only were there few men in New Spain with the requisite knowledge, but also the points involved were delicate, and under such circumstances large groups seldom reached the best decisions.[87]

The printed *Representación* (see note 12) was written by Juan Lucas de Lassaga, an alderman of Mexico City and accountant judge of executorships, and Joaquín Velázquez de León, an attorney before the *Audiencia* and one-time professor of mathematics in the Royal University in Mexico. The pamphlet, 110 pages in length, was dated February 25, 1774, but apparently did not come into Bucareli's hands until the first junta meeting in May. It was an enthusiastic, confident plan, offering a cure for all of mining's ills. Perhaps the outstanding

[86] Bucareli to Arriaga, February 24, 1774, AGN, CVB, 1774, Vol. 48, No. 1290, pp. 22v–25v.
[87] Same to same, May 27, 1774, AGN, CVB, 1774, Vol. 54, No. 1397, pp. 18v–20v.

thing about it was its completeness—it seems to have foreseen every possible contingency and objection.

Its first section was devoted to accounting for the decadent state of the industry as of 1774. Appropriately, it began at the beginning, telling the story of mining in New Spain from pre-Spanish days to the time of writing. After an initial century of prosperity and easy wealth, said the pamphlet, the careless miners began to hit subterranean water reservoirs, which in turn flooded the mines, forcing the exploiters to abandon them. The reason offered for such abandonment was the lack of funds to pay for intelligent draining methods. As proof of their contention that proper methods would pay off, the authors presented two examples of correctly-handled rehabilitation, executed by Pedro Romero de Terreros (Count de Regla) and José Alejandro Bustamante on La Vizcaína vein and by José de la Borda in La Esperanza mine on the Veta Grande.[88]

From this point the deputies turned to a discussion of the possibility of increasing production by means of new discoveries. They dismissed the older, well-settled areas of the viceroyalty as completely explored. They admitted that the interior provinces abounded in deposits of precious metals, but declared that the obstacles to exploitation there were insurmountable. The Spanish population was scanty, the native elements were hostile, food production was inadequate. All manner of goods, such as clothing, steel, mercury, and powder must be transported on muleback from Mexico City, exposed to attack by bandits or Indians, and would arrive inland at such increased prices as to be prohibitive. As possible solutions, the authors suggested the establishment of a maritime transportation system from west coast ports up the Gulf of California to Sonora or Sinaloa anchorages, and greatly increased military protection for the mines against hostile savages. They rejected their own answers, however, as too costly and uncertain.[89]

The only remedy, therefore, was the rehabilitation of the old mines in the settled parts of the viceroyalty, and the prescription called for some method of providing financial backing for the necessary work. In

[88] Lucas de Lassaga and Velázquez de León, *Representación*, pp. 322–329.
[89] *Ibid.*, pp. 329–331.

the past, such money had been secured from *Bancos de Platas,* or mining-loan agencies, whose capital came from merchant investors; but in 1770 the last of these banks had closed its doors, and since then the miners had been without a source of loans. Major mining enterprises were being carried on by a comparatively few independently wealthy operators, such as the Count of Regla, the Count of San Matéo de Valparaíso, the Count of Peñasco, the Marqués de Pánuco, the Marqués de San Miguel de Aguaya, José de la Borda, Juan Lucas de Lassaga, and several others. Most of these men were elderly, and experience showed that their heirs would not continue their mining activities. The remainder of the mining in New Spain was done by an "innumerable multitude" of poor families, whose members gleaned the metal from old dumps, worked abandoned shafts above the water line, or sought small, briefly productive pockets. The persistence and the growing number of such persons had led to a temporary increase in silver production, according to the pamphlet. Nevertheless, the number of major mines was decreasing, large new discoveries were unlikely, and the future of the industry in general was extremely discouraging. Again the mining deputies pounded home their point—the basic cause of mining decadence was a lack of financial backing for rehabilitation.[90]

The *Representación* pointed out, however, that there were other contributing factors. The Miners' Guild or Community of Miners of New Spain was not only headless—it lacked any vestige of organization. The two deputies insisted that any group of men of a common occupation needed a directing head, possessed of an intimate knowledge of it, its nature, and its constitution. This was, they said, ". . . a dogma of politics, the son of reason, proved in all ages and nations, in civil, military, secular, and religious states." Without such guidance the result was confusion, disorder, and self-ruin. The general government, remote and inadequately informed, could not provide the proper supervision. The normal source of more immediate government was found in the mining ordinances, but they were two centuries old and concerned with circumstances no longer prevailing. They were con-

[90] *Ibid.,* pp. 331–334v.

fusing, contradictory, open to multiple interpretations and consequent injustices. New ordinances were needed, and their source should be the reorganized Miners' Guild mentioned above.[91]

The two authors pointed out further hindrances to a revival of the mining industry. In judicial disputes, first instance was held by local *alcaldes mayores*. Ignorant of the problems involved, they frequently handed down bad decisions. The result was usually an appeal to the Royal *Audiencia,* with a consequent waste of time and money. Miners suffered economic disadvantages because of transportation difficulties which occasioned a scarcity of essential commodities and inevitably high prices. Another obstacle was the prevalence of ignorance in the operation of a business as technical and as demanding of professional competence as mining. So-called "experts," jealous of their position, mutually supported one another's mistakes, stubbornly refusing to acknowledge any advances in mining knowledge or technique. As a result, mining in New Spain, according to the *Representación,* was three hundred years behind that of Europe.[92]

Having thus portrayed the status of New Spain's prospects for mineral production, Lucas de Lassaga and Velázquez de León turned next to a detailed consideration of remedies for the various ills. They dealt first with financial backing for rehabilitation. The use of outside capital they rejected for numerous reasons, the most important of which was that capital so invested was subject to individual caprice and ignorant application. It was essential, they said, that the money belong to the miners and that its investment be directed by men learned in the pursuit. An additional tax on some phase of mining would not serve the purpose. The answer lay in a tax already being collected, but which, by error, was being doubly imposed. This was the duplicate seigniorage.[93]

Seigniorage was the tax on bullion delivered to the royal smeltery and destined for coinage. Prior to 1733, private individuals had leased the right to coin money, with the result that bullion was again taxed at the mint before it was converted. In 1733 the Crown took over the

[91] *Ibid.,* pp. 334v–337v.   [92] *Ibid.,* pp. 337v–343.
[93] *Ibid.,* pp. 343–347.

coinage process, but continued to exact this duplicate imposition. Gálvez argued that the duty was unjust and urged that it be stopped. The mining deputies agreed that it was unfair, but it was in the product of this tax that they saw the source of their fund for mining rehabilitation. They recommended that the royal officials at the sub-treasuries continue to collect the seigniorage, but that instead of turning it in as royal income they deliver it to the account of the Miners' Guild. They estimated the income at 200,000 pesos annually. Subtracting 50,000 pesos for the support of various other activities of the guild left 150,000 pesos to serve as interest payments on a possible total of 3,000,000 pesos lent at 5 per cent. To provide for possible misfortunes they proposed that only 2,000,000 pesos be borrowed, leaving a 50,000-peso buffer. With this money available for loans to miners, silver production would increase, seigniorage income would grow, and the guild could repay the principal with the surplus.

The *Representación* then recited a multitude of optimistic possibilities and refutations of probable and improbable objections to the plan. It approached the situation from numerous angles and, by a series of arithmetical jugglings, attempted to prove that not only mining, but the entire viceroyalty would profit from the proposed enterprise. Idle capital from such sources as churches and *cabildos* would be put to use, the amount of money in circulation would increase, trade would prosper, agriculture would thrive, and the treasury would benefit far beyond repayment of its loss of the double seigniorage. The prospect was breath-taking.[94]

Inasmuch as the core of all this beneficial activity was to be the Mining Tribunal at the head of the reorganized Miners' Guild, the two deputies turned next to proposals for this body. They suggested a three-man governing tribunal composed of an administrator general and two general deputies. The first set of appointees were to serve for life, or from ten to fifteen years at least, in order to establish the court firmly, and also because there were so few persons qualified to serve. Thereafter, they were to be elected every three years. It was required that they be mineowners who had actually engaged in the business for

[94] *Ibid.*, pp. 347–353v.

more than three years and had produced more than ten thousand marks of silver. Election was to be by deputies of the miners, one from each district. Below this supreme tribunal were to be parallel district organizations. Within this system all problems concerning mining, including judicial disputes, could be settled. The personnel was to come completely from the guild membership. Several other administrative positions, such as the factor and the assessor, were described.[95]

In view of the need for a greater number of genuine experts in mining, the *Representación* next proposed the establishment of a metallurgical seminary in New Spain. Under a five-man faculty, selected students would study their chosen fields of mining in a course lasting two years. This was to be followed by two years of practical study in the mines, after which would come the final examination. Successful students were to be guaranteed positions commensurate with their learning. Following this schooling proposal, the two deputies dealt briefly with their suggested method for handling loans, after which they concluded their writing with a final reassertion of the many benefits their plan would bring to New Spain.[96]

Bucareli, ever the conservative, reacted decisively. He opposed the entire plan. The proposals for the tribunal, the lending system, the school, and the new ordinances he characterized as "vast ideas," jeopardized by insurmountable obstacles, impracticable and offensive to the public. He defined as a "special difficulty" the desire to create a fund from the seigniorage tax with which to "pay the interest on three or four million pesos which they suppose it would be easy to get at interest for the miners' fund from the convents, communities, or individuals." It was based, he said, on a "disrespectful and irreverent anticipation" of what the King's pleasure might be. He questioned further that even if the King did thus renounce the duplicate seigniorage, was it fair to continue its imposition on all for the benefit of the few who might make use of it? Also, was it wise to attempt to create a *consulado* of subjects scattered throughout the kingdom and notoriously unsociable in character? He suggested that the more

[95] *Ibid.*, pp. 353v–356.   [96] *Ibid.*, pp. 356v–364v.

experienced *Consulado de Comercio* handle the funds, if there be funds. A series of new ordinances would create limitless confusion, he said, and he looked with disfavor on the diversion of so much money from regular trade channels. As related previously, he also opposed the junta's recommendation for a lower mercury price. He therefore suspended the body, "in order to avoid perplexities or contrariness in the decisions." [97]

This was the report, written in September, 1774, which apparently was ignored in Spain and which started the series of misunderstandings. Several times the King reminded Bucareli that he was awaiting action on the mining situation. It was not until June, 1776, that the Viceroy dictated his letter of defense in which he reminded the Crown that he had suspended the junta and was still awaiting further royal instructions on the matter. At about the time this document left Veracruz, however, the matter was being settled in Madrid, and Bucareli was to come out second best. A Royal *Cédula,* dated July 1, approved the *Representación* submitted by Lucas de Lassaga and Velázquez de León. It ordered an end to the double seigniorage, with the money to go henceforth to the credit of the *Cuerpo de Minería,* and the early establishment of the new-style Miners' Guild.[98]

The members of the mining junta which Bucareli had suspended were still in Mexico City. In April, 1777, they petitioned the Viceroy for permission to reconvene and proceed with the organization of the tribunal. As was his cautious custom, Bucareli first passed the request to the fiscal and the assessor general for comment, after which he authorized the junta to meet for the stated purpose. On May 24 the deputies presented to the Viceroy the results of the elections and the rules that the new tribunal was to follow. Juan Lucas de Lassaga became administrator general, while Joaquín Velázquez de León assumed the duties of director general. Thus the authors of the *Representación* became the leaders in the establishment of their own plan. Two deputies general and a secretary were also chosen. Bucareli

---

[97] Bucareli to Arriaga, September 26, 1774, AGN, CVB, 1774, Vol. 58, No. 1534, pp. 30v–33.

[98] Bucareli to Gálvez, January 27, 1777, AGN, CVB, 1777, Vol. 87, No. 2730, p. 42v. Same to same, August 27, 1777, *ibid.,* Vol. 94, No. 3164, p. 6v.

approved the selections and the rules by a decree on August 11.[99] The Miners' Guild was ready for business.

One task remained to be done—the writing of the new ordinances. The King had repeatedly urged their promulgation and he continued to do so.[100] Bucareli had nothing to do with the finished product, however, inasmuch as they were completed by the Tribunal members and sent to Spain in August, 1779, some five months after his death. Charles III approved them in May, 1783. They were extraordinarily comprehensive, establishing procedure for the adjudication and operation of mines, the fiscal and juridical organization of the industry, the constitution of the guild, the regulation of labor, trade in precious metals, banking and credits, technical training for mining engineers, and special privileges for miners.[101]

The *Cuerpo de Minería,* as it developed, became a powerful body. Its members enjoyed the privileges of nobles, including exemption from arrest for debt and from personal-property seizure. They received preferment in political, military, and ecclesiastical appointments. They were guaranteed supplies of such items as provisions and timber, at a minimum price, and could draft as laborers certain idle persons. But the guild was bitterly opposed by the *Audiencia* and by conservatives, and in spite of its power, it failed. There was little improvement in the administration of justice. Because of financial mismanagement and forced loans, little capital was left for mining development, and the bank was finally ruined. Although silver production steadily increased, the guild apparently did not contribute much to mining practice. The provincial or district deputations were corrupt and inefficient. The School of Mines established in 1792 was a good one, but its graduates were unable to defeat tradition and prejudice.[102] Perhaps Bucareli's disapproval of the original plan was founded on a deeper wisdom than is apparent from a mere consideration of his stated objections.

[99] Same to same, August 27, 1777, and inclosures, *ibid.,* pp. 6v–8v, 64–75v. The inclosures comprise a complete *expediente* on the subject of erecting the new body.

[100] Gálvez to Bucareli, January 20, 1778, AGN, RC, 1778, Vol. 113, No. 43, p. 56.

[101] Priestley, *José de Gálvez,* p. 74. Haring, *The Spanish Empire in America,* p. 264.

[102] Haring, *The Spanish Empire in America,* pp. 265–268.

On the other hand, there were certain benefits which stemmed from the existence and activities of the *Cuerpo de Minería* and from the general readjustment of the mining industry, although their demarcation is neither easily nor clearly accomplished. Motten effectively supports his suggestion that it was via this industry that the Enlightenment was more easily introduced and extended in New Spain in the final quarter of the eighteenth century.[103] Also, having weighed the evidence for both sides, Howe finds that the scales settle in favor of the Miners' Guild as a constructive force.[104] To be sure, these ultimate contributions were made over a period of time, and largely during the decades following the 1770's. Nevertheless, important beginnings were made during Bucareli's viceregency.

Ironically, perhaps, Bucareli's reputation is not greatly enhanced by his actions and policies with respect to mining. Conceivably, his record in the matter might be regarded as discreditable, not so much because of what he did as because of what he did not do. He cannot be accused of being overzealous or too aggressive; but there is evidence that aggressiveness and initiative were what the mining industry needed most in the 1770's. A progressive program was laid out for him by Gálvez, and the only deviation he permitted himself was to oppose several of the *Visitador's* recommendations. He contributed nothing original. His own words are an explanation of this dominating conservatism, for, as we recall, he said, in discussing the *partido* system, "I hold as one of the principal maxims of good government to make no change in old customs when they are not harmful . . ." A study of Bucareli's character, however, leads one to believe that anything which could qualify as an "old custom" probably would only rarely be classified by him as "harmful."

[103] *Mexican Silver.*
[104] *Mining Guild.*

General Financial Administration

THE MOST IMPORTANT responsibility borne by a viceroy derived from his capacity as superintendent general of *Real Hacienda*. The term *"Real Hacienda"* must be translated to mean more than "Royal Exchequer" or "Royal Treasury" (*"erario"* is more nearly correct for this latter meaning). The *Real Hacienda* in reality included everything which the Crown possessed, and thus perhaps "Royal Estate" is the clearest English expression of the term, although it is still somewhat lacking in the full connotation which it had for the inhabitants of the Spanish empire. Two sentences by Priestley express succinctly the vital nature of this phase of the viceroy's job. First he says, "It was to create revenues that the colonies existed." He continues, "The *real hacienda* was the organic institutional expression of the *raison d'être* of the Spanish colonial world."[1]

The chief concern of the administrators of the *Real Hacienda* in New Spain was the care, development, collection, and disbursement of

[1] Priestley, *José de Gálvez*, p. 76. The account of the working of the *Real Hacienda* which is presented in the following pages is an extract and summarization of the excellent job done by Priestley in Chapter X, "The *Real Hacienda* and the Reforms of Gálvez." Other sections of Priestley's book dealing with financial matters are Chapter IV, "The Tobacco Monopoly"; and Chapter V, "Customs Reforms at Veracruz." For more extensive treatment of the subject, see the five-volume work, previously cited, by Fonseca and Urrutía. A digest of this account is found in Joaquín Maniau Torquemada, *Compendio de la história de la real hacienda de Nueva España*, cited hereafter as *Compendio de la real hacienda*. Useful also is the *Informe general* or *Informe instructivo* by Gálvez, cited in note 7, below.

Crown revenues. In the late eighteenth century these public funds were divided into four major groups. The first two groups had a common source in that they consisted of the returns upon all the ordinary and extraordinary activities of the people from which a net profit was expected, that is, after the expenses of collection were deducted. Group 1 consisted of thirty-five branches (*ramos*) or sources of revenue. The net profit from these *ramos* went into the *masa común,* or general fund. Group 2 was composed of only three *ramos,* and their profits were deposited separately in the *masa remisible a España.* This meant that such funds went directly and entirely to Spain and were not ordinarily used to meet expenses in the New World.

Group 3 was distinct from the above divisions in that its funds came from a different source and were not entered in the general fund. It was composed of five branches, which were devoted to specific objectives. Group 4, the *ramos agenos,* was made up of thirty-nine funds derived from special sources and dedicated to specific purposes. They were in reality more nearly liabilities than assets, coming under Crown protection because of the paternalistic nature of the government.

There were three possible ways of handling each of the thirty-eight *ramos* in the first two groups. Prior to Gálvez' *visita* the commonest way was by lease to individuals (*arrendamiento*) for an initial payment and/or an annual payment. Leases were sold at auctions after their availability for purchase had been publicly advertized. A second method was the modified lease system, or *encabezamiento,* whereby a leading city (*cabezón*) took upon itself the handling of one or more revenues within the area of its influence in return for a share of the proceeds. The third method, and the one which Charles III favored, was that of administration, that is, direct management by the government, with treasury officials doing the collecting.

Certain revenues, either leased or administered, were held as monopolies. In such cases, production of a widely-used commodity was restricted to certain persons or areas under contracts which fixed the purchase price, the sale price, and details of delivery. The monopoly system led to considerable conflict and, naturally, fraud.

The lease system was extensively used by the Habsburgs. The Spanish Bourbons, however, regarded it as a sign of weak government and therefore were reluctant to allow its growth or continuation. Direct administration was favored when profits were certain, but if the profit was not assured, the Crown preferred to lease the revenue for a fixed amount, thereby making sure of some income and, at the same time, eliminating a number of salaried officials.

Of greatest importance, of course, were the revenues which comprised the first two groups. The three in the second division, which went into the *masa remisible,* are easily explained. They were from tobacco, playing cards, and mercury, all of which were Crown monopolies. Since the works previously cited contain detailed discussions of the thirty-five *ramos* which made up the *masa común,* it does not seem necessary to explain here each of them at length. It may contribute to an understanding of the extent and completeness of the Spanish taxation system, however, to list these branches. The *masa común,* then, received its funds from the following *ramos:*

Derecho de ensaye—a duty on assays of gold and silver.
Derecho de oro—a tax on mined gold.
Quinto—the "fifth" (but really only one-tenth during Bucareli's time) paid on all silver bullion.
Bajilla—a tax on gold and silver used in the manufacture of jewelry.
Amonedación—a tax paid on precious metals made into coins.
Alumbre, cobre, plomo, estaño—revenue from baser metals: alum, copper, lead, and tin.
Tributos—tribute.
Censo—a land tax, paid only on certain areas.
Oficios vendibles y renunciables—certain positions which were sold.
Cancillerías vendibles y renunciables—certain other positions which were sold.
Papel sellado—stamped paper, legally essential in many transactions.
Media anata—half annates, or one-half the first year's salary, paid by most government officials.
Lanzas—money collected from the nobility in lieu of furnishing a body of armed men for the royal service.
Licencias—various licenses.
Composición de tierras—sales of Crown lands.

Pulperías—a tax on retail grocers.

Comisos—fines and confiscations of contraband goods.

Tintos—export taxes on cochineal, indigo, and vanilla.

Caldos—entry duties on wines, brandies, and vinegars.

Nieve—revenue from the leased monopoly on the sale and storage of snow.

Cordobanes—an excise tax on leather goods.

Gallos—cockfighting monopolies.

Pólvora—revenue from the gunpowder monopoly.

Lotería—the lottery.

Novenos—royal share of the tithe.

Alcabalas—sales taxes on goods involved in most commercial transactions.

Pulques—a tax on pulque entering cities.

Armada, avería, almojarifazgo—major export and import duties.

Salinas—revenue from the salt monopoly.

Aprovechamientos—the profit-and-loss account, i.e., goods bought for government use and not consumed.

Alcances de cuentas—balances of accounts.

Anclaje—anchorage, which included various harbor charges.

Lastre—revenue from stone ballast sold to vessels outward bound from Veracruz.

Bienes mostrencos—profit from unclaimed goods.

Donativos—gifts to the king.

Group 3 was composed of five revenues which came chiefly from ecclesiastical sources and were devoted to particular objectives. They were: *bulas de la Santa Cruzada,* or money from the sale of indulgences; *vacantes,* or salaries of church positions which reverted to the Crown in case of vacancies; *medias anatas* and *mesadas* (one month's income) of ecclesiastics; *diezmos,* or tithes; and *penas de cámara y gastos de justicia,* or court fines and expenses of justice.

Group 4 consisted of special funds under treasury protection. Typical of these are: estates of deceased employees of the government; funds of insurance associations (*montepíos*) among government employees; the California Pious Fund; estates of deceased ecclesiastics; the Indian hospital fund; the fund for native courts; funds for expenses of justice; funds for repair of the palace; bridge tolls; seigniorage for the miners' court; the tax on cacao, for military uniforms and barracks; and the fund for the extinction of prohibited beverages.

The fiscal system of New Spain clearly was one of considerable size and complexity. Furthermore, in spite of the wide range of products and activities upon which the Crown levied taxes, it was seldom that a surplus resulted after all ordinary and extraordinary expenses and allotments were paid. The status of the Royal Estate as of September, 1771, is revealed in a reminiscence which Bucareli recorded after he had been viceroy for more than three years: [2]

On assuming command of these vast provinces, among the difficulties which made me regard as of small likelihood my justification of the royal confidence, one of the primary ones was the tremendous indebtedness of the treasury and the appeals of . . . creditors that they be paid. . . . I learned that each day the debts would increase as a necessary consequence of the income's being less than the expenditures. . . . These sad facts inclined me more than once to represent the impossibility that . . . the job would be done properly; and, since someone who might have more talent and intelligence than I, could rectify the situation, I judged it as proper that His Majesty should name him to relieve me.

Fortunately for Spain, Bucareli did not succumb to this early temptation to abandon his post, because there is little doubt but that his greatest achievement as viceroy was his management of the royal finances. Under his guidance the public revenues of New Spain climbed steadily upward. So successful was his administration that he was able to pay off a forbidding debt extending clear back to the reign of Philip V.[3] Of course, such success was not achieved single-handedly by Bucareli, and especially significant in this respect was the work done by *Visitador* Gálvez just before the new Viceroy took over his command.

Since Priestley's excellent work on the accomplishments of the *Visitador* makes it unnecessary to repeat such information in detail at

[2] Bucareli to Arriaga, June 27, 1775, in Velasco Ceballos, *La administración de ... Bucareli*, Vol. II, pp. 59–60.

[3] Statement of arrears debts which the *Real Hacienda* of New Spain had paid . . . , October 26, 1776, AGN, CVB, 1776, Vol. 85, inclosure No. 2 in No. 2585, pp. 68–68v.

this point, a summary will suffice. Gálvez spent nearly six years in New Spain, in the course of which he covered an amazingly large portion of the viceroyalty. Everywhere he went he either instituted reforms or noted what changes should be made and passed such recommendations along to Bucareli. He endeavored to put an end to corrupt practices in the major customhouses of Veracruz, Mexico City, and Acapulco. He introduced the tremendously profitable tobacco monopoly. He and his subordinates investigated the conduct of a multitude of public officials, either preferring charges against the errant ones or leaving them to run their offices more efficiently and honestly for fear of the consequences if they did otherwise. He did not effect a reorganization or a fundamental change in the operation of the fiscal machinery. Instead, he aimed at and achieved a more rigid adherence to the rules. Any potential improvement was within the existing framework; no change was made in the old pattern.[4]

Bucareli reached New Spain late in September, 1771. Gálvez, in compliance with orders from Spain, remained in Mexico until the closing days of November, acquainting the new Viceroy with the results of the *visita* and the workings of the *Real Hacienda*. The two officials held numerous conferences, of which, unfortunately, no record appears to have been kept. It is evident, however, that these meetings, although helpful to Bucareli, were not as enlightening as Gálvez perhaps intended that they should be, for Bucareli commented to O'Reilly that ". . . in my daily conversations with the *Visitador* he gives me an account of antecedents, but they will never be sufficient."[5] If not as fruitful as expected, the conferences appear to have been harmonious, since Bucareli was moved to comment, "He [Gálvez] has not had the least dispute with me—and you know that I am not among those who say Amen to everything—such is his care and such his penetration."[6] The *Visitador* did leave with Bucareli for the latter's guidance his lengthy *Informe instructivo,* previously cited.[7]

[4] Priestley, *José de Gálvez,* passim.

[5] Bucareli to O'Reilly, October 27, 1771, AGI, Mex., Leg. 1242.

[6] Same to same, December 27, 1771, *ibid.*

[7] This document was published in Mexico in 1867 with a single variation in the title, using *Informe general* rather than *Informe instructivo.* It is composed of four major divisions, in which Gálvez discusses the administrative organization of the

The Viceroy's other main source of information on the job he had just taken over was the Instrucción written by his predecessor, the Marqués de Croix. In his section on finance the Marqués indicated the scope of this phase of administration and the worry it had caused him when he said: [8]

The viceroy is superintendent general of all the *ramos* of *Real Hacienda,* including in this particular jurisdiction over New Galicia and New Vizcaya. And since in his care is not only payment for whatever may be needed for the kingdom, but also the payment of subsidies for the Windward Islands and other matters which, since my entry to command have been increased excessively, all my attention was on increasing the *Real Hacienda,* without regard for fatigue.

In order not to duplicate information, Croix then referred Bucareli to what Gálvez would reveal to him. There followed a brief account of those features of the major *ramos* which the Marqués felt were noteworthy. Finally he said: [9]

I conclude the point by saying that although in the time of my government the *ramos* of *Real Hacienda* increased by 3,200,000 pesos, nevertheless, what has been paid out in said time for arrears debts, the drainage *ramo,* deposits of the *Real Audiencia* and others, and especially the increase of subsidies to the Windward Islands and to troops, and the cost of the expedition to Sonora and Monterey, the cost of the shipyard at San Blas and the construction of ships, have resulted in the coffers' not being as full as they will be following the increase of income, the progress of mining, and when the expeditions are finished.

Bucareli probably recognized this as a euphemistic way of saying that the treasury was in debt and was apparently going to stay that way. One of his first investigations concerned this precise point, and his fears were confirmed. A statement which he sent to Spain on

---

fiscal system; the various *ramos* of *Real Hacienda;* municipal finance; and the expeditions to the interior provinces and the Californias. A lengthy appendix of documents, such as statistical tables, follows. In addition to the MS already cited in the Huntington Library, there is another copy in AGI, Mex., Leg. 1509, labeled "Instrucción dada por el Exmo. Sr. Dn. Josef de Gálvez al Virrey Dn. Antonio Bucareli y hallada entre los papeles de aquel."

[8] Croix, Instrucción, AGN, CVB, 1772, Vol. 24, pp. 428v–429.

[9] *Ibid.,* pp. 436v–437.

October 3, 1771, revealed that in the main treasury office in Mexico City funds on hand totaled slightly less than 130,000 pesos. Against this were arrayed the following pressing debts:

Balance remaining on loans made to the treasury since 1761	178,939 pesos
Loans made by the *Comercio* in January, 1771	600,000
Subsidies for the interior presidios for the year 1770 and up to August 31, 1771	735,018
Stipends to missionaries in New Spain	76,660
Subsidy for the Philippines	334,168
Subsidy for the Marianas Islands	22,784
Various charges against the subtreasuries	256,436
Subsidy for Santo Domingo for completion of 1770 allotment and for 1771 to the end of August, 1771	139,228
Subsidy for Cumaná, same conditions as for Santo Domingo	27,933
Subsidy for Puerto Rico for remainder of 1771	258,639
Subsidy for Havana for remainder of 1771	1,906,692
	4,536,497 pesos

A note at the end of the statement warned that this list of debts did not include the as yet unknown cost of the California settlements and their supporting ships, since these remittances were made from Guadalajara. Finally, it was estimated that the funds on hand in the various subtreasuries in the mining regions would send to Mexico City during the remainder of 1771 about 550,000 pesos.[10] When the King received this report, he replied simply that he was awaiting the more formal statements which came at the end of the year in order to get a clearer overall picture.[11]

It must be pointed out that the 130,000 pesos in the Mexico City main treasury did not comprise the total funds free of encumbrance in New Spain. As mentioned earlier, the profits from three Crown monopolies—tobacco, playing cards, and mercury—constituted a separate division of the fiscal system, the *masa remisible a España,*

[10] Inclosures in Bucareli to Arriaga, October 3, 1771, in Velasco Ceballos, *La administración de . . . Bucareli,* Vol. II, pp. 1–4.

[11] Arriaga to Bucareli, January 22, 1772, AGN, RC, 1772, Vol. 100, No. 17, p. 50.

which could not be spent in New Spain, but must go entirely to the mother country. Consequently, Bucareli was able to send to the King at this early date more than 450,000 pesos on deposit in the offices of the tobacco *renta.*[12] Furthermore, sharply aware of the need for funds in Havana, he ordered 400,000 pesos which were being held in the mint in Mexico City sent at once to his former command.[13]

Bucareli then set about determining how best he could overcome the obstacles which confronted him. Several years later, in discussing his attitude during these early depressing months, he said that the thought that the King had entrusted him with such a difficult job served to encourage him, and that with this thought, "fear gave way to duty, and with this I turned to an examination of the remedies, and I decided that everything depended on only two of them, which are: saving in expenses whenever possible, and faithful collection and increase of the treasury, with measures so smooth that, far from producing complaints from these faithful vassals of the King, I would dissipate all the vexation I found in them." [14]

What Bucareli accomplished under these two rules is much more easily ascertained than the methods whereby he accomplished it. With respect to certain major branches of the *Real Hacienda* he administered broad changes in their management, although not in every case did such changes lead to increased revenue during his term. These adjustments will be considered in the following chapter. The only writer who has given any noteworthy consideration to this phase of the viceregency is Velasco Ceballos, and he offers no analysis of the methods used. His principal point is that Bucareli resented or even feared change, and that such changes as came about under him were done only on order from Spain. His conclusion is that [15]

there was not, then, during the eight parsimonious years of Bucareli's administration, any measure of reorganization, but rather simple disposi-

[12] Bucareli to Arriaga, October 3, 1771, in Velasco Ceballos, *La administración de . . . Bucareli,* Vol. II, pp. 4–5.
[13] Velasco Ceballos, *La administración de . . . Bucareli,* Vol. II, p. x.
[14] Bucareli to Arriaga, June 26, 1775, in Velasco Ceballos, *La administración de . . . Bucareli,* Vol. II, p. 60.
[15] Velasco Ceballos, *La administración de . . . Bucareli,* Vol. II, p. xlvi.

tions of order; we must conclude that the stupendous success achieved of making the revenues rise to a point which they never had had since the beginning of the Domination, was due to economy, an economy which, certainly, touched the limits of niggardliness, and, above all, due to the incorruptible, pure hands of this singular viceroy, who needed only the brief time of three years nine months to repay the great debts with which he found the Royal Estate.

He concludes, some pages later, "The increase of the Public *Hacienda,* we repeat, was for Viceroy Bucareli his most legitimate point of pride." [16]

With the overtones of scorn eliminated, Velasco Ceballos is essentially correct. The answer to Bucareli's successful fiscal management apparently does lie in his meticulous attention to the details of income and expenditure, his insistence on observance of the rules, and his own economical example. In two long, rather boastful letters which he wrote in 1775 and 1776 about his accomplishments, he himself does not explain how he did it, aside from reaffirming the two general policies previously cited and making reference to certain statistical statements which were attached. A study of these documents again reveals only what he did, not how he did it. [17]

A partial idea of his method and, more particularly, of his attitude may be derived from his reaction to the King's projected program for establishing the intendancy system throughout his American dominions. [18] This new method of administration lessened considerably a viceroy's powers, especially in the line of finance. It was already under trial in Cuba and in one area, Sonora-Sinaloa, in New Spain, when Bucareli became viceroy. In April, 1772, Charles III sent to Bucareli a file of documents bearing on the possibility of establishing the system in New Spain, and asked him to offer suggestions on how to facilitate such a program. [19]

In reply Bucareli stated that he had been interested in the subject

---

[16] *Ibid.,* Vol. II, p. L.

[17] See financial statements in the Appendix.

[18] For a thorough, scholarly account of this subject, see Fisher, *The Intendant System in Spanish America.*

[19] Arriaga to Bucareli, April 15, 1772, AGN, RC, 1772, Vol. 100, No. 125, p. 221.

from the very first, and that it was a favorite topic of discussion among the people. He indicated, however, that he could not write such a report in the near future because he wished to inquire further into the matter and to talk with certain persons whose opinions he valued. He then listed the objectives he wished to achieve in his investigation whereby he might arrive at a conclusive answer.[20]

Bucareli did not finish his report until March, 1774, but his attitude, when finally expressed, was decisive. He opposed the introduction of the intendancy system into New Spain, offering long and detailed arguments in support of his point of view.[21] The Viceroy first stated his basic premise by asserting that the people of New Spain were not "in a state which permits a variation in the system of government," and that the establishment of the intendancy system, rather than improving the situation, would cause confusion, occasion greater expenses, decrease the revenues for many years, make collections uncertain, and do away with the security contained in the joint-responsibility (*mancomunada*) system then in effect.

Past failures and weaknesses, he said, did not spring from the present system, but rather from the quality of the former employees, whose philosophy was based on favoritism, profiteering, and making their fortune quickly, with a consequent prevalence of corruption and petty tyranny. He felt that it was conditions such as these which had obliged the Council of the Indies in recent years to limit the faculties of the overseas administrators at the same time that they raised salaries and created new positions in order to ensure more honest collections of the revenues through reducing the temptations facing the office-holder and providing a closer check on the governmental process.[22]

Bucareli then discussed how the laws were enforced under his management, and here perhaps is a clue to how he achieved such successful results. Each week he received a report on the income and expenses of each major treasury office, with the various *ramos* sepa-

---

[20] Bucareli to Arriaga, July 26, 1772, AGN, CVB, 1772, Vol. 28, No. 467, pp. 29v–31.
[21] Same to same, March 27, 1774, in Velasco Ceballos, *La administración de . . . Bucareli,* Vol. I, pp. 186–204.
[22] *Ibid.,* pp. 187–188.

rately accounted for.[23] Every month the *ramos* which were administered by the Crown, that is, not under the lease system (*arrendamiento*), submitted statements. The outlying treasuries reported every three months, sending to Mexico City at the same time by registered transport all the funds they had on hand, thus becoming "swept clean" (*barrida*). Finally, at the end of the year all Crown agencies submitted their annual statements, which were audited by the Tribunal of Accounts. Any shortages discovered were promptly paid, inasmuch as all officials were bonded (*afianzada*).

No official could dispense Crown funds without authorization from the Viceroy. The Viceroy himself could not make any extraordinary expenditure of royal money except in emergencies. In such event the royal officials and the Tribunal of Accounts made special note of the occurrence and the Viceroy answered for the act in his *residencia* unless the Crown had approved the expenditure prior to that time.

With such safety precautions as these, Bucareli said, he did not understand how intendants could prove to be of any use. For one thing, they were not to be bonded. Furthermore, he felt that the intendants would be unable to find a sufficient number of subordinates among the upper class (*gente de razón*) in the various towns to carry out the contemplated tasks. Also, he said, the poor condition of New Spain's roads would make it difficult to accomplish the numerous *visitas* which the intendants were supposed to make. Slow and delayed travel would occasion heavy expenses which the intendant could not bear, even with an increased salary. Therefore with all these difficulties and problems the intendants would be unhappy in their work, "because all of them are men, and the name of 'intendant' will not free them of their passions." [24] With reference to the fact that the intendancy system had been in effect in Spain for some time, and that the plan for extending it to the Americas was based on this model, Bucareli

[23] At this time the Mexico City treasury office, called the *Caja Mátriz*, was the main one. Other subtreasuries, called *cajas reales*, were located in Veracruz, Acapulco, Pachuca, Guanajuato, Zacatecas, Sombrerete, Bolaños, Guadalajara, San Luis Potosí, Zimapán, and Los Alamos. Frontier *cajas*, or *cajas marcas*, were at Parral, Tasco, and Zacualpa. Croix, Instrucción, AGN, CVB, 1772, Vol. 24, p. 435v.

[24] Bucareli to Arriaga, March 27, 1774, in Velasco Ceballos, *La administración de . . . Bucareli,* Vol. I, pp. 188–189.

averred that "the nature of these provinces still demands distinct handling from the mother country, and little by little it is moving ahead as it should, gaining uniformity." [25]

Bucareli then adverted to one of his earlier statements and proceeded to amplify it, and from this extension further insight is gained into how he administered his command. He said that the *ramos* which at that time made up the *Real Hacienda* could not be better administered by intendants than by the present corps of royal officials, such as the accountants (*contadores*) of tribute and *alcabala,* the superintendents of mercury, the mint, and the half annate. As proof he called attention to recent comparative financial statements which showed steady increases in revenue year by year. The above officials were, he said, just like so many intendants, endowed with ample faculties to avoid having the Viceroy constantly bothered with detail, but also subject to him, and to the Tribunal of Accounts, to the pre-evaluation of what was due to be collected according to census lists, auction boards (*juntas de almonedas*), account books, and so forth, and whose returns or shortages were bonded. These officials could be no more carefully supervised by intendants, said Bucareli, than they already were by the juntas of *hacienda,* the accountants of the various *ramos* to whom they must report, the auction boards which controlled leases, the civil fiscal who interpreted the law, and by appeals to the *Audiencia.*[26]

Bucareli next offered a consideration of the status and problems of administration of various *ramos,* including among them tribute, *alcabala,* the mint,[27] playing cards, *azogues,* pulque, stamped paper, *bulas,* half annates, *lanzas,* Crown lands, mail, lottery, drainage of Huehuetoca, cockfights, snow, leather goods, salable offices, *diezmos* of gold and silver, and tobacco. He had several suggestions to make for the remedy of such ills as the management of these *ramos* suffered. A major fault lay in the nonobservance of the law which provided that judges from the *audiencias* should make frequent tours of inspection, a practice which was not being effected because of the small number

[25] *Ibid.,* p. 189.   [26] *Ibid.,* p. 190.
[27] He called the mint "the best-known in the world, the best-arranged office, the best-founded security." *Ibid.,* p. 192.

of members on the *audiencias*. The regular *audiencia* business kept these few men so busy that they could not be called upon for a number of outside tasks for which, in theory, they were to be used. Bucareli suggested increasing the personnel on the Mexico *Audiencia* from five to ten judges and making certain increases with respect to subordinate positions. He recommended similar additions to the Guadalajara court.[28]

The Viceroy suggested that from this augmentation of personnel there would result faster handling of financial affairs, the completion of required inspections, greater knowledge of the country by the judges, closer supervision of revenue collection in the lower phases of the system, and a consequent source of advice for the Viceroy with respect to the productive potentialities of the kingdom.[29]

Bucareli then turned to a consideration of the trial intendancy established in Sonora during the viceregency of the Marqués de Croix. He found little that could be said in its favor. Not only had it not produced any advantages, he said, but it had occasioned confusion and had given the central government more concern than any other province. The problems created by its existence had resulted in immense files on points of procedure and diffuse legal opinions from the fiscal, and it had made necessary the creation of a special junta to consider the one problem alone. If only one intendancy could cause this much trouble, he said, "how can I recommend the establishment of many of them, which may risk the fortunate progress which hindered it [the management of the *Real Hacienda*] in the past through the lack of observance of the laws, through profiteering, and through the insatiable thirst of interest?"[30]

In conclusion Bucareli stated that he had devoted a great deal of attention and thought to the intendancy question. He had delayed

[28] *Ibid.*, pp. 192–197. Bucareli to Arriaga, March 25, 1772; April 26, 1773, and June 26, 1773, AGN, CVB, 1772, Vol. 22, No. 288, pp. 57–58; AGN, CVB, 1773–1775, Vol. 11, Libro 9, No. 48 or 901, pp. 41–43v; and *ibid.*, No. 55 or 1003. These three letters deal with Bucareli's problems with the inadequate personnel on the Mexico *Audiencia*.

[29] Bucareli to Arriaga, March 27, 1774, in Velasco Ceballos, *La administración de . . . Bucareli*, Vol. I, pp. 198–199.

[30] *Ibid.*, p. 202.

his report to see whether he could find in his experience as viceroy, in the multitude of papers which passed through his hands, and in the opinions of experienced persons, a possible way to establish the new system without exposing the viceroyalty to confusion and upheaval. He did not find it. He judged it a risk, and feared that the results of such a sweeping change would be dismal. He pointed out that the Laws of Castile had not been adaptable to the government of the Americas because the mother country and the New World were different. By the same token, he concluded, the intendancy system based on the Spanish model would not work in New Spain.[31]

Several conclusions may be derived from this account of Bucareli's attitude toward the intendancy system. His devotion to the old system is, of course, obvious. It may be assumed that his administration of this system was the primary reason for his success, and apparently this method involved simply a close application of the rules wherever possible, frequent checks and safeguards with respect to the processing of the royal revenues, and meticulous attention to detail on the part of the Viceroy, the Tribunal of Accounts, and the various top men in the several *ramos*. In addition, certain major *ramos* increased their revenues through higher imposts, such as that on pulque, while others showed greater profits by virtue of the extinction of competition, legal or illegal, such as with tobacco, and by a readjustment in the method of administration, such as the sales taxes. These will be discussed in the following chapter.

One of the obvious problems inherent in any governmental function is the fact that it is performed by human beings, subject as they are to making errors. The Tribunal of Accounts, through which passed, for auditing purposes, all manner of statements from the multitude of government agencies in New Spain, was an important entity of rather fearsome reputation. Because of the human factor, however, Bucareli was scarcely well settled in his new command before he received an order from Spain to see to it that this tribunal demonstrate greater efficiency in the future. The specific cause for complaint in this case involved a financial statement for 1769 in which an entry showed

[31] *Ibid.*, pp. 202–203.

more than 3,500,000 pesos expended for subsidies to Havana and the Windward Islands, but which offered no explanation for: the years that were involved; the amount that remained to be paid, if any; the major divisions within the total amount; the viceregal decrees authorizing the expenditures; the time of departure and the names of ships on which the funds were dispatched; and several other items of information customarily revealed in such a report.[32]

Because of his personal concern over the matter, Bucareli had already begun to seek clarification of the confusion with respect to Havana's subsidy status, but it took him nearly nine months to get it straightened out. He found that the royal officials in the main *caja* and the members of the Tribunal of Accounts were unaware of numerous important documents. He himself was forced to list certain royal orders and reports from Havana which would clear things up.[33] The undoubtedly-embarrassed officials were a long time in running these papers to earth. Not until August, 1772, did the Viceroy declare the situation clarified. Money shipments had been accounted for with relative ease, but records of remittances of flour, food, powder, and other goods were missing. In fact, Bucareli apparently submitted his report when he did because he decided that certain records would never be found.[34]

Just as he was finishing this task he received another notice from Spain concerning the failure of the Tribunal of Accounts to perform its proper functions, and again the period concerned was prior to his time. The tribunal had been auditing, apparently for a long time, the accounts and ledgers of all *ramos* for the years clear back to 1765. As the audits were completed, reports were sent to Spain, but apparently the process was haphazard and piecemeal, as a result of which there was in Spain no complete set of reports for all *ramos* for any single year from 1765 through 1771. The matter had come up before,

[32] Arriaga to Bucareli, December 4, 1771, AGN, RC, 1771, Vol. 99, No. 98, pp. 153–153v.

[33] Bucareli to Arriaga, November 26, 1771, in Velasco Ceballos, *La administración de . . . Bucareli,* Vol. I, pp. 12–14. Royal approval of his actions is contained in Arriaga to Bucareli, March 16, 1772, AGN, RC, 1772, Vol. 100, No. 91, p. 162.

[34] Bucareli to Arriaga, August 27, 1772, AGN, CVB, 1772, Vol. 29, No. 529, pp. 111–113.

inasmuch as Arriaga relayed the King's judgment that the excuses and pretexts which the tribunal had offered previously were not worthy of consideration. It was made clear to Bucareli that he was to rectify the situation.[35]

Cumulative evidence indicates that Bucareli did see to it that the Tribunal of Accounts improved its processing of the *ramos'* reports. This was precisely the sort of administrative problem which appealed most to him. During the rest of his term, annual financial reports went to Spain right on schedule in the January mail. During the last three years they were dated at the end of December, indicating that the accounts were all drawn up and ready to go well ahead of time. Only one instance of failure appears. In 1773 the tribunal approved an account relative to the costs of the Sonora expedition, but numerous errors were found in the document when it was checked in Spain. The King indicated his displeasure,[36] and although the tribunal was able to explain some of the apparent errors, Bucareli was advised, in effect, not to let it happen again.[37] Apparently he never did.

Another situation affecting the efficiency of the financial administration which involved weaknesses both human and governmental concerned the Guadalajara subtreasury office. In June, 1774, the Tribunal of Accounts recommended to Bucareli that he appoint a commissioner to investigate this *caja.* The royal officials working there, Domingo del Barco and Francisco López, were submitting accounts which had been improperly drawn up. This had been going on since 1767. Bucareli named Bartolomé Pico Palacio of the Mexico City *Caja Mátriz* to make the inspection.

Pico soon reported that although there was some fault in the method with which the Guadalajara officials submitted their accounts, it was due to illness, and there was no shortage or discrepancy with respect to royal funds. When the Tribunal of Accounts read Pico's account, it protested that the investigator was softening his reports

[35] Arriaga to Bucareli, June 11, 1772, AGN, RC, 1772, Vol. 100, No. 188, pp. 482–483v.

[36] Same to same, June 22, 1775, AGN, RC, 1775, Vol. 106, No. 134, pp. 229–233.

[37] Gálvez to Bucareli, April 11, 1776, AGN, RC, 1776, Vol. 107, No. 138, pp. 246–246v.

because of the illness of Del Barco and López. Bucareli therefore ordered Pico to be more realistic in his investigation and to report on the seriousness of the illnesses from which the two men were suffering, to the end that if such illnesses interfered too much with their work they must choose lieutenants to carry on in their places or else Bucareli would do the selecting. Pico then revealed that López was nearly blind and could do his work only with difficulty. Del Barco suffered from a chest ailment which kept him confined at home nearly all the time. Pico therefore instructed the two officials to name younger men to take their places.

Why Bucareli went through this whole procedure is not clear. The preceding January he had reported to the King that López was incapable of doing his job and that he had petitioned for his release and permission to return to Spain. If the King granted these requests, it was Bucareli's intention to name Pico to the position, but until word arrived from Spain such measures could not be taken.[38] The incident serves to illustrate one of the weaknesses of the system which depended on Madrid for so many petty decisions. It also suggests that such a situation was not rare. Probably a great number of governmental agencies were run by men as incapable of doing their jobs, for one reason or another, as were these two. Perhaps Bucareli would have liked to apply a remedy, but his chances of doing so seem negligible. The fact that he achieved success in the face of such conditions adds to the credit he deserves.

The extent to which Bucareli improved the financial status and establishment of New Spain is largely a matter of figures. On three occasions he sent to Spain compilations of the debts which the treasury owed as of September 23, 1771, the day on which he assumed command. The amount grew larger each time, perhaps because old debts previously forgotten continued to come to light. As figures given earlier in this chapter show, an initial, hurriedly-compiled statement of arrears debts revealed a total of 4,536,497 pesos owed by the Crown. By a second listing completed in May, 1775, the amount had

[38] Bucareli to Arriaga, October 27, 1774, AGN, CVB, 1774, Vol. 60, No. 1577, pp. 40v–43v.

risen to 7,374,773 pesos.[39] Finally, as a sort of observance of the completion of five years as viceroy, Bucareli had a statement drawn up in October, 1776. The grand total was 9,405,877 pesos.[40]

These statements reveal that the Crown owed money to a wide variety of persons, organizations, and dependent governmental units. Included were: individual creditors or their heirs, living in Havana, who were still receiving 6 per cent interest on loans made during the reigns of Philip V and Ferdinand VI; one José Urrutía, who was due salary for a job which had been suppressed in 1753; an order of friars that was the heir of a position long extinct; various persons who had lent money to finance Gálvez' Sonora expedition; the *Consulado* of Manila, which had been overcharged for export duties in 1768 and 1770; a former superintendent of *Azogues,* who was still waiting for his salary for 1763; various other officeholders whose salaries were in arrears; and, finally, numerous troop units.[41]

Bucareli attached to both of these later compilations, which revealed his success, a prideful letter pointing out the merit of what he had done. In the earlier letter of the two he stressed the fact that during his viceregency he had not resorted either to the merchants or to the general public for loans in emergencies, as had been the practice of other viceroys. On the contrary, the old debts had been paid in a manner that permitted the money to continue in circulation. Consequently, trade was flourishing and the reputation of the government was so well established that in case such public loans did become necessary, the response would be the best that could be desired. He pointed out also that not only had he avoided using any funds of the tobacco monopoly in his debt-clearance program, but that he had even repaid the monopoly some 400,000 pesos which it had supplied for the Sonora expedition.[42]

[39] May 11, 1775, AGN, CVB, 1773–1775, Vol. 11, Libro 9, inclosure in No. 115 or 1851, pp. 247–250.

[40] October 26, 1776, AGN, CVB, 1776, Vol. 85, inclosure No. 2 in No. 2585, pp. 66–74.

[41] *Ibid.*

[42] Bucareli to Arriaga, June 26, 1775, in Velasco Ceballos, *La administración de . . . Bucareli,* Vol. II, pp. 60–61. The King expressed his appreciation for his

In the 1776 letter he concentrated on what he had accomplished in the way of increased revenues and on future prospects for further increases. In doing so, he engaged in some of the arithmetical juggling of which he was so fond whenever the news was good. In 1771, the last year of Croix's government, all the general *rentas* (that is, exclusive of tobacco and the other monopolies) had produced a gross income of 6,904,611 pesos. In the four years from 1772 through 1775 the total gross income had been 32,708,758 pesos. This revealed, he pointed out, an average annual increase of 1,272,578 pesos, or a total increase in the four years of 5,090,314 pesos. According to his estimate, the year 1776 would produce a still greater increase, resulting in a five-year gross increase of 6,500,000 pesos over the 1771 figure.[43]

Referring to the 9,405,877 pesos in old debts which the Crown owed before Bucareli's arrival, and revealing that he had managed to accumulate a surplus fund of nearly 2,000,000 pesos, Bucareli summarized his accomplishments thus: in five years all current expenses of the treasury had been paid without burdening the people with new imposts or loans; nearly 10,000,000 pesos in back debts had been repaid; a surplus had been set aside; all this had been done in spite of the expense of increased subsidy allotments, construction on San Juan de Ulúa and Perote, expanded housing for the mint, the California settlements, land and sea explorations, continuous frontier warfare, and the establishment of the new line of presidios.[44]

The Viceroy then brought into consideration the increased income from tobacco in these same five years. Its net profit in 1771 was 886,757 pesos. The increase in 1772 was small, but in the following three years it had been larger, and Bucareli estimated that in 1776 it would reach 1,500,000 pesos. (As figures in the following chapter show, it exceeded his estimate by 14,790 pesos.) He then figured out a five-year increase of 1,781,500 pesos and added this to the 6,500,000-peso increase cited above, to reach a total of more than

---

viceroy's services in Arriaga to Bucareli, October 17, 1775, AGN, RC, 1775, Vol. 106, No. 248, pp. 464–464v.
[43] Bucareli to Gálvez, November 26, 1776, AGN, CVB, 1776, Vol. 85, No. 2585, pp. 1–5v.
[44] *Ibid.*

8,000,000 pesos greater revenue in five years, based on the figures for 1771. Even better revenues were predicted for 1777. He concluded this message of self-praise by saying,[45]

The anxieties and worries which the unburdening of the treasury has cost me, and giving the *rentas* revenues which they have never had since the Conquest, today produce for me the consolation of giving Your Lordship this news, so that, . . . making it known to His Majesty, it may merit his royal pleasure, which is what I seek in all my activities.

In June, 1777, the Tribunal of Accounts sent Bucareli a financial statement for 1776. Its contents reveal a number of significant facts concerning the use which was made of the money the Viceroy strove to accumulate for the Crown. The *ramos* contributing to the *masa común,* or general fund, produced a total gross revenue of 8,637,189 pesos. Adding the tobacco monopoly income of 3,818,580 pesos produced a total revenue of 12,450,769 pesos. The *ramos* of the *masa común* reported their total expenses of administration as 973,626 pesos. This left a liquid surplus of 7,030,007 pesos. The tobacco monopoly's expenses were 2,329,500 pesos, leaving a profit of 1,489,080 pesos, almost exactly what Bucareli had anticipated. This money, however, went intact to Spain, and therefore did not go to help defray the costs accounted for as extraordinary expenses and labeled *pensiones.* It was from the 7,030,007-peso surplus from the *masa común* that these were deducted. They totaled 5,521,101 pesos, and included such expenses as presidio and missionary subsidies, construction on Perote, military salaries and other defense costs, subsidies to various other subordinate governments, support of San Blas, and royal gifts. Therefore, although Bucareli managed a vast business concern with such skill that it was able to show a profit of more than 7,000,000 pesos in one year, extraordinary expenses cut this surplus to only 2,122,436 pesos.[46]

Consistently foremost as a single entry among these added expenses were the subsidies which went every year from New Spain to Havana,

[45] *Ibid.*

[46] Bucareli to Gálvez, June 26, 1777, and inclosure, AGN, CVB, 1777, Vol. 92, No. 3026, pp. 1–5, 75–80.

the Philippines, and the Marianas. Havana was the distributing point for the subsidies which were allotted to Louisiana, Santo Domingo, Puerto Rico, and Cumaná. All these Spanish colonies were technically subordinate to the Mexican viceroy, all operated at a deficit, and, as a result, the people of New Spain, via the *Real Hacienda,* paid for the financial inadequacy of these lesser dominions. The money thus paid out went for diverse purposes, and although the amount expended varied from time to time, the revision was generally upward. For the years 1772, 1774, and 1778—the years for which complete figures are available—the respective total amounts in pesos sent to the above places were: 3,146,332; 4,324,347; and 4,531,910.[47]

Bucareli was always prompt in making these payments. Indeed, because of his affection for Havana, his old command, one of his earliest acts upon arriving in New Spain was to ferret out 300,000 pesos on deposit in the mint. To this he added 100,000 of the 130,000 pesos on hand in the Mexico City main *caja* and dispatched the entire amount to Havana because he was aware that its coffers were nearly empty.[48]

As suggested above, these funds were used for a wide variety of purposes. Those for Havana were usually assigned for three major uses: building fortifications, support of the naval squadron, and the purchasing of tobacco for the royal monopoly. The Puerto Rico and Santo Domingo shares went largely for defense. Cumaná received nearly 50,000 pesos each year for cutting timber to be used in ship construction.[49] Perhaps the most interesting special subsidy concerned the Philippines. In November, 1777, Gálvez informed Bucareli, in a letter marked "Very Confidential," that a preliminary treaty of peace

[47] Figures cited were compiled from the following sources: for 1772—Bucareli to Arriaga, March 26, 1772, AGN, CVB, 1772, Vol. 22, No. 315, pp. 88v–89, 181, and same to same, same date, *ibid.,* No. 316, pp. 99, 182; for 1774—same to same, April 26, 1774, AGN, CVB, 1774, Vol. 52, Libro 1, No. 1360, pp. 13v–14v, 37–38, and same to same, same date, *ibid.,* No. 1361, pp. 15–17, 39; for 1778—Bucareli to Gálvez, February 24, 1778, AGN, CVB, 1778, Vol. 100, No. 3572, pp. 3–3v, 41.

[48] Bucareli to Arriaga, October 4, 1771, in Velasco Ceballos, *La administración de . . . Bucareli,* Vol. I, pp. 11–12. Royal approval was expressed in Arriaga to Bucareli, January 23, 1772, AGN, RC, 1772, Vol. 100, No. 18, p. 51.

[49] Documents concerning subsidies are found in a great many—perhaps 50 per cent—of the volumes of Bucareli's correspondence.

had been arranged with Portugal. By its terms Spain was to receive two islands off the Guinea Coast which the Spaniards intended to use as a base for the slave trade. For this trade Spain needed a large quantity of goods from China, of which cotton cloth was particularly mentioned. The Philippines governor was to act as agent in securing these goods, and to pay for them Gálvez ordered Bucareli to send the governor from 35,000 to 40,000 pesos in addition to the regular subsidy for the year. Bucareli immediately dispatched 30,000 pesos, which was all the treasury could spare at that time.[50]

Consideration of the subsidies phase of financial administration accentuates the fact that New Spain was one of the major supports of the Spanish empire. Consequently, the Mexican viceroy was a man of singular importance because of the magnitude of what depended on the success or failure of his financial management. This was undoubtedly his most important function, inasmuch as the empire existed almost wholly for the benefits it could produce for the mother country. It is readily apparent that Bucareli recognized this fact, and it follows that his major concern within his command was the increase of the royal revenues. As Velasco Ceballos has said, the fact that he succeeded is "his most legitimate point of pride." How much of his success was due to the reforms and suggestions of Gálvez, the general increased prosperity of Spain and her empire under Bourbons in general and Charles III in particular, and how much was due to Bucareli's own talents, it would be difficult to assess. It is clear, however, that a considerable amount of credit must be allotted to Bucareli for his energy, his attention to detail, his knowledge of what he was doing, and, above all, for his integrity.

[50] Bucareli to Gálvez, February 24, 1778, AGN, CVB, 1773–1779, Vol. 7, Libro 5, No. 242 or 2571, pp. 18–20. In this letter, as in so much of the correspondence on which this book is based, the letter writer obligingly repeats verbatim the letter he is answering before he begins his reply.

Problems in Financial Administration

IN THE PRECEDING CHAPTER it was stated that Bucareli effected no fundamental change in, or reorganization of, New Spain's financial administration, that his endeavors were directed instead toward making the existing machinery work more efficiently and more in accordance with regulations. As a result, most of the individual *ramos* show little evidence of having undergone any significant changes or startling developments during his period. Certain branches, however, merit closer attention, either because broad adjustments were made in the method in which they were handled or because they appear frequently in Bucareli's correspondence, indicating that they gave him special problems with respect to their management.

The tribute branch was of the latter type. Although it was a variable thing in terms of time and place, the tribute, generally, was a capitation tax paid by the Indians to the King in token of his overlordship. Normally, it was paid only by married males and by unmarried males after age twenty-five. In some instances, Indian women, free Negroes, and mulattoes were also subject to the tax.

One of Charles III's many attempted reforms concerned this revenue. After the usual false starts and delays, the King finally approved in 1770 an entire new set of ordinances for the collection of tribute in New Spain.[1] These regulations were printed in Mexico in 1771, and

[1] *Regulaciones y ordenanzas . . . para el gobierno y administración del ramo de Tributo en Nueva España. 1770.* Printed in Mexico in 1771, the copy here used was

the problems attendant upon putting them into effect were largely Bucareli's. The first and perhaps the most important thing to be done was to produce a long-overdue new census of persons liable to pay the tribute. This job fell primarily on *corregidores, alcaldes mayores,* and local justices. It was to be handled through a mass re-registration of tributaries, and the subordinate official concerned was to attend personally to its consummation. Furthermore, from other officials these lesser agents were to secure such censuses and registration lists as they might have, and from curates they were to get copies of parochial registers. All of these were then to be compared with each other and with the new registries before a final census list was drawn up.[2]

Although this would appear to be a tremendous job, it seems to have been managed without dissension; at least Bucareli's papers reveal no complaints. Instead, the *alcaldes mayores* selected as objects of their disfavor several of the ordinances which they claimed were unfair when given the current interpretation. To decide the matter, Bucareli convoked a junta of *hacienda* in June, 1772, but the decisions reached by this council were of only temporary duration. It was ruled that tributaries employed as field hands or servants on ranches should continue to pay the tax through their employers. If these employees were registered in an adjoining village, however, they were to pay the local government agent, who in turn would deliver the money to the district *alcalde mayor.* But, if such tributary lived on the ranch, he should pay a lesser amount through the owner, inasmuch as he was not enjoying the benefits which came with living in the community. It was also ruled that, because the *alcaldes mayores* in certain districts for some reason did not receive the customary salary for their jobs, they were to withhold 9 per cent of the tribute they collected person-ally. Ranchowners who collected tribute from their employees were

found in a volume devoted otherwise to documents of the year 1774. The printed pamphlet includes a brief relation of the several sources of the ordinances, the com-plete regulations, and a royal explanatory decree addressed to the governmental subordinates who were to put them into effect. AGN, CVB, 1774, Vol. 50, Nos. 8 and 9, pp. 364–403v.

[2] *Ibid.,* pp. 397–403v.

allowed to keep 3 per cent of the tax, but the *alcalde mayor* could make no deduction from the money these *hacendados* turned over to him. Finally, any *alcalde mayor* who managed to gather a greater amount than was called for by the tax rolls was allowed to keep 12 per cent of such excess.[3] Poor Lo seems to have been little better off south of the Río Bravo than he was later in lands farther north.

The *alcaldes mayores* did not like these decisions. They mistakenly assumed that they would be held responsible for the amount of tribute theoretically due from the ranches in their districts, and that in case less was turned in they would have to pay the difference. On December 4, 1772, therefore, Bucareli called another junta of *hacienda* to consider the problem. The council ruled that the *alcaldes* were not responsible for such shortages, but that they were morally obliged to endeavor to procure full collection.[4] The *alcaldes* were still not satisfied. A third junta met, therefore, on June 22, 1773, and decided to do away with the system of collection by employers and to leave the entire field open to the efforts of the *alcaldes*.[5]

In his search for increased revenue from the tribute, Bucareli adopted a suggestion of Gálvez—as he did in so many cases. He sought to extend the collection of this tax into the Sonora-Sinaloa frontier area where it had not yet been made effective. Early in his viceregency he advised Intendant Pedro Corbalán of his ideas on the subject. He counseled the use of gentleness and persuasion with these Indians, employing local agents who were trusted by the natives and making full use of the influence which the curates had with their charges.[6] A junta was convened one year later to discuss the matter, and it was decided to warn the Intendant against using violence with these Indians. Also, the policy of taking full advantage of the curates' influence was again stressed. Finally, the tribute was ruled payable in

[3] Bucareli to Arriaga, June 26, 1772, AGN, CVB, 1772, Vol. 25, No. 454, pp. 42–46.
[4] Same to same, December 27, 1772, AGN, CVB, 1772, Vol. 33, No. 717, pp. 44–49.
[5] Same to same, July 27, 1773, AGN, CVB, 1773, Vol. 40, No. 1025, pp. 22v–26.
[6] Bucareli to Corbalán, February 12, 1772, in Velasco Ceballos, *La administración de . . . Bucareli,* Vol. II, p. 7.

silver bullion, food, grain, gold, or such other goods as might be available. Food collected under this plan was either to be sent to California or used as rations for settlement Indians.[7]

Several months later, however, Bucareli was obliged to suspend tribute collections among most of these tribes because of severe food shortages resulting from drought.[8] Velasco Ceballos, who seems to have overlooked this action, says, with respect to the idea of extending the tribute to this area, "The situation of these places was disastrous, despite which he [Bucareli] undertook the collection." [9]

Another idea for increasing the revenue from tribute came from the *Audiencia.* This plan contemplated the taking of a new census in two of the lower-class districts in Mexico City inhabited largely by Negroes and mulattoes of slave status who had long avoided the tax by virtue of the fact that they were not registered, but were passed off by their owners as tax-exempt freemen. The *Audiencia* recommended that two special ministers be appointed to execute the plan. Bucareli passed the plan to the fiscal, who agreed that these Negroes represented a valuable source of revenue, but he advocated copying the system of control used in Madrid, which involved a new census, a reapportionment of the city into new and more numerous districts, and the appointment of a number of precinct *alcaldes* (*alcaldes de barrio*). The current loss of revenue, not only in Mexico City but in other cities of New Spain, was blamed by the fiscal on disorderly and confused administration. Under his plan, he said, Mexico City alone would produce annually more than 100,000 pesos in tribute. He concluded by recommending that Bucareli issue a decree ordering the owners of Negro and mulatto slaves to deduct the tribute from the slaves' wages and deliver it to the royal collector.

The Viceroy passed the growing *expediente* to the *Real Acuerdo,* which agreed in essence with the fiscal's proposals. Bucareli did not, however, reach a decision; instead, he sent the entire file to Spain,

[7] Bucareli to Arriaga, January 27, 1773, AGN, CVB, 1773, Vol. 34, No. 739, pp. 39v–42.
[8] Same to same, March 27, 1773, AGN, CVB, 1773, Vol. 36, No. 836, pp. 28–29v.
[9] Velasco Ceballos, *La administración de . . . Bucareli,* Vol. II, p. XLV.

soliciting royal advice.[10] Apparently the government continued to lose money because of the disorderly situation in Mexico City, since no reply by the Crown has come to light, and Bucareli himself seems not to have brought the matter up again.[11]

Priestley points out that the entire tribute system needed revision and reorganization. There was no uniformity in the amount collected, the time of collection, or the material used in payment, although perhaps it should be noted that these observations need not necessarily be regarded as critical in all situations. Gálvez made a series of recommendations designed to correct these and other deficiencies, but Bucareli took no action on them. In fact, Gálvez' ideas had to await the establishment of the intendancy system before they became law.[12]

It is interesting to turn once more to Velasco Ceballos for an opinion. "Reorganization, basic or even superficial, for the collection of Tribute? Never. Much was said about it during the government of the Marqués de Croix, and Gálvez supported it solidly; but, as we have already seen, all innovation terrified Viceroy Bucareli." [13] Perhaps this is true, at least in part, although one is tempted to say, "Terrified? Never." The system did need reformation, but Bucareli did not normally or easily follow such a course. Furthermore, in spite of Gálvez' recommendations Bucareli did have at hand a complete new set of ordinances to install. It is possible that he felt that these were a sufficient change. With respect to Mexico City, however, he apparently allowed a good source of revenue to go untouched, an action which was genuinely out of keeping with his usual method.

In another instance, however, when a similar unexploited source of income came to light, Bucareli saw to it that the deficiency was remedied. By way of a junta of *hacienda* which met in December, 1772, the Guadalajara *Audiencia* was requested to report why tribute was not being collected in the mining districts of Rosario, Maloya, and Copala, while it was being collected in Culiacán, which was

[10] Bucareli to Arriaga, December 27, 1773, AGN, CVB, 1773, Vol. 46, No. 1227, pp. 25v–29v.

[11] Velasco Ceballos is also of this opinion. *La administración de . . . Bucareli,* Vol. II, p. 44 n.

[12] Priestley, *José de Gálvez,* pp. 325–329.

[13] Velasco Ceballos, *La administración de . . . Bucareli,* Vol. II, p. XLVI.

farther toward the interior than the other three. The Guadalajara body replied that the exaction had not been made because some of the areas were recognized as frontier districts whereas the others were mining districts and therefore exempt. After meeting again in May and June, 1774, to consider this reply, the junta decided that the theory that mine workers were exempt from the tribute was fallacious. The Guadalajara tribunal was therefore ordered to see to the imposition of this royal levy immediately.[14]

One further decision with respect to tribute policy was made voluntarily by Charles III. As was the case with almost every financial activity of the Crown, there always existed numerous legal disputes in the various tribunals. Such disputes occasioned long delays and, in the eyes of the King, were generally harmful. Tributaries were accustomed to bring before the *audiencias* a great many appeals for rebates, discounts, and exemptions. In 1776 Charles III ordered that thereafter the collection of the impost would not await any pending legal decision, but that the money would be gathered and refunded later if the court decided that it should be. The only exception was to be in case there occurred a "general calamity," in which event the Viceroy, as superintendent of *Real Hacienda,* could declare collections suspended, having first solicited an opinion from the fiscal, of course.[15]

After a drop in 1772, caused apparently by the confusion attendant upon putting the new ordinances into effect, the income from tribute showed a fairly consistent increase under Bucareli's supervision. From 1771 through 1778, except for 1774, for which no figures were found, the annual gross revenues in pesos were: 824,528; 699,598; 817,511; 834,014; 846,188; 912,161; and 862,468. It is difficult to compute the combined deductions for expenses of collection and *pensiones* because such figures are not available in every case. A general estimate would place the combined figure at between 75,000 and 90,000 pesos annually.[16]

[14] Bucareli to Charles III, July 27, 1774, AGN, CVB, 1771–1778, Vol. 14, No. 174, pp. 65–71.

[15] Gálvez to Bucareli, October 20, 1776, AGN, RC, 1776, Vol. 109, No. 64, pp. 233–234.

[16] Figures taken from inclosures in the following cover-letters. Bucareli to Arriaga, January 27, 1773, in Velasco Ceballos, *La administración de . . . Bucareli,* Vol. II,

One profitable agency of the Crown with which Bucareli concerned himself throughout his viceregency was the mint (*Casa de Moneda*). Established in 1535, the mint in Mexico City was one of the oldest in the New World. The revenue which the Crown obtained from the operation of this agency came from the profits on coining money, that is, from the tax on bullion to be coined, and from using alloys of the precious metals to make specie. From its inception until the second quarter of the eighteenth century, the mint and the coinage process were leased to individuals for a fixed amount. In the early 1730's, however, the process of making the mint a possession of the Crown was begun, although it was not completed until Bucareli's time. Experts came to Mexico from Spain with machinery, a new 200,000-peso building was constructed, ordinances were drawn up, and in 1733 the mint came under royal administration. Thereafter there was no more private coinage. The government purchased on its own account nearly the entire output of the mines, for which purpose a reserve fund of 1,000,000 pesos was maintained.[17]

When the Crown took over the mint in 1733, however, it had to abrogate a number of leases held by individuals on the various offices which made up the organization. Instead of paying these persons off and finishing the transaction, the Crown continued to pay interest of 5 or 6 per cent on the evaluations which were made of these various positions. The single suggestion that Gálvez made to Bucareli concerning the mint was that he pay off this principal and bring an end to the interest payments.[18] Croix made only a few brief comments on the administrative organization of the mint, saying nothing about its condition or its problems.[19]

---

pp. 30–34. Bucareli to Gálvez, November 26, 1776, AGN, CVB, 1776, Vol. 85, No. 2585, pp. 1–5v, 65. Same to same, December 31, 1776, AGN, CVB, 1776, Vol. 86, No. 2695, pp. 117v–118v, 610–611. Same to same, February 24, 1778, AGN, CVB, 1778, Vol. 100, No. 3576, pp. 7–8, 119. Same to same, May 27, 1778, AGN, CVB, 1778, Vol. 106, No. 3809, pp. 60v–61v, 338–338v. Same to same, December 27, 1778, AGN, CVB, 1778, Vol. 114, No. 4205, pp. 14–14v, 214.

[17] Priestley, *José de Gálvez*, pp. 318–320.

[18] *Ibid.*, p. 321.

[19] Croix, Instrucción, AGN, CVB, 1772, Vol. 24, p. 418v.

Judging from Bucareli's initial report on the status of the mint upon his arrival, it appears to have been flourishing. The gross profit for 1771 was 1,231,156 pesos. Its regular expenses totaled 219,924 pesos, and it had paid 400,000 pesos to the tobacco *renta* which the latter had lent for the Gálvez expeditions. On hand from the end of 1770 was 1,410,461 pesos. The total cash on hand, therefore, was 2,021,693 pesos, according to the superintendent's statement which Bucareli forwarded to Spain early in 1772.[20]

In spite of the availability of this fund, Bucareli took no step to clear the mint of its old debts, as Gálvez had suggested. Charles III does not seem to have been interested in the idea either, until 1775, when, on July 1, he ordered the Viceroy to begin paying on the principal owed to the heirs of a certain Medina family as the former lessees of the office of treasurer of the mint. The evaluation was 424,673 pesos. On April 15, 1776, the King reiterated the order and extended the plan to include all offices for which the mint was still indebted.[21]

Bucareli replied that he had not been able to send news that the Medina situation had been concluded because the several heirs had been squabbling in court as to who was to get how much, and the whole thing had been held up. Nevertheless, the debt could be regarded as paid, he said, since the principal and accrued interest had been placed on separate deposit in the mint and earmarked as such while the court fight went on.[22]

With respect to the amounts owed on the other offices incorporated into the Crown mint, Bucareli asked the superintendent for a report. This official revealed that the total principal was 406,100 pesos, on which the Crown was paying 5 per cent interest. Of this amount, 200,000 pesos pertained to the offices of the assayer (*ensayador*) and smelter (*fundidor*). By virtue of a royal order of Ferdinand VI, issued

[20] Bucareli to Arriaga, January 27, 1772, and inclosure, AGN, CVB, 1772, Vol. 20, No. 149, pp. 111–114.

[21] Bucareli to Gálvez, July 27, 1776, AGN, CVB, 1776, Vol. 81, No. 2410, pp. 61v–62. This letter is another in which Bucareli obligingly repeats all antecedent correspondence before getting down to the case at hand.

[22] *Ibid.*, pp. 62–62v.

in 1754, the interest on this 200,000-peso debt was paid to the Carmelite nuns of Santo Desierto, and it was the superintendent's opinion that the King would not want this principal to be paid off. The remaining 206,100 pesos was divided among the offices of the engraver (*tallador*), the weighmaster (*balanzario*), the actuary (*escribano*), and the chief guard (*guarda mayor*).[23]

Three months later, September, 1776, Bucareli reported that, in accordance with his plan, the amount owed to the heirs of the engraver lessee was already paid off, that to the weighmaster would be completed by the end of the month, that to the actuary by the end of October, and that to the chief guard by the end of November. Meanwhile, the fiscal had offered his opinion that in spite of Ferdinand VI's royal order, the principal owned by the Carmelite nuns could be redeemed. Bucareli agreed and, as a consequence, ordered the mint superintendent to inform the Carmelite provincial that payments on this sum would begin very soon.[24]

The King approved all of Bucareli's actions in this matter. In April, 1777, the Viceroy reported that closer investigation revealed that the entire amount due the Carmelite nuns, including interest, was 225,000 pesos, but that this would be completely paid by the end of May and that the mint would then be wholly free of these old debts.[25]

There still remained, however, one office concerned with the processing of precious metals which did not yet belong to the Crown. Furthermore, it had not been assimilated into the royal organization by means of the lease-abrogation method as had been the case with the other offices, although the reason for this exception is not clear. The only apparent reason which can be offered is that of oversight, but it seems inadequate. The office thus treated was that of the separator of gold and silver (*apartador de oro y plata*), whose services were needed when bullion came to the mint in mixed form. The bullion from Sonora had a special tendency to present such a problem. It was

[23] *Ibid.*, pp. 63–65. The only amount specifically cited with respect to these latter offices is 116,000 pesos for the *tallador*.

[24] Same to same, September 27, 1776, AGN, CVB, 1776, Vol. 83, No. 2532, pp. 65–67v.

[25] Same to same, April 26, 1777, AGN, CVB, 1777, Vol. 90, No. 2909, pp. 55–57.

the *apartador's* function to separate the two metals by smelting processes, for which service he charged a specified fee.[26]

The matter came to Bucareli's attention when he received a royal order of November 14, 1777, which revealed that one Francisco de Fagoaga had presented a claim to the Crown in which he averred that the office of the *apartador* had been auctioned off in 1689 for 70,000 pesos to one José de Retes. One of the conditions was that the royal grant was for perpetuity. Retes' last heir, Francisco Antonio Bernardino de Zaldivar, received the office in 1697, but, upon joining a religious order in 1718, had transferred the grant to Fagoaga. In 1735 the Crown ordered an investigation made to see if this office could be incorporated into the mint as a royal agency, but the King's order had not been carried out.[27]

The question did not arise again until 1770, when, on the recommendation of the Council of the Indies, Charles III gave a title of confirmation for the office to Francisco Manuel Cayetano de Fagoaga. In 1776, however, the King decided that his earlier measure had been erroneous, and as a consequence he ordered Bucareli to proceed secretly to form a council of trustworthy men to discuss possible methods for returning this office to royal control.[28]

Before convoking the council, Bucareli requested a file of documents on the matter, but discovered that through "carelessness or perhaps malice," the requisite papers could not be found. As a result, he decided to entrust Superintendent of the Mint Pedro de Villavicencio with the investigation because he had faith in his discretion and because in this manner he would have to reveal the project to fewer people.[29]

The Superintendent did a great deal of spade work on the problem and managed to piece together a rather lengthy history of the *apartador's* office. He discovered that it had been created in 1626 upon the request of the miners, and that its services had been rendered

[26] Same to same, May 27, 1777, AGN, CVB, 1777, Vol. 13, Libro 14, No. 205 or 2953, p. 23.

[27] *Ibid.*, p. 23v.

[28] *Ibid.*, pp. 24–24v.

[29] *Ibid.*, pp. 24v–25v. Bucareli's letter of instruction to Villavicencio, dated May 12, is found in the same volume on p. 143.

free of charge until, in one of its traditional searches for money, the Crown had auctioned off the process. After a long technical discussion, Villavicencio concluded that the *apartador's* office, as it was run at that time, was harmful to the welfare of both the miners and the general public, and that the present owner was making a highly unreasonable profit. He recommended that the lease be redeemed by the Crown, submitting a complete list of persons and the jobs they were to fill if and when the office did become royal property. The cost of the incorporation was set at 76,000 pesos for buying up the lease and 25,000 pesos for the purchase of the building in which the office was located, although it was deemed possible that an adjoining building might also have to be obtained in order to have adequate space.[30]

From the Superintendent's report Bucareli deduced two major points: the miners would benefit from Crown ownership because they would pay less for the separation service and would receive their pure bullion more quickly; and, the royal revenues would be increased considerably over the 1,333 pesos which the *apartador* had been paying annually to the Crown under the old contract. Not only were these two points "persuasive," said Bucareli, but the method by which he had arrived at them had saved him from the confusion attendant upon the variety of opinions which would have resulted had he proceeded to form a council to handle the question. He pointed out, however, that the office was held by Fagoaga not as a gift, but by a legal contract entered into by the King. Whether or not the Crown chose to break this contract, the King must decide.[31]

By a Royal *Cédula* of July 21, 1778, Charles III ordered that the *apartador's* office be incorporated with the rest of the mint as a clear Crown possession. This was being done, the King said, "with the just

[30] Bucareli to Gálvez, July 27, 1777, AGN, CVB, 1777, Vol. 13, Libro 14, No. 215 or 3096, pp. 32–37v.

[31] *Ibid.*, pp. 38–39. The inclosures in this letter are three: No. 1—Villavicencio's long reply to Bucareli's instruction of May 12, dated July 5, *ibid.*, pp. 147–177v; No. 2—a copy of the conditions under which the *apartador's* office was first auctioned off, dated October, 1651, *ibid.*, pp. 179–184v; No. 3—a Royal *Cédula* of January 29, 1708, which granted the office of *tallador* to one Pedro Sánchez de Tagle, *ibid.*, pp. 185–190. The relationship of the last document is not clear.

and pious design of avoiding the harm to the royal treasury, to the public, and to the mining industry which resulted from the *apartador's* being in the hands of private persons." Bucareli issued the corresponding decree on October 16 and ordered the new mint superintendent, Fernando José Mangino, to see to its execution. Mangino swore in Second Assayer José Ignacio Bartolache as the new royal *apartador* on the seventeenth, and on the nineteenth he read the royal order and Bucareli's decree to the Marqués de Apartado Francisco Fagoaga. The Marqués offered no objection, but he advised Mangino that his cousin, José Fagoaga, really performed the service and that he would have to answer such questions as the new official might have. The 76,000 pesos for the abrogated lease was to be paid within three days.[32]

In February, 1779, Bucareli reported that all the necessary transfers of papers and instructions had been accomplished, the new *apartador* and his staff were doing business, and all that remained to finish the incorporation was the formation of a set of ordinances for the office and a decision on whether to buy the old offices or to build new ones.[33] For all practical purposes, the deed was done.

Mint Superintendent Villavicencio proposed another change in policy which was discussed and accepted during Bucareli's viceregency. It concerned the working fund which the mint kept on hand for the purchase of bullion from miners. This fund had been maintained at 2,000,000 pesos for some time until Charles III, acting on the advice of the Marqués de Croix, had lowered it by nearly a fourth. In the spring of 1775 Villavicencio suggested to the Crown that the amount be restored to its former level. The King sent the suggestion to Bucareli, soliciting his opinion.[34]

Before this dispatch reached the Viceroy, however, the Superintendent had turned to Bucareli with his suggestion, apparently because the reply from Spain was not as quickly forthcoming as he had hoped. His

[32] Bucareli to Gálvez, October 27, 1778, AGN, CVB, 1778, Vol. 111, No. 4102, pp. 56–57.

[33] Same to same, February 24, 1779, AGN, CVB, 1779, Vol. 116, No. 4262, pp. 4–6v. Another letter (same to same, same date, *ibid.*, No. 4263, pp. 6v–9) discusses the problem of the old or new offices.

[34] Arriaga to Bucareli, August 4, 1775, AGN, RC, 1775, Vol. 106, No. 175, p. 324.

point was simply that 1,500,000 pesos was not an adequate amount, especially when several large shipments of bullion from various regions all reached the mint at nearly the same time. Bucareli agreed, pointing out that although the proposal would have been out of the question during the period when the treasury was heavily in debt and operating at a deficit, now that these problems had been remedied the idea was feasible. Furthermore, he favored the increase because it provided a ready source from which money could be borrowed in case of emergency without causing any particular economic or administrative upheaval, and to which repayment could be made when it was most convenient.[35]

By the time the King's request for an opinion reached the Viceroy, however, Bucareli had also received the royal order to repay the Medina family for the lease it held on the mint treasurer's office. In view of this, he suggested that the fund increase be postponed until such burdens as the Medina lease were all cleared away. His attitude toward the higher reserve fund was still favorable, however.[36] There then ensued the period of nearly a year and a half during which most of the profits from certain of the mint's operations that could reasonably be applied to redeeming the various leases against that institution were so used. During this period Charles III approved the 2,000,000-peso fund, and by January, 1778, Bucareli could report that the fund had been built up to 1,800,000 pesos and that the remaining 200,000 pesos would be obtained from the first profits which the mint produced in that year.[37] This amount was reached by April 1.[38]

A *ramo* which was not in a flourishing condition when Bucareli took command—which was, in fact, on the downgrade—was that of pulque, the alcoholic, fermented liquor made from the maguey plant. The right to manufacture and sell it in New Spain was leased until 1763, when

[35] Bucareli to Arriaga, September 26, 1775, AGN, CVB, 1775, Vol. 71, No. 1976, pp. 9v–10v.

[36] Same to same, November 26, 1775, AGN, CVB, 1775, Vol. 73, No. 2060, pp. 24–24v.

[37] Bucareli to Gálvez, January 2, 1778, AGN, CVB, 1777, Vol. 98, No. 3477, pp. 35v–37.

[38] Same to same, April 26, 1778, in Velasco Ceballos, *La administración de . . . Bucareli,* Vol. II, pp. 105–106.

the industry was placed under Crown administration. Controlling pulque production was a difficult task for the authorities inasmuch as the wide cultivation of maguey made possible a great deal of illicit manufacture of the drink. It was (and remains) the poor man's liquor, and therefore the criminal courts were clogged with cases of disorders wherein pulque was held the responsible element. Priestley observed that "the viceroys would have gladly eradicated the evil, as would the clergy, but the beverage was an immemorial heritage of the indigenes, and its use could not be prevented." [39]

The validity of this statement depends on how much faith may be placed in a viceroy's preference for public virtue over monetary income. The pulque business was a profitable one, bringing into the royal coffers about 300,000 pesos each year during the viceregency preceding Bucareli's. In fact, one of the earliest communications Bucareli received on the subject expressed the King's concern over the fact that the pulque revenue had been steadily declining. Charles III charged that the main reason for the decrease was to be found in Mexico City, where the soldiers were drinking and dispensing various illegal and nontax-paying liquors, such as *chinguirito*.[40] So widespread was this practice that a comparison of the net profits from pulque in 1764 and 1770 revealed a decrease of 67,733 pesos. The King therefore ordered the Viceroy to enforce the law in this matter and raise the revenue to its former level.[41]

Bucareli replied, typically, that as soon as he had investigated the antecedents he would take the proper steps.[42] This was in March, 1773. Once more it is easier to ascertain what Bucareli accomplished rather

[39] Priestley, *José de Gálvez*, pp. 358–359.

[40] A rum made from the lees of sugar. There were numerous liquors of this type, made from whatever fermentuous liquid that came to hand.

[41] Arriaga to Bucareli, November 4, 1771, AGN, RC, 1771, Vol. 99, No. 74, pp. 108–109. The figures that Charles III used in his computation have not been found. It is presumed that they included the entire viceroyalty. Figures for Mexico City alone for these two years are: net profit for 1764—264,315 pesos; for 1770— 221,081 pesos; decrease—43,234 pesos. Statement which shows the liquid product of the pulque *ramo* of Mexico . . . , in Velasco Ceballos, *La administración de . . . Bucareli*, Vol. II, p. 70.

[42] Bucareli to Arriaga, March 20, 1772, AGN, CVB, 1772, Vol. 22, No. 243, pp. 1–1v.

than precisely how he did it. Late in 1774, when the returns were all in for the preceding year, Charles III congratulated the Viceroy on "the considerable increase in this [pulque] *ramo* in the same year [1773] in the amount of 40,000 pesos." (This increase was from Mexico City alone.) The King then urged Bucareli to even more intensive efforts to wipe out illegal sales in order to achieve thereby "the conservation of the public health, and . . . the increase of a legal revenue." [43] Bucareli must have used police methods to suppress the sale of prohibited liquors, and it is probable that in this case and during the remainder of his term he availed himself of the services of the *Acordada,* or special police, which he supported and to some extent strengthened while he was viceroy. [44]

In trying to reconstruct the financial side of Bucareli's viceregency by using figures, in many instances it is difficult to secure consecutive similar statements. Therefore, a precise accounting for what the pulque *ramo* produced during his time cannot be presented. In some cases figures are lacking, while in others there are too many numbers. Nevertheless, a general idea of the progress he made can be attained. From February, 1763, through December, 1771, the annual net profits from pulque in Mexico City only, in thousands of pesos were: 242, 264, 251, 239, 236, 230, 235, 221, and 216. For the seven full years of Bucareli's viceregency, that is, 1772 through 1778, the corresponding figures are: 217, 264, 285, 319, 344, 435, and 419. [45]

Not all of this increase came from the enforcement of the laws. From 1776 on, as Spain moved ever closer to war, first with Portugal and then with England, Charles III continuously asked for more money, and pulque was one of the sources from which he suggested that it be raised. It was his stated intention to seek the needed addi-

[43] Arriaga to Bucareli, November 30, 1774, AGN, RC, 1774, Vol. 105, No. 125, pp. 280–281. As can well be imagined, the various bootleg liquors sold did constitute a genuine menace to the consumer's physical well-being.

[44] See, for example, Bucareli to Gálvez, August 27, 1776, No. 2465, AGI, Mex., Leg. 1375.

[45] The figures for the pre-Bucareli period are from Velasco Ceballos, *La administración de . . . Bucareli,* Vol. II, p. 70. For the later figures, see the following volumes and letters in Bucareli's correspondence in the AGN: Vol. 34, No. 754; Vol. 48, No. 1281; Vol. 62, No. 1695; Vol. 87, No. 2732; Vol. 99, inclosure in No. 3517; Vol. 115, No. 4227.

tional revenue from "unnecessary products," such as pulque and tobacco. With respect to pulque he suggested a slight increase in the tax, to be so prudently administered that it would be barely perceptible to the public.[46]

Pulque was originally taxed at the rate of one real (piece of eight) per arroba (twelve English quarts). In 1767 the rate was raised by one and one-sixth grains.[47] In order to decide how much the new increase should be, Bucareli consulted the superintendent and the accountant of the Mexico City customs office, and the fiscal. Although these three officials agreed that "the drinking of pulque, besides not being of the first necessity, is also enervating, vicious, and from which are derived horrible excesses," they could not agree on how much the tax should be increased. It was proposed, however, that the increase be imposed by means of a reduction in the amount of each serving rather than through a direct increase in the price.[48]

Superintendent Miguel Páez felt that an increase of two and five-sixths grains would not be burdensome on the consumer. Using the 2,471,134.5 arrobas of pulque which entered Mexico City in 1775 as a basis, he figured it would increase revenue by the amount of 72,932 pesos, and, estimating that 2,700,000 arrobas would enter in 1776, he computed the increase at 79,687 pesos. Accountant Felipe Clere was "more timid." He advocated a tax increase of only one and one-third grains, with parallel increases of 34,321 pesos and 36,000 pesos. The fiscal (either Domingo Arangoyti or José Antonio Areche) was more interested in income than in popular reaction. He averred that four and two-thirds grains would be a proper increase, which, again using the above figures, would produce 123,914 pesos or 135,937 pesos.[49]

Bucareli felt that the government should proceed slowly and cautiously with new taxes, and therefore Páez' figure of two and five-

[46] Gálvez to Bucareli, July 27, 1776, AGN, RC, 1776, Vol. 108, No. 56, pp. 121–121v. The King reiterated this order and added the *alcabala* to the list in same to same, January 23, 1777, in Velasco Ceballos, *La administración de . . . Bucareli,* Vol. II, p. 85.

[47] Priestley, *José de Gálvez,* p. 359.

[48] Bucareli to Gálvez, December 31, 1776, AGN, CVB, 1776, Vol. 86, No. 2694, pp. 110–111v, 113–114v.

[49] *Ibid.,* pp. 111v–113.

sixths grains was his choice as the most reasonable suggestion. By instructing pulque retailers to deduct a proportionate amount from their servings, it was intended that the new impost should fall directly on the drinker. The new increase was to go into effect on January 1, 1777.[50]

At the end of January the Viceroy received a report comparing the pulque entry for that month with that of the same month in 1776. Despite a decrease of 15,705 arrobas, the revenue had increased by 4,276 pesos. He predicted, however, that the decline would not continue, because pulque had a strong hold on the natives, and importations would therefore rise again.[51] His prediction was correct, for 1777 saw the entry of 2,744,593 arrobas of pulque, which was slightly more than had been anticipated. In 1778 the figure climbed to 2,891,-651 arrobas.[52]

Next to tobacco, the *alcabala* was the most fruitful source of revenue in the entire *Real Hacienda* and the top contributor to the *masa común*. This impost was a sales and turnover tax payable on raw materials, consumer goods, chattels, and real and personal property with every change of ownership. It was a legal essential of the process of sale.[53]

In spite of a royal promise not to do so, the *alcabala* was introduced into New Spain and the rest of Spanish America in 1574. Originally amounting to only 2 per cent, the rate was doubled in 1632 when the

[50] *Ibid.*, pp. 113–114v.

[51] Same to same, January 27, 1777, AGN, CVB, 1777, Vol. 87, No. 2748, pp. 66–67.

[52] Felipe Clere to Bucareli, January 3, 1778, AGN, CVB, 1778, Vol. 99, of No. 3517, pp. 78–79. Bucareli to Gálvez, January 27, 1779, AGN, CVB, 1779, Vol. 115, No. 4224, pp. 12–12v.

The most startling suggestion concerning the pulque situation came from Charles III, who ordered Bucareli to convene certain officials and consider the possibility of building a strong, permanent wall around Mexico City in order to stop smuggling. It could be paid for, he said, with receipts from the pulque tax. Bucareli held a meeting and turned the problem over to a crew of engineers, whereupon the project disappeared into limbo, which was perhaps the Viceroy's intention. Bucareli to Gálvez, April 26, 1777, No. 2861, AGI, Mex., Leg. 1275.

[53] Robert Sidney Smith, "Sales Taxes in New Spain, 1575–1770," *Hispanic American Historical Review*, Vol. XXVIII, No. 1, Part I (February, 1948), p. 14. This work is cited hereafter as "Sales Taxes." Priestley, *José de Gálvez*, p. 353.

Crown sought additional revenue to help defray the cost of the military and naval forces used to protect America. This added 2 per cent, called *unión de armas*—on the theory that it united the forces of Castile with those of the colonies—was initially scheduled to last for only fifteen years, but it became a permanent part of the impost. A few years later, in 1635, searching for still more money for defensive purposes, the Crown added another 2 per cent. This time it was labeled the *armada de Barlovento,* and was ostensibly devoted to forming and maintaining a fleet of coast-guard vessels. From 1644 to 1754 and from 1780 to 1790 the rate was 8 per cent, in the first instance because of the *reventa,* or resale theory, and in the latter because of the demands of war.[54]

As was the case with so many laws, taxes, regulations, methods, and systems in New Spain, however, the *alcabala* was not uniformly exacted in all places at all times. Some of this variance was regulated and some of it was due simply to confused administration. For example, there were many exemptions. Indians, at varying times and on diverse products, paid no sales tax. The clergy and religious institutions enjoyed certain exemptions, a privilege which was frequently abused. The Tribunal of the Santa Cruzada had a partial exemption. Specific commodities moved on and off the exemption lists. Finally, in certain frontier areas the duty was either not collected at all or was held to a 2 per cent impost.[55]

From 1602 until 1753—except for the period 1677 to 1693 when the Crown handled it—the *alcabala* was farmed out in Mexico City, the most important revenue area. The contracts were held either by the city government or by the *Consulado de Comercio.* In 1753 the Crown began to administer the revenue on its own account as the various leases expired. Finally, a royal order of February 6, 1764, made this direct-administration program definitive. Gálvez' Instructions directed him to investigate the question of which method—lease or administration—would bring greater revenue into the royal coffers. He found that the transfer to the administration system was under way, but that a

---

[54] Robert Sidney Smith, "Sales Taxes," pp. 3–4, 9, 34–35. Priestley, *José de Gálvez,* p. 354. Maniau, *Compendio de la real hacienda,* p. 18.

[55] Robert Sidney Smith, "Sales Taxes," pp. 14–16.

number of leases were still in existence. Popular reaction was equally unfavorable to both methods. He finally settled on the *encabezamiento,* that is, lease by towns and districts, as the best solution for certain situations, whereas Crown management appeared best for others. He preferred the lease system for provincial centers where local officials could handle the collection. For large towns, however, where trade was more active, he felt that administration by treasury officials was superior.[56]

Aside from recurrent encounters with merchants over interpretations of minor points in the *alcabala* ordinances, the first major policy-adjustment which Bucareli had to administer in this *ramo* concerned certain other branches of the *Real Hacienda.* The problem began when the chief accountant of *alcabalas,* interested in increasing the revenue of his *ramo,* asked Bucareli whether the mail branch should pay sales tax on the iron and steel it brought from Spain on its ships and whether the tobacco and playing-card monopolies should do the same on the paper and similar goods which they imported. The Veracruz minister of *Real Hacienda* made a like query at about the same time.

Not sure of the answer himself, Bucareli asked for the opinions of the chiefs of the three branches concerned. All of them made nearly the same reply—it was like transferring money from one royal pocket to another, and would serve only to increase the *alcabala* revenue. In a law-citation contest which ensued, the Tribunal of Accounts supported the *alcabala* chief's point of view, while the fiscal impartially quoted legal precedents for both sides. He concluded, however, by suggesting that no change be made until the King had been consulted. Since this was one of Bucareli's favorite administrative methods, he readily complied.[57]

On November 11, 1773, Charles III ruled that the three *ramos* must pay the tax just as though they were private business concerns.[58] The result was a deluge of petitions, suggestions, and questions. The cus-

[56] *Ibid.,* pp. 4, 35–37. Priestley, *José de Gálvez,* p. 354.

[57] Bucareli to Arriaga, June 26, 1773, and inclosures, AGN, CVB, 1773, Vol. 39, No. 988, pp. 21–22v, 99–108.

[58] Fonseca and Urrutía, *Historia general de real hacienda,* Vol. II, p. 69.

toms superintendent wondered what to do about tobacco imported from Havana. The tobacco administrator complained that the operation of his offices was being dangerously slowed down by the actions of the customs officials. The fiscal gave lengthy opinions on the matter. The mail administrator petitioned for exemptions on certain goods lying in storage in Puebla. The chief of the playing-card *ramo* acted puzzled. Bucareli, backed by the fiscal, settled each question with commendable good sense and summarized the whole thing in a report to the Crown. Nothing further was heard on the matter aside from a report on a brief bit of stubbornness on the part of the mail administrator.[59] Fonseca and Urrutía note simply that the Viceroy put the King's ruling into practice.[60]

The most important change in *alcabala* administration during Bucareli's term had its beginning with the death of Accountant General of *Alcabalas* Juan Antonio de Arce y Arroyo early in 1776. As a result of his demise, Charles III ordered the entire accountant's section done away with and its functions taken over by the superintendency and accountant's office of the Mexico City customs office. Extending the adjustment of the *ramo* even further, the King ordered that, as the leases expired which Gálvez had made with the various cities, towns, and districts, *alcabala* management in these places was to be placed under administration, that is, directly on the account of the *Real Hacienda.*[61]

According to Bucareli's account of December 27, 1776, the union of the accountants' offices was easily enough accomplished, although it created a problem as to what was to be done with the surplus personnel thus created. The fact that the *alcabala* collection for Guadalajara had just been leased also presented a difficulty. With respect to other leases which were at that moment being offered for sale but which had not as yet been purchased, Bucareli ordered all auctions immediately discon-

[59] Bucareli to Arriaga, November 26, 1774, AGN, CVB, 1774, Vol. 61, No. 1617, pp. 29–39v. Same to same, December 27, 1774, AGN, CVB, 1774, Vol. 62, No. 1663, pp. 64–67.

[60] Fonseca and Urrutía, *Historia general de real hacienda*, Vol. II, p. 69.

[61] *Ibid.*, p. 71.

tinued.[62] He then turned to various subordinates for advice on what to do next.

Instead of advice he received summaries of the administrative arrangements which must be made and of doubtful points raised by the royal order. In the first category were such things as: what to do with the leftover employees; the need for a new set of *alcabala* ordinances and special *reglamentos* for each *alcabala* district; decisions on the number and definition of administrative districts (*partidos*) which must be created. Of the doubtful points, one concerned whether the *alcabala* collection in small, provincial centers should be administered or auctioned, in view of the fact that the amount of revenue they produced was nearly inadequate to pay the salaries of the royal officials who would be needed. The second point bothered Bucareli most. He worried because the royal order, although clear enough as to what to do with expired leases, did not expressly state what was to be done about those which had been made during his viceregency and which still had a long time to run. Finally, the Guadalajara lease question was upsetting.[63]

With respect to these last two points, former Fiscal José Antonio Areche, waiting for transportation to Peru as *visitador* general to that viceroyalty, and Fiscal Domingo Arangoyti both felt that the contract for the Guadalajara *alcabalas* which the Crown had made was binding, although the latter admitted that there was some doubt about the matter and recommended consultation with the *Real Acuerdo*. Seven of the eight ministers on this body declined to advise, however, because they considered it a matter which only a court of justice could settle.[64]

Justifiably worried about the effect which the rescission of these contracts would have on the government's reputation, Bucareli decided that he would make no change until he had learned the King's desire on the matter. He did, however, send notes to all *alcabala* lessees asking that they consider giving up their leases voluntarily in view of the

[62] Bucareli to Gálvez, October 27, 1776, AGN, CVB, 1776, Vol. 84, No. 2556, pp. 31v–32v. A simple acknowledgment of receipt with no additional comment is in Gálvez to Bucareli, February 9, 1777, AGN, RC, 1777, Vol. 110, No. 95, p. 148.
[63] Bucareli to Gálvez, December 27, 1776, AGN, CVB, 1776, Vol. 86, No. 2687, pp. 93–97. See note 70, below, for citation of the royal reply.
[64] *Ibid.*, pp. 97–98.

King's wish that their districts be directly administered. Furthermore, he ordered *alcaldes mayores* and local justices in areas in which leases were in force to institute a record of all *alcabala* payments made in these places, to the end that if the King should decide that these leases were to be rescinded, an account of what was due the Crown would be available.[65]

Although Charles III did express his will in direct reply to the above letter from Bucareli, the Viceroy was writing another report on the problem even before the first one had reached Spain. He revealed that in answer to his request to the *alcabala* lessees that they consent to rescission of their contracts, some, including the Guadalajara lease-holder, presented many arguments and pleas as to why they could not give up their contracts. Others readily consented, but it turned out that they controlled in most cases only small, unproductive districts or else their leases had only a few months to run. Bucareli was not even certain that it would be worthwhile to accept their offers. The rest had not replied. An additional worry resulted from the fact that the *alcaldes* and justices who had been ordered to keep a record of *alcabala* payments assumed that they were now royal employees and thus should be drawing a salary from the treasury. Bucareli quickly put a stop to that nonsense.[66]

Because the Jalapa Fair was going on and trade was brisk, with a consequent promise of high *alcabala* revenues, Bucareli wanted to move rapidly and also to protect the King's interest in case the contracts were deemed ended as of an earlier date. He therefore convened a special junta of top financial ministers and presented it with a list of specific questions on which he wanted recommendations. He also issued a decree that a royal decision was pending on whether or not the leases were still in effect.[67]

Because of the slowness of communications, Bucareli continued to make decisions on the *alcabala* question before he had received replies to the queries he made in his monthly reports. With respect to the

[65] *Ibid.,* pp. 98–100.
[66] Same to same, January 27, 1777, AGN, CVB, 1777, Vol. 87, No. 2734, pp. 52–53v.
[67] *Ibid.,* pp. 53v–55v.

small *alcabala* districts whose lessees had consented to rescission of their contracts, the Viceroy dispatched royal officials to administer those which might be temporarily profitable because of the movement of goods from the Fair, while others he simply added to the nearest district already under administration. In a few instances he saved money by adding the *alcabala* collection to the duties of officials of the tobacco *renta* already in the district concerned, making similar use of this monopoly's guard corps. It was difficult to convene the junta because its members were too busy with their regular jobs. To counterbalance this, Bucareli sent notes to each one, asking in what way he could help them in order that they might have time to get together.[68]

This was in February, 1777. Month by month during that spring and summer the junta either could not meet or moved too slowly and raised too many questions. Consequently, although Bucareli continued to make decisions on minor matters, major issues remained unsolved.[69] Not until September did he receive the royal reply, dated March 18, in answer to his second letter on the matter, dated December 27, 1776. These Instructions from Charles III covered most of the questions which had been disturbing the Viceroy. As a basic premise the King stated that the *alcabala* was to be placed under general and uniform administration for the good of the royal service. Minor districts and towns were to be united with the nearest administrations unless distance or scanty revenue made leasing by the town or district preferable. In no instance were leases to be granted to private citizens. Therefore, the contract in existence with the Count de la Torre Cosio, who held the Guadalajara lease, and all similar lessees were to cease immediately. Only Veracruz was to remain an exception to the plan which called for central control from the director in Mexico City. Finally, Bucareli was instructed to accept no appeal or petition which would hinder execution of these orders.[70]

[68] Same to same, February 24, 1777, AGN, CVB, 1777, Vol. 88, No. 2768, pp. 25–26v.

[69] Same to same, March 27, April 26 (4), and May 27, 1777, AGN, CVB, 1777, Vol. 89, No. 2828, pp. 41–42; Vol. 90, Nos. 2864–2866, pp. 17–19v, and No. 2908, pp. 54v–55; Vol. 91, No. 2959, pp. 5–7v.

[70] Gálvez to Bucareli, March 18, 1777, AGN, RC, 1777, Vol. 110, No. 216, pp. 337–338.

Upon receipt of this royal order Bucareli passed it to the fiscal, as was his custom. The fiscal proposed that all *alcabala* lessees cease handling collections immediately and that the chief of this *ramo* propose men to serve as administrators in the districts affected. Until such men could be chosen, it was suggested that control be temporarily given to royal-treasury officials where there were such, or to administrators of other *ramos,* local justices or some similar satisfactory citizen. Subordinates in these *alcabala* offices were not to be disturbed. Bucareli agreed and ordered these measures put in practice. He then returned the file to the fiscal for an opinion on when the leases should be adjudged as expired.[71]

It was the fiscal's conclusion that these contracts were ended as of October 3, 1776, the day on which Bucareli had received the original July 26 letter calling for general administration of the *ramo* and for the extinction of the accountant's office. Therefore, all sales taxes collected by the lessees since that time were the property of the Crown, legitimate expenses deducted. The assessor general was of a contrary opinion. He argued that this money was legally the property of the lessees, and that they had committed no offense for which they should be so penalized. He felt that the leases should be adjudged expired at the time the persons named to take them over from the lessees did so. The *Real Acuerdo* refused once more to give an opinion, or at least nine of the ten members did. The tenth chose still a third date as the time of expiration, selecting the day on which, in accordance with Bucareli's order, the *alcaldes mayores* or justices began keeping a record of collections in the leased districts.[72]

In view of the general disagreement, Bucareli reserved the matter to the King's decision, but in order to protect both the lessees and the Crown he ordered that the former present to the new administrators within twenty days of the change-over a sworn statement of the revenue collected between October 3, 1776, and the day the justices

---

[71] Bucareli to Gálvez, September 26, 1777, AGN, CVB, 1777, Vol. 95, No. 3243, pp. 18–19v. The data used are from Bucareli's summary of events, which comprises the cover-letter. The opinions of the fiscal and various other advisers constitute an inclosure, which is located in the same volume, pp. 152–167.

[72] *Ibid.,* pp. 19v–21.

began their records, and between the latter day and the day on which the change-over was made.[73]

The King's decision, dated January 20, 1778, declared that the fiscal was correct—the contracts expired on October 3, 1776, and all revenue collected by the lessees since that date belonged to the Crown. With respect to this point and to whatever other problems of a similar nature that might arise in the future, the director of the *ramo* was to act as a privative judge, with appeals from his decisions to go only to the Viceroy, as superintendent general. There was to be no appeal to any tribunal, inasmuch as the regular courts had no cognizance of points involving the *Real Hacienda.*[74] Bucareli received this royal order in April, 1778, and at the end of May he reported that the King's decision had been fulfilled.[75]

How much the Crown gained by this whole maneuver is not apparent. No further comment on the subject was found, while reference to figures reveals no startling increase in the *alcabala* income, as the following statements of the annual net profits (in pesos) from this *ramo* demonstrate: [76]

1772	.	.	.	.	1,121,718
1773	.	.	.	.	1,844,993
1774	.	.	.	.	1,325,667
1775	.	.	.	.	1,262,869
1776	.	.	.	.	1,285,997
1777	.	.	.	.	1,975,460
1778	.	.	.	.	2,590,222
1779	.	.	.	.	2,099,253

[73] *Ibid.,* pp. 21–22. The decree concerning the sworn statements is found in AGN, Bandos, 1777–1778, Vol. 10, No. 24, pp. 61–61v.

[74] Gálvez to Bucareli, January 20, 1778, AGN, RC, 1778, Vol. 113, No. 33, pp. 43–44. This includes Bucareli's endorsement. The Viceroy acknowledged receipt of this royal order in Bucareli to Gálvez, April 26, 1778, AGN, CVB, 1778, Vol. 104, No. 3698, pp. 3v–4v.

[75] Bucareli to Gálvez, May 27, 1778, AGN, CVB, 1778, Vol. 106, No. 3794, pp. 1v–4v.

[76] Figures for years 1772–1775 are from inclosure No. 1 in Bucareli to Gálvez, November 26, 1776, AGN, CVB, 1776, Vol. 85, No. 2585, p. 65. For years 1776–1779, from Fonseca and Urrutía, *Historia general de real hacienda,* Vol. II, p. 94.

It is possible that the increase of more than 500,000 pesos in 1778 over 1777 and the subsequent drop in 1779 reflect the adjustment, but 1773 shows a similar variation between figures for 1772 and 1774.

The point is not here especially important, however. The entire incident has significance in so far as it is another signpost on the road to Bourbon centralization. With respect to Bucareli, it was one of his most confident and deft administrative actions. His hesitation in the face of contrary opinions from his advisers was only normal. For him to make decisions without specific royal guidance was atypical.

Of all the *ramos* in which Bucareli intervened more or less personally, the tobacco revenue was the one which gave him the most satisfaction. His pleasure was justified, because during his viceregency this monopoly made genuine progress. How the Crown came into possession of the profitable tobacco business is too long a story to relate here in any detail. The government first entered the field simply as a competitor of the private tobacco interests in 1764, but beginning in 1765 steps were initiated which were ultimately to force all nongovernment merchandizers out of the field.[77]

This objective had by no means been achieved when Bucareli assumed command. Although the growing of tobacco was restricted to a group of planters around the towns of Córdova, Orizaba, and Tesuitlán, with the government purchasing the entire crop, there was still much tobacco grown illegally. Furthermore, there were not as yet enough royal factories in existence to supply the needs of the viceroyalty. As a result, many private citizens were still engaged in processing and retailing tobacco. It was Bucareli's intention either to put such people out of business or to put them to work for the monopoly.

Shortly after he became viceroy he discovered that there existed a sort of feud among various officials in the upper brackets of the General Direction, the tobacco administrative organization. On one side were several influential men who opposed complete Crown control of the industry. Among the objects of their opposition was the recently-established cigar and cigarette factory in Mexico City. In

---

[77] For the story of the first years of the tobacco monopoly and a relation of the difficulties which Gálvez had in its establishment, see Priestley, *José de Gálvez,* pp. 142–155.

order to decide the matter, Bucareli made a personal inspection of the place.[78]

He came away enthusiastic about its prospects in general, and was particularly pleased with two things. First, after all expenses were deducted, a 50 per cent profit remained. Second, the factory provided a "most appropriate remedy for the nakedness and misery" of the lower classes. Even in its present early stage, he said, it employed nearly sixty-five hundred workers, thus clearing the streets of so many beggars and troublemakers. He predicted that in the future it would use nearly three times this number of employees, without any necessity for making additions to the large building in which it was housed. He recognized, however, that such expansion could not come about until the numerous private tobacco shops had been done away with, a matter which demanded cautious action.[79]

In July, 1772, Bucareli submitted a lengthy report on what he had discovered about the monopoly and on his measures for its improvement. The letter demonstrates both the problems he faced and the methods he used. In the first place, the Durango district was not producing the revenue it should. To correct this situation, Manuel Fernández Jubera was appointed *visitador* and given adequate powers to effect appropriate adjustments. Ever concerned with economy, Bucareli gave the *visitador* the additional duty of investigating the powder and the playing-card *ramos* in the area he would cover on his tour. Jubera was to carry general directives to all parochial curates, justices, and presidio commandants to supply him with all required information on the people of their districts. Secondly, measures were taken to provide a more extensive and specialized administration of the tobacco monopoly in Sonora and Sinaloa, until then handled by Intendant Pedro Corbalán. Two other questions were decided by the Viceroy when he granted a salary increase to tobacco officials in the busy Orizaba and Córdova districts and ordered that tobacco sowings

---

[78] Bucareli to Arriaga, December 23, 1771, in Velasco Ceballos, *La administración de . . . Bucareli,* Vol. II, p. 5.

[79] *Ibid.,* pp. 5–6. Royal acknowledgment of this report charged Bucareli "anew" to see to the progress of the monopoly. Arriaga to Bucareli, March 20, 1772, AGN, RC, 1772, Vol. 100, No. 102, p. 177.

be increased to the extent that a reserve supply sufficient for two years be maintained.[80]

Finally, indicative of his long-range plan, Bucareli reported that he had ordered the General Direction to submit a report on how many private tobacco shops existed in all of New Spain. The first court revealed only that there were 1,505 such shops as of mid-1772, with no indication of the number of persons employed in them. Bucareli ordered that thereafter the report be made annually, showing how many shops still remained and how many had been suppressed in the past year. He regarded the peaceful extinction of these private shops as one of the most important and most delicate objectives to be achieved.[81]

Bucareli was thorough in his efforts to improve the tobacco revenue. On January 1, 1773, he issued two decrees appealing for better popular support of the monopoly. In one he explained that the King's object in establishing the monopoly was to pay for the defense of his colonies, thus avoiding additional taxation. With reference to the prevalence of contraband tobacco, he exhorted the people to be more zealous in their duties and to be alert for the introduction of illegal tobacco. He even offered to pay the expenses of punitive expeditions which would ferret out and destroy illicit sowings.[82]

Meanwhile, Administrator General José de la Riva of the tobacco *renta* had been working on a plan for doing away with the private shops in Mexico City, which he submitted to the Viceroy in September, 1774. A limited number of registered tobacco retailers still existed, but as long as any of them were in business, fraud was made easier and the monopoly was neither genuine nor efficient. Bucareli agreed with the home government that direct suppression of these shops was not the solution because it would be unjust to the shopowners and their families. For a while the Viceroy thought that he could achieve the desired end simply by allowing no new shops to open and waiting for the old ones to disappear gradually. It soon became apparent, however, that this method would be too slow and uncertain, and he therefore

---

[80] Bucareli to Arriaga, July 26, 1772, AGN, CVB, 1772, Vol. 28, No. 468, pp. 31–36.

[81] *Ibid.,* pp. 37–38.

[82] AGN, Bandos, 1771–1774, Vol. 8, Nos. 81 and 82, pp. 333–334v.

sought a better solution from the head of the *ramo*. De la Riva's proposal contemplated converting the private shops into *estanquillos,* or, literally, little monopolies, employing to run them the same persons who now owned them. Additional jobs for other members of their families would be made available in the tobacco factories. It was felt that the former owners would be better off and that the public would be pleased with the prospect of cleaner and less expensive tobacco products. The Viceroy approved the plan, but promised the Crown that it would not be put into practice until all the details had been worked out and all contingencies anticipated.[83]

Nevertheless, the system was applied almost immediately. As of January 1, 1775, private tobacco shops had been replaced by 110 government *estanquillos.* The change had been achieved quietly, the Viceroy said, with no harm to the former owners inasmuch as all of them had been given employment in their old shops or elsewhere in the tobacco organization. To his own credit, Bucareli cited De la Riva for his excellent work in originating and executing the plan.[84]

De la Riva submitted a report to Bucareli in August which spoke encouragingly of the benefits the full monopoly was bringing in the way of revenue and optimistically about the future income of the *renta.* The extinction of private shops had resulted in the employment of thirty-four hundred more workers in the capital factory, most of whom had formerly been suspected of dealing in contraband tobacco. He pointed out that in Querétaro and other cities private dealers were still in business, and that as their shops were converted or closed, the *renta* would make still more profit.[85]

More than a year and a half elapsed before any action was taken to

---

[83] Bucareli to Arriaga, September 26, 1774, AGN, CVB, 1774, Vol. 58, No. 1551, pp. 55v–58. The King approved the plan, but warned Bucareli that the public must be satisfied and that the families affected must be taken care of. Arriaga to Bucareli, February 25, 1775, AGN, RC, 1775, Vol. 106, No. 53, pp. 82–82v.

[84] Bucareli to Arriaga, January 27, 1775, AGN, CVB, 1775, Vol. 63, No. 1704, pp. 38–39. Charles III expressed his pleasure with the move and his gratitude to De la Riva in Arriaga to Bucareli, May 1, 1775, AGN, RC, 1775, Vol. 106, No. 99, p. 179.

[85] De la Riva to Bucareli, August 19, 1775, AGN, CVB, 1775, Vol. 70, of No. 1961, pp. 178v–179.

achieve this end. Not until April, 1777, did Bucareli reveal that the officials of the branch had recently instituted or were about to effect in Valladolid, Guadalajara, Querétaro, and Puebla a program similar to that used in Mexico City. The delay had been occasioned by their desire to secure full information on the situations in these areas and to be certain that the persons affected by the change would be taken care of in the matter of employment.[86]

At the same time that this general program for expanding the monopoly was going on, Bucareli was receiving the series of appeals from the King, already cited several times, originating in the deteriorating European situation and the imminence of war. One of the sources of revenue which Charles III cited as preferable for such increase was tobacco, and the program just described may be regarded as having been part of Bucareli's efforts in this direction. Another obvious step was simply to increase the price of tobacco products, but it was judged best to delay this move until the *estanquillos* had become established and accepted by the public. This desirable end appears to have been achieved as of May, 1777, for at that time the General Direction presented the Viceroy with a schedule of price adjustments. The method involved both decreases in the amount of goods delivered for the same old price in some instances, and a straight price increase in others. Bucareli approved the suggestions without change.[87]

Again it is enlightening to turn to figures for evidence of the fruits of Bucareli's administration with reference to income from tobacco. The figures for 1766 and 1771 are given to demonstrate the tremendous growth which this monopoly enjoyed. The amounts are in pesos.[88] It should be pointed out that beginning in 1774 the tobacco *renta* paid sales tax on the paper it imported from Spain, thus adding to the expenses. The only figures available on such payments reveal the cost to have been about 50,000 pesos in 1776 and about 40,000 pesos in 1777.[89]

[86] Bucareli to Gálvez, April 26, 1777, AGN, CVB, 1777, Vol. 90, No. 2872, pp. 25–27.

[87] Same to same, May 27, 1777, AGN, CVB, 1777, Vol. 91, No. 2958, pp. 3–5.

[88] Fonseca and Urrutía, *Historia general de real hacienda,* Vol. II, p. 437.

[89] Bucareli to Gálvez, March 27, 1778, and inclosure, AGN, CVB, 1778, Vol. 101, No. 3681, pp. 54v–55, and Vol. 102, p. 783.

Year	Gross	Expenses	Net Profit
1766	1,417,846	1,178,748	239,097
1771	2,501,015	1,614,257	886,757
1772	2,859,268	1,899,680	959,588
1773	3,089,270	1,839,882	1,249,388
1774	3,192,111	1,950,572	1,241,538
1775	3,702,839	2,451,881	1,250,957
1776	3,845,742	2,330,951	1,514,790
1777	4,355,307	2,412,112	1,943,194
1778	5,094,362	2,661,211	2,433,151

The preceding discussion has considered Bucareli's approach to various problems he encountered in his administration of New Spain's fiscal system, with special reference to only the major branches of the *Real Hacienda*. They serve merely as examples. Bucareli disposed of many more financial questions in each of the branches here referred to, as he did in nearly every phase of the revenue system. The supervision of things monetary was undoubtedly the Viceroy's primary concern.

Nearly every *ramo* showed a progressively greater income and net profit during his time. How much of this was due to his peculiar talent, how much to the reforms of Gálvez, and how much to the general trend of the late Bourbon period cannot be precisely stated. After Bucareli's death the revenues continued to increase in approximately the same proportions, although year by year more of them began to level off, probably because they had reached their optimum status. Nevertheless, Bucareli certainly deserves credit for his part in keeping the trend going, and very probably his efforts and ability rate praise in some degree beyond this basic award.

The Man and the Office

EVALUATING the accomplishments of a Spanish viceroy in the New World is, in several respects, an unusually difficult task. The heart of the difficulty lies in the fact that the act of evaluation depends frequently on the use of comparison, and comparisons are impossible when there is no opportunity to place the object of one's study next to another similar object. Unfortunately, the attainments of historians in the field of viceregal biography are meager. Only two authoritative works fit this biographical category—Arthur S. Aiton, *Antonio de Mendoza, First Viceroy of New Spain,* and A. F. Zimmerman, *Francisco de Toledo, Fifth Viceroy of Peru.* These biographies are but two out of more than one hundred possibilities of such studies, and both deal with sixteenth-century officials.

There is, of course, a considerably more extensive bibliography than this which can be presented as relevant to inquiry into viceregal personnel.[1] There are a good many works in Spanish, but unfortunately too many of them lack adequate documentation by scholarly standards, and investigation of their content usually reveals a sufficient number

---

[1] See, for example, Lillian E. Fisher, *Viceregal Administration in the Spanish-American Colonies,* and Donald E. Smith, *The Viceroy of New Spain.* Both of these, however, are of the survey type and, consequently, are of limited use for individual studies.

of demonstrably erroneous statements to make the reader distrust, without the support of documentation, such statements as may be valid.[2]

For these reasons, then, it does not seem warranted to declare, on the basis of the investigations underlying the preceding chapters, that Bucareli was the greatest viceroy New Spain ever had, or the third best, or to place him in any such definite niche. Keeping in mind the maxim that a man should ordinarily be judged by the standards of his time, about the only classification of this nature which may now be conscientiously made is that he was an excellent viceroy. It is probable that in the future, as a result of investigations by reputable scholars in the field of viceregal administration, a more precise evaluation will be possible. Until then, such conclusions as are reached here which involve comparative values must be regarded as somewhat tentative.

Before embarking on this analysis, however, certain qualifications or observations should be made with respect both to the position of viceroy generally and to specific aspects of the job as of Bucareli's time. Most notably, it must be emphasized that the viceroy was necessarily concerned with many more matters than have been considered in this book. Reason and the sheer limits of time and space have dictated a process of selectivity whereby feasible limits for the extent of the study may be set. Several additional topics could be considered and the number of chapters thereby increased through the analysis of such phases of administration as, for example, justice, trade, public welfare, education, and local government, all of which, to some degree, demanded the attention of the viceroy. A brief commentary on various aspects of this nature may demonstrate the diversity of problems, in

[2] In the Mexican field, good examples of this type are Rivera Cambas, *Los gobernantes de México;* Padre Andrés Cavo and Carlos María de Bustamante, *Los tres siglos de México durante el gobierno español, hasta la entrada del ejército trigarante,* cited hereafter as *Los tres siglos de México;* Niceto de Zamacois, *Historia de Méjico desde sus tiempos mas remotos hasta nuestros dias,* cited hereafter as *Historia de Méjico;* Pedro Soler Alonzo, *Virreyes de la Nueva España;* and Vicente Riva Palacio, *México a través de los siglos.* A distinct exception to this categorization is the recently-published *Introducción al estudio de los virreyes de Nueva España,* by Jorge Ignacio Rubio Mañé.

itself probably baffling and frustrating, with which the viceroy must be concerned and to which only casual reference may have been made in preceding chapters.

Perhaps the most interesting of these subjects, and the one most reluctantly omitted from the category of detailed consideration, was the *Acordada,* a special law-enforcement agency with wide jurisdiction and virtually summary authority.[3] Its principal function in Bucareli's time was the suppression of crimes of violence and smuggling. Bucareli supported it enthusiastically and upheld its side in a dispute with the regular criminal courts. He credited it with achieving a significant diminution in the number of murders, assaults, and robberies being committed, especially in Mexico City, and with breaking up an extensive smuggling ring operating in Pánuco and Tampico, with the connivance of several Spanish officials.[4]

Another source of viceregal concern—and one which was a corollary problem interwoven with defense, the California settlements, and trade—was that of international affairs. Madrid kept Bucareli well-posted on relevant official developments in this field, and O'Reilly supplied him with court gossip and useful behind-the-scenes commentary. During the period of peace in the early 1770's, the Crown issued detailed instructions for the handling of the problem of English ships, either merchant or naval, which might show up in Mexican coastal waters.[5] As England's troubles with her North American colonies began to become serious, as the struggle with Portugal over the Banda Oriental was intensified, and as a general renewal of war in Europe threatened in the second half of the decade, instructions to Bucareli concerning his part in the implementation of Spanish policy came thick and fast. He was warned not to trust England's declared neutrality in the Platine matter, not to allow Cook's vessels to enter

[3] Haring, *The Spanish Empire in America,* pp. 133–134.
[4] The goods were English and were coming principally from Pensacola. For representative documents on these matters see: Bucareli to Arriaga, July 27, 1773, No. 1904, AGI, Mex., Leg. 1372; same to same, March 27, 1776, No. 299 (confidential file), *ibid.,* Leg. 1274; and Bucareli to Gálvez, October 27, 1776, No. 2537, *ibid.,* Leg. 1376.
[5] Arriaga to Bucareli, January 14, 1772, AGI, Mex., Leg. 1509.

New Spain's ports, how to treat ships of the English rebels, and how to maintain a properly neutral attitude and policy toward England, France, and the American rebels as the situation worsened.[6] Obviously, this was an important area of concern to the Viceroy and demanded much of his time and attention.

Finally, there was a multitude of lesser and occasionally even petty affairs which the Viceroy must attend to. Repairs on the royal palace, the opening of a new insane asylum, and the approval of a new fire ordinance are but three examples of this sort of thing.[7] Also in the same category was Bucareli's function as a sort of odd-jobs man, as demonstrated by his compliance with instructions to send to Madrid such things as live pelicans, certain wood samples, a notably large gold nugget, and to find and order to return to Spain an errant husband whose wife clearly had the ear of someone in the Spanish court.[8]

The point of all the above is, perhaps, obvious. The Viceroy of New Spain was a very busy man, responsible for, and concerned with, such a wide variety of things that a complete account of any viceregency of significance is clearly impossible within the limits of a single volume. No pretense is made, therefore, that this study is exhaustive. Instead, it is hoped that the topics and the chapters which present them offer a proper selection and consideration of such meaningful aspects of the viceregency as to provide both a valid exposition of the events and a sufficient basis for evaluating the time and the man.

A study such as this one involves the perusal of thousands of manuscripts, frequent recourse to appropriate monographs, and a considerable amount of reflection. In the course of following this process the student begins to become aware of certain faults or weaknesses in Bucareli's character and methods. Prominent among these were undue

---

[6] Again, let the citation of representative documents suffice. Bucareli to Gálvez, October 27, 1776, Nos. 2534 and 2535, AGI, Mex., Leg. 1376; same to same, January 27, 1777, *ibid.,* Leg. 1276; same to same, July 27, 1778, No. 263 or 2848, AGN, CVB, Vol. 7, Libro 15, 1773[8]–1779, pp. 41v–42v.

[7] Arriaga to Bucareli, November 16, 1775, AGI, Mex., Leg. 1509. Bucareli to Arriaga, November 26, 1774, No. 1618, *ibid.* Bucareli to Gálvez, January 27, 1777, No. 2736, *ibid.,* Leg. 1379.

[8] Bucareli to Arriaga, January 25, 1772, No. 178, AGI, Mex., Leg. 1509. Same to same, November 26, 1775, *ibid.,* Leg. 1373; same to same, February 24, 1775, *ibid.*

caution, the relative inability to take decisive action in the face of contrary opinion from his advisers, a lack of aggressiveness, and a notable sparsity of original thought or initiative. An abundance of good characteristics were discernible also, of course, which will be discussed later. Nevertheless, these deficiencies seem sufficient in number and importance to obviate any chance of Bucareli's achieving any rating approaching greatness. However, such a conclusion is shaken by the things which other writers say about him and by virtue of which he enjoys, generally, an enviable reputation.

Whether these encomiums are documented or not—and usually they are not—is in part beside the point, an apparent contradiction which is perhaps best explained on the principle of the simultaneous existence of smoke and fire. His reputation began to rise in Cuba. One writer points to Bucareli's policy of giving two hours a day to hearing complaints from the common people, whereby special benefits accrued to the slaves, "whose rights he endeavored to protect and insure." This author concludes by asserting that Don Antonio was one of the few governors who never gave cause for complaint and that the Cubans were loath to part with him.[9] Other students of the Cuban phase of his career adopt similar attitudes.[10]

The story of his work in New Spain is told only in laudatory terms by a majority of the Mexican historians, although, as has been pointed out, none of them has written an extensive and authoritative work on his viceregency. However, what they have written about him tends to consist essentially of a repetition of the same stories, most of which are concerned with lesser and rather odd facets of his activities, and it is reasonable to suspect that many of the writers simply copied from their predecessors. Tracing this chain, one finds C. M. de Bustamante, writing in 1836, to be the apparent first link. Without citing any sources, documentary or other, he relates the tale of the locust plague, in which Bucareli cut the cost of the campaign to eliminate the pests, and also reveals that the Viceroy allegedly borrowed 2,500,000 pesos from the

[9] Willis Fletcher Johnson, *The History of Cuba*, Vol. II, pp. 112, 118. Johnson uses the spelling Buccarelli, a corruption not easily understood.

[10] Calcagno, *Diccionario biográfico cubana*, Vol. I, pp. 130–131. Luis J. Bustamante, *Enciclopedia popular cubana*, Vol. I, pp. 279–280.

Consulado with no other security than his own word.[11] Zamacois repeats these two stories and lavishes praise on Bucareli for the prosperity of the viceroyalty under his command.[12] In their enthusiasm some writers, including the two just cited, credit Bucareli with accomplishments which are not rightfully his. They assert that he founded the *Cuerpo de Minería,* created the revolving fund of the mint, finished the Acapulco fortress, and instituted scientific expeditions into the interior.[13]

Other historians, however, despite their lack of documentation, apparently merit greater consideration. Such, for example, is Rivera Cambas, who says, in his summary:[14]

The period during which Bucareli governed was one of uninterrupted tranquillity for New Spain. It appeared that Providence wished to reward the virtues of the Viceroy by lavishing on his subjects everything that contributed to their well-being. He was one of those men whose memory never will be erased from the hearts of Mexicans and whose administration is a palpable example of what this soil can be when a virtuous and able man undertakes with decision the difficult task of developing its elements of richness.

It is possible to depreciate the claims of historians such as these on the grounds that some are merely following the lead of the man originally in error, or that others are simply asserting obvious preconceptions. But, in seeking the sources of Bucareli's reputation and in endeavoring to show that he was perhaps less than has been claimed, there is one man who certainly must have known whether Don Antonio did a better-than-average job. This is Charles III, and by his statements and actions the skeptic is given pause. Several times during Bucareli's term the King expressed his pleasure with his viceroy's work, and it will be remembered that the King insisted on Bucareli's remaining as viceroy for nearly three years after he had submitted his

[11] Cavo and Bustamante, *Los tres siglos de México,* Vol. III, pp. 14–15.

[12] Zamacois, *Historia de Méjico,* Vol. V, pp. 612–624.

[13] José R. Benítez, *Historia gráfica de la Nueva España,* pp. 81–82. Soler Alonzo, *Virreyes de la Nueva España,* pp. 57–58. These works were found in the library of the *Secretaría de Hacienda* in the National Palace in Mexico City.

[14] Rivera Cambas, *Los gobernantes de Mexico,* Vol. I, p. 422.

resignation. Finally, after Bucareli's death the King decreed, "In view of the noted zeal, integrity, and equity with which the deceased Viceroy of New Spain, . . . Bucareli, governed that kingdom, His Majesty has decided to dispense entirely with the *residencia* for the time of his command, and . . . has declared himself fully satisfied with his faithful and important services."[15] Elimination of the *residencia* was very rare, and provides strong proof of the high regard of the King for one of his most devoted servants.

Recalling, then, the suggested faults attributed above to Bucareli, the King's statement and attitude lead to the alternative deductions that either these characteristics did not really apply, or that they were not regarded as faults by the man most concerned with the abilities of the viceroys. The latter interpretation seems more logical; that is, that the Crown preferred executives who were more concerned with a careful implementation of royal directives than with displaying originality and independence of thought and action.

The delineation of what kind of man and what caliber viceroy Bucareli really was is further confused by the variety of adjectives and nouns which have been applied to him. A compilation of such descriptive words, combined with a consideration of their various sources, should serve as an excellent object lesson to historians. Bucareli's viceregal career offers a fine subject for a discussion of this nature because, although his biography has not been written, certain aspects of his conduct and activities have been studied and reported on, and studies of other persons whose lives touched his have been written.

It was argued in the chapter on the California colonization that Chapman's eulogies of Bucareli may have stemmed from the writer's historical point of view, geographically considered, his desire to see the men about whom he wrote succeed, and his conviction that the developments about which he wrote were intrinsically good, whereby the men who brought them about partook of this merit. He applied the words "greatest hero who has ever appeared in the field of California history," "greater than Gálvez in many respects, and certainly a more noble character," and he characterized Don Antonio as "one of the

[15] Gálvez to Mayorga, October 12, 1779, AGN, RC, 1779, Vol. 116, No. 177, p. 324.

greatest rulers it [New Spain] ever had." In summary he used the words "simple, straightforward, unselfish, clear-thinking, sincerely religious man, without a shadow of conceit or pretense, and even without personal ambition except to perform his duty to the full. Finally, he was . . . an indefatigable worker." [16]

Of interest is what others have said and what their motivations were. Engelhardt, a religious, in describing the expulsion of the Jesuits in 1767, relates how a group of them, sick and tired, disembarked at Havana, where Bucareli gave them kindly treatment. Engelhardt therefore calls him "humane and pious." [17] Thomas C. Russell, concerned with the California colonization, is another who used the phrase "great viceroy." [18] Richman uses the same words to apply to a similar situation, adding that when Serra went to Mexico City in 1773, "he met a chief capable of understanding and appreciating the Croix-Gálvez tradition." [19] Johnson praises him for his "affable disposition," and calls him "a man of rare nobility of character." [20] Many more similar cases could be cited.

On the other hand, there are those who regard him with less favor. Vito Alessio Robles wrote an introduction to a document by Nicolás de Lafora, who was on the Rubí expedition. When, in a later incident of Lafora's life, Bucareli did not treat him with the consideration which Alessio Robles felt was proper, the latter portrayed Don Antonio as "the dry and inflexible Viceroy Bucareli." [21] The attitude of A. B. Thomas toward Bucareli has been discussed in the chapter on the interior provinces. Although in one place he does call him "the greatest viceroy since Mendoza," he concludes the sentence by saying that this same viceroy "had, of course, done nothing!" Thomas had reference to the desperate situation in New Mexico from 1772 to 1777. [22] In

[16] Chapman, *Spanish California*, pp. 94–96.

[17] Fr. Zephyrin Engelhardt, O.F.M., *The Missions and Missionaries of California*, Vol. I, p. 275.

[18] In his introductory notes to Francisco Antonio Mourelle, *Voyage of the Sonora in the Second Bucareli Expedition*.

[19] Irving Berdine Richman, *California under Spain and Mexico, 1535–1847*, p. 94.

[20] Johnson, *The History of Cuba*, Vol. II, p. 117.

[21] Nicolás de Lafora, *Relación del viage que hizo a los Presidios Internos situados en la frontera de la América Septentrional pertenecientes al Rey de España*, p. 22.

[22] Thomas, *Plains Indians*, p. 49 n.

another place Thomas says that in so far as the northern frontier was concerned, Bucareli was "an armchair executive filled with petty resentment." He further characterized Don Antonio as being "meticulous in keeping his prerogatives intact." [23]

The other writer whose general attitude toward Bucareli is unfavorable is Velasco Ceballos, whose work is the only one which is concerned exclusively with Don Antonio. Although he has some complimentary remarks to make, such as calling the Viceroy "honest" and "an indefatigable worker," Velasco Ceballos reserves his strongest words for derogation. He pictures Bucareli as "rigidly economical," "touched with vanity," "accustomed to fall into minute trivialities," and "profoundly deceived about the majority of the inhabitants of New Spain." [24] He says that although Bucareli was "one of the less bad governors," he also had an "inflexible and austere" soul, and was possessed of a "rigid morality." Velasco Ceballos is clearly a product of the Mexican Revolution generation, which resents the inhumane aura of exploitation which characterized the Spanish domination. His attitude is revealed when he says of Bucareli, "He had neither the eyes of charity nor the penetration of a statesman to see in the misery, in the nakedness of the people anything other than the effect of the climate or the lack of good police regulations in earlier times; that is, either racial faults or the lack of force." [25] These words inevitably remind one of the astute commentary of José Clemente Orozco in his *Autobiografía,* partially reproduced in translation in Hanke's *Mexico and the Caribbean.*[26] Orozco castigates with satire the indigenists who tend, in effect, to blame the Spaniards for not believing in, and abiding by, the tenets of the Constitution of 1917.

The preceding paragraphs indicate, therefore, that a fair diversity of words has been applied to Bucareli. He was one of New Spain's greatest rulers, but also one of its less bad governors. He had not a shadow of show or pretense, but he was touched with vanity. He was

[23] Thomas, *Teodoro de Croix,* pp. 28–29.
[24] Velasco Ceballos, *La administración de . . . Bucareli,* Vol. II, pp. X, XV, XVII, XLI, LVII.
[25] *Ibid.,* pp. XV, XVI, XXXIX, LXIV.
[26] Lewis Hanke, *Mexico and the Caribbean,* pp. 177–180.

clear-thinking, but he was profoundly deceived about a majority of the people of New Spain. He was straightforward and unselfish, but he was an armchair executive filled with petty resentment. He was without great personal ambition, but he was meticulous in keeping his prerogatives intact. He was humane, but he was inflexible and austere.

Clearly, and unfortunately, it all depends upon the topic with which the individual writer is concerned. It has been my endeavor to appraise Bucareli objectively, without the hindrance of a historical point of view, be it geographical or ideological. Not surprisingly, Bucareli emerges as a human being, with all the complexities of motivations, capacities, and weaknesses which the phrase connotes. A summary categorization reveals in him virtually nothing of the villain, but equally denies him heroic stature.

The more precise question is, of course, what Bucareli's standing should be, both as a man and as a high government official. In deciding this, one could wish for an abundance of private correspondence, newspapers, pamphlets, diaries, and contemporary unofficial chronicles; but only a limited amount of a few of these kinds of sources exist or have been found, which prevents the characterization from being recognizedly complete. Bucareli's correspondence with O'Reilly has proved to be the most helpful in this respect. However, one result of a lengthy study of a man, of going through thousands of pages of his correspondence, official and private, is the gradual achievement of a feeling and understanding about him. It is in part on such a basis that the following character reconstruction is presented.

Bucareli was essentially a kindly, courteous, considerate person, a Spanish aristocrat with a strong sense of *noblesse oblige.* His dominant motivation in life was to serve his nation and his King well. Some of his laudable traits were tempered by the atmosphere in which he lived; in other words, he was a product of his times. He was class- and race-conscious, and believed in the theory of peninsular superiority. There is little evidence that he possessed a strong sense of humor. He tended to be a generous person, but his own personal relative poverty and his addiction to governmental economy prevented any lavish enjoyment of, or submission to, this tendency. His integrity was not to be questioned. Legend has it that he was called *Padre del Pueblo, Flor de los Virreyes,* and *Padre de la Patria.*[27] There is little doubt that the people of New Spain, and especially those of Mexico City, were genuinely fond of him.[28]

Among his special virtues as viceroy which merit praise are two. First, he engaged in no continuing feuds with other persons, officials or others, as government personnel are wont to do. The single possible exception involves Teodoro de Croix, and the two-sided nature of this situation is not apparent. Second, he never stole the credit for any accomplishment when such credit was properly due a subordinate. He inevitably related the sources of new plans or ideas, and he was also careful to commend to the Crown any of his aides who merited praise.

The preceding evaluations are concerned largely with Bucareli personally. From a broader point of view, certain other considerations should be presented, and in most cases Don Antonio's reputation is enhanced, although qualifications must be made in certain instances.

A comparison of the condition of the viceroyalty as he received it from Croix and as he left it is in his favor. With respect to the important matter of defense, although it is questionable whether or not New Spain could have withstood a determined English assault in 1779, there is no doubt that such a conquest would have been a much more formidable proposition at this later date than it would have been in 1771. Similarly, the extension and strengthening of the northern frontier as administered by Bucareli goes on the credit side of the ledger. Furthermore, his part in the California colonization, although not of his own initiative, was well handled, particularly with reference to the development of San Blas and the maintenance of a good supply system. His management of the *Real Hacienda* was almost spectacularly successful.

It is well to remember that an astute monarch such as Charles III undoubtedly had specific ideas about what he wanted from New Spain and how he wanted the Viceroyalty handled. His instructions to

[27] See, for example, a letter from Antonio Eugenio Melgarejo, head of the College of San Ildefonso, to the regent of the *Audiencia,* April 12, 1779. AGN, Historia, Vol. 306, No. 1, p. 39.

[28] Zúñiga y Ontiveros, the printer, wrote a particularly moving account of the reaction of the people to Bucareli's death. Rubio-Argüelles, "Zúñiga, Impresor del Siglo XVIII en México," pp. 523–524. See also an unsigned note in AGN, Historia, Vol. 306, pp. 36–37.

Gálvez indicate clearly that the King knew whereof he spoke. It is obvious that Bucareli served satisfactorily. He did oppose the intendancy system, but he offered little resistance to any other aspect of Charles III's reform program. Indeed, he supervised many administrative improvements, particularly in the matter of financial management, which contributed not only to the efficiency and reputation of the viceroyalty, but also to the firmness with which the King was able to carry out his policies. Much of the Spanish empire was dependent upon New Spain, a fact which Bucareli accepted without question, and a burden which he carried without faltering. This he did without alienating any section of the population, without resorting to forced loans, and without reward for himself other than the respect of the people and the satisfaction of having served his king well. It is possible that if there had been more viceroys like Bucareli, Spanish subjects in America would not have followed so willingly the rebellious example set by their English prototypes to the north. Probably Charles III was justified in his regard for Don Antonio.

Let it be reiterated once more, however, that the great majority of Bucareli's successes stemmed from his efficient and capable performance of his duty. Basically, he did only what he was told to do, or what had been suggested to him by José de Gálvez. But, as was pointed out in the first chapter, these things he was told to do and these suggestions of Gálvez had singular importance, because they were not merely more of the same old policies, but instead were part of a program of change, and Bucareli's skillful effectuation of the new order contributed materially to the significance of the era and his viceregency.

INSCRIPTION ON BUCARELI'S TOMB IN THE
SHRINE OF THE VIRGIN OF GUADALUPE, MEXICO

AQUI YACE

Aquel Heroe Inmortal,
Tan Amante, Como Amado del Pueblo
Cuya Memoria Vivirá Indeleble
En los Corazones Mexicanos
Por el Paternal Amor, conque los abrigó Virrey
En las Voces de la Fama
Por la Rectitud conque gobernó politico
En el temor de los enemigos
Por el Valor conque triunfó militar
En la admiracion de los buenos
Por las virtudes que exercitó, Christiano
En las paredes de este Santuario
Por devocion conque las veneró, Piadoso

EL EXM̃O SEÑOR BAILIO FREY DON
ANTONIO MARIA BUCARELI Y URSUA
HENESTROSA, LASO DE LA VEGA VILLACIS
Y CORDOBA, CABALLERO GRAN CRUZ, Y
COMENDADOR DE LA DE TOCINA
EN EL ORDEN DE MALTA, GENTIL
HOMBRE DE CAMARA DE S.M. CON
ENTRADA, THENIENTE GENERAL DE
LOS REALES EJERCITOS, VIRREY GOBERNADOR
Y CAPITAN GENERAL DE ESTA NUEVA
ESPANA Y PRESIDENTE DE SU REAL AUDIENCIA

Que haviendo nacido en Sevilla a los veinte y quatro
De Enero de 1717, falleció en Mexico a nueve de
Abril de 79 del mismo siglo
Fué su ultima voluntad
Ser sepultado a los umbrales de este templo
Adonde siempre se dirijian sus pensamientos
Para confundir la vanidad humana
Para conciliarse la protección divina
Para protestar su humilidad, y rendim.to a estas sagrad.s puert.s
En las quales fundó su mayor grandeza
É las que siempre lo alabar.an
En las que justamente esperó
Hallar las de la gloria

APPENDIX

FINANCIAL STATEMENT, 1771 [1]
(Amounts in Pesos)

Branches	Credits	Debits
On hand, December 31, 1770 . . .	525,471	. . . . . .
Salaries & gifts	. . . . . .	212,173
Interest	. . . . . .	14,648
Expenses of war & troop salaries . .	. . . . . .	1,091,172
Ordinary and extraordinary expenses of war	. . . . . .	3,606,535
Interior presidios	. . . . . .	293,313
Synods & missions	. . . . . .	28,439
Diezmos of gold	86,623	. . . . . .
Diezmos of silver	1,459,572	400
Diezmos of *bajilla*	3,001	. . . . . .
Diezmos of Pánuco	4,285	. . . . . .
Quicksilver	663,376	451,200
Balances of accounts	6,136	1,509
Alcabalas	873,346	7,625
Armada de Barlovento	83,937	400
Cruzada	218,057	7,395
Major vacancies	770⎱	24,667
Minor vacancies	26,917⎰	
Censo	730	. . . . . .
Sales of Crown lands	2,763	. . . . . .
Remissible to Spain.	34,327	30,322
Snow	10,937	. . . . . .
Regular deposits	2,300	57,034
Fines	050	. . . . . .
Extraordinary expenditures . . .	2,249,621	1,515,312
Playing cards	27,299	. . . . . .
Powder	30,000	. . . . . .

Financial Statement, 1771 (*continued*)

Branches	Credits	Debits
Cockfights	22,155	. . . . . .
Leather goods	1,820	. . . . . .
Alum	1,200	. . . . . .
Copper	1,400	. . . . . .
Palace	2,391	144
Half annates	34,519	9,230
Mesadas	16,037	. . . . . .
Novenos	88,035	26,391
Salable offices	36,020	17,320
Drainage	22,844	104,854
Pulque	291,827	3,102
Stamped paper	33,656	2,844
Seigniorage	130,073	. . . . . .
Court fines	. . . . . .	4,096
Tribute	824,548	38,173
Encomienda vacancies	. . . . . .	5,315
Donations	621	. . . . . .
Mint	300,000	. . . . . .
Audiencia supplements	. . . . . .	20,823
Comisos	303	. . . . . .
Ownerless goods	159	. . . . . .
Mail	. . . . . .	4,989
Arrears debts	. . . . . .	44,717
Totals	8,117,126	7,624,142

[1] AGN, CVB, 1772, Vol. 20, inclosure in No. 147, p. 102.

FINANCIAL STATEMENT, 1772 [1]
(Amounts in Pesos)

Branches	Credits	Debits
On hand, December 31, 1771 . . .	493,536	. . . . . .
Salaries & gifts	. . . . . .	196,108
Interest	. . . . . .	15,199
Expenses of war & troop salaries . .	. . . . . .	664,358
Ordinary and extraordinary expenses of war	. . . . . .	4,042,033
Interior presidios	. . . . . .	580,271
Synods & missions	. . . . . .	50,407
Diezmos of gold	84,867	. . . . . .
Diezmos of silver	1,244,052	400
Diezmos of *bajilla*	2,090	. . . . . .
Diezmos of Pánuco	4,285	. . . . . .
Quicksilver	574,047	434,800
Balances of accounts	1,183	1,509
Alcabalas	907,732	20,197
Armada de Barlovento . . .	45,420	400
Cruzada	220,275	19,388
Major vacancies	23,496	23,640
Minor vacancies	37,546	. . . . . .
Censo	730	. . . . . .
Sales of Crown lands	2,778	. . . . . .
Remissible to Spain.	15,435	667
Snow	17,590	. . . . . .
Regular deposits	6,000	2,249
Fines	1,132	. . . . . .
Extraordinary.	2,321,426	877,183
Playing cards	76,314	. . . . . .
Powder	47,000	. . . . . .
Cockfights	22,259	. . . . . .
Alum	1,200	. . . . . .
Leather goods	1,820	. . . . . .
Copper	1,400	. . . . . .
Palace	2,167	1,782
Half annates	46,669	3,090
Mesadas	31,952	600

Financial Statement, 1772 (*continued*)

Branches	Credits	Debits
Novenos	115,785	26,391
Salable offices	20,294	2,679
Drainage	35,663	1,976
Pulque	330,414	3,102
Stamped paper	26,308	4,510
Court fines	. . . . . .	3,832
Seigniorage	109,908	. . . . . .
Tribute	699,598	52,080
Donations	061	. . . . . .
Pearls	385	. . . . . .
Ownerless goods	370	. . . . . .
Lottery	40,000	. . . . . .
Encomienda vacancies	. . . . . .	4,000
Audiencia supplements	. . . . . .	19,987
Mail	. . . . . .	2,614
Arrears debts	. . . . . .	43,010
Totals	7,616,173	7,098,502

[1] AGN, CVB, 1733, Vol. 34, inclosure in No. 749, p. 132.

FINANCIAL STATEMENT, 1773 [1]
(Amounts in Pesos)

Branches	Credits	Debits
On hand, December 31, 1772 . . .	517,871	. . . . . .
Salaries & gifts	. . . . . .	221,236
Interest	. . . . . .	15,720
Expenses of war & troop salaries . .	. . . . . .	848,743
Ordinary and extraordinary expenses of war	. . . . . .	3,886,415
Interior presidios	. . . . . .	865,937
Synods and missions	. . . . . .	58,331
Diezmos of gold	107,074	. . . . . .
Diezmos of silver	1,392,453	400
Diezmos of *bajilla*	1,883	. . . . . .
Diezmos of Pánuco	4,285	. . . . . .
Quicksilver	520,552	464,800
Balances of accounts	7,905	1,409
Alcabalas	1,668,113	6,600
Armada de Barlovento	46,814	. . . . . .
Cruzada	174,969	25,702
Major vacancies	43,534⎫	58,696
Minor vacancies	42,855⎭	
Censo	730	. . . . . .
Sales of Crown lands	3,789	. . . . . .
Remissible to Spain.	56,250	53,412
Snow	30,547	. . . . . .
Regular deposits	87,647	3,875
Fines	016	. . . . . .
Extraordinary.	1,042,831	1,784,053
Mint	1,651,825	. . . . . .
Playing cards	43,000	. . . . . .
Powder	48,000	. . . . . .
Cockfights	22,255	. . . . . .
Alum	1,200	. . . . . .
Leather goods.	0,820	. . . . . .
Copper	1,419	. . . . . .
Palace	1,994	2,733
Half annates	50,084	3,158

Financial Statement, 1773 (*continued*)

Branches	Credits	Debits
Mesadas	21,331	300
Novenos	137,313	26,391
Salable offices	29,011	11,428
Drainage	21,942	1,648
Pulque	396,843	3,102
Stamped paper	41,646	5,958
Court expenses	. . . . . .	7,315
Seigniorage	127,719	. . . . . .
Tribute	817,511	58,437
Encomienda vacancies	. . . . . .	4,000
Donations	377	. . . . . .
Comisos	1,942	. . . . . .
Ownerless goods	246	. . . . . .
Lottery	22,000	. . . . . .
Mail	. . . . . .	1,192
Arrears debts	. . . . . .	51,709
Totals	9,189,396	8,472,700

[1] AGN, CVB, 1774, Vol. 50, Libro 2, No. 3, p. 346.

FINANCIAL STATEMENT, 1774 [1]
(Amounts in Pesos)

Credits	7,492,997
Debits	6,949,087
Existencia	543,910

[1] A detailed statement for 1774 was not found, probably because the documents for this period are those which have been most heavily damaged by water. The above short statement is located in AGN, CVB, 1775, Vol. 63, inclosure in No. 1693, p. 74. It is dated December 31, 1774.

FINANCIAL STATEMENT, 1775 [1]
(Amounts in Pesos)

Branches	Revenues	Expenses	Pensiones [2]
Diezmos of gold	100,432	......	......
Diezmos of silver	1,611,956	93,271	......
Diezmos of *bajilla*	14,816	383	......
Coinage	1,144,989	314,787	37,179
Quicksilver	650,116	51,791	404,000
Alum, copper, lead	3,013	666	338
Diezmos of Pánuco	4,290	......	......
Tribute	834,014	22,992	58,438
Censo	1,417	......	......
Salable offices	35,740	......	7,309
Stamped paper	45,504	1,814	......
Cruzada	135,277	7,191	36,100
Major & minor vacancies	51,192	......	38,784
Mesadas	14,492	......	300
Novenos	124,586	......	26,391
Media Anata	41,679	4,482	6,388
Licenses	7,470	242	30
Sales of Crown lands	1,213	......	......
Palace	1,221	......	2,998
Guadalajara water project	8,631	......	6,000
Drainage	24,470	1,431	2,925
Donations	620	......	......
Comisos	11,638	......	3,931
Fines	320	......	......
Court expenses	535	......	5,156
Brandy	2,776	......	......
Snow	20,767	......	......
Leather goods	1,820	......	......
Cockfights	26,700	......	......
Pulque	468,888	11,212	3,102
Powder	315,019	190,230	41,512
Playing cards	112,872	41,090	......
Lottery	80,623	22,687	......
Alcabalas	1,312,056	106,675	3,259

Financial Statement, 1775 (*continued*)

Branches	Revenues	Expenses	Pensiones
Armada de Barlovento . . .	60,007	666	142,420
San Blas duties . . .	28,588	10,220	048
Chihuahua duties . . .	5,483	2,400	. . . . . .
Almojarifazgo—Tabasco & Goazcoalcos	7,905	762	300
Acapulco duties . . .	177,750	5,741	. . . . . .
Veracruz duties . . .	497,552	54,145	100,810
Mérida & Campeche duties .	27,164	6,971	14,657
Extraordinary	112,652	9,676	5,784,183
Balances of accounts . .	12,362	131	1,504
Totals	8,138,615	961,646	6,728,062

[1] AGN, CVB, 1778, Vol. 100, inclosure in No. 3573, p. 119.
[2] The *pensiones* column was a new entry. It was used originally in a 1776 report (not located), and the King requested that a similar statement be drawn up for 1775. Its value lies in the fact that it breaks down the debits entry one more step. A further breakdown is made in the entry labeled "*Desmembración* . . . ," which lists the items included under "*Extraordinario*," which always totaled several million pesos (see end of this statement).

Breakdown of Extraordinary branch

Presidios.	744,795
Missions	89,296
Arrears debts	40,707
Interest	15,206
Factoriá of Mexico . . .	187,518
Work on Perote	128,941
Food storage in Puebla	125,679
Salaries & gifts	219,579
Troop salaries & other expenses of war .	1,016,227
Subsidy—Philippines	303,227
Subsidy—Marianas	3,000
Subsidy—Windward Islands . . .	2,282,335
Subsidy—Isla del Carmen . .	53,296
Registered to Castile	40,156
Commissary of San Blas	112,464
Chihuahua military expedition. . .	155,603
Extraordinary	266,153
Total	5,784,183

FINANCIAL STATEMENT, 1776 [1]
(Amounts in Pesos)

Branches	Credits	Debits
On hand, December 31, 1775 . . .	987,050	. . . . . .
Salaries & gifts	. . . . . .	241,118
Interest	. . . . . .	14,522
Expenses of war & troop salaries . .	. . . . . .	444,854
Ordinary and extraordinary expenses of war	. . . . . .	3,983,009
Interior presidios	. . . . . .	527,238
Synods & missions	. . . . . .	55,324
Diezmos of gold	75,321	. . . . . .
Diezmos of silver	1,559,836	400
Diezmos of *bajilla*	1,615	. . . . . .
Diezmos of Pánuco	4,290	. . . . . .
Quicksilver	859,860	467,800
Balances of accounts . . .	17,653	1,509
Alcabalas	986,579	5,068
Armada de Barlovento	36,779	400
Cruzada	248,546	19,202
Major vacancies	2,960⎫	98,829
Minor vacancies	26,595⎭	
Encomienda vacancies . . .	. . . . . .	5,312
Censo	1,417	. . . . . .
Sales of Crown lands	3,631	. . . . . .
Remissible to Spain	139,693	73,749
Snow	21,809	. . . . . .
Regular deposits	26,020	19,917
Extraordinary	808,157	376,270
Mint	642,671	. . . . . .
Playing cards	115,000	. . . . . .
Powder	100,000	. . . . . .
Cockfights	26,700	. . . . . .
Alum	1,225	. . . . . .
Leather goods	1,820	. . . . . .
Copper	1,450	. . . . . .
Palace	1,578	1,825
Half annates	35,996	6,388

Viceregency of Bucareli

Financial Statement, 1776 (*continued*)

Branches	Credits	Debits
Mesadas	14,142	300
Stamped paper	23,143	5,986
Novenos	117,183	26,391
Salable offices	22,134	7,896
Drainage	39,377	11,503
Pulque	450,370	3,102
Court expenses	. . . . . .	4,811
Seigniorage	61,728	. . . . . .
Tribute	846,188	94,045
Donations	050	. . . . . .
Arrears debts	. . . . . .	52,897
Ownerless goods	178	. . . . . .
Lottery	57,935	. . . . . .
Fines	375	. . . . . .
Inválidos	9,060	10,567
Monte Pío Militar	16,305	1,613
Totals	8,392,579	6,561,445

[1] AGN, CVB, 1776, Vol. 86, inclosure in No. 2695, p. 610.

FINANCIAL STATEMENT, 1777 [1]
(Amounts in Pesos)

Branches	*Revenues*	*Expenses*	*Pensiones* [2]
Diezmos of gold . . .	64,673	. . . . . .	. . . . . .
Diezmos of silver . . .	1,965,651	103,039	. . . . . .
Diezmos of *bajilla* . . .	20,665	400	. . . . . .
Coinage	1,632,488	339,226	431,100
Quicksilver	728,989	81,757	404,000
Alum, copper, lead . .	3,376	333	428
Diezmos of Pánuco . . .	4,290	. . . . . .	. . . . . .
Tribute	912,161	29,172	61,089
Censo	1,371	. . . . . .	. . . . . .
Salable offices. . . .	28,478	. . . . . .	8,518
Stamped paper . . .	44,624	2,674	750
Cruzada	174,266	6,698	69,109
Major & minor vacancies .	38,720	. . . . . .	46,063
Mesadas	4,959	. . . . . .	. . . . . .
Novenos	122,834	. . . . . .	26,391
Media Anata	60,548	6,841	1,700
Licenses.	17,629	227	042
Sales of Crown lands . .	1,021	. . . . . .	. . . . . .
Palace	2,079	. . . . . .	2,631
Guadalajara water project .	12,455	. . . . . .	2,000
Drainage	20,404	1,496	82,029
Donations	18,042	. . . . . .	. . . . . .
Comisos	67,623	4,509	. . . . . .
Fines	8	. . . . . .	. . . . . .
Court expenses . . .	503	. . . . . .	7,045
Brandy	4,221	. . . . . .	. . . . . .
Pulque	617,564	12,475	3,102
Snow	23,889	. . . . . .	. . . . . .
Leather goods . . .	1,820	. . . . . .	. . . . . .
Cockfights	26,700	. . . . . .	. . . . . .
Powder	391,249	192,319	73,425
Playing cards . . .	115,879	26,869	1,759
Lottery	106,495	37,967	. . . . . .
Alcabalas	1,933,972	109,088	3,259

Financial Statement, 1777 (*continued*)

Branches	Revenues	Expenses	Pensiones [2]
Armada de Barlovento . .	59,767	5,199	299,976
San Blas duties . . .	50,353	7,041	889
Chihuahua duties . . .	4,956	. . . . . .	. . . . . .
Almojarifazgo—Tabasco &			
Goazcoalcos . . .	6,837	537	300
Acapulco duties . . .	8,835	8,226	. . . . . .
Veracruz duties . . .	367,340	59,260	43,296
Mérida & Campeche duties .	26,350	9,220	18,497
Extraordinary . . .	34,826	10,728	7,003,756
Balances of accounts . .	18,165	1,136	1,991
Totals	9,746,475	1,056,437	8,593,145

[1] AGN, CVB, 1778, Vol. 106, inclosure in No. 3809, pp. 338–338v.
[2] See 1775 statement, note 2, for explanation of *Pensiones* column.

Breakdown of Extraordinary branch

Presidios	796,447
Missions	56,278
Arrears debts	41,734
Interest	14,872
Factoría de México . . .	176,239
Work on Perote . . .	50,491
Food storage in Puebla . .	151,169
Salaries & gifts . . .	315,143
Troop salaries & other expenses of war	1,559,539
Subsidy—Windward Islands	2,938,781
Subsidy—Isla del Carmen . Salt develop.	69,139
Registered to Cartagena . .	196,147
Commissary of San Blas . .	154,028
Chihuahua military expedition .	220,571
Extraordinary	263,178
Totals	7,003,756

FINANCIAL STATEMENT, 1778 [1]
(Amounts in Pesos)

Branches	Credits	Debits
On hand, December 31, 1777 . . .	534,991	......
Salaries & gifts	......	290,487
Interest	......	15,419
Expenses of war & troop salaries . .	......	590,414
Ordinary and extraordinary expenses of war	......	4,699,994
Interior presidios	......	457,121
Synods & missions	......	46,131
Diezmos of gold	40,784	......
Diezmos of silver	1,618,148	400
Diezmos of *bajilla*	3,857	......
Diezmos of Pánuco	4,290	......
Quicksilver—Castile	644,365	470,346
Quicksilver—Peru	789	......
Balances of accounts	4,678	1,939
Alcabalas	1,952,793	26,290
Armada de Barlovento	7,292	......
Cruzada	243,772	21,545
Major vacancies	756⎫	
Minor vacancies	20,495⎭	39,344
Censo	1,363	......
Sales of Crown lands	2,617	......
Remissible to Spain	59,129	138
Snow	20,253	......
Regular deposits	58,070	19,869
Extraordinary	733,693	174,677
Mint	877,508	......
Playing cards	85,379	......
Powder	194,000	......
Cockfights	26,700	......
Alum	1,225	......
Leather goods	1,820	......
Copper	1,450	......
Palace	2,372	3,470
Half annates	50,782	4,894

Financial Statement, 1778 (*continued*)

Branches	Credits	Debits
Mesadas	13,477	423
Novenos	97,976	26,391
Salable offices	20,609	4,938
Drainage	21,077	84,960
Pulque	584,154	3,830
Excise on pulque	25,524	6,266
Stamped paper	20,806	2,519
Court expenses	......	5,862
Seigniorage	4,412	......
Tribute	862,468	96,877
Donations	338	......
New tax on cacao	26,075	......
Arrears debts	......	31,882
Ownerless goods	434	......
Lottery	35,527	......
Inválidos	44,381	10,453
Monte Pío Militar	24,326	3,497
Totals	8,954,951	7,140,379

[1] AGN, CVB, 1778, Vol. 114, inclosure in No. 4205, p. 214.

BIBLIOGRAPHY

PRIMARY SOURCES

Manuscript Material

This study is based in large measure on unpublished manuscript materials contained principally in two major repositories—the *Archivo General de la Nación* in Mexico City and the *Archivo General de Indias* in Seville. The bulk of these materials consists of correspondence between the viceregal establishment in Mexico City and the Spanish court in Madrid. Attached to the letters themselves which passed between the correspondents was a great volume of reports, subsidiary correspondence, and allied material. Such documentation does not lend itself readily to bibliographic categorization, inasmuch as each document is an entity within itself. Hence, meaningful identification of material of this nature can be supplied only in the footnotes, where the contents of each manuscript are indicated by the material in the text, and where the data on the precise location of each manuscript are set forth. In this bibliography, therefore, it has seemed feasible merely to indicate the general archival sources from which these documents have been drawn.

I. Documents from the following sections and volumes located in the Archivo General de la Nación, Mexico:

Archivo Histórico de Guerra. Tomos 1 (1706–1781), 2 (1770–1887).

Bandos. Volúmenes 8 (1771–1774), 9 (1775–1776), 10 (1777–1778, 11 (1779–1781).

Correspondencia de los virreyes. Bucareli. Volúmenes 5–116.

Historia. Tomos 3, 15–30, 41, 61, 66, 84, 89, 126, 136–138, 154, 172, 306, 327, 335, 339–390, 429, 494, 574.

Alcabalas y Aduanas. Volumen 121

Justicia y Subdelegados. Volumen 132

Monjas. Volumen 134

Indiferente de Guerra. Volumen 389, Tomo 10 (1779–1780).

Inquisición. Indice del Ramo, Numero 11 (Volúmenes 1083–1169), Numero 12 (Volúmenes 1170–1252).

Volúmenes 1098, 1100, 1114, 1134, 1162, 1170, 1179.

Marina. Tomos 20 (1762–1777), 32 (1770–1776), 32A (1771–1778), 34 (1774–1783), 37 (1775–1781).

Astilleros. Tomo 39 (1776–1777).

Ordenanzas. Volúmenes 18 (1768–1775), 19 (1776–1779).

Reales Cédulas. Volúmenes 99–119.

Temporalidades. Tomos 64 (1767–1774), 110 (1774–1781).

Tribunal de la Acordada. Tomo 3 (1765–1777).

II. Documents from the following sections and legajos located in the Archivo General de Indias, Seville:

Audiencia de México. Legajos 1129, 1239, 1242, 1269, 1272–1276, 1370–1385, 1509.

Indiferente General. Legajos 63–65, 3026A, 3026B, 3043.

Located in the Huntington Library, San Marino, California:

Gálvez, José de. Informe instructivo del Visitador Gener.l de Nueva España al Exmo. S.or Virrey de ella don Antonio Bucareli y Ursúa, en cumplimiento de Real Orden de 24 de Mayo de 1771. 2 vols.

Printed Documents

Ajofrín, Francisco de. *Diario del viaje que hicimos a México.* (Biblioteca Histórica Mexicana de Obras Inéditas, Vol. I) México: Antigua Librería Robredo, de José Porrúa e Hijos, 1936.

Barrio Lorenzot, Francisco del. *Ordenanzas de gremios de la Nueva España.* México: Secretaría de Governación, 1920.

Beleña, Eusebio Bentura (ed. & comp.). *Recopilación sumaria de todos los autos acordados de la Real Audiencia y Sala del Crimen de esta Nueva España.* 2 vols. México: Felipe de Zúñiga y Ontiveros, 1787.

Bonilla, Antonio de, "Breve Compendio de la Historia de Texas, por Don Antonio Bonilla. 1772," *Boletín del Archivo General de la Nación,* Vol. IX, No. 4 (1938), pp. 677–729.

———, "Brief Compendium of the Events which have occurred in the Province of Texas from its conquest, or reduction, to the present date (1772)," Elizabeth Howard West (trans.), *Texas State Historical Association Quarterly,* Vol. VIII (1905).

Bolton, Herbert Eugene. *Anza's California Expeditions.* 5 vols. Berkeley: University of California Press, 1930.

————. See Palou, Francisco. *Historical Memoirs of California.*

"División política de Nueva España hasta la promulgación de la Real Ordenanza de Intendentes. (4 de diciembre de 1786)," anonymous, *Boletín del Archivo General de la Nación,* Vol. II, No. 3 (Mayo-Junio, 1931), pp. 328–334.

"El ejército de Nueva España a fines del siglo XVIII," anonymous, *Boletín del Archivo General de la Nación,* Vol. IX (1938), pp. 236–275.

Gálvez, José de. *Informe general que en virtud de real orden instruyó y entregó al exmo. sr. marqués de Sonora, siendo visitador-general de este reyno, al Exmo. Sr. virrey, Frey D. Antonio Bucarely y Ursúa, con fecha de 21 de diciembre de 1771* . . . México: Imprenta de S. White, 1867.

Hackett, Charles W. (ed.). *Historical Documents relating to New Mexico, Nueva Vizcaya and Approaches thereto, to 1773.* 3 Vols. Washington, D. C.: The Carnegie Institution, 1923–1937.

Lafora, Nicolás de. *Relación del viage que hizo a los Presidios Internos situados en la frontera de la América Septentrional pertenecientes al Rey de España.* Con un liminar bibliográfico y Acotaciones por Vito Alessio Robles. México: Editorial Pedro Robredo, 1939.

"Memorial sobre las misiones de Sonora. 1772," anonymous, *Boletín del Archivo General de la Nación,* Vol. IX, No. 2 (1938), pp. 276–320.

Ministerio de Trabajo y Previsión (ed. & comp.). *Disposiciones complementarias de las leyes de Indias.* 3 vols. Madrid: Imprenta Sáez Hermanos, 1930.

Mourelle, Francisco Antonio. *Voyage of the Sonora in the Second Bucareli Expedition.* Introductory notes by Thomas C. Russell. San Francisco: Thomas C. Russell, 1920.

Ordenanzas de minería y colección de las ordenes y decretos de esta materia. Dispuesta por C. N. Méjico: Librería de J. Rosa, 1846.

"organización de milicias provinciales en Nueva España, La," anonymous, *Boletín del Archivo General de la Nación,* Vol. IX, No. 3 (1938), pp. 408–438.

Palou, Francisco. *Historical Memoirs of California.* 4 vols. Edited by Herbert E. Bolton. Berkeley: University of California Press, 1926.

————. *Francisco Palou's Life and Apostolic Labors of the Venerable Father Junípero Serra.* Introduction and notes by George Wharton

James. Translated by C. Scott Williams. Pasadena: G. W. James, 1913.

Rubio-Argüelles, Angeles, "Zúñiga, Impresor del Siglo XVIII en México," *Anales de la Asociación Española para el Progreso de las Ciencias,* Vol. XXII, No. 3 (1957), pp. 507–561.

Sedaño, Francisco. *Noticias de México . . .* Joaquín García Icazbalceta (ed.). México: Imprenta de J. R. Barbedilla y Comp.a, 1880.

Thomas, Alfred Barnaby (ed. & trans.). *Forgotten Frontiers: A Study of the Spanish Indian Policy of Don Juan Bautista de Anza, Governor of New Mexico, 1777–1787.* Norman: University of Oklahoma Press, 1932.

——— (ed. & trans.), "Governor Mendinueta's Proposals for the Defense of New Mexico, 1772–1778," *New Mexico Historical Review,* Vol. VI, No. 1 (January, 1931).

——— (ed. & trans.). *The Plains Indians and New Mexico, 1751–1778.* Albuquerque: University of New Mexico Press, 1940. (Coronado Historical Series, Vol. XI)

——— (ed. & trans.). *Teodoro de Croix and the Northern Frontier of New Spain, 1776–1783.* Norman: University of Oklahoma Press, 1941.

Velasco Ceballos, Rómulo. *La administración de D. Frey Antonio María de Bucareli y Ursúa.* 2 vols. (Publicaciones del Archivo General de la Nación, Tomos XXIX–XXX) México: 1936.

Williams, C. Scott. See Palou, Francisco. *Francisco Palou's Life and Apostolic Labors of the Venerable Father Junípero Serra.*

West, Elizabeth Howard. See Bonilla, Antonio de, "Brief Compendium of the Events which have occurred in the Province of Texas from its conquest, or reduction, to the present date (1772)."

SECONDARY SOURCES

Guides, and Bibliographies, Encyclopedias, and Dictionaries

Bolton, Herbert Eugene. *Guide to the Materials for the History of the United States in the Principal Archives of Mexico.* Washington, D. C.: The Carnegie Institution, 1913.

Bustamante, Luis J. *Enciclopedia popular cubana.* 2 vols. La Habana, Cuba: Cultural, S. A., no date.

Calcagno, Francisco. *Diccionario biográfico cubano.* 2 vols. New York: Imprenta y Librería de N. Ponce de León; and Habana, Cuba: D. E. F. Casona, 1878–1886.

Castañeda, Carlos E., and Jack A. Dabbs. *Guide to the Latin American Manuscripts in the University of Texas Library.* Cambridge: Harvard University Press, 1939.

Chapman, Charles Edward. *Catalogue of Materials in the Archivo General de Indias for the History of the Pacific Coast and the American Southwest.* Berkeley: University of California Press, 1919. (University of California Publications in History, Vol. VIII)

——, "A Description of Certain Legajos in the Archivo General de Indias," *Hispanic American Historical Review,* Vol. I (1918), pp. 209–230.

Dabbs, Jack A. See Castañeda, Carlos E.

Iguíniz, Juan B. *Bibliografía biográfica mexicana* . . . México: Imprenta de Secretaría de Relaciones Exteriores, 1938. (Monografías bibliográficas mexicanas, No. 18)

Indice de documentos de Nueva España existentes en el Archivo de Indias de Sevilla. —— vols. México: Imprenta de Secretaría de Relaciones Exteriores, 1938. (Monografías bibliográficas mexicanas, Nos. 12, 14, 22, 23)

Medina, José Toribio. *La imprenta en México, 1539–1821.* 9 vols. Santiago de Chile: the author, 1909–1911.

Spain and Spanish America in the Libraries of the University of California. 2 vols. Berkeley: University of California Press, 1928–1930.

Pezuela y Lobo, Jacobo de. *Diccionario geográfico, estadístico, histórico de la Isla de Cuba.* 4 vols. Imprenta del Establecimiento de Mellado, 1863.

Vigil, José M. (ed.). *Catálogos de la Biblioteca Nacional de México.* 9 vols. México: Tipografía Secretaría de Fomento, 1889——.

Wagner, Henry R. *The Spanish Southwest, 1542–1794.* Albuquerque: 1937. (Quivira Society Publications, Vol. VII, in two parts)

Books

Aiton, Arthur Scott. *Antonio de Mendoza, First Viceroy of New Spain.* Durham: Duke University Press, 1927.

Alamán, Lucas. *Disertaciones sobre la historia de la república mejicana.* 3 vols. Méjico: Imprenta de Lara, 1844–1849.

Alessio Robles, Vito. *Coahuila y Texas en la época colonial.* México: Editorial Cultura, 1938.

Bancroft, Hubert Howe. *History of Arizona and New Mexico, 1530–1888.* San Francisco: The History Company, 1889.

Bancroft, Hubert Howe. *History of Mexico.* 6 vols. San Francisco: A. L. Bancroft & Company, 1883–1888.

———. *History of the North Mexican States and Texas.* 2 vols. San Francisco: A. L. Bancroft & Company, 1884–1889.

Benítez, José R. *Historia gráfica de la Nueva España.* México: 1929.

Bolton, Herbert Eugene. *Athanase de Mézierès and the Louisiana-Texas Frontier, 1768–1770.* 2 vols. Cleveland: The Arthur H. Clark Company, 1914.

———. *Texas in the Middle Eighteenth Century.* Berkeley: University of California Press, 1915. (University of California Publications in History, Vol. III)

Bustamante, Carlos María de. See Cavo, Padre Andrés.

Carmen Velázquez, María del. *El Estado de guerra en Nueva España, 1760–1808.* México: El Colegio de México, 1950.

Caughey, John Walton. *California.* New York: Prentice-Hall, 1940.

Cavo, Padre Andrés, and Carlos María de Bustamante. *Los tres siglos de Mexico durante el gobierno español, hasta la entrada del ejército trigarante.* 4 vols. México: Imprenta de Luis Abadiano y Valdés, 1836–1838.

Chapman, Charles Edward. *The Founding of Spanish California.* New York: The Macmillan Company, 1916.

———. *A History of California: the Spanish Period.* New York: The Macmillan Company, 1928.

Coan, Charles F. *A History of New Mexico.* 3 vols. Chicago and New York: The American Historical Society, 1925.

√ Dahlgren, Charles B. *Minas históricas de la república mexicana.* México: Oficina Tipográfica de la Secretaría de Fomento, 1887.

Dánvila y Collado, Manuel. *Reinado de Carlos III.* 6 vols. Madrid: El Progreso Editorial, 1893–1896.

Desdevises du Desert, G. *L'Espagne de L'Ancien Régime.* 3 vols. Paris: Societé Francaise D'Imprimerie et de Librairie, 1897–1904.

Engelhardt, Fr. Zephyrin, O.F.M. *The Missions and Missionaries of California.* 4 vols. San Francisco: The James H. Barry Company, 1908–1915.

Ferrer del Río, Antonio. *Historia del reinado de Carlos III en España.* Madrid: Imprenta de Los Señores Matute y Compagni, 1856.

Fisher, Lillian Estelle. *The Intendant System in Spanish America.* Berkeley: University of California Press, 1929.

———. *Viceregal Administration in the Spanish-American Colonies.*

Berkeley: University of California Press, 1926. (University of California Publications in History, Vol. XV)

√ Fonseca, Fabián de, and Carlos de Urrutía. *Historia general de real hacienda.* 6 vols. México: Imprenta de Vicente García Torres, 1845–1853.

√ Gamboa, Francisco Xavier de. *Comentarios a las ordenanzas de minas.* Madrid: En la Oficina de Joachín Ibarra, 1761.

García Gutiérrez, Presbítero Jesús. *Apuntamientos de historia eclesiástica mejicana.* México: Imprenta Victoria, 1922.

Gómez Hoyos, Presbítero Rafael. *Las leyes de Indias y el derecho eclesiástico en la América española e Islas Filipinas.* Medellín, Colombia: Ediciones Universidad Católica Bolivariana, 1945.

González Obregón, Luis. *Epoca Colonial. México Viejo.* México: Editorial Patria, 1945.

———. *México en 1768.* México: Imprenta de *El Nacional,* 1897.

Griggs, George. *Mines of Chihuahua.* Chihuahua, México: Imprenta El Norte, S. A., 1911.

Hanke, Lewis. *Mexico and the Caribbean.* New York: D. Van Nostrand Company, 1959.

Haring, Clarence H. *The Spanish Empire in America.* New York: Oxford University Press, 1947.

Howe, Walter. *The Mining Guild of New Spain and its Tribunal General, 1770–1821.* Cambridge: Harvard University Press, 1949.

Johnson, Willis Fletcher. *The History of Cuba.* 5 vols. New York: B. F. Buck & Company, 1920.

Kinnaird, Lawrence. *The Frontiers of New Spain: Nicolás Lafora's Description, 1766–1768.* Berkeley: 1958. (Quivira Society Publications, Vol. XIII)

Lea, Henry Charles. *The Inquisition in the Spanish Dependencies.* New York: The Macmillan Company, 1908.

Macedo, Pablo. *Tres monografías.* Mexico: J. Ballesca y Comp.a Sucesores, Editores, 1905.

Maniau Torquemada, Joaquín. *Compendio de la historia de la Real Hacienda de Nueva España.* México: Sociedad Mexicana de Geografía y Estadística, Imprenta de la Secretaría de Industria y Comercio, 1914.

McAlister, Lyle N. *The "Fuero Militar" in New Spain, 1764–1800.* Gainesville: University of Florida Press, 1957.

Medina, José Toribio. *Historia del tribunal de la Inquisición en México.* Santiago de Chile: Imprenta Elzeviriana, 1905.

Mora, José-María Luis. *Méjico y sus revoluciones.* 3 vols. Paris: Librería de Rosa, 1836.

Motten, Clement G. *Mexican Silver and the Enlightenment.* Philadelphia: University of Pennsylvania Press, 1950.

Orozco, Wistano Luis. *Legislación y jurisprudencia sobre terrenos baldíos.* 2 vols. México: Imprenta de *el Tiempo,* 1895.

Orozco y Berra, Manuel. *Historia de la dominación española en México.* 4 vols. (Biblioteca Histórica Mexicana de Obras Inéditas, Vols. VIII–XI) México: Antigua Librería Robredo, 1938.

Parkes, Henry Bamford. *A History of Mexico.* Boston: Houghton Mifflin Company, 1960.

Priestley, Herbert Ingram. *José de Gálvez, Visitor-General of New Spain, 1765–1771.* Berkeley: University of California Press, 1916. (University of California Publications in History, Vol. V)

Richman, Irving Berdine. *California under Spain and Mexico, 1535–1847.* Boston and New York: Houghton Mifflin Company, 1911.

Riva Palacio, Vicente. *México a través de los siglos.* 5 vols. Barcelona: Espasa y Comp.a, 1888–1889.

Rivera Cambas, Manuel. *Los gobernantes de México.* 2 vols. México: Imprenta de J. M. Aguilar Ortiz, 1872.

Rodríguez Casado, Vicente. *Primeros años de dominación española en la Luisiana.* Madrid: Consejo Superior de Investigaciones Científicas Instituto Gonzalo Fernández Oviedo, 1942.

Roeder, Ralph. *Juárez and his Mexico.* 2 vols. New York: The Viking Press, 1947.

Romero de Terreros y Vinent, Manuel. *Bocetos de la vida social en la Nueva España.* México: Editorial Porrúa, 1944.

Rousseau, Francois. *Regne de Charles III d'Espagne, 1759–1788.* 2 vols. Paris: Librairie Plon, 1907.

Rubio Mañé, Jorge Ignacio. *Introducción al estudio de los virreyes de Nueva España.* Tomo I. México: Universidad de México, 1957.

Sierra, Justo. *Evolución política del pueblo mexicano.* México: Fondo de Cultura Económica, 1940.

Simpson, Lesley Byrd. *Many Mexicos.* New York: G. P. Putnam's Sons, 1946.

Smith, Donald E. *The Viceroy of New Spain.* Berkeley: University of California Press, 1913. (University of California Publications in History, Vol. I, No. 2)

Soler Alonzo, Pedro. *Virreyes de la Nueva España.* México: Secretaría de Educación Pública, 1945.

Torres Quintero, Gregorio. *México hacia el fin del virreinato español.* México: Librería de la Vda. de Ch. Bouret, 1921.

Urrutía, Carlos de. See Fonseca, Fábian de.

Valle-Arizpe, Artemio. *La muy noble y leal ciudad de México, según relatos de antaño y hogaño.* México: Editorial Cultura, 1924.

Vasconcelos, José. *Breve historia de México.* México: Ediciones Botas, 1938.

Wagner, Henry R. *Cartography of the Northwest Coast of America.* 2 vols. Berkeley: University of California Press, 1937.

Whitaker, Arthur Preston. *The Huancavelica Mercury Mine.* Cambridge: Harvard University Press, 1941.

——— (ed.). *Latin America and the Enlightenment.* New York: D. Appleton-Century Co., 1942.

Zamacois, Niceto de. *Historia de Méjico desde sus tiempos mas remotos hasta nuestros días.* 18 vols. Barcelona and Méjico: J. F. Parres y Comp.a, 1877–1882.

Zimmerman, Arthur Franklin. *Francisco de Toledo, Fifth Viceroy of Peru, 1569–1581.* Caldwell, Idaho: The Caxton Printers, 1938.

Articles

Bobb, Bernard E., "Bucareli and the Interior Provinces," *Hispanic American Historical Review,* Vol. XXXIV, No. 1 (February, 1954), pp. 20–36.

Chapman, Charles E., "The Alta California Supply Ships, 1773–1776," *Southwestern Historical Quarterly,* Vol. XIX, No. 2 (October, 1915), pp. 184–194.

———, "Difficulties of Maintaining the Department of San Blas," *Southwestern Historical Quarterly,* Vol. XIX, No. 3 (January, 1916), pp. 261–270.

Fisher, Lillian Estelle, "Teodoro de Croix," *Hispanic American Historical Review,* Vol. IX (1929), pp. 488–504.

Hammond, George P., "Pimería Alta after Kino's Time," *New Mexico Historical Review,* Vol. IV (1929), pp. 220–238.

Hussey, Roland D., "Traces of French Enlightenment in Colonial Hispanic America," in *Latin America and the Enlightenment,* pp. 23–51. See Arthur Preston Whitaker.

McAlister, Lyle N., "The Reorganization of the Army of New Spain, 1763–1767, *Hispanic American Historical Review,* Vol. XXXIII, No. 1 (February, 1953), pp. 1–32.

Mendizábal, Miguel O. de, "Los Minerales de Pachuca y Real del Monte en la época colonial," *El Trimestre Económico,* Vol. VIII (1941), pp. 253–309.

Smith, Robert Sidney, "Sales Taxes in New Spain, 1575–1770," *Hispanic American Historical Review,* Vol. XXVIII, No. 1, Part I (February, 1948), pp. 2–37.

Tavera Alfaro, Xavier, "Periodismo Dieciochesco," *Historia Mexicana,* Vol. II, No. 1 (Julio-Septiembre, 1952), pp. 110–115.

Thomas, Alfred Barnaby, "Antonio de Bonilla and Spanish Plans for the Defense of New Mexico, 1772–1778," in *New Spain and the Anglo-American West.* Vol. I. Lancaster, Pennsylvania: Lancaster Press, 1932.

Whitaker, Arthur Preston, "The Dual Role of Latin America in the Enlightenment," in *Latin America and the Enlightenment,* pp. 3–21. New York: D. Appleton-Century Co., 1942.

INDEX

Abarca, Silvestre: and Castle of San Diego, 125

Acapulco: Castle of San Diego at, 125, 264; as possible seaport, 170

Acordada (special police): accomplishments of, 11, 261; and military forces, 106; and Bucareli, 242, 261

Acuerdo, Real: nature of, 43; and ecclesiastical controversy, 43, 67–68; and collection of tribute, 231; and leasing of *alcabala*, 248, 251

Agonizantes, Order of: 40

Ahumada, Agustín de: and Presidio del Carmen, 123

Ais, Mission of: extinction of, 140

Aiton, Arthur S.: book by, 259

alcabala (tax): nature of, 244; history of, 244–245; exemptions from, 245; leasing of, 245–252; and Bucareli, 246, 247, 249–250; and Charles III, 246, 249, 251; and other government branches, 246–247; administration of, 247; and Jalapa Fair, 249–250; and the fiscal, 251; revenues from, 252–253; accounts of, 273, 275, 277, 279, 281, 283, 285

alcaldes mayores: collection of tribute by, 229–230

alcaldías: as divisions of New Spain, 4

Alessio Robles, Vito: on Bucareli, 266

Alexander VI: Royal Patronage under, 34

Alfaro, Xavier Tavera: on censorship, 17

Almadén mines: mercury from, 188; mining school at, 193; experts from, 193–194

Alta California. SEE California

Alzate y Ramírez, José: as publisher, 17

American Revolution: 261

Andrés de la Santísima Trinidad, Fray: as *visitador,* 40–43

Antonio de la Madre de Dios, Fray: and Bethlemite conflict, 40–41

Antonio de Mendoza, First Viceroy of New Spain: by Arthur S. Aiton, 259

Anza, Juan Bautista de: on Indian problem, 149; route of, to California, 163–166, 170

Apache Indians: depredations by, 130, 134; José Fayní on, 132; attacks on, 135, 140–143. SEE ALSO Eastern Apache Indians; Gila Apache Indians; Lipan Apache Indians; Mescalero Apache Indians

apartador de oro y plata: Bucareli's problems with, 236–239; and Charles III, 238–239

apartador, royal: creation of, 239

Aranda, Conde de: on San Juan de Ulúa, 118

Arangoyti, Domingo: and tax on pulque, 243; and *alcabala,* 248

Arce y Arroyo, Juan Antonio de: as Accountant General of *Alcabalas,* 247

Archbishop of Mexico: feud of, with Marqués de Croix, 36, 38; and Bucareli, 38–39, 45, 49, 51, 115; and ecclesiastical conflicts, 45; and secularization of curacies, 49; and right of asylum, 52; and *Vida Común* controversy, 64, 68–69, 74

Areche, José Antonio: and Archbishop Lorenzana, 39; and Bethlemite conflict, 41, 43; and tax on pulque, 243; and leasing of *alcabala,* 248. SEE ALSO fiscal, the

Arizpe: 145

armada de Barlovento (tax): imposition of, 245; accounts of, 273, 275, 277, 280–281, 284–285

and *Vida Común* controversy, 63,
66, 69, 71–73, 78–79, 81, 83
Bucareli, Luis, Marqués de Valleher-
mosa: father of Bucareli, 19
Bull of 1748: 66
Bustamante, C. M. de: on Bucareli, 263
Bustamante, José Alejandro: rehabili-
tation of mines by, 197

cabildos: as divisions of New Spain, 4
Cádiz, *Consulado* of: donation of
money by, 115
California: as part of New Spain, 4,
165; colonization of, 14, 156–171;
as part of Interior Provinces, 144–
145, 160, 165–166; and Bucareli,
148–149, 156, 159, 160–162, 165–
166, 265–266, 269; and Charles III,
149, 157–158, 163; geographical
area of, 156 n.; and José de Gálvez,
157–159, 165; and Marqués de
Croix, 157–158; governors of, 148,
158, 162; Catholic Church in, 158–
159, 162, 165; military powers in,
159; Indian problem in, 159, 166;
supplies for, 159, 162, 165–166,
170–171, 269; *reglamento* of July
1773 on, 163; voyages along coast
of, 164, 168; benefits to Spain from,
165
California, Baja. SEE California, Lower
California, Lower: geographical area
of, 156 n.; José de Gálvez in, 158–
159
Campeche: 23, 52, 123
Carlota, Princess: birth of, 55
Carmelites, Order of: *visita* to, 43–44
Carmelite nuns of Santa Desierto: mint
debt to, 236
Carmen, Presidio del: plan for, 123–
124
Casa de Moneda. SEE mint
caste system: in New Spain, 5–7, 33,
103
Cataluña, Volunteers of: 90, 105, 108
Catholic Church: bishops of, 21; and
class structure, 33; finances of, 33,

57, 59; influence of, 33, 50; and the
religious peace, 33; relationship of,
with State, 33–35, 48, 59–61, 83–
84; King as head of, 33–35, 48, 58–
59; and Bucareli, 34, 36–38, 41–50,
58–62; and the Enlightenment, 34;
proposed reform of, 34, 40; administration of, 35; and Marqués de
Croix, 36, 44; refuge of criminals
in, 50–52; and Inquisition, 53; taxing of, 58, 245; and *Vida Común*
controversy, 63–84; and military
powers, 129, 159; in California,
158–159, 162, 165
Caughey, J. W.: on Bucareli and California, 157–158, 161–163
censorship: in New Spain, 17–18, 54
census: of payers of tribute, 229
Cermeño, Antonio: on San Juan de
Ulúa, 118
Chafalote Indians: in New Vizcaya, 153
Chapman, Charles E.: on Bucareli and
California, 156–157, 160–163, 171,
265–266
Charles III: achievements of, 13; foreign policy of, 13–14, 98; reforms
of, 15; and locust plague, 24; and
Catholic Church, 34, 48, 58–59; and
the Fourth Mexican Provincial Council, 39; and Bethlemite conflict, 41;
and Carmelite *visita*, 43–44; and
Franciscans, 48; expulsion of Jesuits
by, 56–57; and *Vida Común* controversy, 65, 68–69, 70–71, 76–78, 80,
82; and militia, 86–87, 89, 99; and
Bucareli's military policy, 90; and
defenses of New Spain, 97–98, 104–
105, 107–108; on establishment of
foundry, 110; on establishment of
shipyard, 112–113; and fortresses,
118–119, 120, 122, 124–125; and
Indian problem, 129, 135–137, 143–
144; and separation of Interior Provinces from New Spain, 144–145;
and California, 149, 157–158, 163;
financial demands of, 151; and Teodoro de Croix, 154; and San Blas,
168, 170; and mining industry, 174,
179, 181, 183, 185, 192, 202–203;
and mining of mercury, 190–191,

nunneries: and *Vida Común* controversy, 63–84; life in, 64; children in,
64, 70–72, 74; secular women in,
64, 70–72, 74; servants in, 64, 70,
74

Oaxaca: bishop of, 21, 52; secularization of curacies in, 49–50
O'Conor, Hugo: and Indian problem,
131–135, 140–143, 154–155; as
commandant inspector of Interior
Provinces, 137; troops for, 138; duties of, 138–139; as governor of
Guatemala, 143; Teodoro de Croix
on, 150, 153; and La Cieneguilla
mines, 184–185
Oliver, Antonio: and Presidio del Carmen, 124
O'Reilly, Alejandro: friendship of, with
Bucareli, 19 n.–20 n., 161, 268; Bucareli to, 19–20, 23, 27, 29, 30, 32,
36, 37, 88, 90–91, 93, 94–95, 97,
105, 131, 147, 160–161, 210; to Bucareli, 91
Orizaba: 111; militia from, 94–95; garrisons at, 107; tobacco monopoly in,
254
Orozco, José Clemente: on indigenists,
267
Ortúzar, Francisco: on establishment of
foundry, 111–112

Pachuca: 168; represented at mining
junta, 195
Pachuca, Apostolic College of: 47
Páez, Miguel: and tax on pulque, 243
Palacios, Juan Fernando: and discharge
of militia, 89; on San Juan de Ulúa,
119
Panes, Diego: and establishment of
foundry, 111–112
Panón, Ramón: and Castle of San
Diego, 126
Pánuco, Marqués de: mining by, 198
Papagoe Indians: in Sonora, 150
Parkes, H. B.: on José de Gálvez, 15
partido system: Bucareli on, 177–178,

204; in mining industry, 177–178;
Count of Regla on, 178
Patronato Real. SEE Royal Patronage
Peñasco, Count of: mining by, 198
penas de cámara y gastos de justicia:
revenues from, 208
Pérez, Juan: exploratory voyage of,
164, 168
Perote fortress: 117; Bucareli at, 24;
defenses of, 24; garrisons at, 95, 106;
foundry near, 111; construction of,
122; costs of, 224–225
Peru: 42; mercury production in, 188
Philip II: Royal Patronage under, 34
Philip V: accomplishments of, 13
Philippines: and New Spain, 226–227
Pico Palacio, Bartolomé: and Guadala-
jara subtreasury, 221–222
Pima Indians: attacks against, 129; in
Sonora, 150
Pimiento, ——: and Bucareli, 93
Pious Fund: 162
Pius VI: and expulsion of Jesuits, 57.
SEE ALSO Pope
playing cards: as Crown monopoly,
207; and *masa remisible,* 207; accounts of, 273, 275, 277, 279, 281,
283, 285
police, special. SEE *Acordada* (special
police)
polygamy: frequency of, 53; convictions
for, 56
Ponze, Pedro: on establishment of
foundry, 111–112
Pope: and Fourth Mexican Provincial
Council, 39; and Bethlemite conflict,
41; and *Vida Común* controversy,
76–77, 83. SEE ALSO Clement XIV;
Pius VI
Portolá, Gaspar de: and *Vida Común*
controversy, 67, 71, 78; as governor
of Puebla, 78, 101; on militia, 101;
as governor of California, 158
Portugal: Bucareli fights in, 19; and
Spain, 98, 242, 261
Poyanos, Ignacio: and Bucareli, 28,
242, 261

Prado y Ulloa, Josef de: donation of money by, 115
praetorian tradition: in Mexico, 103
presidios: 123, 124; relocation of, 129–135, 137, 139, 153; establishment of, 132–133, 143; Pedro de Rivera on, 138
Priestley, H. I.: on José de Gálvez' reforms, 14–15; on collection of tribute, 232
Puebla: volcanoes of, 8; *ayuntamiento* of, 60–61; militia from, 99–102; private tobacco shops in, 257
Puebla, Bishop of: 21; and secularization of curacies, 49; and right of asylum, 52; conflict of, with *ayuntamiento*, 60–61; and *Vida Común* controversy, 64–65; donation of money by, 115. SEE ALSO Fabián y Fuero, Francisco; López Gonzalo, Victoriano
pulque: as Crown monopoly, 240–244; nature of, 240–241; illicit manufacture of, 241; Bucareli and, 241–244; and Charles III, 241–243; revenues from, 241–242, 244; tax on, 243–244; accounts of, 274, 276, 278–279, 282–283, 286

Quebradilla mine: rehabilitation of, 180, 185; and Charles III, 181
Querétaro: Teodoro de Croix in, 148–149; private tobacco shops in, 256–257
Querétaro convent: and Carmelite *visita*, 44
quicksilver. SEE mercury

Ramo de Azogues: 189
ramos: nature of, 206; leasing of, 206–207; administration of, 217; auditing of accounts of, 220–221
rationalism: effect of, on Inquisition, 52. SEE ALSO Enlightenment; liberalism, eighteenth-century
Real Acuerdo. SEE *Acuerdo, Real*
Real Audiencia. SEE *Audiencia, Real*
Real del Monte mines: Army units at,

105; rehabilitation of, 175, 177–180, 185, 197; workers' rebellions at, 177; and Bucareli, 177–180; and Charles III, 179; labor for, 179
Real Hacienda. SEE *Hacienda, Real*
rebellion: factors causing, 15; Bucareli on, 103–104; at Real del Monte mines, 177–178
Regiments: of Granada, 99, 106, 108; of Mexico, 100, 104, 108; of Querétaro, 101; of Spain, 104, 108; Crown, 106, 107, 108; Asturias, 106–107, 108
Regla, Count of: donation of money by, 144; rehabilitation of mines by, 175, 178–180, 185, 197; and rebellion of workers, 177; on *partido* system, 178; mining by, 198
Representación of mining junta: contents of, 175–176, 196–201; presentation of, 190; preparation of, 196; Bucareli on, 201–202; and Charles III, 202
residencia: nature of, 25–26; elimination of, 265
Retes, José de: as *apartador*, 237
revenues: from gold mines, 182, 185; from silver mining, 185; José de Gálvez on handling of, 206; leasing of *ramos* for, 206; use of, for special funds, 208–209; from collection of tribute, 233; from the mint, 234–235; from pulque, 242, 244; from *alcabala*, 252–253; from tobacco monopoly, 257–258. SEE ALSO fiscal system of New Spain; *Hacienda, Real*
revenues, Crown. SEE fiscal system of New Spain; *Hacienda, Real;* revenues
Revillagigedo, Juan Vicente de Güemes: rehabilitation of Mexico City by, 7, 9–10, 11; on periodicals, 17
revolution: effect of colonial milita on, 102–103
Ricardos, Antonio: and San Juan de Ulúa, 118
Richman, I. E.: on Bucareli, 266
Ripperdá, Juan María de: on Indian problems, 6, 130, 136, 140–141